T0320877

ORGANIZING RESISTANCE AND IMAGINING ALTERNATIVES IN INDIA

This volume examines the political economy of neoliberalism in India and offers cases of resistance and alternative organizing. It departs from existing conversations that focus on the state's policies and decisions, and attends to the violence unleashed by corporate forces. It should be of interest to anyone curious about the collapse of crucial infrastructures such as healthcare and the news media, or the rhetoric of corporate social responsibility, and why there are people's movements and organizations rising from different geographies.

While offering in-depth case studies of oraganizations within India, such as *The Wire*, the People's Archive of Rural India, Kudumbashree, and LeftWord Books, it also informs conversations across the world on alternative forms of organizing. These accounts have two imperatives: First, to train our attention on corporations and where capitalism produces its vast waste lands. Second, to imagine the possibilities of another world. The contributors to this volume write to resist the status quo, explore alternative ways of organizing, re-imagine social relations, and rekindle hope.

Rohit Varman is Professor of Marketing and Consumption at the University of Birmingham. He is currently working in the areas of modern slavery, exploitation, and corporate violence. He has co-edited *Alternative Organizations in India: Undoing Boundaries* (Cambridge University Press, 2018).

Devi Vijay is Associate Professor in Organizational Behavior at the Indian Institute of Management Calcutta. Her research explores questions of inequality, institutions, and collective action, with a focus on healthcare. She has co-edited *Alternative Organizations in India: Undoing Boundaries* (Cambridge University Press, 2018).

ORGANIZING RESISTANCE AND IMAGINING ALTERNATIVES IN INDIA

Edited by

ROHIT VARMAN

DEVI VIJAY

CAMBRIDGE
UNIVERSITY PRESS

CAMBRIDGE
UNIVERSITY PRESS

University Printing House, Cambridge CB2 8BS, United Kingdom

One Liberty Plaza, 20th Floor, New York, NY 10006, USA

477 Williamstown Road, Port Melbourne, vic 3207, Australia

314 to 321, 3rd Floor, Plot No. 3, Splendor Forum, Jasola District Centre,
New Delhi 110025, India

103 Penang Road, #05–06/07, Visioncrest Commercial, Singapore 238467

Cambridge University Press is part of the University of Cambridge.

It furthers the University's mission by disseminating knowledge in the pursuit of
education, learning and research at the highest international levels of excellence.

www.cambridge.org
Information on this title: www.cambridge.org/9781009193412

© Cambridge University Press 2022

This publication is in copyright. Subject to statutory exception
and to the provisions of relevant collective licensing agreements,
no reproduction of any part may take place without the written
permission of Cambridge University Press.

First published 2022

Printed in India by Thomson Press India Ltd.

A catalogue record for this publication is available from the British Library

ISBN 978-1-009-19341-2 Hardback

Cambridge University Press has no responsibility for the persistence or accuracy
of URLs for external or third-party internet websites referred to in this publication,
and does not guarantee that any content on such websites is, or will remain,
accurate or appropriate.

To the brave farmers who have rekindled hope through their resistance. And in memory of more than 700 martyrs who died saving India at the borders of Delhi.

CONTENTS

IMAGES

TABLES

1

CAPITALIST DEATHWORLDS, ALTERNATIVE WORLDMAKING

ROHIT VARMAN
DEVI VIJAY

kaleja phuñk rahā hai aur zabāñ kahne se aarī hai
batā.ūñ kyā tumheñ kyā chiiz ye sarmāya-dārī hai
ye vo āñdhī hai jis kī rau meñ muflis kā nasheman hai
ye vo bijlī hai jis kī zad meñ har dahqāñ kā ḳhirman hai
ye apne haath meñ tahzīb kā fānūs letī hai
magar mazdūr ke tan se lahū tak chuus letī hai

My heart is singed by its flame, capitalism is its name
When it turns into a storm, it uproots many a cobbled tent
As lightening, it destroys the harvest of the peasant
It dazzles the world with its cultural pedigree
But thrives on the workers' blood, it's free

In this powerful poem titled 'Sarmayadari' (Capitalism), progressive poet Asrarul Haq Majaz[1] repeatedly invokes the tropes of 'monstrosity' to portray how capitalism sucks the blood of, strangulates, and walks on the bodies of the poor and builds with their bones the chariots of the rich. Capital devours human beings and nature in an endless drive for profits. This insatiable drive for profiteering in recent times has been particularly intensified by finance capital. We live in times when bankers and the financial elite, who are in unprecedented control of the capitalist world, take the monstrosity of capitalism to new levels (Hudson, 2015; Lapavitsas, 2013).

Never in the history of humankind has such a tiny financial elite exercised so much control over the fate of humanity and caused so much mass destruction. Phillips (2018: 31) describes how the transnational capitalist class of bankers and corporate managers speculates on human lives and profits from deathworlds,

> Each year, poor nutrition kills 3.1 million children under the age of 5. Twenty five thousand per day, more than 9 million people per year die from starvation and malnutrition. This slaughter is occurring around the world every day.... So while millions suffer, the TCC [transnational capitalist class] financial elites focus on seeking returns on trillions of dollars, which can and does include speculation on the rising cost of food and land. They do this in cooperation with each other in a global capitalist system of TCC power and control that structurally entraps them in cycles of economic growth and contraction, with mass humanitarian consequences.

This transnational capitalist class manipulates laws, policies, and governments to its advantage. Based on a close analysis of the financial giants and ownership of finance capital, Phillips (2018: 58) further informs that 'the global financial Giants are laying the foundation for the privatization of the world. If public, democratic institutions ... become privately owned entities, then corporate interests will truly dominate. As that happens we become a neo-feudal society'. Several others have pointed to how liberal capitalism, as we have understood over the last few decades, is giving way to a new order. For instance, Varoufakis (2021) calls it a techno-feudal order in which a small set of financial and technology firms controls the world. Hudson (2017) adds, 'These bankers (and bondholders) are the main exploiters today. So finance capitalism is overwhelming industrial capitalism. Instead of industrial capitalism evolving into socialism as was expected, it is retrogressing back to neo-serfdom and neo-feudalism.' While we may debate these labels and transformations, it is hard to deny that we are in an interregnum that Gramsci (2020) insightfully noted as a period in which the old order is dying but the new one is yet to be born. And we are witnessing various morbid tendencies that are direct results of the increasing financialization of a neoliberal world order.

Neoliberalism is a political and ideological project that propels an agenda of deregulation and privatization of public resources 'from above', through financial institutions, corporations, and governments. Patnaik (2020: 39) notes that 'neoliberal economic policies are the outcome of a regime of hegemony of international finance capital'. From below, neoliberalism popularizes rationalities of individualistic hyper-competition and entrepreneurialism to bootstrap oneself out of structural violence (Gago, 2020). In its current inflection, neoliberalism is marked by financialization wherein the 'logic of finance – that is of lending, speculation, and investment – penetrates all areas of economic activity to the benefit of a small financial elite and to the detriment of the working people' (Blakeley, 2019: loc. 168). Hudson (2015: 375) writes, 'The financial sector has the same objective as military conquest: to gain control of land and basic infrastructure, and collect tribute. To update von Clausewitz, finance has become war by other means. What formerly took blood and arms is now obtained by debt leverage.' As a result, this neoliberal phase of capitalism is particularly destructive of the liberal versions of democracy that many countries, including India, had put in place in the twentieth century.

This destructive aspect of capitalism's current trajectory gives rise to another spectre that haunts India today. Neoliberalism destroys democracies and reduces them to post-democratic orders with an increase in the possibilities of fascification of societies (Patnaik, 2019). Fascism, borrowing from Paxton (2005: 218), is a political behaviour marked by 'obsessive preoccupation with community decline, humiliation, or victimhood and by compensatory cults of unity, energy, and purity'. It helps monopoly capital use authority, centralization, and violence to further accumulation (Rosenberg, 2016). Indeed, Dimitrov (1938: 6) warned that 'fascism is the power of finance capital itself. It is the organization of terrorist vengeance against the working class and the revolutionary section of the peasantry and intelligentsia'. Dimitrov (1938) further adds that it is not that a committee of finance capital puts fascists in place, but their support is crucial when fascists struggle to outmanoeuvre old bourgeois parties. Indeed, it was a Cologne banker, Kurt von Schröder, who served as a crucial link between Adolf Hitler and Franz von Papen, facilitating the rise of the Nazi Party to power in 1933 (Paxton, 2005).

Corporations and finance capital may not support fascism from the outset, but as fascists start gaining political momentum and as their anti-working-class agenda becomes clearer, corporate support for fascists swells. As Rosenberg (2016: 90) observes, 'leading big industrialists and bankers funded the growing financial needs of the Brown House (the Nazi Headquarters).…. What mattered most was Hitler's drive to destroy Marxism and ward off a Bolshevik revolution in Germany'. Economic crisis, large-scale unemployment, and disenchantment with liberal politics are some conditions that contribute to the popular support for fascist forces (Paxton, 2005). In neoliberal India, many of these conditions have been present and have allowed the Bhartiya Janata Party (BJP) to gain popular support. Patnaik (2016) warns,

> In the context of crisis-induced mass unemployment, the corporate-financial oligarchies that rule many countries actively promote divisive, fascist, and semi-fascist movements, so that while the shell of democracy is preserved, their own rule is not threatened by any concerted class action. And the governments formed by such elements, even when they do not move immediately towards the imposition of a fascist state as in the case of classical fascism, move nonetheless towards a 'fascification' of the society and the polity that constitutes a negation of democracy.

Roy (2019: 121) adds that right-wing fascism and corporate capital work in synergy – 'while one arm is busy selling the nation off in chunks, the other to divert attention, is orchestrating a baying, howling, deranged chorus of cultural nationalism'. Roy further contends that the 'inexorable ruthlessness of one process results in the naked, vulgar terrorism perpetrated by the other. There's no separating them'.

We write this book on alternatives in India when the country is in the grip of these two ruthless forces – financiers and fascists. The destructive effects of these twin forces that shape India have been cast in sharp relief during the COVID-19 pandemic. For months now, images have circulated of burning mass pyres and corpses floating down rivers or buried in shallow graves by river banks. These images evidence the onslaught of neoliberalism that has been concealed in the everyday structures of violence against the poor. Social media pleas intensified for oxygen, ventilators, testing kits, medicines, and intensive care beds (Rana, 2021). With the near collapse of the economy and rising unemployment, reports emerge of starvation deaths and suicides (SWAN, 2020).

If one has the privilege to pause in the midst of illness, grief, and trauma, one may ask: 'Can anything at all survive in this miasma of death and depletion?' And yet, much like the virus itself, what has circulated and mutated across nation-state borders is triumphant finance capitalism and the rising forces of fascism. In India, we witness the onward march of finance and fascism – the stock market soars and bankers and the corporate elite increase their bonuses, as the state tramples dissent with impunity.

We offer this edited volume in this conjuncture of a devastating humanitarian crisis where a few elites prosper from the disposability of large swathes of the population. While we began curating this volume before the pandemic surfaced, the unfolding catastrophe magnifies the urgent need to rethink the unviable capitalist order in which we find ourselves. Although we point to the twin spectres of finance and fascism and their relatedness in our introduction, this book is about people's determination to dissent, and it is a writing that is firmly grounded in hope. Despite being haunted by these two oppressive forces, people continue to resist in India. In the face of the threat of contagion, death, and incarceration, people have protested from their homes, on the streets, and even under water (as seen in Lakshadweep, Koshy, 2021). The farmers' movement at Delhi's borders sharply framed corporate oligarchs like the Adanis and the Ambanis as responsible for their predicament. Activists and public intellectuals have repeatedly foregrounded the breakdown of public healthcare and the Indian state's governance failures in curbing private profiteering and mismanaging vaccination production and distribution (for example, Pandhi, 2021; Roy, 2021). Some journalists have diligently traced the official under-reporting of deaths that reveal the horror of the unfolding crisis (for example, Rukmini, 2021a; Venkataramakrishnan, 2021).

In a similar spirit of defiance, the contributors to this volume seek to interrogate and interrupt the monstrosities of contemporary neoliberal capitalism. This volume has two imperatives: First, to train our attention on capitalism and its agents. To understand the current crisis, we must expand our spatial, temporal, and ecological visions beyond the hospital, the crematoriums, the death counts, and the state to where capitalism produces its vast wastelands. Second, to imagine the possibilities of another world. Together with the contributors to this edited volume, we write to resist the status quo, explore alternative ways of organizing, and re-imagine social relations and hope in this world.

This chapter is organized into three sections. We first delineate some features of contemporary capitalism. We follow this with a discussion of the ongoing illusions and deceptions of nationalism and rising fascism in India. Finally, we think through what it would mean to imagine another world. Here we introduce the book chapters to outline how our contributors imagine alternatives to the current hegemony.

CAPITALIST MONSTROSITIES

Examining the relation between capital and labour, Marx anticipated the high levels of cruelty, violence, and exploitation that were to take deep systemic roots and spread across the globe in the twentieth and twenty-first centuries. Theorizing 'The Working Day', Marx (2013: 317) pointed out that the capitalist division of labour converted the worker 'into a living appendage of the machine'. In its insatiable lust of accumulation, capital squeezes every ounce of life from workers – 'To appropriate labour during all the 24 hours of the day is, therefore, the inherent tendency of capitalist production' (Marx, 2013: 175). There was little space for human kindness or compassion in such a capitalist order. Marx (2013: 195) noted,

> [O]ur labourer comes out of the process of production other than he entered. In the market, he stood as owner of the commodity 'labour-power' face to face with other owners of commodities, dealer against dealer. The contract by which he sold to the capitalist his labour-power proved, so to say, in black and white that he disposed of himself freely. The bargain concluded, it is discovered that he was no 'free agent', that

the time for which he is free to sell his labour-power is the time for which he is forced to sell it, that in fact the vampire will not lose its hold on him so long as there is a muscle, a nerve, a drop of blood to be exploited.

Marx deploys the metaphor of vampire to convey the power of capital as an abstract form of domination that is not easy to identify or act against. In the last 150 years, the factory at the service of capitalists has become a more generalized form of organizing human life in almost every sphere of existence. Feminists exploring the social reproduction of labour point to the entire factory of care work – domestic work, elder and childcare, janitorial work – that feeds capitalist extractions (Bhattacharya, 2017; Gago, 2020). In their *Feminism for the 99%: A Manifesto*, Arruzza, Fraser, and Bhattacharya (2019: 53) explain,

[C]apitalism is not just an economic system, but something larger: an institutionalized social order that also encompasses the apparently 'noneconomic' relations and practices that sustain the official economy. Behind capitalism's official institutions – wage labor, production, exchange, and finance – stand their necessary supports and enabling conditions: families, communities, nature; territorial states, political organizations, and civil societies; and not least of all, massive amounts and multiple forms of unwaged and expropriated labor, including much of the work of social reproduction, still performed largely by women and often uncompensated. These, too, are constitutive elements of capitalist society – and sites of struggle within it.

McNally (2011: 4) adds that those who are exploited and injured become 'labouring zombies'; in the camp of the victims, we find disfigured creatures 'who have been turned into mere bodies ... exploitable collections of flesh, blood, muscle and tissue'.

Capitalism thrives on making a killing in profits off the bodies of the destitute. Yet there is no responsibility for these holocausts. Žižek (2009: 14) notes, 'All this seems just to have happened as the result of an "objective" process, which nobody planned and executed and for which there was no

"Capitalist Manifesto".' As a result, the monstrosity of the system operates as a baseline condition of normalcy that allows capitalists to suck the blood of working people as a natural phenomenon. Consider emerging accounts of heightened precarities and deaths among gig workers deemed as 'essential services' during the pandemic (IFAT-ITF, 2020; Raj and Gurmat, 2021) even as the companies earned multibillion-dollar valuations from the global power elite. Corporate academics further naturalize capitalist monstrosities through euphemisms of 'asset-light' successful modern tech companies that achieve 'scale and scope at breakneck speeds' through 'customer intimacy' and 'digital disruption' (for example, Govindarajan and Srivastava, 2021). Such endorsements are disconnected from the literal implications of breakneck speed and disruption for the gig workers.

Contemporary neoliberal violence is an attempt to mask its structural weaknesses. Harvey (2004: 74–75) observes,

> Stock promotions, ponzi schemes, structured asset destruction through inflation, asset stripping through mergers and acquisitions, the promotion of levels of debt encumbrancy that reduce whole populations, even in the advanced capitalist countries, to debt peonage, to say nothing of corporate fraud, dispossession of assets (the raiding of pension funds and their decimation by stock and corporate collapses) by credit and stock manipulations – all of these are central features of what contemporary capitalism is about.

Calling this as new imperialism and accumulation by dispossession, Harvey reads neoliberalism as a political project carried out by the corporate capitalist class to intensify their gains in the face of the threat posed by the labour movements in the 1960s and 1970s. The International Monetary Fund (IMF) and the World Bank, as brokers of US imperialism, conscripted the Third World, often at gun point, to debt and neoliberal regimes through structural adjustment programmes (Prashad, 2007).

The parasitic characteristics of high finance shape the current neoliberal trajectory (Crosthwaite, Knight, and Marsh, 2014). The financialization of the global economy, which began in the 1970s, is now a deeply entrenched form of capital accumulation and extraction distinct from other modes of industry and commerce. Financialization manifests most evidently in the growth of the finance sector and its symbiotic relationship between insurance and real estate. Under financialization, the logic of shareholder value maximization reigns supreme, financial institutions are more likely to own businesses, and businesses are more likely to invest in financial markets (Blakeley, 2019). Financial institutions provide the capital for big businesses to acquire smaller rivals. Financialization is anchored around market concentration and short-term orientation. Profit, not production, is the dominant rationale.

The pernicious effects of financialization have been experienced well before this pandemic. In the aftermath of the 2008 recession, Matt Taibbi (2010), writing for the *Rolling Stone*, described Goldman Sachs as 'a great vampire squid wrapped around the face of humanity, relentlessly jamming its blood funnel into anything that smells like money'. Montgomerie and Cain (2018) elaborate, 'The vampire is an undead monster that embodies the image of an elite aristocrat with wealth and power capable of violence without fear of repercussions.' Exploiters – financiers, corporate managers or owners, consultants – as vampires injure different aspects of the living world in the process of profiteering by capturing and dissecting bodies and bringing their bits to market (McNally, 2011).

One concrete consequence of finance capitalism is visible in the Indian healthcare sector today. Certainly, the post-Independence welfare state's commitment to public health was abysmally short of the nationalist movement's initial espousal of state healthcare provision (Amrith, 2007). However, India had made significant investments in public health interventions with improvements in indicators such as infant mortality rate, crude birth rate, and life expectancy over the years (Ganggoli, Duggal and Shukla, 2005). Yet, in 1987, championing corporate interests, the World Bank (1987: 3) stated in its report titled *Financing Health Services in Developing Countries: An Agenda for Reform*, 'The more common approach to healthcare in developing countries has been to treat it as a right of the citizenry and to attempt to provide free services to everyone. This approach usually does not work.' Shortly after this, India adopted a structural adjustment programme, opening up a period of publicly funded private-sector provisioning of healthcare, rapid privatization, and corporatization of public hospitals

(Chakravarthi et al., 2017). This unregulated privatization of the healthcare sector has created large-scale disenfranchisement, distrust, and deathworlds (Gadre and Shukla, 2016). India is now ranked 5th on the Medical Tourism Index and 145th among 195 countries on the *Lancet* index in terms of healthcare quality and accessibility (Oxfam, 2019; RUPE, 2020).

Another immediate manifestation of the logic of finance is the ongoing vaccine apartheid. Eighty-five per cent of vaccines administered have been in richer countries (Progressive International, 2021). Meanwhile, low- and middle-income countries are left wrangling over intellectual property rights with pharmaceutical giants and their henchmen, such as the philanthro-capitalists and the World Trade Organization (Nileena, 2021). After all, how can the holy ideology of profit be violated? Nine new pharma billionaires were crowned as shares in companies skyrocketed, and chief executive officers (CEOs) defended the right to profit because of the 'risk' vaccine companies assumed by investing in research and development (Isidore, 2021; Ziady, 2021). As Hudson (2015: 377) observes,

> Having gained enough control over government policy to privatize public assets, the financial sector provides credit to buy the right to install tollbooths on hitherto public roads, railroads, airlines and other transport infrastructure, phone and communications systems. The aim is to extract monopoly rent instead of providing basic services freely or at subsidized rates. Financialization means using this rent extraction for debt service.

The IMF's Chief Economist, Gita Gopinath, recently co-authored a report (Agarwal and Gopinath, 2021: 2) titled *A Proposal to End the COVID-19 Pandemic*, which estimates that national and international efforts at vaccination, tracking, and testing will cost only $50 billion 'of which $35 billion should be paid by grants from donors and the residual by national governments potentially with the support of concessional financing from bilateral and multilateral agencies' – in other words, conscripting the Global South into further cycles of debt (see also Oxfam, 2021). This proposal is but one example of how the logic of finance capital parasitically penetrates the world and bleeds the most vulnerable to death.

Hudson (2015: 15) adds,

> Bankers and bondholders desiccate the host economy by extracting revenue to pay interest and dividends. Repaying a loan – amortizing or 'killing' it – shrinks the host. Like the word amortization, mortgage ("dead hand" of past claims for payment) contains the root mort, 'death.' A financialized economy becomes a mortuary when the host economy becomes a meal for the financial free luncher that takes interest, fees, and other charges without contributing to production.

This outcome is often achieved by perpetuating a widespread belief that the rentier class is helping rather than depleting lives – as exemplified by the IMF discourse. The logic is designed to make it appear that austerity, rent extraction, and debt deflation are necessary for the victim and are not killing the economy. Hudson (2015: 23) labels finance as the mother of all monopolies and considers that 'future generations may see the degree to which this self-destructive ideology has reversed the Enlightenment and is carving up today's global economy as one of the great oligarchic takeovers in the history of civilization'.

Under these conditions, the controls over state power are subtly manoeuvred from democratic means to the demands of the oligarchs. The oligarchs oppose any direct intervention by the state for increasing aggregate demand and hence employment and output (Ghosh, 2020). Patnaik (2020: 40) observes, '[N]o matter whom the people elect to form the government, unless that government takes the country out of the vortex of globalized finance, the same set of policies continues to be pursued.' Not only do we have the same set of policies, but we also have the same set of agents of finance capital who continue to rule us. We end up with the worst of all worlds in which the poorest people of the world end up feeding the rentier class. Here Dimitrov (1938: 9) warns that 'fascism delivers up the people to be devoured by the most corrupt and venal elements, but comes before them with a demand for "honest and incorruptible government". Speculating on the profound disillusionment of the masses in bourgeois-democratic governments, fascism hypocritically denounces corruption'. Yet the most corrupt and venal elements are the corporate elite for whom fascism delivers vast masses of people to devour. As one of the global power elites in Phillips's (2018:138) study states, government leaders are the pilots flying 'our airplane'.

Haiven (2020) describes this current system of violence as 'revenge capitalism'. Revenge explains the irrational, blood-curdling systemic violence of capitalism that reduces the vast majority of people to complete worthlessness and disposability. The word 'revenge' also encapsulates capitalism's foundations in the cruelties of empire, colonialism, fascism, and the racial ordering of humanity. Haiven (2020: 5) points out that revenge capitalism surfaces in the monstrous ways surplussed populations encounter direct and systemic violence: 'as humans are, completely unnecessarily, warehoused in prisons, left to die in slums, worked to death in mines, abandoned to the border, or denied the care they require'.

In recent times, we have seen several examples of such monstrosity in India. For instance, the draconian lockdown of 2020 forced millions of workers to walk for hundreds of miles to return to their homes. RUPE (2020: 31–34, emphasis in original) caustically observes,

> It appears that India is a global leader *in inflicting policy-based pain on its citizens* in response to COVID-19 … measures such as sweeping lockdowns without warning or preparation can have a particularly devastating impact, since nine-tenths of the workforce is informal; *yet the government imposed the most draconian lockdown in the world; and provided the least material succor or compensation in the world to those hit by these measures.*

In May 2021, the heinous oxygen shortage in New Delhi and subsequently in other parts of the country made international headlines. However, in August 2017, 60 children died within 72 hours because of oxygen shortage during an encephalitis outbreak in Gorakhpur (Uttar Pradesh), one of the poorest regions in the country. Arguably, COVID-19 mainstreamed the ongoing structural violence against the poor. Varman and Vijay (2021) temporally and spatially distended and displaced the event of oxygen shortage to surface the structural violence against the precariat. This structural violence manifests in the form of crumbling primary and community health centres and the absence of water and sanitation alongside rising costs of healthcare privatization and land dispossession. Where there is dissent, the precariat primarily holds the state responsible for the tragedies without identifying or implicating privatization or corporate-finance capital that makes further gains from such crises.

We understand from Klein (2007) that every crisis is an opportunity for the capitalist class to extract more and to increase profits. The pandemic has deepened the ongoing economic crisis in India. However, instead of providing a stimulus to generate demand, the state has refused to provide any substantial package for economic revival (Ghosh, 2020). Patnaik (2020) argues that finance capital does not allow governments in the Global South to support the poor and exacerbates crises for its benefit. RUPE (2020: 143, emphasis in original) observes, '[T]he government's refusal to spend even during the present dire economic and public health crisis can partly be explained by its anxiety to get listed on global bond indices and to display its adherence to principles of fiscal austerity.' In such situations, private investors extract various concessions from the government as they are asked to implement 'reforms' in favour of corporations and sell off valuable public assets at distress prices in the name of bridging fiscal deficits (RUPE, 2020). Salivating at the prospect of making a killing, the Boston Consulting Group, a key advisor to the Indian government on the COVID-19 crisis, spelled out in 2018 what it called 'the $75 Trillion Opportunity in Public Assets',

> Governments around the world are under enormous financial pressure. Budgets remain constrained in many countries while the need for investment – particularly in infrastructure – is growing. A solution, however, is hiding in plain sight. Central governments worldwide control roughly $75 trillion in assets, according to conservative estimates – a staggering sum equal to the combined GDP of all countries.... Government leaders must take aggressive action to harness the value of the public assets under their control.... Governments should consider three main transaction models: corporatization ... partnerships ... [and] privatization. (Khanna et al., 2018)

The recent decision of the Indian government to monetize public assets through privatization appears inspired by such corporate consultants

(Ranade, 2021). Similar stories of monstrosity, destruction, and dispossession are legion. Tata's and Essar's role in arming the Salwa Judum militia in Chhattisgarh (Shrivastava and Kohari, 2012), Hindustan Unilever's mercury poisoning in Kodaikanal (Bhargava et al., 2001), and Coca Cola's depletion of groundwater in Mehdiganj (Varman and Al-Amoudi, 2016) exemplify ever-expanding corporate profiteering that has stockpiled bodies and destroyed ecologies in the path of capitalist growth and the nation-state's 'development'. Rather than a retreat of the state as free-market gurus sell, corporations need the state to do the dirty work of clearing lands, conscripting the police to bulldoze or even fire on protesting Adivasis or Dalits, so that corporate profiteering can proceed unhindered (Shrivastava and Kothari, 2012; Varman, Skålén, and Belk, 2012; Varman and Vijay, 2018).

Apart from precipitating and using crises for corporate profiteering, neoliberalism creates a crisis of imagination and fosters its own trajectory of further violence and revenge. Haiven (2020: 12) suggests that 'Enclosure 3.0, or hyperenclosures', plays a significant role in the process. He describes the seizure of common lands and resources as Enclosure 1.0, which was followed by Enclosure 2.0 in which we witnessed capital's theft of social wealth through privatization of public services, the deregulation of industry that destroyed ecosystems, and the extractive politics of unpayable debt. Hyperenclosure, as Enclosure 3.0, represents the use of media and technology to seize upon the commons of the imagination, cognition, communication, and creativity. This hyperenclosure manifests most glaringly with social media control over political discourse and the rise of WhatsApp University to spread disinformation, misinformation, fake news, and propaganda. For instance, *gau rakshaks* (cow protectors), self-labelled vigilantes, allegedly use the WhatsApp network to spread fake news and doctored videos, typically targeting discriminated groups such as Dalits, Muslims, Adivasis, and Christians for cow smuggling or beef consumption (Mukherjee, 2020). The habitual micro-practices of everyday forwarding of fake news build a *mahaul* (atmosphere) of rumour and suspicion, culminating in monstrous events. Such stereotypes also proliferate in mainstream media and films, and television series (Banaji and Bhat, 2019).

Haiven (2020: 13) contends that in this crisis of imagination, we may embrace the hyperenclosure as 'fractal capitalists', adopting the 'freedom' to compete and consume. Alternatively, we opt for a neofundamentalism outside the hyperenclosure, striving for an 'authenticity' through religious, racial, ethnonational, political, or personal registers. Such authenticity may be derived from seemingly harmless spirituality such as yoga, mindfulness, or minimalism, but can also morph into religious or rational fundamentalism. However, Haiven (2020: 13) considers that both fractal capitalists and neofundamentalists are revenge capitalism's children: 'each, in their own way, is filled with easily misdirected vengeance that furnishes revenge politics with its terrible energies'.

This 'misdirected vengeance' must be understood in the context of finance capital where there is no identifiable exploiter. Prashad (2018) contends that workers and the unemployed *know* they are exploited, disposable, and cast aside as bare lives. Unlike industrial capitalism, where one could strike outside factory gates, how can the exploited hold exploiters accountable under the fictitious shadows of finance capital? Prashad (2018) adds that the millions who struggle to find employment will be made into the living dead: 'they exist so that they will soon not exist; they are born, but purpose has been taken from their lives. But what to do with their anger? ... The guns are mostly turned against strangers, the rage phantasmagoric' (p. 18). Strong men rise in this society, 'telling the hemorrhaging middle-class and the unemployed workers that it is neither the rich nor the state apparatus that are to blame for social failure.... The way ahead is to disparage the marginal, the vulnerable. It is those people who are at fault' (Prashad, 2018: 16).

Thus, neoliberalism and finance capital produce and are furthered by a regime that requires close attention. It is fascism based on the phantasms of the Other and nationalism.

THE FASCIST PHANTASMS OF THE OTHER AND NATIONALISM

Neoliberal destruction of human lives has been accompanied by a particular phantasmagoria – a parade of ghosts that distracts from the real monstrosity of finance capital. This is a phantasmagoria of Hindutva. 'Phantasmagoria' was a term coined by Étienne-Gaspard Robert in 1797 to connote the spectacular depiction of phantasms in plays that used moving lanterns to create a parade of ghosts (Cohen, 1989). More recently, several authors have applied the idea of phantasmagoria 'to surface invisible, unacknowledged or shadowy aspects of modernity and to explore the contents of contemporary social imaginaries' (Schwabenland and Tomlinson, 2015: 1914; see also De Cock, Baker, and Volkman, 2011). Apart from being a form of theatre, the phantasm has a long lineage as a conceptual tool, with Karl Marx and Walter Benjamin using the concept to describe the transfixing power of commodity culture. Our analysis of the present phase of Indian neoliberalism as a phantasmagoric realm partly draws on Agamben's (1993) reading of Freud, who points out that phantasms are often created to overcome a loss that is unbearable. Accordingly, ego breaks its links to reality and accepts phantasms of desire as a superior reality under such conditions of loss.

As we have established in the previous sections, neoliberal capitalism is one such source of loss and dispossession that robs people of their economic means of subsistence, selfhood, and identity and forcefully inserts them into markets as either buyers or sellers (Harvey, 2004). Patnaik (2020: 42) notes,

> Neoliberalism, in short, has brought the world economy into a crisis, from which no bourgeois, or even social democratic, political formations are in any position to extricate their respective national economies. They can do so only by delinking, in some measure, from globalization, that is, by going beyond the current phase of capitalism, marked by the hegemony of globalized finance; but they are immanently incapable of doing so by their class orientation.

In order to overcome this loss, people show a great urge 'to shape the maximum reality seizing on the maximum unreality' through an 'obstinate phantasmagoric tendency' (Agamben, 1993: 26). In this dialectic of real and unreal, phantasmic othering and nationalism become, as Benjamin (1969: 82) incisively concluded about Parisian arcades, 'a phantasmagoria into which people entered in order to be distracted ... they yielded to its manipulations while savoring their alienation from themselves and from others'. Although Benjamin interprets phantasmagoric not just as a form of mystification, we see a particular illusory function in its fascist creation.

In contemporary India, specific phantasms are part of the Hindutva ideology of the Rashtriya Swayamsevak Sangh (RSS). There is an explicit attempt to glorify a Hindu past, vilify Muslims as traitors, and mobilize nationalist sentiments to restrict the egalitarian impulses of socialist ideals (Basu et al., 1993). Zachariah (2020) suggests that India has the longest-running fascist movement in the world – the RSS. As Sarkar (2016: 143) notes,

> central to Hindutva as a mass phenomenon (or for that matter to Fascism) is the development of a powerful and extendable enemy image through appropriating stray elements from past prejudices, combining them with new ones skilfully dressed up as old verities, and broadcasting the resultant compound through the most up-to-date media techniques.

Such agenda finds resonance with middle and upper classes, primarily drawn from upper-caste Hindus, who are eager to be conscripted into the global flows of capital and support the growth of the BJP (Poruthiyil, 2021). Moreover, as in the case of Europe, we witness the unleashing of storm troopers in the form of mobs that invade the public sphere in a controlled manner to intimidate and inflict violence (Simeon, 2016). Like their European counterparts, these storm troopers have thrived under the corporate–state patronage (Lalwani, 2021; Srinivasan, 2016).

Such fascist impulses and violence have democratic legitimacy (Banaji, 2016; Rosenberg, 2016; Sassoon, 2021). Fascism in Italy and Germany took control of the state not through coups but through legitimate constitutional processes that included active electoral politics (Rosenberg, 2016). We see similarities in India today. Paxton (2005: 37) notes, '[F]ascists need a demonized enemy against which to mobilize followers.' The deployment of phantasms of Muslim invasions, a glorious Hindu past, or muscular nationalism does not merely indicate mystification but also signifies attempts by fascists to offer another afterlife beyond the earlier liberal vision of India. These phantasms create a heady cocktail of populism, nationalism, authoritarianism, and majoritarianism (Chatterji, Hansen, and Jaffrelot, 2019). In eerie similarities with European fascism, the BJP, as the political arm of the RSS, claims to speak for the masses and against the elite (Paxton,

2005). Hindu nationalism is depicted as the true destiny of the people of India, thwarted time and again by Muslim invaders and the British. Majoritarianism is driven by augmenting the numbers who subscribe to the nationalist ideology (Sarkar, 2016), including Dalits and Adivasis, who are the most dispossessed and derealized by the pro-corporate ideology (Sundar, 2019). Those marginalized or critical of this agenda are then anti-national. This potent combination surfaces in other contexts, such as Trump's America, Erdogan's Turkey, and Bolsanaro's Brazil. In its new Indian inflection, this mixture is uninhibitedly seasoned with pro-corporate policies and practices (Chatterji, Hansen, and Jaffrelot, 2019).

Ivy (1995: 22) describes the phantasm as an 'epistemological object whose presence or absence cannot be definitively located'. Accordingly, a phantasm is neither internal and subjective nor external or objective, but 'an area of illusion'. This area of illusion is not fixed in space and time and keeps shifting through imagination, desire, and experiences. The phantasm is an especially appropriate analytical instrument to capture the nature of fascism under financialized capitalism. The current ruling dispensation creates the phantasmagoria we witness with the active support and participation of corporations and corporate media. Banaji (2016, ix–x) reminds that corporations facilitated Narendra Modi's image makeover after the 2002 Gujarat riots,

> [a]nd as with Hitler's growing acceptability in wider social circles after 1924, his [Modi's] sordid image has since been refurbished to transform a hardened RSS functionary into prime-ministerial material, thanks to the Washington-based PR and lobbyist firm APCO, hired at tax-payers expense to obliterate the memory of 2002. The forces aiding this image makeover include major sycophants in India's business community, leaders of industry who have chosen to make Gujarat and Modi the platform of a state fanatically committed to capitalism.

As a result of these corporate–state deceptions, there is a blurring of boundaries between the real and the imaginary. Such a blur furthers the circulation of phantasms. These phantasms in the context of the current regime shift attention away from the monstrosity of vampire capital and to the imagined play of ghosts that haunt the saffron imagination of majoritarian India.

These phantasms link the saffron imagination with geography and history to produce a regime of truth that blurs real and false or authentic and simulated (Favero, 2003). Moreover, a phantasm is ghostly as it is about life beyond the current one. Agamben (1993: 112) suggests, '[E]very culture is essentially a process of transmission and of *Nachleben*'. In this reading of culture and phantasm, *Nachleben* means life that is after the current one or a world beyond the current one. Thus, the current right-wing phantasm is a ghostly production of an entity that is marked by illusions (Ivy, 1995). It is this reading of culture by Agamben (1993) and Ivy (1995) that brings elements of desire, illusion, and afterlife together in our interpretation of phantasmagoria. Although phantasmic is illusory and ghostly, as Mankekar (2015: 73) points out, it has 'material and tangible implications for lives and subjectivities'.

In this fascist phantasmagoria, the Indian nation is the land of the Hindus, whose glory crumbled because of Muslim invaders and the colonial encounter. While neoliberalism generates disenchantment and alienation among the 99 per cent (Arruzza, Fraser, and Bhattacharya, 2019), the anger is tragically directed at the wrong targets (Haiven, 2020). Rather than an interrogation of the mode of production that dispossesses, anger is directed towards those more dispossessed. Chatterji, Hansen, and Jaffrelot (2019: loc. 285) observe,

> Among the active supporters attending Modi's meetings and taking part in the most militant sections of the Sangh Parivar, including the Bajrang Dal, were lumpenised 'angry young men'. Some of them are resentful, jobless, upper caste members who epitomise a new political culture based on the quest for self-esteem.

Like the *Sturmabteilung* (SA or Brown Shirts) in Germany (Rosenberg, 2016), these sites of lumpenized angry young men become recruiting grounds of storm troopers, who are supported by the state and sponsored by corporations. A concrete outcome of the current phantasmagoria of fascist nationalism is visible in rising vigilantism, lynchings, and militant uprisings by dominant castes to protect perpetrators of crimes against not only the working classes but, specifically, also Muslims, women, Dalits, and Adivasis (Chatterji, Hansen, and Jaffrelot, 2019). What is significant is not just the rise in crimes but that they are 'openly committed heinous crimes' (Thorat, 2019: loc. 4291), such as *gau rakshaks* thrashing Dalit youth in Una or the lynching of Tabrez Ansari in Jharkhand. Instead of hospitalization, the police later charged Tabrez Ansari as a thief and produced him before a magistrate who remanded him to custody. He died in custody later. The combined force of nationalists in government and storm troopers engaged in cultural policing and vigilantism co-opts other institutions of democracy such as the police apparatus, judiciary, and the media (Simeon, 2016). As Bardhan notes (2019: loc. 3623), '[t]he current regime is presiding over the creeping degeneration of Indian democracy into a kind of thugocracy: the leaders are mostly unconcerned, even shameless, about this'.

This fascist nationalism corrodes all democratic institutions. Rajnish Rai (2019: 111), in his auto-ethnographic account as a serving officer of the Indian Police Services for more than 25 years, documents the ascendance of violence and the complicity of the police forces through illegal killings that normalize and promote majoritarian violence (see also Jagannathan and Rai, 2018). This phantasmagoria becomes more shocking each day, and a key element of this phantasmagoria is the 'foreign conspiracy'. In September 2019, the RSS chief Mohan Bhagwat stated that lynching was a 'Western concept' alien to the Hindu community and that people were using the term to defame India by imposing such terms (Banerjee, 2019). We witnessed the 'international conspiracy' turn in the rape and murder of a 19-year-old Dalit woman in Hathras, allegedly by the dominant caste Thakurs of her village. In response, it is alleged, to suppress dissent among the Dalits, the dominant caste Thakurs mobilized the police to cremate the body in the middle of the night without the presence of the victim's family (*The Caravan*, 29 October 2020). Responding to the media frenzy and international attention on this incident, Chief Minister Ajay Bisht, also known as Yogi Adityanath, deemed the entire episode an 'international conspiracy'. Aided and abetted by a compliant and sycophantic mainstream media, 'distract and rule' becomes a governance practice, garnering popularity for a right-wing, securing middle-class support, and circumventing organized opposition (Roy, 2020; see also Palshikar, 2019).

In sum, in this age of monstrosity of finance capital and corporations, it is vital to see how fascism is furthered to aid profiteering. These ways of seeing put in place praxis that helps us imagine the world differently. To borrow from McNally (2011: 7), these alternative pathways require 'developing a dialectical optics, ways of seeing the unseen ... to chart the cartography of the invisible'.

IMAGINING ALTERNATIVES

The fascist phantasmagoria is not a dream that can be merely opposed by awakening but by creating reflexive and critical practices (Benjamin, 1969). As much as the task of reimagining another world is imperative at this moment, it seems daunting and hopeless for numerous reasons. First, dominant knowledge production across the world embraces the end of history and inevitability of capitalism (see also Vijay and Varman, 2018). As Jameson (2003: 76) observes, 'it is easier to imagine the end of the world than to imagine the end of capitalism'. Second, this contemporary crisis of capitalism is magnified in India by the ascendant fascification of our imaginations through print and electronic media, and social media. This fascist tendency is a perennial presence in the current conjuncture of neoliberalism (Patnaik, 2020). In the struggle to come out of this interregnum between the old and the new, the chief characteristic is uncertainty. Sassoon (2021: 2) notes, 'It is like crossing a wide river: the old riverbank is left behind, but the other side is still indistinct; currents might push one back, and drowning cannot be ruled out.'

Various authors in this volume present theoretical reflections and experiments impelled by imaginations that challenge the current neoliberal monstrosity. It is important to note that it is insufficient that alternative organizations are merely distinct from the mainstream or dominant capitalist forms. In this volume, most contributors confront the demonic nature of the capitalist logic and engage with the need to overcome the hegemonic common sense with what Gramsci (2020) labelled as a 'good sense'. Such a task is so much more urgent in a world ravaged by COVID-19. Here, we agree with Giroux (2021) that

[t]he pandemic has exposed neoliberal capitalism's criminality, cruelty, and inhumanity. It has become clear in the age of plagues and monsters that any successful movement for resistance must be not only for democracy and anti-capitalist; it must also be anti-fascist. We owe such a challenge to ourselves, to future generations, and to the promise of a global socialist democracy waiting to be born.

The chapters in this volume are underpinned by a unifying imperative for social transformation and an urgent need to reimagine the world. Yet this is not a book of a single grand theory. Rather, this volume assembles multiple interdisciplinary narratives and plural, open-ended imaginations through specific case studies of alternatives in the Indian context.

These chapters join several urgent conversations on alternatives across the world (for example Cruz, Alves, and Delbridge, 2017; Dawson, 2016; Gibson-Graham, 2006; Kothari and Joy, 2017; Parker et al., 2014; Zanoni et al., 2017). This body of work has drawn attention to alternative organizing through forms such as workers' cooperatives (for example Cheney et al., 2014), communes (for example Ciccariello-Maher, 2016), and solidary economy initiatives (for example Meira, 2014). These forms of organizing strive to bring into being a different world, emphasizing human emancipation, equity, and justice (Vijay and Varman, 2018). We outline how this volume contributes to extant understanding by drawing attention to the questions of social relations, rights and representations, and subaltern struggles that constitute alternative forms.

ALTERNATIVE IMAGINATION OF SOCIAL RELATIONS

Any struggle for radical social transformation must contest the capitalist imagination of social relations that is fundamentally constituted through colonialism, patriarchy, and exploitation of workers and nature. Alternative imaginations offer different possibilities for organizing social relations (Gago, 2020; Vergès, 2021; Yengde, 2019). The opening chapters of the book offer such alternative visions.

In the second chapter, Maidul Islam brings Mohandas Gandhi and Antonio Gramsci into conversation through Kojin Karatani to explore how their ideas might formulate an alternative imagination to capitalism. Islam specifically attends to the local exchange trading system (LETS) as a site of resistance to capitalism. A LETS engages both producers and consumers through workers' cum consumers' cooperatives. These cooperatives are based on mutual aid and are partly inspired by Gandhi's political consumerism that emphasized the boycott of foreign goods as a tool of popular mobilization. Islam also borrows from Karatani's reading of Gramsci, who pointed in his *Prison Notebooks* to the power of the Gandhian boycott movement that linked it with the war of position, which at times could become a war of manoeuvre. In so doing, Islam argues that the limitations of the nineteenth- and twentieth-century working-class mobilizations against capital at the site of production have to be overcome with alternative forms of mobilization at the site of consumption. Islam foregrounds the possibilities of such producer-cum-consumer mobilizations and the creation of local exchange trading networks. In these ways, Islam imagines alternative organization and political agency that have the potential to resist capitalism.

In the third chapter, Prabhir Vishnu Poruthiyil engages with the phantasmagoria of the right-wing nationalism that confronts India. Poruthiyil argues that, unlike countries where inequality-fuelled resentments against the elite are primary triggers, in India, it is the plutocracy itself that is driving sectarianism to preserve its economic and cultural interests. The resistance to this sectarian plutocracy has been ineffective as it predominantly uses a rights framework noted for its troubling coexistence with neoliberalism. Specifically, such a rights-based approach engineers a shared consensus and aims for sufficiency or staving off destitution while neglecting material inequality. Although neglecting material equality may be a bargain for a minimum floor protection of rights in some contexts, in India this means more resources within a sectarian plutocracy. A plutocracy infused with sectarianism implies not just that the elite interests are prioritized but also the programmatic denial of rights to minorities and other oppositional groups. Rights-based activism and analyses of discrimination against minorities rarely trace the causes to the increasing wealth concentration within groups aligned with sectarianism. The chapter argues that democratic socialism offers a coherent philosophical alternative to dislodge human rights from minimalism and counter both the sectarian and plutocratic dimensions of the hegemony. Key features of democratic socialism such as the protection of labour rights, creating solidarities based on economic exploitation, and the adoption of scientific temper can jointly address the critical processes that sustain the sectarian plutocracy – that is wealth concentration, polarization, and the acceptance of supremacist propaganda.

In Chapter 4, Ashish Kothari critiques the current agenda of development and the capitalist monstrosity of environmental degradation. Kothari challenges the destructive neoliberal discourse of development. With its roots in the desire of imperial powers to find new ways of exploiting and dominating after the Second World War to aid in the reconstruction of their economies, this development model is based on a unilinear notion of how nations should 'progress' (farming/fishing/pastoral to industrial and post-industrial; traditional to modern, and so on). This predatory model considers measures like gross domestic product (GDP) as the most important indicators of the stage and rate of development and promotes unrestrained industrialization, commercialization, extraction of resources, and urbanization. Its impacts have been disastrous worldwide with the creation of deathworlds, evidenced by how human activity has crossed several critical planetary thresholds, with the extinction of species, widespread water and air pollution, and potentially runaway climate change as some of the results. Kothari examines the current predation of capitalism that operates through forces of injustice, oppression, ecological unsustainability and delineates the fundamental faults of the 'model' of development foisted upon India's poor. He describes Vikalp Sangam, an alternative platform he has co-founded, which creates a common ground for people to voice their deprivation and discrimination, displacement, and dispossession. Vikalp Sangam reminds us that people struggle and resist to create new futures even when in the grip of oppressive conditions.

ALTERNATIVE VISIONS OF RIGHTS AND REPRESENTATIONS

In a milieu where the right to dissent is suppressed and snatched away, it is important to reiterate, *ad nauseam, ad absurdum*, that the very birth of the Indian nation-state was through dissent and struggle. As Pawar and Moon (2008) remind us in their account of Dalit women's forgotten role in the

Ambedkarite movements – *We Also Made History* – even the most oppressed resisted and wrote new worlds into existence, under all conditions of subordination, dehumanization, and humiliation. People's struggles and the destructive effects of financialization rarely enter public discourse or surface in distorted ways because of financiers' control of media and representations through their labyrinth of investments in various corporations engaged in thought control. Social media and most print and electronic media normalize the phantasms of the Other and nationalisms, viciously circulating fake news and criminally staging spectacles (Palshikar, 2019; Varman and Vijay, 2021). The following three chapters in the book document social struggles and attempts to reorganize voice and visibility through democratic representations to resist the imperatives of neoliberal capitalism and fascism.

In Chapter 5, Priyanshu Gupta documents the struggle of Hasdeo Aranya Bachao Sangharsh Samiti – an Adivasi community-led movement to resist displacement and protect their densely forested and biodiversity-rich region. Gupta mobilizes the knowledge that activists produce in the form of popular writings, *gram sabha* resolutions, and dialogues across scales of governance (local to state and central government). He shows how the movement has successfully resisted capitalist expansion of mining and infrastructure projects by exploiting the available policy and constitutional spaces. The use of decentralized governance provisions along with continuous and often proactive engagement with policy processes for environmental and social clearances has become the focal point of resistance. Gupta argues that the strategy of careful framing that amalgamates environmental and social dimensions of resource conflict, and tactically leverages the broader civil society network to amplify local voices, has allowed Hasdeo Aranya forests to emerge at the centre stage of energy-conservation policy debates in India. The chapter showcases the potential and limits of harnessing the institutional spaces for organized resistance, as available in a constitutional democracy.

In the sixth chapter, Srinath Jagannathan and Rajnish Rai examine how the independent media platform *The Wire* presents an alternative to corporate media that are compliant and sycophantic to the current government (Bardhan, 2019; Roy, 2020). *The Wire* was birthed in this very fascist phantasmagoria to offer a subversive imagination and resist, combating the shrinking freedom of the press head-on despite threats to their editors and journalists (B. Sharma, 2020; The Wire Staff, 2020). Jagannathan and Rai spotlight the February 2016 police action in which Jawaharlal Nehru University (JNU) students were arrested and charged with sedition. Several media outlets collaborated with the BJP to build a discourse of national hysteria against a section of JNU students. In this context, the authors focus on *The Wire*'s discursive work. By engaging with narrative fragments of *The Wire*'s coverage of the JNU crisis and conversations with numerous stakeholders, Jagannathan and Rai argue that it is possible to resist the muscularity of majoritarian nationalism by paying attention to issues of gender and problematizing the politics of presence. They contend that the case for a slow, democratic temporality and the recognition of the fictionality of presence is enabled by deepening the process of witnessing. Such a practice of witnessing is an intertextual act filled with the subjectivities of craft, discontent, and lament that countervails the ongoing monstrosity.

In a similar vein, in Chapter 7, Apoorv Khare and Ram Manohar Vikas describe the case of the People's Archive of Rural India (PARI), an open-source digital archive and a living journal dedicated to rural India. Like *The Wire*, PARI resists the phantasmagoria of corporate media and its stranglehold on information and public discourse. The authors show how people-centric media can be a source of vibrant democratic possibilities. Khare and Vikas surface ways in which PARI offers a corrective to the predatory politics of the mainstream media. They show that rural India, which is in the midst of a deep agrarian crisis and where hundreds of thousands of farmers have committed suicide in the last three decades, is invisibilized by the mainstream media and exists as ellipsis in most media debates. A key reason is the corporatization of media and the weakening of the public sphere in India. They draw on Jürgen Habermas's idea of public sphere to offer PARI as an alternative media platform. A well-functioning democratic public sphere is an important institutional mechanism to ensure the political participation of its people. Simultaneously, PARI also showcases the sheer creativity and cultural heterogeneity of the other India that the fascist phantasmagoria wishes us to forget.

Social infrastructures such as libraries, neighbourhood groups, theatre spaces, playgrounds, and hospitals are the physical places and organizations where people forge social connections, engage in proximate, face-to-face interactions, and nurture mutual support (Klinenberg, 2018). Financialization destroys these social infrastructures and robs people of their rights to represent themselves and their concerns. Rohit Varman and Devi Vijay, in Chapter 8, describe the case of LeftWord publishers in Delhi. LeftWord gains salience in a context where any intellectual infrastructure is anathema to fascist regimes (Paxton, 2005). When to think warrants punishment and where publishers fiddle for the ruling dispensation (*The Wire*, 2020), LeftWord offers a radical alternative that evades enclosure. Varman and Vijay draw on Lefbevre's idea of heterotopic sites to examine this alternative. LeftWord as a site of resistance inverts and challenges the twin evils of finance and fascism. The authors point out that a heterotopia can contain multiple, contradictory emplacements. They show that LeftWord emplaces communist ideals alongside capitalist market-based transactions. If imagining inheres past, present, and future temporalities (Haiven, 2014), LeftWord is a site of heterochrony. It is shaped around communist ideals that inspired many progressive movements across the world in the twentieth century. It negates the present as capitalist and hopes to emplace a future that is equal, just, and fair for all. As much as neoliberal capitalism that dominates our imagination celebrates class-based hierarchies and profiteering, LeftWord is an attempt to be outside it and to create a greater sense of equality.

ALTERNATIVE INTERROGATIONS OF SUBALTERNITY

Alternative futures cannot be imagined without interrogating how capitalism reduces large swathes of populations to subalterns confined to abject poverty. Corporations and neoliberal states produce a governmentality in which there is a facade of off-setting the ill-effects of capitalist destruction of lives and nature. This facade, actively deployed by corporate consultants, non-governmental organizations, and neoliberal regimes, relies on discourses of poverty alleviation through social enterprises and self-help groups. These discourses further corporate profiteering while allowing the state to abdicate any responsibility towards those who are made vulnerable because of capitalist destruction. The last two chapters of the book critically examine such discourses to offer alternative imagination of addressing economic marginalization and subordination.

Neoliberal governments, corporations, and non-profit organizations have fervently competed to insert the business logic into poverty alleviation programmes through discourse of the bottom-of-the pyramid (BOP) formulated by C. K. Prahalad (2006). In Chapter 9, Suparna Chatterjee critiques the representation and refashioning of the state within the BOP discourse. Chatterjee points out that with the ascendant neoliberal political rationality, the state is no longer conceived as an active, or even desirable, agent in redressing societal challenges. The BOP proposition offers a prism to understand how neoliberal social projects constitute the state as the enforcer of the rule of law, especially contractual law focused on maintaining the sanctity of contractual obligations and entitlements between large corporations and poor communities. In this neoliberal avatar, the state is recast as a neutral market overseer or facilitator providing the necessary infrastructure for the survival and sustenance of the 'enterprise society' and is explicitly positioned as secondary to markets in the fight against global poverty. What is ironic, however, is that even as the state is delegitimized and posited as antithetical to innovation, competition, and efficiency, it is nonetheless harnessed to share the costs and burdens of market-making at the BOP. The state's 'public' commitment and reach, its symbolic and material resources, and legal mandate are drawn on strategically to create market conditions conducive to profit generation. In this sense, the state is not so much receding or waning as it is rendered subservient to global capital while the poor are cast into deathworlds. Even as critics question formulations of the state within BOP narratives, they leave unchallenged the underlying normative neoliberal rationality which informs the BOP characterizations of the state. The notion that the state might be reclaimed and revitalized (with all its contradictions and differentiations) to promote collective social emancipation and well-being based on considerations other than those permitted by globalizing capital remains outside the permissible BOP metanarratives.

Much like the BOP discourse, the self-help group movement has been an instrument of 'global crisis management', which seeks recourse in capitalist reform and remediation (Banerjee and Jackson, 2017; Varman, 2016). In particular, the idea of 'women's emancipation' through market-based activities is a key neoliberal trump card (A. Sharma, 2008). The micro-credit and entrepreneurial self-help movements allow global capital to masquerade as progressive, compassionate, and emancipatory, legitimizing neoliberal regimes while building 'economies of affect' through women's immaterial labour (Chatterjee, 2019; Varman, 2016). Kerala's Kudumbashree initiative – a state-instituted programme with the stated objective of women empowerment – is one such site, where it is the working-class women's 'invisible hand' which creates and sustains various infrastructures, including cleaning and care (Devika and Thampi, 2007). George Kandathil, Poornima Varma, and Ram Mohana Turaga, in Chapter 10, critically interrogate the possibilities afforded by Kudumbashree. The authors acknowledge that a central thematic in the search for alternatives to a patriarchal corporate capitalist order has to be women's emancipation. Their multi-site case study reveals the (re)production of a neoliberal self-caring autonomous subject who can be governed at a distance and is inscribed with a masculine hegemony that provides the ideological and material support for the reproduction of capitalistic patriarchal labour relations. In Kudumbashree, they uncover a struggling communitarian subject who positions inconsistently as anti-patriarchal within some experiences and capitalistic patriarchal yet empowered within some other experiences. The authors surface a rupture within the totalitarian web of capitalist patriarchal relations. Within this rupture, day-to-day micro-resistance creates conditions for possibilities of alternative imaginations.

CONCLUSION

In these times of exploitation, destruction of nature, thought control, and hyperenclosures when it is difficult to imagine alternatives, this book provides accounts of resistance and hope. We offer neither a blueprint nor a manifesto. The plural approaches contained in this book speak to the need for organizing on multiple fronts and of the possibilities of interdependent collaborative survival. This book documents but a few instances of dissent and struggles.

As much as the chapters in this volume are firmly grounded in the contemporary Indian context, they highlight the mutilations of contemporary lifeworlds that are likely to leave similar scars and wounds across geographies in the Global North and the Global South that are penetrated by global capitalism. Consider the corporate media conglomerates and publishing houses across the world that do not allow anti-capitalist imaginaries. Indeed, some of the path-breaking work done by the organizations analysed in this volume have transcended nation-state boundaries. For example, LeftWord's publications and May Day event forge internationalist solidarities. Similarly, *The Wire* was a member of the 17 international media organizations under the 'Pegasus Project' that revealed governments' espionage using the Pegasus Spyware.

Cumulatively, these contributions offer some insights into the spatialities and temporalities of alternative organizing. Across chapters, authors foreground how alternative organizations produce spaces that invert, resist, and subvert dominant social relations (for example, Gupta; Kothari; Islam; Kandathil, Varma, and Turaga, this volume). Further, chapters in this volume illustrate scale-jumping wherein connections are made between local, national, and global issues to expand the reach of contentious politics (for example, Khare and Vikas; Varman and Vijay, this volume). These chapters remind us that people create these alternative spaces even when confronted with the military might of the state and powerful corporations. Such alternative spaces are interpenetrated by non-capitalist value regimes, nurtured by solidarity, the gift of life's work, and care, enabling the production of other worlds.

The chapters also surface multiple temporalities. Even as the COVID-19 virus circulates through India and even as we brace for a third wave, many are already writing about a post-pandemic world. And yet there are so many temporalities at play – those in the Aranya forests seeking to undo the ruins and ravages of the past and the present in order to secure a future; the past, present, and futures of *The Wire* and PARI's journalism and archiving; the Kudumbashree workers caring for the wounds of the past for a better tomorrow. In other words, these writings are not just an act of re-imagining for a future. This is a re-imagining that is already underway, already in practice.

We hope that they open up possibilities of greater solidarities within the country and outside. As Sassoon (2021: 239) emphasizes, 'after all, if matters have improved over the previous centuries, it is precisely thanks to those who do not lose hope, who did not give up, and who fought on and on, however morbid the times'. We receive hope from Father Stan Swamy, the 83-year-old ailing activist killed in custody because he was a threat to India's ruling establishment. Stan Swamy wrote: 'But we will still sing in chorus. A caged bird can still sing.'[2]

NOTES

1. Majaz, 'Sarmayadari', translated by Jawed Naqvi, https://www.dawn.com/news/720840/majaaz-on-wall-street, accessed 31 December 2021.
2. From Mander (2021).

REFERENCES

Agamben, G. (1993). *Stanzas: Word and Phantasm in Western Culture.* Minneapolis: University of Minnesota Press.

Agarwal, R., and G. Gopinath (2021). A proposal to end the COVID-19 Pandemic. 19 May. Accessed on 9 September 2021: https://www.imf.org/en/Publications/Staff-Discussion-Notes/Issues/2021/05/19/A-Proposal-to-End-the-COVID-19-Pandemic-460263.

Amrith, S. (2007). Political culture of health in India: A historical perspective. *Economic and Political Weekly* 42 (2): 114–121.

Arruzza, C., N. Fraser, and T. Bhattacharya (2019). *Feminism for the 99%.* London: Verso.

Banaji, J. (2016). *Fascism: Essays on Europe and India.* New Delhi: Three Essays Collective.

Banaji, S., and R. Bhat (2019). *WhatsApp Vigilantes: An Exploration of Citizen Reception and Circulation of WhatsApp Misinformation Linked to Mob Violence in India.* London, UK: Department of Media and Communications, London School of Economics and Political Science.

Banerjee, S. (2019). Lynching alien to India, says RSS chief Mohan Bhagwat. *The Hindu*, 8 October. Accessed on 2 October 2020: https://www.thehindu.com/news/national/rss-chief-says-lynching-is-a-western construct/article 29616428.ece.

Banerjee, S. B., and L. Jackson (2017). Microfinance and the business of poverty reduction: Critical perspectives from rural Bangladesh. *Human Relations* 70(1): 63–91.

Bardhan, P. (2019). Merchants of hype and hate: A political-economic evaluation of the Modi Regime. In *Majoritarian State: How Hindu Nationalism Is Changing India*, ed. A. Chatterji, T. B. Hansen, and C. Jaffrelot. Noida: Harper Collins India, Kindle Edition, 173–192.

Basu, T., P. Datta, S. Sarkar, T. Sarkar, and S. Sen (1993). *Khakhi Shorts Saffron Flags*. New Delhi: Orient Longman.

Benjamin, W. (1969). Paris: The capital of the nineteenth century. *Perspecta* 12: 163–172.

Bhargava, S. N., A. Nair, Ramakrishnan, and R. K. Singh (2003). *The Indian People's Tribunal Report: On the Alleged Environmental Pollution and Health Impacts Caused by the Hindustan Unilever Mercury Thermometer Factory at Kodaikanal.* Online: Combat Law Publications Ltd. for Indian People's Tribunal on Environment and Human Rights. Accessed 4 January 2022: https://hrln.org/publication/indian-peoples-tribunal-report-on-the-alleged-environmental-pollution-and-health-impacts-caused-by-the-hindustan-lever-mercury-thermometer-factory-at-kodaikanal-indian-peoples-tr.

Bhattacharya, T., ed. (2017). *Social Reproduction Theory: Remapping Class, Recentering Oppression*. New York: Pluto Press.

Blakeley, G. (2019). *Stolen: How to Save the World from Financialisation*. London: Repeater.

Chakravarthi, I., B. Roy, I. Mukhopadhyay, and S. Barria, S. (2017). Investing in health. *Economic and Political Weekly* 52(45): 50–60.

Chatterjee, S. (2020). A suitable woman: The coming-of-age of the 'third world woman' at the bottom of the pyramid: A critical engagement. *Human Relations* 73(3): 378–400.

Chatterji, A., T. B. Hansen, and C. Jaffrelot, eds. (2019). *Majoritarian State: How Hindu Nationalism Is Changing India*. Noida: Harper Collins India.

Cheney, G., I. Santa Cruz, A. M. Peredo, and E. Nazareno (2014). Worker cooperatives as an organizational alternative: Challenges, achievements and promise in business governance and ownership. *Organization* 21 (5): 591–603.

Ciccariello-Maher, G. (2016). *Building the Commune: Radical Democracy in Venezuela*. New York: Verso.

Cohen, M. (1989). Walter Benjamin's phantasmagoria. *New German Critique* 48: 87–107.

Crosthwaite, P., P. Knight, and N. Marsh (2014). *Show Me the Money: The Image of Finance, 1700 to the Present.* Manchester: Manchester University Press.

Cruz, L. B., M. A.Alves, and R. Delbridge (2017). Next steps in organizing alternatives to capitalism: toward a relational research agenda. *M@n@ gement* 20 (4): 322–335.

Dawson, M. (2016). *Social Theory for Alternative Societies.* London: Palgrave MacMillan.

De Cock, C., M. Baker, and C. Volkman (2011). Financial phantasmagoria: Corporate image-work in times of crisis. *Organization* 18 (2): 153–172.

Devika, J., and B. V. Thampi (2007). Between 'empowerment' and 'liberation': The Kudumbashree initiative in Kerala. *Indian Journal of Gender Studies* 14 (1): 33–60.

Dimitrov, G. (1938). *The United Front: The Struggle against Fascism and War.* London: Lawrence and Wishart.

Favero, P. (2003). Phantasms in a starry place: Space and identification in a central New Delhi market. *Cultural Anthropology* 18(4): 551–584.

Gadre, A., and A. Shukla (2016). *Dissenting Diagnosis.* New Delhi: Random House India.

Gago, V. (2020). *Feminist International.* New York: Verso.

Ganggoli, L., R. Duggal, and A. Shukla (2005). *Review of Healthcare in India.* Mumbai: Centre for Enquiry into Health and Allied Themes, Research Centre of Anusandhan Trust, Survey No. 2804 & 2805.

Ghosh, J. (2020). A critique of the Indian government's response to the COVID-19 pandemic. *Journal of Industrial and Business Economics* 47 (3): 519–530.

Gibson-Graham, J. K. (2006). *A Postcapitalist Politics.* Minnesota: University of Minnesota Press.

Giroux, H. A. (2021). *Resistance Is Not Futile: Fighting Back in an Age of Manufactured Ignorance.* Accessed on 24 August 2021: https://www.counterpunch.org/2021/07/08/resistance-is-not-futile-fighting-back-in-an-age-of-manufactured-ignorance/

Govindarajan, V., and A. Srivastava (2021). What Zomato's $12 billion IPO says about tech companies today. *Harvard Business Review,* 6 August. Accessed on 8 September 2021: https://hbr.org/2021/08/what-zomatos-12-billion-ipo-says-about-tech-companies-today.

Gramsci, A. (2020). *Selections from the Prison Notebooks*. New Delhi: Orient Blackswan.

Haiven, M. (2014). *Crises of Imagination, Crises of Power: Capitalism, Creativity and the Commons*. New York: Zed Books.

—— (2020). *Revenge Capitalism: The Ghosts of Empire, the Demons of Capital, and the Settling of Unpayable Debts*. London: Pluto Press.

Harvey, D. (2004). The new imperialism: Accumulation by dispossession. *Socialist Register* 40: 63–87.

Hudson, M. (2015). Killing the Host: How Financial Parasites and Debt Bondage Destroy the Global Economy. California: Islet.

—— (2017). How bankers became the top exploiters of the economy. *Counterpunch*, 15 March. Accessed on 24 June 2021: https://www.counterpunch.org/2017/03/15/how-bankers-became-the-top-exploiters-of-the-economy/.

IFAT-ITF (2020). *Locking Down the Impact of COVID-19*. Accessed on 24 August 2021: https://cis-india.org/raw/ifat-itf-locking-down-the-impact-of-covid-19.

Isidore, C. (2021). Here's what Covid vaccines are worth to Big Pharma. CNN, 15 March. Accessed on 1 September 2021: https://edition.cnn.com/2021/03/13/business/business-of-covid-vaccine/index.html.

Ivy, M. (1995). *Discourses of Vanishing Modernity, Phantasm, Japan*. Chicago: Chicago University Press.

Jagannathan, S., and R. Rai (2018). Formal and informal technologies of alternative organisational spaces within the state. In *Alternative Organisations in India: Undoing Boundaries*, ed. Devi Vijay and Rohit Varman. New Delhi: Cambridge University Press, 26–58.

Jameson, F. (2003). Future city. *New Left Review* 21 (May–June): 65–80.

Khanna, D., LaBresh, J., Kengelbach, J., Selikowitz, D., Argent, J., and Burke, E. (2018). The 75 trillion opportunity in public assets. BCG, 18 October. Accessed on 24 July 2021: https://www.bcg.com/publications/2018/75-trillion-dollars-opportunity-public-assets.

Klein, N. (2007). *The Shock Doctrine: The Rise of Disaster Capitalism*. New York: Macmillan.

Klinenberg, E. (2018). *Palaces for the People: How Social Infrastructure Can Help Fight Inequality, Polarization and the Decline of Civic Life.* New York: Broadway Books.

Koshy, S. M. (2021). Lakshadweep filmmaker faces sedition FIR for 'bio-weapon' remark. NDTV, 11 June. Accessed on 1 September 2021: https://www.ndtv. com/india-news/lakshadweep-filmmaker-named-in-sedition-fir-for-criticising-administrators-covid-policy-bio-weapon-remark-2461330.

Kothari, A., and K. J. Joy (2017). *Alternative Futures: India Unshackled.* New Delhi: Authors Upfront.

Lalwani, V. (2021). Viral terror: Why the perpetrators of anti-Muslim assaults are broadcasting their own crimes. *Scroll.in,* 2 September. Accessed on 6 September 2021: https://scroll.in/article/1004272/viral-terror-why-the-perpetrators-of-anti-muslim-assaults-are-broadcasting-their-own-crimes.

Lapavitsas, C. (2013). *Profiting without Producing: How Finance Exploits Us All.* New York: Verso.

Mander, Harsh (2021). The song of a caged bird: A tribute to Fr Stan Swamy. *Scroll. in,* 7 July. Accessed on 1 September 2021: https://scroll.in/article/999486/the-song-of-a-caged-bird-a-tribute-to-fr-stan-swamy.

Mankekar, P. (2015). *Unsettling India: Affect, Temporality, Transnationality.* Durham: Duke University Press.

Marx, K. (2013). *Capital.* London: Wordsworth Classics.

McNally, D. (2011). *Monsters of the Market: Zombies, Vampires and Global Capitalism.* Leiden: Brill.

Meira, F. B. (2014). Liminal organization: Organizational emergence within solidary economy in Brazil. *Organization* 21 (5): 713–729.

Montgomerie, J., and R. Cain (2018). The zombie economy and the aesthetic of austerity. *Angles: New Perspectives on the Anglophone World.* https://doi.org/10.4000/angles.582.

Mukherjee, R. (2020). Mobile witnessing on WhatsApp: Vigilante virality and the anatomy of mob lynching. *South Asian Popular Culture,* 18(1): 79–101.

Nileena, M. S. (2021). Pharma companies driving policy led to vaccine apartheid: Mohga Kamal-Yanni. *The Caravan,* 9 May. Accessed on 1 September 2021: https://caravanmagazine.in/health/pharma-companies-driving-policy-led-to-vaccine-apartheid-mohga-kamal-yanni

Oxfam (2019). *Public Good or Private Wealth.* Accessed 10 September, 2021, https://oxfamilibrary.openrepository.com/bitstream/handle/10546/620599/ bp-public-good-or-private-wealth-210119-en.pdf?utm_source=indepth.

——— (2021). *Adding Fuel to Fire: How IMF Demands for Austerity Will Drive Up Inequality Worldwide.* Oxford, UK: Oxfam International.

Palshikar, S. (2019). Toward hegemony: The BJP beyond electoral dominance – majoritarian state. In *Majoritarian State: How Hindu Nationalism is Changing India,* ed. A. Chatterji, T. B. Hansen, and C. Jaffrelot. Noida: Harper Collins India, 101–116.

Pandhi, N. (2021). India's rights panel wants law for dignity in death – but marginal groups first need dignity in life. *Scroll.in,* 8 June. Accessed on 1 September 2021: https://scroll.in/article/995531/indias-rights-panel-wants-law-for-dignity-in-death-but-marginal-groups-first-need-dignity-in-life.

Patnaik, P. (2016). Capitalism and its current crisis. *Monthly Review,* 1 January. Accessed on 9 September 2021: https://monthlyreview.org/2016/01/01/ capitalism-and-its-current-crisis/.

——— (2019). Shadow of fascism. *Monthly Review,* 8 April. Accessed on 9 September 2021: https://mronline.org/2019/04/08/the-modi-years/.

——— (2020). Neoliberalism and fascism. *Agrarian South: Journal of Political Economy* 9(1), 33–49.

Parker, M., G. Cheney, V. Fournier, and C. Land, eds. (2014). *The Routledge Companion to Alternative Organization.* London: Routledge.

Pawar, U. and M. Moon (2008). *We Also Made History: Women in the Ambedkarite Movement.* Translated by Wandana Sonalkar. New Delhi: Zubaan.

Paxton, R. O. (2005). *The Anatomy of Fascism.* London: Vintage.

Phillips, P. (2018). *Giants: The Global Power Elite.* New York: Seven Stories,

Poruthiyil, P. V. (2021). Big business and fascism: a dangerous collusion. *Journal of Business Ethics* 168(1): 121–135.

Prashad, V. (2007). *The Darker Nations: A Biography of the Short-lived Third World.* New Delhi: Leftword Books.

——— (2018). Introduction: The return of the monster. In *Strongmen: Trump, Modi, Erdoğan, Putin, Duterte,* V. Prashad. New Delhi: Leftword Books, 1–11.

Progressive International (2021). Summit for vaccine internationalism hails a 'new international health order'. Accessed on 25 July 2021: https://

progressive.international/wire/2021-06-21-progressive-international-hails-the-beginning-of-a-new-international-health-order-as-global-south-states-commit-to-share-covid-19-vaccine-technology-and-production/en.

Rana, C. (2021). Culpable carnage: How the Modi Government's failure to act led to India's COVID-19 catastrophe. *The Caravan*, 1 June. Accessed on 18 June 2021. https://caravanmagazine.in/health/modi-government-failure-led-india-covid-19-catastrophe.

Ranade, S. (2021). How will asset monetisation help the government? *The Wire*, 24 August. Accessed on 9 September 2021: https://thewire.in/economy/how-will-asset-monetization-help-the-government.

Rai, R. (2019). The production of precariousness for the dissenting subject at the intersections of neoliberal and cultural nationalist practice. *Decision* 46(2): 111–126.

Raj, K. and S. Gurmat (2021). As India's gig workers died of Covid-19, their families received neither govt nor company aid. *Article14*, 6 September. Accessed on 7 September 2021: https://article-14.com/post/as-india-s-gig-workers-died-of-covid-19-their-families-receive-neither-govt-nor-company-aid-6135842b68c1a.

Roy, A. (2019). *My Seditious Heart*. New Delhi: Penguin.

———— (2020). *Azaadi: Freedom, Fascism, Fiction*. New Delhi: Penguin Books.

———— (2021). It's not enough to say the govt has failed: We are witnessing a crime against humanity. *The Wire*, 29 April. Accessed on 9 September 2021: https://thewire.in/government/india-covid-19-government-crime-against-humanity

Rosenberg, A. (2016). Fascism as a mass movement. In *Fascism: Essays on Europe and India*, ed. J. Banaji. New Delhi: Three Essays Collective, 19–96.

Rukmini, S. (2021). Madhya Pradesh saw nearly three times more deaths than normal after second wave of Covid-19 struck. *Scroll.in*, 12 June. Accessed on 8 August 2021. https://scroll.in/article/996772/madhya-pradesh-saw-nearly-three-times-more-deaths-than-normal-after-second-wave-of-covid-19-struck.

RUPE (2020). *Crisis and Predation: India, COVID-19, and Global Finance*. New York: Monthly Review Press.

Sarkar, S. (2016). The Fascism of the Sangh Parivar. In *Fascism: Essays on Europe and India*, ed. J. Banaji. New Delhi: Three Essays Collective, 135–151.

Sassoon, D. 2021. *Morbid Symptoms: An Anatomy of a World in Crisis*. London: Verso

Schwabenland, C., and F. Tomlinson. (2015). Shadows and light: diversity management as phantasmagoria. *Human Relations* 68(12): 1913–1936.

Sharma, A. (2008). *Logics of Empowerment: Development, Gender, and Governance in Neoliberal India*. Minnesota: University of Minnesota Press.

Sharma, B. (2020). Siddharth Varadarajan on police summons: Coronavirus has deepened the worst tendencies of Indian governance. *HuffPost*, 15 April. Accessed on 9 September 2021: https://www.huffingtonpost.in/entry/siddharth-varadarajan-police-coronavirus_in_5e969f88c5b6ead140049377.

Shrivastava, A., and A. Kothari (2012). *Churning the Earth: The Making of Global India*. New Delhi: Penguin.

Simeon, D. (2016). The law of killing: A brief history of Indian fascism. In *Fascism: Essays on Europe and India*, ed. J. Banaji. New Delhi: Three Essays Collective, 153–213.

Srinivasan, K. (2016). A subaltern fascism? In *Fascism: Essays on Europe and India*, ed. J. Banaji. New Delhi: Three Essays Collective, 99–134.

Sundar, N. (2019). Hindutva incorporation and socio-economic exclusion: The Adivasi dilemma. In *Majoritarian State: How Hindu Nationalism Is Changing India*, ed. A. Chatterji, T. B. Hansen, and C. Jaffrelot. Noida: Harper Collins India, Kindle Edition, 249–258.

SWAN (2020). No data, no problem: Centre in denial about migrant worker deaths and distress. *The Wire*, 16 September. Accessed on 15 December 2020: https://thewire.in/rights/migrant-workers-no-data-centre-covid-19-lockdown-deaths-distress-swan.

Taibbi, M. (2010). The great American bubble machine. *Rolling Stone*, 5 April. https://www.rollingstone.com/politics/politics-news/the-great-american-bubble-machine-195229/.

The Caravan (2020). Prosecute the dominant-caste men and police who committed crimes in Hathras: India Civil Watch International. 29 October. Accessed on 9 September 2021: https://caravanmagazine.in/noticeboard/india-civil-watch-prosecute-dominant-caste-men-and-police.

The Wire Staff (2020). UP Police registers FIR against journalist Supriya Sharma for report on PM's adopted village. *The Wire*, 18 June. Accessed on

9 September 2021: https://thewire.in/media/up-police-fir-supriya-sharma-journalist-domari.

The Wire (2020). Bloomsbury withdraws book on Delhi riots launched by BJP's Kapil Mishra. 22 August. Accessed on 9 September 2021: https://thewire.in/books/bloomsbury-withdraws-book-on-delhi-riots-launched-by-bjps-kapil-mishra.

Thorat, S. (2019). Dalits in post-2014 India: Between promise and action. In *Majoritarian State: How Hindu Nationalism Is Changing India*, ed. A. Chatterji, T. B. Hansen, and C. Jaffrelot. Noida: Harper Collins India, Kindle Edition, 217–236.

Varman, R. (2016). Mystifying development: Marketing capitalist enterprise as compassionate caring in a postcolonial society. *Marketing Theory* 16(3): 410–414.

Varman, R. and D. Vijay (2018). Dispossessing vulnerable consumers: Derealization, desubjectification, and violence. *Marketing Theory* 18(3): 307–326.

Varman, R., and I. Al-Amoudi. (2016). Accumulation through derealization: How corporate violence remains unchecked. *Human Relations* 69(10): 1909–1935.

Varman, R. and D. Vijay (2021). The Thanatopolitics of neoliberalism and consumer precarity. In *Consumer Culture Theory in Asia: History and Contemporary Issues*, ed. Yuko Minowa and Russell Belk. London: Routledge, 179–201.

Varman, R., P. Skålén, and R. W. Belk (2012). Conflicts at the bottom of the pyramid: Profitability, poverty alleviation, and neoliberal governmentality. *Journal of Public Policy and Marketing* 31(1): 19–35.

Varoufakis, Y. (2021). Techno-feudalism is taking over. *Project Syndicate*, 28 June. Accessed on 10 September 2021: https://www.project-syndicate.org/commentary/techno-feudalism-replacing-market-capitalism-by-yanis-varoufakis-2021-06.

Venkataramakrishnan, R. (2021). Is the Modi government admitting it messed up India's vaccine policy just to spite the states? *Scroll.in*, 28 May. Accessed on 9 September 2021: https://scroll.in/article/995973/is-the-modi-government-admitting-it-messed-up-indias-vaccine-policy-just-to-spite-the-states.

Vergès, F. (2021). *A Decolonial Feminism*. Northampton, UK: Pluto Press.

Vijay, D. and R. Varman (2018). Introduction: Undoing boundaries. In *Alternative Organisations in India: Undoing Boundaries*, ed. D. Vijay and R. Varman. New Delhi: Cambridge University Press, 1–25.

World Bank. (1987). Financing health services in developing countries: An agenda for reform. Accessed on 9 September 2021: http://documents1.worldbank. org/curated/en/468091468137379607/pdf/multi-page.pdf.

Yengde, S. (2019). *Caste Matters*. New Delhi: Penguin Random House India Private Limited.

Zachariah, B. (2020). India has the longest running fascist movement in the world – the RSS. *The Wire*, 22 January. Accessed on 10 September 2021. https://thewire.in/politics/benjamin-zachariah-fascism-sangh-parivar.

Zanoni, P., A. Contu, S. Healy, and R. Mir (2017). Post-capitalistic politics in the making: The imaginary and praxis of alternative economies. *Organization* 24(5): 575–588.

Ziady, H. 2021). Covid vaccine profits mint 9 new pharma billionaires. CNN, 21 May. Accessed on 9 September 2021: https://edition.cnn.com/2021/05/21/ business/covid-vaccine-billionaires/index.html.

Žižek, S. (2009). *Violence*. London: Profile Books.

PART I

ALTERNATIVE IMAGINATIONS OF SOCIAL RELATIONS

2

LETS AND THE POSSIBILITIES OF A TWENTY-FIRST-CENTURY ALTERNATIVE ECONOMIC SYSTEM

MAIDUL ISLAM

In the twenty-first century, several initiatives for the search of alternatives in the form of 'economic democracy' that could move beyond capitalism have been theoretically articulated (Shantz and Macdonald, 2013; Solimano, 2014). However, the success of an alternative economic system partly depends on whether capitalism has become obsolete or whether it still has enough elasticity to resolve its periodic crises and accommodate various demands articulated within it. So far, in the last century, alternatives in the form of public ownership of means of production, self-management, planning, market socialism, universal basic income, state support for basic capital, shareholder socialism, and a compromise of a market economy with a workable welfare state have been noticed in various parts of the world. At present, there is hardly any positive social system that could ensure that a post-capitalist system will necessarily be more humane, just, and efficient than the alternatives that could be arrived at by reforming capitalism instead of altering the basic social structure of the capitalist economy (Corneo, 2017). The point is that if contemporary capitalism is reproducing uncouth economic inequality and unemployment of magnanimous proportion as witnessed during the COVID-19 pandemic, then a search for an alternative to capitalism is something worth pursuing given the fact that the exploitative and unequal character of contemporary capitalism is not going to change even in a post-COVID world.

PROBLEMS OF CONTEMPORARY CAPITALISM

The lifestyle and consumption patterns of the top 1 percentile population of the world comprising of the economic elites, super-wealthy business tycoons, upper-middle-class technocrats, and productive entrepreneurs have been distinctively different from the rest of the global population (Solimano, 2014). The tremendous inequality within contemporary capitalism is due to the excessive returns on capital over the rate of growth of output and income ($r > g$) and the money gained from inheritance accumulated over time.[1]

In imagining an alternative to the capitalist system, three fundamental issues have to be addressed. The first is the identification of the domain of resistance to the capitalist order. The second is the nature of agency that can resist capital and state with an agenda to transcend capitalism. The third task is the construction of an alternative imagination of a viable post-capitalist system. This third aspect is essential because, without a preliminary sketch of an alternative economic system, the role of the political agency in resisting capital and the capitalist state will only be grounded on the negative aspects of identifying the antagonistic frontiers of the capitalist system. In other words, the political agency that might mobilize people against the antagonistic frontiers of capital and the capitalist state has nothing positive to offer but only rally people on the ground of negation of specific dislocatory effects of capitalism. Such a trend is already being noticed in the xenophobic character of right-wing populist mobilizations where the anger of the aggrieved population against inequality and joblessness is not channelized against the capitalist system as such but by targeting the immigrants, vilifying, and attacking specific population groups instead of an agenda of transcending capitalism. In the last two centuries, there have also been numerous movements against capital, based on various demands at the domain of production like wage increase, better working conditions, and work security followed by various tactics of workers' strikes and gherao by the political agency of trade unions and working-class parties. Some of them have been successful, while others have not been as successful in achieving their demands. Moreover, those struggles have been at best economistic in nature that were absorbed by the welfare state in the West in the twentieth century in the name of reforming capitalism and presenting a humanist face of capitalism within the ideological framework of liberal and social democracies.

In the last two centuries, capitalism has been a flexible system in which various governmental forms as distinct as monarchy, liberal democracy, military dictatorship, and fascism have sustained the basic structure of the capitalist mode of production and exchange. Social democracy in various parts of Europe in the twentieth century and populist governments in the twenty-first century in various parts of the world have been primarily situated within the entire economic system of capitalism. The twentieth-century experiments of state socialism, which was seen as a concrete alternative to capitalism, gave rise to totalitarian systems that undermined individual liberty and did not effectively challenge global capitalism. The nationalization and state control of the economy in the Soviet Union and Maoist China led to bureaucratization. The existence of the socialist bloc also ensured the consolidation of Western capitalist countries under the leadership of the United States. By the end of the twentieth century, the collapse of the Soviet Union was decisive to the end of the state socialist experiments. After the disintegration of the former Soviet Union in the early 1990s, China and Vietnam have been mostly open to capitalist market reforms while North Korea and Cuba, off late, are also following such trajectories.

However, in the twenty-first century, the nature of capitalism has itself transformed from the nineteenth and twentieth centuries. The proletariat, in the classic Marxian sense of the factory or industrial worker, is no more a majority under conditions of contemporary capitalism. This was already noticed by the end of the twentieth century in the West (Islam, 2022: 75–76). By the second decade of the twenty-first century, various forms of occupational groups have emerged that could be put within the larger segment of surplus population and informal sector labour force both in the advanced capitalist countries in the Euro-American world and in the Afro-Asian and Latin American countries. Such a set of population is unemployable within the growth engines of contemporary corporate capitalism. At the same time, the capitalist system has so far managed the surplus population either by various forms of welfare policies through the welfare state that was strong in the middle decades of the twentieth century and still exists in Nordic countries or by implementing dole-centric governmental schemes under the modern architecture of neoliberal governmentality through the neoliberal state (Sanyal, 2007). The redundant surplus population, as described by Kalyan Sanyal as a constitutive outside of global capital, also has a significant proportion of the lumpenproletariat, which is increasing in both urban and suburban areas of developing countries. Along with such a class, a new vulnerable heterogeneous class of the precariat is emerging who have no secured and permanent jobs and whose behavioural patterns have strong expressions of anger, anomie, anxiety, and alienation (Standing, 2011).

In the context of twenty-first-century capitalism, humanity is experiencing three fundamental challenges. The first is the global trend of growing income inequality. The second challenge to contemporary capitalism is the ecological crisis and the potential exhaustion of the earth's mineral, water, and energy resources. The third problem of contemporary capitalism is the technological breakthrough of automation in the form of artificial intelligence, machine learning, robotics, and supercomputers that together have created a condition where contemporary capitalism will effectively produce another round of surplus population on the one hand and job loss growth on the other hand.

How can capitalism accommodate a large pool of surplus population with no jobs and no money? Already two strategies are in place in the twenty-first century. First, the anxieties and rage of the unemployed and underemployed population have been used to create a ruckus of xenophobia and political violence on racial and religious grounds. This has created tensions within nation states, where the constitutive character of nation states has been now getting redefined by the singular identity of large homogeneous groups instead of composite and heterogeneous populations forming the nation states. This process has been broadly captured by the global political phenomenon of the rise of right-wing populism. In many cases, the right-wing populist mobilization has taken the shape of authoritarianism as a governmental form sustaining the initial political mobilization with xenophobic agenda. Second, there has been a call for redistribution of social surplus in the form of universal basic income along with state protection for education, health care, and unemployment benefits with an agenda of a social state in the twenty-first century as argued by Piketty (2017: 597–699).

Any search for an alternative to capitalism in the form of post-capitalist possibilities must be practised in everyday political activism. Since the arrival of neoliberal capitalism in the decade of the 1970s, several 'transnational alternative policy groups' (TAPGs) have been working as intellectual networks for altering and countering neoliberal globalization from above, which in effect is dictated by global corporate elites. The TAPGs encourage innovative forms of North–North, South–South, and North–South dialogues as components of global civil society. Such initiatives have generated strategies for a 'globalisation from below' with visions of post-capitalist alternatives (Carroll and Sapinski, 2013). Case studies from the United Kingdom in the first decade of the twenty-first century have already shown that everyday activism has immense possibilities and potentialities for building post-capitalist progressive alternatives of 'autonomous geographies' against uneven geographical development inherent in the very structural logic of capitalism (Chatterton and Pickerill, 2010). One way of challenging corporate capital is to boycott goods and services provided and controlled by it. This will be in line with Gandhi's boycott strategy that he learned from the Swadeshi movement in Bengal.

GANDHI AND THE POTENTIAL OF BOYCOTT MOVEMENT

Gandhi learned the tactic of boycott movements from the Swadeshi movement in Bengal (1905–1911) against the first partition of the province by the British colonial administration. While responding to the reader as an editor in the dialogic text of *Hind Swaraj*, Gandhi writes the following:

[W]hat you call the real awakening took place after the Partition of Bengal. For this, we have to be thankful to Lord Curzon.... The shock that the British power received through the Partition has never been equalled by any other act. This does not mean that the other injustices done to India are less glaring than that done by the Partition. The salt-tax is not a small injustice. We shall see many such things later on. But the people were ready to resist the Partition. At that time, the feeling ran high. Many leading Bengalis were ready to lose their all.

They knew their power; hence the conflagration. It is now well nigh unquenchable; it is not necessary to quench it either. Partition will go, Bengal will be reunited, but the rift in the English barque will remain; it must daily widen. India awakened is not likely to fall asleep. Demand for abrogation of Partition is tantamount to demand for Home Rule. Leaders in Bengal know this, British officials realise it. That is why Partition still remains. As time passes, the Nation is being forged. Nations are not formed in a day; the formation requires years. (Gandhi, [1910] 1997: 19–20)

In responding to the reader about his opinion on the results of partition, Gandhi wrote:

Hitherto we have considered that, for redress of grievances, we must approach the Throne, and, if we get no redress, we must sit still, except that we may still petition. After the Partition, people saw that petitions must be backed up by force, and that they must be capable of suffering. This new spirit must be considered to be the chief result of Partition. That spirit was seen in the outspoken writings in the press. That which the people said tremblingly and in secret began to be said and to be written publicly. The Swadeshi movement was inaugurated. People, young and old, used to run away at the sight of an English face; it now no longer awed them. They did not fear even a row, or being imprisoned. Some of the best sons of India are at present in banishment. This is something different from mere petitioning. Thus are the people moved. The spirit generated in Bengal has spread in the North to the Punjab, and, in the South, to Cape Comorin. (Gandhi, [1910] 1997: 20–22)

Thus, Bengal became the lead example of the Swadeshi movement during the anti-colonial struggle and had inspired other parts of India to follow a new method of combating the British rulers. But what was Swadeshi? Anthony Parel, the editor of selected writings of Gandhi in the Cambridge Texts in Modern Politics, including that of *Hind Swaraj*, notes from the writings of historian Ramesh Chandra Majumdar and the collected works of Gandhi, and clarifies the meaning of Swadeshi in a footnote:

Swadeshi: things pertaining to one's own country. A many-faceted national movement which arose in reaction to the Partition of Bengal. At the economic level it involved the boycott of British imports. At the educational level, it introduced national educational institutions in Calcutta. In 1906 Aurobindo Ghose resigned his post at Baroda College to take up the post as professor of history and political science and principal of Bengal National College in Calcutta. At the political level, it led to resignations from legislative councils. [See Majumdar 1975. 33–64]. As early as 1905, Gandhi saw the revolutionary potential of the Swadeshi movement: 'The movement in Bengal for the use of swadeshi goods is much like the Russian movement' [CW 5: 132]. In 1907 he compared the Swadeshi movement to Sinn Fein, which 'literally translated into Gujarati, means exactly our Swadeshi movement' [CW 7: 213]. (Gandhi, 1997: 21)

Further, Parel notes about Swadeshi from another passage from the writings of Gandhi embodied in the collected works in which the essence of Gandhi's political struggle becomes clear.

No cause for unhappiness would remain if swadeshi were to replace everything foreign. We can easily attain happiness if we exert ourselves to that end during the year that has just commenced. Swadeshi carries a great and profound meaning. It does not mean merely the use of what is produced in one's own country. That meaning is certainly there in swadeshi. But there is another meaning implied in it which is far greater and much more important. Swadeshi means reliance on our own strength. We should also know what we mean by 'reliance on our own strength'. 'Our strength' means the strength of our body, our mind and our soul. From among these, on which should we depend? The answer is brief. The soul is supreme, and therefore soul-force is the foundation on which man must build. Passive resistance or satyagraha is a mode of fighting which depends on such force. That, then, is the only real key (to success) for the Indians [CW 9: 118]. (Gandhi, 1997: 21)

If one carefully reads Gandhi, then it is amply clear that the power of boycott movements had tremendous potential to challenge both British trade and the state. If, today, such a movement is sustained for a longer period of time, then it can create havoc results in making losses to corporate capital, which is dominant in the domain of contemporary globalized form of neoliberal capitalism. At the same time, the move to boycott foreign and corporate capital funded educational institutions and instead build a national educational movement to set up new indigenous colleges and universities also has the potential to fight corporate capital in the education sector. Aurobindo Ghose's resignation from Baroda to join the National College in Calcutta is a classic example of renunciation for a higher goal of building a self-reliant higher education system in the country free from the ideological prejudice of the colonial masters and far away from the financial manipulation of British rulers in funding universities and colleges in colonial India. At present, when foreign-funded higher education along with private capital is opening their shops in India with the greater goal of privatization of higher education, a deliberate move to boycott such educational institutions by both students and talented teachers by not going to study or teach in such universities and colleges will be a smart tactic of passive and non-violent resistance to corporatization and profitization of higher education in India.

In Kerala's Palakkad district, during the first decade of the twenty-first century, the boycott of Coca Cola was witnessed as a protest against the installation of the Plachimada plant of the company. The protest was for several reasons. First, the plant had lowered groundwater levels in the surrounding neighbourhoods, which created water shortage in the area. The Adivasis (tribals) were the most affected. Second, the plant also needed to dump the carbonated water components, which produced hazardous chemical wastes. Third, the Coca Cola authorities had lied to the ordinary Adivasis that such wastes were useful fertilizers, which were not even donated for free but sold to Adivasis. The poor tribals believed that the corporate company must be giving them good fertilizers for an amount. But agricultural fields were devastated when those harmful chemical wastes were used. In such a context, several organizations came to form a wider platform ranging from environmental activists like Sunita Narain and Vandana Shiva against water privatization, the Swatantra Matsyathozhilali Federation (Independent Fishworkers Federation), and a frontal youth organization of the Kerala unit of the moderate Islamist party, the Jamaat-e-Islami, namely the Solidarity Youth Movement (SYM). Initially, it was a low-profile movement. But later on, a mix of 30 organizations and political parties came together to launch a state-wide anti-Pepsi-Cola campaign. The Communist Party of India (Marxist)–led government, after coming to power in 2006, formally banned the selling of Coca Cola in the state. It certainly had an impact on the sales figures of the company (Islam, 2015: 127–129). The Plachimada campaign was a successful political struggle given the fact that it ensured the state government set up a high-power committee to look at the compensation for each and every person who was negatively affected by the hazardous Cola plant (Mathews, 2011). Moreover, the boycott movement at Plachimada showed the importance of having a local core group in charge of the campaign, along with making use of existing support groups at the regional, national, and international levels. The movement revealed that after reaching its goal, the campaign has further politicized those who actively participated in the agitations, made them politically aware, and has increased their political participation on issues of social concern (Berglund and Helander, 2015).

GRAMSCI AND THE POLITICAL STRUGGLE AGAINST CAPITAL

Antonio Gramsci was a contemporary of Gandhi. His ideas were as powerful as that of Gandhi, particularly those that were expressed from the prison in Italy's dictatorial regime of Benito Mussolini from 1929 to 1935. The late 1920s and the early 1930s fall within the intermediate period of two world wars and the beginning of the retreat of European colonial powers from the colonies in the wake of the global trend of the twentieth-century national liberation movements and decolonization. In such a context, indeed, the originality of Gramscian tactic of political struggle to cripple European colonial capital to fight the circuits of global capital was a brilliant move par excellence. But first of all, an important distinction must be made between military war and political struggle. This is significant because today, military war is not an option to fight global capital. The context has significantly changed from the 1920s and 1930s, when the nature of global capitalism was still colonial with imperialist economic policies. Although the period saw the decisive decline of Britain as the dominant world power, it was nonetheless marred with a struggle among multiple nation-states in the capitalist world, outside the influence of the former Soviet Union, like Germany, France, Great Britain, Japan, and Italy. At the same time, it was the initial phase of the rise of the United States as the global hegemon to lead the bandwagon of capitalist countries against state socialism of Soviet Union during the period of the Cold War roughly from 1930 to 1990. Today, in the second decade of the twenty-first century, the global dominance of the United States has been questioned in the wake of significant challenges from China, Russia, India, Turkey, and Iran.

Gramsci makes a distinction between military war and political struggle. For him, peace arrives when the strategic aim of destroying the enemy's army and occupation of the enemy's territory is achieved. In contrast, political struggle is

enormously more complex: in a certain sense, it can be compared to colonial wars or old wars of conquest – in which the victorious army occupies, or proposes to occupy, permanently all or part of the conquered territory. Then the defeated army is disarmed and dispersed, but the struggle continues on the terrain of politics and of military 'preparation'. (Gramsci, [1971] 1996: 229)

When Gramsci was writing the prison notebooks in Mussolinian jail, the anti-colonial struggle in India under the national-popular leader in the name and figure of Mohandas Karamchand Gandhi was at its peak. The non-violent method of Gandhi's passive resistance, as articulated by him in *Hind Swaraj* (1910), was antithetical to the armed tactics of Indian revolutionaries. In such a context, Gramsci mentioned an important merit of Gandhi's boycott strategy to weaken colonial capital, as can be seen here.

India's political struggle against the English (and to a certain extent that of Germany against France, or of Hungary against the Little Entente) knows three forms of war: war of movement, war of position, and underground warfare. Gandhi's passive resistance is a war of position, which at certain moments becomes a war of movement, and at others, underground warfare. Boycotts are a form of war of position, strikes of war of movement, the secret preparation of weapons and combat troops belongs to underground warfare. A kind of commando tactics is also to be found, but it can only be utilised with great circumspection. If the English believed that a great insurrectional movement was being prepared, destined to annihilate their present strategic superiority (which consists, in a certain sense, in their ability to manoeuvre through control of the internal lines of communication, and to concentrate their forces at the 'sporadically' most dangerous spot) by mass suffocation – i.e. by compelling them to spread out their forces over a theatre of war which had simultaneously become generalised – then it would suit them to *provoke* a premature outbreak of the Indian fighting forces, in order to identify them and decapitate the general movement. (Gramsci, [1971] 1996: 229–230)

It is from such insights of both Gandhi and Gramsci that Karatani, a prominent philosopher-cum-political-activist of Japan, has formulated an alternative imagination to contemporary capitalism.

KOJIN KARATANI AND THE ANARCHO-MARXIST ALTERNATIVE OF NEW ASSOCIATIONISM

Recently, Kojin Karatani has proposed an associationist model of communism beyond the trinity of the nation, state, and capital by carrying forward the Marxian idea of communism as an association of associations (Karatani, 2003: 265–306; Karatani and Wainwright, 2012). Karatani describes associationism as socialism that rejects the state, and which is fundamentally different from 'state socialism' or 'welfare statism' of the twentieth century (Karatani 2014, 234). Karatani's model of associationism is best expressed in his activist model of the LETS, initially designed by Michael Linton with alternative forms of money and with the launch of the New Associationist Movement (NAM) in Japan right at the start of the twenty-first century (Karatani, 2003: 23–25, 298–301, 346–347). In this respect, his conviction is that only through the mechanism of LETS, which abolishes labour value itself, that a ground for communism can be approached without having a transitional phase of socialism, which is nothing but a form of state capitalism that will never be shifted to communism (Karatani, 2003: 346).

Karatani blends both Marx's analysis of capitalism and Proudhon's creative anarchism of Exchange Bank or People's Bank (Karatani and Wainwright, 2012: 50). He advises that to resist capital, we could learn the boycott strategies and the nurturing of consumers' or producers' cooperatives from Gandhi as well (Karatani, 2003: 302). Antonio Gramsci had already acknowledged Gandhi's passive resistance and boycotts as 'a war of position, which at certain moments becomes a war of movement', quite distinct from the underground warfare of armed revolutionaries (Karatani, 2003: 292).

Karatani correctly reads Gramsci by pointing out that the crucial shift from 'war of maneuver' to 'war of position' had already begun in the late nineteenth century (Karatani, 2003: 291). Gramsci maintains that

> the problem of the political struggle's transition from a 'war of manoeuvre' to a 'war of position' certainly needs to be considered at this juncture. In Europe, this transition took place after 1848 and was not understood by Mazzini and his followers, as it was on the contrary by certain others: the same transition took place after 1871, etc. (Gramsci, [1971] 1996: 110)

Here, Karatani innovatively reads Gramsci by linking Gramsci's insights on Gandhi's boycott strategies. Karatani suggests that 'the "war of position" should be interpreted as much more than just the struggle of hegemony' that becomes clear if one is aware of Gramsci's understanding of Gandhi's agenda (Karatani, 2003: 292). Karatani argues that Gramsci 'sought the crux of the war of position in the boycott movement' (Karatani, 2003: 292). Thus, Karatani points out that after the European revolutions of 1848, there was not only a transition from the war of manoeuvre to the war of position, but it also implies that when Marx was writing *Capital* in the second half of the nineteenth century, 'the struggle of the proletariat had already been shifted to acts of boycott, namely, acts that affected the process of circulation; nevertheless the shift was not thoroughly registered' (Karatani, 2003: 292). In Britain, such a transition from war of manoeuvre to war of position was conspicuous when the Chartist movement was run by the Ricardian socialists (Karatani, 2003: 292). In appreciation, Karatani makes the following comments.

What we call nonviolence is exemplified by the strategy of Mahatma Gandhi. But it cannot be reduced to so-called civil disobedience. Mahatma Gandhi's principle of nonviolent resistance is well known, but less known are his 'resistances' of boycotting English products and nurturing consumers'/producers' cooperatives. If not for this nurturing, the boycott could not be what Gramsci called the war of position. If not for the will to noncapitalist cooperatives, the boycott would be a nationalist movement that cared only for the well-being of national capitals. (Karatani, 2003: 302)

In this context, Karatani links how the boycott movements of Gandhi had inspired the African American activists like Martin Luther King Jr. and Malcolm X.

For individual capitals, nothing is more damaging than boycotts. The most powerful campaign in the Civil Rights movement of the late 1950s was initiated by the boycotting of the segregated bus services in Montgomery, Alabama. It is said that the leader, Dr. Martin Luther King Jr., learned the spirit of nonviolent resistance from Gandhi. But what needs to be stressed here is that nonviolent resistance was done as a boycott. Without referring to Gandhi, Malcolm X, later in his life, sought to do what Gandhi did in his own context: He was trying to organize consumers'/producers' cooperatives by and for the African American community. It was a tacit boycott against capitalist economy. Since his death, the social welfare system has begun to support many more impoverished, including African Americans; but it does not help their independence. What is imperative here is also not the social democracy that organizes the state's redistribution of wealth, but the autonomous movement to create consumers'/producers' cooperatives.

Today, when the neoliberal state has become more powerful in terms of technological superiority to combat armed insurrection, the only path open for any subversive politics with an alternative to capitalism can be nothing but a non-violent approach. After all, the limitations of Indian Maoists with their

armed tactic and the failure of most armed insurgencies to fight the might
of global capital and the neoliberal state in the contemporary world should
be an eye-opener for any progressive force to counter global capital and the
neoliberal state through the path of sustained people's movement and electoral
democracy (Islam, 2019). The potential for a non-capitalist cooperative as a
war of position is fundamentally different from 'a nationalist movement that
cared only for the well-being of national capitals' (Karatani, 2003: 302). The
limitation of the Gandhian project was that it eventually turned out to be a
programme for promoting the national capital instead of resisting capital in
general and organizing workers' or consumers' cooperatives. Marx correctly
understood that capital does not become capital at the site of production but
on the site of consumption. Money becomes capital at the point of selling.
In other words, capital has to be realized, and it is only possible if one buys
the commodity. In this regard, workers are at the same time consumers, as
brilliantly argued by Karatani.

Instead of treating social systems as modes of production as Marx did
in the nineteenth century, Karatani identifies social systems with modes
of exchange. For him, there are four principal modes of exchange to which
the logic of capital, state, nation, and association are related. Along with
such modes, the core ideological orientations are linked, as demonstrated
here.

(a) plunder and redistribution	(b) reciprocity of gift and return
(c) exchange by money	(d) association

(a) feudal state	(b) agrarian community
(c) city	(d) association

(a) state	(b) nation
(c) capital (market economy)	(d) association

(a) equality	(b) fraternity
(c) liberty	(d) association

Source: Karatani (2003: 276).

For Karatani, association is based on 'mutual aid like that found in traditional communities, yet it is not as closed. It is a network of voluntary exchange organized by those who have once left traditional communities via the commodity economy' (Karatani, 2003: 276). The mutual aid as a mode of exchange in Karatani's model of associationism in the form of mode D could reappear again and again for an attempt to transcend mode A (reciprocity by gift and countergift), mode B (domination and protection), and mode C (commodity exchange). This is because Mode D or X is yet to be realized that has the possibility to transcend the structures of nation, state, and capital and on a grand scale to transcend the structures of min-world system, world empire, and world economy to eventually evolve as a world republic in future (Karatani, 2017: 135–140). However, it will not be easy to attain Mode D or X in the form of transcending modes A, B, and C because the logic of nation, state, and capital as corresponding to the modes of exchange in the form of A, B, and C will always hinder such a process. Thus, a political agency has to be conscious enough to subvert and at the same time strive to transcend the nation-state-capital form with the agenda of creating an alternative form of associationist model of communism based on mutual aid. In this regard, LETS as a possible endeavour for a possible communism in the twenty-first century has some strengths and weaknesses that deserve some attention.

LETS: STRENGTHS AND WEAKNESSES

In this regard, the LETS of Michael Linton (Rudisuela, 2018), the NAM of Kojin Karatani for producing workers'-cum-consumers' cooperatives based on the exchange principle of mutual aid and Gandhi's boycott strategies as a site of popular mobilization are fascinating ideas of alternatives to resist corporate capital if put together in one grid and think about possible alternatives to the hegemony of corporate capitalism. In this respect, noting the limitations of the nineteenth- and twentieth-century working-class mobilization against capital at the site of production with alternative forms of mobilization at the site of consumption by boycotting commodities produced by corporate capital is one of the potential strategies to resist capital in the twenty-first century. Contemporary capitalism is inherently prone to the economic crisis with the relative fall of purchasing power of the consumers who are, in other contexts, workers as well. Marx already noted in the nineteenth century that capital's internal crisis is a result of a demand-constraint economy (Marx, [1867] 1976: 208–209, 235–236). On the ground of such possibilities of popular mobilization of boycott movements and creating local exchange trading networks with workers-run cooperatives, funded by crowdsourcing, as a substitute to corporate capital, Linton's LETS was given an activist turn by Karantani's NAM in Japan that began in 2000 with an innovative idea of an alternative-organization-cum-political-agency that could resist capitalism in the twenty-first century (Harootunian, 2001).

The principle of running the political agency of LETS is Karatani's adoption of the method of lottery in placing talented leaders and organizers to run LETS on a daily basis.

Lottery functions to introduce contingency into the magnetic power center. The point is to shake up the positions where power tends to be concentrated; entrenchment of power in administrative positions can be avoided by a sudden attack of contingency. It is only the lottery that actualizes the separation of the three powers. If universal suffrage by secret ballot, namely, parliamentary democracy, is the dictatorship of the bourgeoisie, the introduction of a lottery should be deemed the dictatorship of the proletariat. The association of associations or *assozierter Verstand* inexorably entails a center; yet the center is constantly replaced by the contingency; the centrality of the center is displaced in this manner. *The center exists and does not exist at the same time.* (Karatani, 2003: 183)

Karatani argues that the merit of the lottery is to substantiate the electoral system to choose better candidates.

Notwithstanding the derogatory nuances attached to the term lottery, lottery is not in the least obstructive to the electoral system, but a sine qua non to maximize its function. In any kind of representative vote – even of a commune – the representative and the represented are split in fixation. The same group of people are always chosen, and factional strife transpires. Can we choose all representatives by lottery in all elections? That is not realistic; the system itself would be too arbitrary to gain the trust of the people.... Speaking of the use of lottery in institutions today, it is used only for posts anyone can do, but no one wants to do, such as jurors. In other words, lottery is used only in the case where the candidates' abilities are equal or do not matter. For us, the point of using it is the opposite. We would use it in order to save the elections from corruption and choose relatively talented leaders. (Karatani, 2003: 183–184)

Karatani further provides an example of how the system of the lottery might work in giving an opportunity to efficient leaders and managers running the organization.

Considering these examples, what is preferable to us would be to choose the most crucial post by lottery: namely, first choosing three candidates by secret vote (three in one choice) and then finally electing one by lottery. Because the last and most crucial stage is determined by contingency, factional disputes or conflicts over successors would not make sense. As a result, a relatively superior, if not the best, representative would take up the post. Furthermore, the one who is chosen could not parade his or her superiority and power, while those who are not chosen have no reason to refuse collaboration. This kind of political technique would be functional and would go beyond the cliché, 'all the power will fall.' Employed in such manner, the lottery would be an ideal method to free the power center from fixation in the long run and choose able managers and leaders when necessary. (Karatani, 2003: 184)

Karatani points out that the system of lottery functions as a balancing act of contingency to avoid stagnation of power in an extracapitalist organization like that of his ideal form of LETS.

[W]e should not assume that the human nature of loving power ever changes, or that the difference and heterogeneity of individual abilities ever disappears. Even in the production systems or cooperatives managed by workers, these elements are sustained. Especially when the extracapitalist production systems have to compete with capitalist enterprises, they are forced either to adopt the organizational principle of corporations for the sake of improving production or lose and disappear. Our ideal organization should assume the existence of hierarchy from the beginning, except that it introduces the election and lottery to escape the stagnation of the power structure. (Karatani, 2003: 184)

At the grand scale of association of associations where several LETS may come together to form a larger network, the same principle of both voting and lottery will be put into practice.

The association of associations should be equipped with a mechanism that avoids the reification of a substantial center. In the concrete, the associations would be united by a central committee consisting of a representative of each dimension. In this case, not only the normal vote but also the lottery must be introduced at the final stage. In this way, an organization with and without a center can be realized. It is evident that if the counter movement against capital and state does not itself embody the principles that go beyond them, there is no way for it to sublate them in the future. To conclude, I emphasize that the two types of struggles – the immanent and ex-scendent – against capital and state can be united only in the circulation process, that is, the place where workers appear as consumers en masse. Only here is the moment that individuals can become subjects. Association is finally the form based on individuals' subjectivity. (Karatani, 2003: 306)

In the Principles of New Associationist Movement, Karatani lays down the objectives and mechanisms of NAM through LETS in the following manner.

NAM intends to intervene … to reorganize the mid-to-small corporations by way of (non-capitalist) cooperatives and LETS. In this sense, the present situation is becoming similar to the age when Marx paid attention to the producers' cooperative in Britain. We are not optimistic about the situation created by the expansion of world capitalism, neither are we pessimistic about it. The osmosis of the capitalist economy is at the same time creating the conditions that abolish it. This dialectic is exemplified by the coming of the Internet. This thing, that was created as a military defense system and used by capitals, is now a necessary means for counter-movements to capitalism and state. The same is true of e-money-an arm for capital and a means to expand LETS globally. NAM could not exist if not for cyberspace. The counter-act against capitalism has nothing to do with romantic nostalgia; it exists amidst the world intercourse engendered by the world capitalism. (Karatani, 2001)

When LETS is put into practice in several contexts, evidence from the ground suggests that it has enormous potential for reactivating the local economy in terms of providing cash in the form of alternative currency and delivers to provide work for the poor and the unemployed (Williams, 1996a; Williams, 1996b; Seyfang, 2001; Williams et al., 2001). In the United Kingdom, there have been local experiments with LETS, and it has produced outstanding results in the form of a localized barter economy that signals towards imagining a post-capitalist alternative by bypassing the M-C-M', the trinity formula of capital and commodity exchange (Williams, 1996c; Thorne, 1996; Granger, Wringe, and Andrews, 2010). Some have suggested that instead of a barter exchange or abolition of money, LETS is a creative venture for parallel currencies and has a moral appeal for building alternative communities with participatory motivation than simple pecuniary gain (Peacock, 2006). LETS does not only give positive results in the city, but it has an impact in the countryside and rural sectors too (Williams, 1996d; Pacione, 1997). More evidence shows that LETS is a new tool for community development in both the United Kingdom and Australia with not-for-profit, voluntary economic associations with a transparent and interest-free system and whose alternative currency is equal in value to the national currency where the system is in place (Caldwell, 2000; Williams, 1997). However, some studies show the limitations of LETS in terms of the low volume of trade and some structural constraints for their further development (Aldridge and Patterson, 2002).

The main challenge for LETS to work successfully is to first convince the members of the local community that an alternative mode of production and exchange is possible outside the capitalist mode of production and exchange that is based on private ownership of major means of production and private control of the capitalist mode of exchange overseen by the capitalist nation-state. Second, LETS is a better model of exchange and trade than a successful model of production through crowdsourcing and building workers' collectives and cooperatives. Third, in order to successfully run LETS in a localized community or neighbourhood, boycotting existing goods and services provided by big multinational corporations must be given priority. The habit of buying goods and services from shops and markets owned or controlled by corporate capital has become a norm, thanks to billions of dollars invested in advertisements in everyday mass media and in billboards in the neighbourhoods. In this respect, convincing a local community to first boycott certain goods and services, to begin with, is a real challenge. Fourth, even if the boycott strategy is successful, an alternative and cheaper version of goods and services must be available without compromising the quality of such goods and services that big multinational corporates offer. Fifth, such an alternative provider of goods and services has to offer substitutes to the boycotted goods and services through building cooperatives run, managed, and distributed, or exchanged, by the workers cum consumers in a localized community. This is a domain of economy that has the potential for what can be called a 'cooperative theory of justice' focused on the production and exchange through cooperation among workers-cum-consumers outside the circuits of global capital. Finally, a motivated political agency has to take initiatives in popularizing boycott strategies as well as building alternative workers' collectives, along with distributing or trading within a given set of the population.

The new search for an alternative to neoliberal capitalism is not provided only by the Anarcho-Marxist scheme of Karatani. A search for an alternative to the rabid inequality of contemporary capitalism has also been provided recently by Piketty in his proposal for a 'participatory socialism' (Piketty, 2020: 966–1041). This is an addendum to his earlier proposal of a social state in the twenty-first century (Piketty, 2017). Piketty suggests that governments throughout the world must take a firm decision to impose progressive wealth taxes along with creating a tax system that will ensure to extract progressive taxes from property, inheritance, and income. Suppose such a proposal is followed apart from a policy of permanent land reform, then a just society where access to the broadest possible range of fundamental goods, including education, health, voting rights, and the right to full participation in social, economic, civic, cultural and political life, can be ensured. He carries forward his initial sketch of the social state in the twenty-first century in his last book with the proposals mentioned here along with his previous suggestions for basic income, just wage, and transparency both within nation-states and at the global institutional level. Piketty is bypassing Marx by reactivating and radicalizing the liberal-egalitarian principles of John Rawls and the liberal-egalitarian and federalist discourses embedded within the liberal democratic tradition. However, if one takes a post-Marxist theoretical stance, then it will immediately warn that a model of associative communism of Karatani or Piketty's 'participatory socialism' is nothing but names of empty signifiers necessary for political mobilization. It does not mean that if such an alternative social system is ever established, it will be a society without antagonisms or the absence of politics. New antagonisms may arise from such an alternative system, and the possibilities of new politics of favouring both change and continuity will also be associated with such systems. In the wake of a surge of cryptocurrency as an alternative form of currency that a model LETS would have otherwise used, new antagonisms between the national governments like that of India and the virtual space of international mode of exchange of the cryptocurrency markets are already being noticed. In future, one will probably witness whether such an antagonism will be resolved by an accomodationist principle of the capitalist nation-state by recognising various forms of cryptocurrencies or cryptocurrencies become a perennial outside of the anarchic mode of global capitalism without alternative modes of worker-run production systems cum cooperatives. In that case, it will be just another form of currency in the money market and will be used for only trading purpose of existing commodities produced by corporate capital instead of creatively used by LETS communities.

NOTE

1. As Piketty formulates that 'r stands for the average annual rate of return on capital, including profits, dividends, interest, rents, and other income from capital, expressed as a percentage of its total value, and g stands for the rate

of growth of the economy, that is, the annual increase in income or output'. See Piketty (2017, 34). For inequality based on merit and inheritance and how such dynamics play a crucial role in reproducing global wealth inequality, see Piketty (2017: 476–543).

REFERENCES

Aldridge, T. J. and A. Patterson (2002). LETS get real: Constraints on the development of Local Exchange Trading Schemes. *Area* 34 (4): 370–381.

Berglund, H. and S. Helander (2015). The popular struggle against Coca-Cola in Plachimada, Kerala. *Journal of Developing Societies* 31(2): 281–303.

Caldwell, C. (2000). Why do people join Local Exchange Trading Systems? *International Journal of Community Currency Research* 4(1): 1–16.

Carroll, W. K. and J. P. Sapinski (2013). Embedding post capitalist alternatives? The global network of alternative knowledge production and mobilization. *Journal of World-Systems Research* 19(2): 211–240.

Chatterton, P. and J. Pickerill (2010). Everyday activism and transitions towards post-capitalist worlds. *Transactions of the Institute of British Geographers* 35(4): 475–490.

Corneo, G. (2017). *Is Capitalism Obsolete? A Journey through Alternative Economic Systems*, trans. Daniel Steuer. London: Harvard University Press.

Gandhi, M. K. (1997). *Hind Swaraj and Other Writings* [1910], ed. Anthony J. Parel. Cambridge: Cambridge University Press.

Gramsci, A. (1996). *Selections from the Prison Notebooks* [1971], ed. and trans. Quintin Hoare and Geoffrey Nowell Smith. Hyderabad: Orient Longman.

Granger, R. C., J. Wringe, and P. Andrews (2010). LETS as alternative, post-capitalist economic spaces? Learning lessons from the Totnes 'Acorn'. *Local Economy* 25 (7): 573–585.

Harootunian, H. (2001). Out of Japan: The New Associationist Movement. *Radical Philosophy* 108 (July–August): 1–5.

Islam, M. (2015). *Limits of Islamism: Jamaat-e-Islami in Contemporary India and Bangladesh*. New Delhi: Cambridge University Press.

Islam, M. (2019). Fortunes of radicalism: Indian Maoists and the dead end of politics. In *Radicalization in South Asia: Context, Trajectories and*

Implication, ed. Mubashar Hasan, Kenji Isezaki and Sameer Yasir. New Delhi: Sage, 27–52.

——— (2022). *Political Theory and South Asian Counter-Narratives*. London: Routledge.

Karatani, K. and J. Wainwright (2012). 'Critique is impossible without moves': An interview of Kojin Karatani by Joel Wainwright. *Dialogues in Human Geography* 2(1): 30–52.

——— (2001). The principles of New Associationist Movement (NAM). 18 May. Accessed on 1 May 2021: https://www.nettime.org/Lists-Archives/ nettime-l-0105/msg00099.html.

——— (2003). *Transcritique: On Kant and Marx*, trans. Sabu Kohso. London: The MIT Press.

——— (2014). *The Structure of World History: From Modes of Production to Modes of Exchange*, trans. Michael K. Bourdaghs. New York: Columbia University Press.

——— (2017). *Isonomia and the Origins of Philosophy*, trans. Joseph A. Murphy. Durham: Duke University Press.

Marx, K. (1976). *Capital: A Critique of Political Economy*, Vol. 1 [1867]. Introduced by Ernest Mandel, translated by Ben Fowkes. London: Penguin.

Mathews, R. D. (2011). The Plachimada struggle against Coca Cola in southern India. *Dialogues, Proposals, Stories for Global Citizenship*. Accessed on 30 December 2021: http://base.d-p-h.info/en/fiches/dph/fiche-dph-8891.html.

Pacione, M. (1997). Local Exchange Trading Systems: A Rural Response to the Globalization of Capitalism? *Journal of Rural Studies* 13(4): 415–427.

Peacock, M. S. (2006). The moral economy of parallel currencies: An analysis of Local Exchange Trading Systems. *American Journal of Economics and Sociology* 65(5): 1059–1084.

Piketty, T. (2017). *Capital in the Twenty-First Century*, trans. Arthur Goldhammer [2014]. London: The Belknap Press of Harvard University Press.

——— (2020). *Capital and Ideology*, trans. Arthur Goldhammer. London: The Belknap Press of Harvard University Press.

Rudisuela, J. (2018). Decades of documents: Michael Linton passes on LETS legacy. *Commox Valley Record*, 30 September. Accessed on 31 October 2020: https://www.comoxvalleyrecord.com/news/decades-of-documents-michae l-linton-passes-on-lets-legacy/.

Sanyal, K. (2007). *Rethinking Capitalist Development: Primitive Accumulation, Governmentality and Post-Colonial Capitalism*. New Delhi: Routledge.

Seyfang, G. (2001). Working for the Fenland Dollar: An evaluation of Local Exchange Trading Schemes as an informal employment strategy to tackle social exclusion. *Work, Employment and Society* 15(3): 581–593.

Shantz, J., and J. B. Macdonald, eds. (2013). *Beyond Capitalism: Building Democratic Alternatives for Today and the Future*. New York: Bloomsbury.

Solimano, A. (2014). *Economic Elites, Crises, and Democracy: Alternatives Beyond Neoliberal Capitalism*. Oxford: Oxford University Press.

Standing, G. 2011. *The Precariat: The New Dangerous Class*. London: Bloomsbury.

Thorne, L. (1996). Local exchange trading systems in the United Kingdom: A case of re-embedding? *Environment and Planning A: Economy and Space* 28(8): 1361–1376.

Williams, C. C. (1996a). Informal sector responses to unemployment: An evaluation of the potential of Local Exchange Trading Systems (LETS). *Work, Employment and Society* 10(2): 341–359.

—— (1996b). Local Exchange and Trading Systems: A new source of work and credit for the poor and unemployed? *Environment and Planning A: Economy and Space* 28(8): 1395–1415.

—— (1996c). The new barter economy: An appraisal of Local Exchange and Trading Systems (LETS). *Journal of Public Policy* 16(1): 85–101.

—— (1996d). Local purchasing schemes and rural development: An evaluation of Local Exchange and Trading Systems (LETS). *Journal of Rural Studies* 12(3): 231–244.

—— (1997). Local Exchange and Trading Systems (LETS) in Australia: A new tool for community development? *International Journal of Community Currency Research* 1(1): 1–11.

Williams, C. C., T. Aldridge, R. Lee, A. Leyshon, N. Thrift, and J. Tooke (2001). Bridges into work? An evaluation of Local Exchange and Trading Schemes (LETS). *Policy Studies* 22(2): 119–132.

3

DEMOCRATIC SOCIALISM

A CHALLENGE TO SECTARIAN PLUTOCRACY

PRABHIR VISHNU PORUTHIYIL

A common theme in the explanations of the mass support for authoritarianism and sectarianism (often interlinked) across the world is an unintended consequence of the entrenching of economic inequalities created by neoliberal capitalism (Brown, 2019; Jackson and Grusky, 2017; Pierson, 2017). Resentments of those left out, this dominant explanation for rising sectarianism holds, was channelled by proto-fascist authoritarians to implicate all constituencies identified with democratic institutions and associated values like pluralism as unworthy and to be discarded (Frank, 2004; Mounk, 2018, Hacker and Pierson, 2020). Nativism was 'not neoliberalism's intended spawn, but its Frankensteinian creation' (Brown, 2019: 9).

The rise of sectarianism in India – Hindutva (Hindu supremacy) – has a different trajectory due to its early entanglement with traditional social hierarchies and the economic elite (Jodhka, 2016; Joshi and Malghan, 2017). The rise of Indian sectarianism to its now hegemonic status is due to the twin benefits it offers the indigenous plutocracy: a claim to cultural supremacy and the reinforcing of its economic interests (Chatterji, Hansen, and Jaffrelot, 2019; Palshikar, 2017). Support for Hindutva rises 'as we go up the class hierarchy, as well as the caste hierarchy' (Sridharan, 2014: 75, described later). It has been supported by the neoliberal state, even prior to its current transformation, through collaboration with Indian plutocrats to oppress challenges to its economic interests (Randeria, 2007; Sundar, 2010). Now with wealth extraction and display serving as evidence of religious supremacy, the sectarian state protects economic interests with an added religious zeal. The electoral successes of the collusion between big businesses and sectarian forces have intensified the state-led oppressions on behalf of plutocrats (Poruthiyil, 2019).

Resistance to sectarian plutocracy in India is being led by human rights groups like the Human Rights Watch, Amnesty International, and a number of Indian civil society groups such as the People's Union of Civil Liberties (PUCL). The focus of these organizations has been on the escalation in violence against weaker groups by majorities (like the spike in the lynching of Muslims), the destruction of democratic institutions such as the politicization of the judiciary, attacks on freedom of expression, unfair incarceration of dissenters, and the blatant favouring of corporate interests (Amnesty International, 2018; Human Rights Watch, 2019; Mander, Badhwar and Dayal, 2018; PUCL, 2021a, 2021b). Human rights activism tends to focus on egregious violations that trigger outrage while rarely addressing processes that widen material inequalities and benefit plutocrats.

Samuel Moyn's tracing of the history of human rights shows that this is a problem that afflicts human rights groups internationally (Moyn, 2018a, 2018b). From around the 1970s, the framework of human rights detached itself from the focus on material equality. Human rights groups lowered ambitions to a floor of minimum rights, just enough to stave off indigence and stop spectacular violations like the type discussed earlier. It is not that the minimal version of human rights was not necessarily pro-market. Rather, that human rights groups have been powerless in checking neoliberalism's destruction of any restraints on inequality and its consequences (Moyn, 2018a, 2018b).

In India, the neglect of wealth concentration results in further concentration of wealth among the core supporters of sectarianism. Even the consensus on minimum protection hoped for by the rights framework will not materialize as the plutocracy is rooted in an ideology – Hindutva – which programmatically denies human rights to minorities and other oppositional groups (Jaffrelot, 2019). The serious challenge to Hindutva – with its limitless sources of funding and ideologically driven propaganda machinery (that first formulated and is now implementing its vision of totalitarian control over every crevice of Indian psyche, civil society, bureaucracy, and judiciary) – requires a coherent ideology with a vision for inter-organizational solidarities. A structural dismantling of the mechanisms of wealth concentration among the elite is, therefore, necessary for genuinely egalitarian access to shared human rights in India.

In the desperate search for political alternatives for India, the revival of interest and partial success of 'democratic socialism' across the world as an alternative to neoliberal capitalism have gone unnoticed (Day, 2019; Desan and McCarthy, 2018; Fraser, 2020; Meyer, 2018). Democratic socialism provides an ideological platform for building an ideological and operational detail to arrest and reverse the unravelling of sectarian plutocracy by (*a*) disrupting the processes that concentrate wealth among sectarian groups and thereby (*b*) limiting the financial resources sustaining the sectarianism. Democratic socialism can inspire human rights groups to raise ambitions to material equality and be prepared for a confrontation with the fundamental premises of both sectarianism and plutocracy.

The balance of this chapter is divided into the following sections. A description of the 'sectarian' nature of plutocracy in India is followed by an elaboration of the critique of human rights in its current form and its inability to curtail the expansion of sectarian plutocracy (Moyn, 2014, 2018a, 2018b). Later, the basics of democratic socialism are introduced as a challenge to sectarian plutocracy. The chapter concludes by summarizing its argument favouring the need to disrupt human rights approaches from its comfortable co-existence with neoliberalism and trigger their transformation into means for material equality.

A SECTARIAN PLUTOCRACY

Neoliberalism is the idea that markets should be allowed to expand into all aspects of human life and property rights, normalizing competition and selfishness, the dominance of private finance, and indifference to inequalities (Harvey, 2005). The rise of nativist movements that accompanies it is 'animated by the mobilized anger of the economically abandoned and racially resentful, but as contoured by more than three decades of neoliberal assaults on democracy, equality, and society' (Brown, 2019: 8). An analysis of anti-democratic movements in advanced democracies notes the irony that populist demagogues who rode the anti-elite wave into power are transforming into authoritarian facilitators of evermore wealth concentration (Hacker and Pierson, 2020; Pierson, 2017). An underlying theme in these perspectives is an assumption that the alliance between plutocracy and religious conservatism was unexpected and opportunistic.

A distinct feature of neoliberalism in India is its strong support in the upper echelons of the class and caste hierarchies, which have a significant overlap (Nanda, 2011; Venkatramakrishnan, 2019). That Hindutva draws from Hindu scriptural legitimations of graded inequality of human beings with the wealth concentration at the top as a 'natural' state of affairs is a significant attraction for the corporate elite. In addition to their economic interests, these religious and caste groups that dominate the plutocracy have their sociocultural interests protected by the rise of cultural nationalism (Jaffrelot, 2019, 2017; Sridharan, 2014). Submission to Hindutva assures the corporate elite, dominated by upper-caste Hindus, a privileged status in the country's political, economic, and social life (Chakravarthy, 1993; Jaffrelot, 2019).

Certainly, in recent decades, the appeal of Hindutva has transcended caste and class boundaries to reach formerly oppressed Hindu castes like the Dalits (Desai and Roy, 2016; Teltumbde, 2005). Its transcendence of class led to one of the major tectonic shifts of the general elections of 2019: the consolidation of Hindu votes in favour of the Bharatiya Janata Party (BJP). Upwardly mobile sections of these formerly oppressed groups have been led, through intelligent social engineering, to consider Hindutva, particularly its support for neoliberalism, an aspirational vehicle to escape their lower-caste and economically deprived status (Chacko, 2019; Gopalakrishnan, 2008; Jaffrelot, 2013). Nevertheless, a non-negotiable requirement for entry into the Hindutva fold is the acquiescence of these formerly oppressed groups to its sectarian tenets (Khan, 2019).

This symbiotic relationship between the economic elite and sectarianism is reminiscent of the early-twentieth-century fascisms, which also benefited from the financial and cultural support of the business elite (Guerin, 1937; Passmore, 2014; Paxton, 2004). Like then, cultural and ethnic identities forged by fascism are effective in preventing the formation of other solidarities (particularly labour mobilizations) that could potentially threaten elite interests (Patnaik, 1993; S. Sarkar, 1993). Further, the submerging of specificities and uniqueness of different groups into an electorally significant dominant group identity also provided an undifferentiated consumer market for selling mass-produced items (Gopalakrishnan, 2008). The interlocking of interests between the religious supremacists and the plutocracy, tightening after the neoliberal turn in the 1990s, has also resulted in the Hindutva shedding its initial (nationalist) opposition to globalized capital and yoking itself to the economic interests of the Hindu elite (Chacko, 2019; Gopalakrishnan, 2008).

This wealth accumulation at the top of a mutually reinforcing class and traditional hierarchy has triggered a viciously consequential process that is unique to India. The generous and continued funding by the corporate sector to reinforce the Hindtuva hegemony, in spite of its blatant imposition of majoritarianism, is a revelation of this ideological alignment (Center for Media Studies, 2019; Desai, 2019; Kumar and Gupta, 2019; Rodrigues, Choudhary, and Dormido, 2019; Venkatramakrishnan, 2019). Increasing the economic and cultural prominence of the elite is generating ever-increasing financial and political resources to entrench a sectarian plutocracy premised upon a denial of basic rights to minorities and other targeted groups.

The increasing violation of human rights by the plutocracy in India has, for many decades and particularly since the onset of neoliberalism, been organized and protested against by scholars and human rights organizations and activists (Randeria, 2007; Sundar, 2010). They are also resisting another range of violations resulting from the recent infusion of sectarianism and targeting minorities, rationalists, and thinkers accused of hurting the cultural sensitivities of the elite (Amnesty International, 2018; Human Rights Watch, 2019). For example, a grassroots movement called Karwan-e-Mohabbat managed to highlight the phenomenon of the 'beef lynchings' – Muslims and Dalits being publicly lynched by vigilante cow-protection groups – that the state authorities and affiliated media were wilfully ignoring (Mander, Badhwar, and Dayal, 2018). Other organizations highlight the concentration of wealth without extending the analysis to include the rise of sectarianism (Oxfam, 2018).

The steady entrenching of sectarian plutocracy, despite the highly visible public awareness campaigns against its excesses, reveals the ineffectiveness of the resistance, however fierce, offered by rights-based groups. One of the reasons for its weak impact is the tendency to challenge either sectarianism or inequality, but rarely in combination (for exceptions, see Chacko 2019; Gopalakrishnan, 2008). This leaves unarticulated the mutually reinforcing processes of wealth concentration and denial of civil liberties facilitated by the rise of a sectarian plutocracy. Legal historian Samuel Moyn has traced this reluctance to a foundational limitation of human rights activism to focus on subsistence rights and spectacular violations without addressing wealth accumulation (Moyn, 2018a, 2018b).

SUFFICIENCY AND SPECTACULAR VIOLATIONS

To illustrate the extent of the limited ambitions of contemporary human rights, particularly with regard to economic and social rights (henceforth social rights), Moyn makes a helpful distinction between two terms – *sufficiency* and *equality*. Sufficiency refers to 'how far an individual is from having nothing and how well she is doing in relation to some minimum of provision of the good things in life', while equality focuses on 'how far individuals are from one another in the portion of those good things they get' (Moyn, 2018a: 3). However, the Universal Declaration of Human Rights (UDHR), often referred to by today's rights groups as the touchstone, was at inception a means of canonizing social rights within a commitment to material equality *within* bounded national communities (Moyn, 2018a: 175). Though large sections of populations were excluded (immigrants and colonial subjects, women), social rights that formed the UDHR were understood as commitments to a state-led egalitarian project (Moyn, 2018a).

The post-war decades were also characterized by competing visions of society – the capitalist and socialist, both of which were committed to welfare while differing on the extent of personal freedom afforded to the individuals. The imperative for liberal states to differentiate their version of welfare from that of communist states created discomfort with social rights, understood as a commitment to egalitarianism (Moyn, 2018a: 98). The severing of the egalitarianism project from human rights discourses occurred in the 1970s.

Organizations now associated with human rights like Amnesty International and Human Rights Watch emerged in this period to focus attention solely on violations in left- and right-wing states. It was this phase that saw the unravelling of the claim that capitalism was essential for freedom and democracy, its hollowness exposed in spectacular fashion when the neoliberal experiment in Chile showed that particularly under conditions of inequality, an authoritarian government was even necessary (Frank, 1976; Letelier, 1976). Simultaneously, the state-led oppression under communist regimes in Eastern Europe provided another front for the emergence of human rights on the world stage.

The break with material equality became definite as the purpose of human rights activism was now to 'save the individual from the state's depredations of civil liberties rather than to empower the state to make individual flourishing and equality a reality' (Moyn, 2014: 121–122). By the 1990s, no longer fettered by the presence of socialism as a viable alternative, international organizations decisively adopted sufficiency as a palliative and an excuse for not confronting the deeper structural flaws of a market economy (Moyn, 2018a).

The idea of the welfare state was offered a window to be internationalized by the liberation of a number of states from the yoke of colonialism in the 1960s. The New International Economic Order (NIEO) wanted to replicate the welfare state as well as demanded the sharing of wealth *between* nations – or global welfare. The egalitarian dream was global welfare, the idea of sharing the wealth from the richer to the poorer countries through repatriation and equitable sharing of trade. However, it was soon clear to the proponents of the NIEO that the entrenched Western powers were not going to allow global redistribution to happen. A strong argument that distribution of welfare would only enrich the elite in the post-colonial nations provided a justification for the refusal of a global redistribution of wealth.

It is at this point in history that the focus shifted to poverty alleviation and minimum guarantees for subsistence in these developing countries. Intellectuals and international organizations such as the United Nations and the International Labour Organization contributed to the recasting of human rights as subsistence (See Moyn, 2018a: 119–172). The outcome of this consolidation is the neglect of material equality and the focus on subsistence, at the most sufficiency: 'Rights and needs were worth talking about; equality not so much' (Moyn, 2018a: 144). This discourse of 'basic needs' would later merge with the global discourse on human rights.

Thus, this increased visibility of human rights on the global stage was at the expense of limited ambitions. The focus on sufficiency (the principle that no person be discriminated on the basis of race, colour, gender, nationality) came at the expense of policies required for material equality such as redistribution of wealth: 'Atrocity prevention, not welfare promotion' confined within the frames of humanitarianism and global charity became the guiding principle of global human rights (Moyn, 2014: 94, Moyn, 2018a). To the extent that social rights were acknowledged, it was within a humanitarian perspective of sufficiency or minimum guarantee for the global indigent and not within an egalitarian perspective.

The new version of human rights 'minimal, individual, and fundamentally moral: not maximal, collective and potentially bloody' (Moyn, 2018a: 82) assured that key mechanisms of wealth accumulation would remain undisturbed and became a key basis for a commitment from plutocrats on social projects across the world (Crabtree, 2018; Giridhardas, 2018; McGoey, 2014). Human rights movements have, by their silence on galloping inequalities and their cooperation with elites, become the 'signature morality of the neoliberal age' (Moyn, 2018b: 32).

DISJOINTED RESPONSE TO SECTARIAN PLUTOCRACY

Plutocrats in advanced democracies are increasingly expressing commitments to ensuring basic rights of subsistence, albeit as an antidote to rising anti-elite sentiments and without commitment to reducing inequality (Giridharadas, 2018). The infusion of sectarianism into the plutocracy makes it less likely that even such inherently faulty engagement with subsistence will be forthcoming in India. In the Global North, the conflicts between plutocrats and the deprived classes are primarily due to their mutually antagonistic economic interests. The groups tend to have shared (or at least not hostile) sociocultural identities (for instance, the white elite and the working class). In contrast, sectarian plutocrats in India, as discussed earlier, are not merely economically removed from the deprived but are also culturally distinct, for instance, on account of race, caste, ethnicity, or religion. They are conditioned to *deny* the basic tenets of equality to groups seen as 'internal enemies'; recent spending of philanthropic funds and political funding reiterates the corporate support for promoting sectarian agendas of the ruling faction (Rodrigues et al., 2019; Sundar, 2018).

The hegemony of sectarian plutocracy need not result in the total absence of welfare measures for the poor. Large-scale welfare measures are being implemented by the BJP that cut across religions, class, and caste. However, social welfare will be fabricated to maintain or even enhance sectarian dimensions. For instance, access to social rights will be graded as excluded groups, particularly the minorities, may receive some rights – minimum wages, water supply, and basic education and health – but will be systematically denied other equally essential rights (for instance, political and civil rights).

This grafting of sectarianism onto an already authoritarian neoliberalism (Bruff, 2014) has created unique challenges for groups and individuals speaking for the rights of the poor and marginalized in India. Even before the establishment of the Hindutva hegemony, human rights groups were already portrayed as inimical to the country's economic interests and subjected to violence from state agencies acting on behalf of corporate interests (Randeria, 2007; Shrivastava and Kothari, 2012; Sundar, 2010). A well-financed and executed propaganda campaign has led to the perception that economic and religious assertions are indistinguishable from 'national interests' (Jaffrelot, 2019). Simultaneously, constituencies committed to human rights, and by extension, pluralism, are branded as inimical to this Hinduized and capitalist version of national interests (Chacko, 2019).

The state has pandered to these prejudices by actively inserting obscurantist ideas, without significant push back, into higher education and scientific organizations (Mathur, 2018; Ramachandran, 2016). The explosion of social media has complemented the methods for entrenching prejudices and reiterating victimhood among youth yearning for economic uplifting (Udupa, 2018). They, in turn, become the foot-solders of a 'militant obscurantism' wherein any critique of religious supremacy is met with violence (Sen, 1993). The uncritical acceptance of claims of historical wrong and imminent threats to the community is the justification of violence against minorities (T. Sarkar, 2019) and the unravelling of the civic solidarity essential for social progress (Bijukumar, 2019).

The result is that significant sections of the public harbour spontaneous suspicion for human rights: a hatred that may not be as frenzied if the threat was perceived only to their economic interests. The outcome of the general elections in 2019 has shown that a significant majority of religious voters, if not supportive, are comfortable with sectarianism and plutocracy (Bal, 2019; Gupta, 2019). This state of public disdain for human rights provides the state legitimacy for actions that would otherwise be deemed undemocratic and dictatorial – deploying tax agencies to lock activists in legal quagmires that consume scarce resources, arresting academics, journalists, and activists on the flimsiest of pretences (Chandhoke, 2018; United Nations, 2018).

There are indigenous rights movements like the PUCL that emerged in the 1970s during an earlier phase of state-led authoritarianism. PUCL's early struggles for civil liberties were rooted in critiques of capitalism, which is in sharp contrast to other human rights organizations addressing sectarianism or inequality in isolation. However, in recent times even PUCL's focus has predominantly been on what Moyn refers to as spectacular violations (lynchings, prisoner's rights, misuses of 'national security' acts by the state) and less on interventions that problematize the neoliberal economic model or the sociocultural characteristics of wealth accumulation in India (see PUCL, 2021a, 2021b).

Nevertheless, it is a vindication of their commitment to human rights groups that these relentless onslaughts have not drawn civil rights activists in India away from their commitment to defend democratic institutions from majoritarianism; in fact, civil activism has been reinvigorated with a range of small and large movements erupting against sectarianism. However, the return of the BJP in the general elections of 2019 with a much larger mandate than in 2014 suggests that this resistance, along with that of allied groups of activists, artists, and academics, has been less than effective (Poruthiyil, 2019).

Democratic socialism, however, can equip defenders of rights with the material and ideological means to sectarian and plutocratic dimensions of the emerging hegemony in India. The increasing global attention to inequality, triggered in no small part by the rise of populist authoritarians, suggests a model for human rights to rediscover its original roots within a vision of material equality.

DEMOCRATIC SOCIALISM

Socialism is 'the tendency inherent in an industrial civilization to transcend the self-regulating market by consciously subordinating it to a democratic society' (Polanyi, 1944: 242). Socialism has many variants, but four common characteristics are (a) commitment to equality, (b) an optimistic view that human beings are not driven by self-interest alone, (c) the possibility of tapping solidarity and cooperation to create an egalitarian society, and (d) the ability of human beings to effect changes without being bogged down by religion, culture, and tradition (Newman, 2005).

Contemporary proponents of socialism imagine a world where 'everyone has a right to food, healthcare, a good home, an enriching education, and a union job that pays well ... this kind of economic security is necessary for people to live rich and creative lives – and to be truly free' (Meyer, 2018: 2). They see equality of 'chances to life and the ability to flourish' and solidarity wherein people 'care about and care for each other' as guiding principles (Desan and McCarthy, 2018: 3).

The current upsurge of interest in socialism attaches the label 'democratic' to underline its commitment to democracy, sharply rejecting the totalitarian dictatorships under Stalin or Mao (Desan and McCarthy, 2018). The 'democratic' dimension underlines the vision of a society that 'preserves individual liberty and democratic procedures while simultaneously extending the values of democracy to the economic sphere' (Iber, 2016: 1).

Democratic socialism should also not be confused with social democracy or welfare liberalism of the type in Nordic countries, characterized by economic security, high standards of living, high levels of state ownership, and union participation in corporate boards (McCarthy, 2018). These social democracies remain committed to capitalism albeit cushioned with welfare, that is, the kind of society that conforms to the contemporary human rights position discussed earlier. Democratic socialism involves a 'more decisive break with capitalism ... the goal is not just relative equality and generous social spending, but a radical, democratic, and participatory reorganization of economic control' (Iber, 2016: 1).

That is, democratic socialism goes beyond the bare minimums required for a dignified life (decent work, adequate nutrition, employable education, pensions, and so on) that keep human rights from confronting the dominance of plutocrats: 'The core aim of socialism is not just the state gaining control of industry, but empowering the broad masses of people – in their workplaces, in their communities, in their homes, in their schools, in their politics – to be in the driver's seat of society' (Desan and McCarthy, 2018: 4).

Socialism involves radical transformations of society at the level of both structure and ideas that can offer an alternative vision for organizing Indian society. Three broad aspects of this transformation into a socialist society that challenging the sectarian plutocrats should simultaneously embrace are (a) dismantling labour markets, (b) promoting solidarities based on vulnerability to economic exploitation, and (c) challenging obscurantism. These three transformations are concrete steps for human rights activists aiming for material equality and thereby posing a meaningful challenge to sectarianism.

DISMANTLING LABOUR MARKETS

Commodification of labour, the idea that labour power can be bought and sold, is central to capitalism. Being a subject of a capitalist society implies the loss of autonomy and alienation of human beings and is the leading cause of exploitation as the dependence on private capital is absolute. Socialism would remove an essential feature of neoliberalism, 'the sordid necessity of living for others' (Wilde, 1891), and involves 'nothing less than creating conditions for the truly free, rational, active and independent' person (Fromm, 1961: 43).

Socialism does not mean, contrary to popular perceptions, the negation of individual freedom (James, 2017; Klagge, 1986). A socialist society has conditions for what Marx called the 'development of human energy which is its own end, the true realms for freedom' (Marx, 1864) and is one in which the 'right to nonconformity must be institutionally protected' (Polanyi,

1944: 265). This kind of freedom is possible only when an individual is not manipulated by capital or bureaucracy and 'participates actively' in the creation of conditions of production (Fromm, 1961: 52).

De-commodification of labour will certainly not automatically lead to a world without struggle. It is only when workers 'collectively control their own time, their own labor processes and their own product' that alienation is avoided (Harvey, 2014: 66). Private ownership of capital means 'what labor wins in the domain of production can be stolen back' through entrapment in the extractive mechanisms of the credit and housing markets (Harvey, 2014: 67). When socialist public policies such as higher taxes and abolition of labour markets are implemented, private capital has withheld investments or created social instability and supported authoritarian coups (as in Chile) to protect their interests. Investment choices in the hands of capitalists have resulted in decisions that are detrimental to both society and nature (Fraser, 2020). Without robust societal control over capital, which involves the abolition of the billionaire classes, labour cannot be genuinely free.

PROMOTING SOLIDARITY AND FAIRNESS

Commoditization of labour would mean that individuals are alienated not just from themselves but also from other humans. This form of individualization, placing people in intense competition with each other for basic survival, is not conducive to solidarity. It separates people from their labour, from their 'life activity', from their 'species-being', and from each other (Marx, 1844: 7). 'Socialists believe that people should care about and care for each other.... A socialist vision of emancipation is one where our institutions help us care about and for each other' (Desan and McCarthy, 2018: 3). Socialist solidarity leads to a world where individuals are not vying for control over others for profits but seek to cooperate for the flourishing of society as a whole (Fromm, 1961).

Sectarianism, it should be recognized, is also a form of solidarity. It is a reactionary response to globalization and modernity and triggered by a sense of loss of traditions that binds individuals into a community nostalgic for 'the debris of paradise drifting past' (Lilla, 2016: xiii). Though the serenity and gloriousness of this nostalgic past are often imagined, it provides a sectarian vision for organizing the contemporary society glued together by resentments and hatred for groups that challenge the traditional hierarchies of race, caste, and religion. Democratic socialism offers an alternative basis for social solidarity based on shared vulnerabilities to the violence of capital.

DEMOCRATIZING SCIENCE

All sectarian movements are driven by narratives with loose connections to facts (Snyder, 2017). Idealization of a glorious past tarnished by the invasion and infiltration of the 'other', supremacist beliefs and claims unsupported by scientific evidence, concocted histories of religious, ethnic, or racial purity, and a larger-than-life leader committed to the restoration of cultural glory are some of the essential ingredients for the realization of sectarianism (Stanley, 2018).

Neoliberalism, for example, has had profound impacts on the practice of science (Oreskes, 2019). Privatization of science and education tends to facilitate a greater concentration of wealth, while at stake is 'the social contract that cultivates science for the common good' (Broad, 2014: 3). Control over the gathering and interpretation of data and the formulation of facts is an emerging terrain where commercial interests prevail over societal interests (Kelly and McGoey, 2018; Paul and Haddad, 2019).

Socialists recognize the importance of adherence to facts and the role of science in abolishing hunger, curing diseases, and reversing climate change. Socialist movements were historically aligned with significant contributors to Indian scientific establishments (Purkayastha, 2020). Such movements and the democratization of science cannot be disentangled from class struggles, as science and technology controlled by market forces will be deployed primarily for profits with social welfare as an afterthought.

DISCUSSION

Low ambitions to ensure sufficiency at the expense of equality have resulted in the human rights perspective becoming part of an 'apparatus of justification' for neoliberalism (Piketty, 2014: 264). Adopted in this reduced form, human rights have the potential to ensure a minimum floor of rights in most countries under most plutocracies. However, in India, even sufficiency is unlikely as the plutocracy in India has a distinct dimension – sectarianism – that is premised on the denial of even basic rights to minorities. Rights-based groups working under a sectarian context cannot ignore processes that allow the wealth to concentrate in the hands of groups aligned with sectarianism. The near-complete obliteration of all alternatives to sectarian plutocracy in India has brought socialist movements face to face with the reality of its obsolescence in contemporary politics.

Democratic socialism offers a comprehensive framework under which rights-based groups can align and cooperate as a genuine alternative to sectarian plutocracy. Three ways in which the adoption of democratic socialism poses a significant challenge to sectarian plutocracy in India are suggested.

First, socialism highlights the fact that stronger labour protections, as Polanyi (1944) observed, 'can achieve freedom not only for a few, but for all.... Such a society can afford to be both just and free' (265). In contrast, capitalist control over the means and nature of employment – the focus on flexibility and informalization of labour, is one of the key contributors to wealth concentration (Agarwala, 2019; Harvey, 2014). The limited and companion stance of human rights in neoliberalism (with its focus only on minimums like the living wage and workplace abuse) becomes explicit through silence on the systematic decimation of the ability of the employed classes to defend themselves through mass action (Gopalakrishnan and Sundar, 2018; Jenkins, 2004; Mathew and Jain, 2018).

Meanwhile, increasingly digitized workplaces are not immune to radical consciousness and need not be ceded to sectarianism. Organizing workers, even in highly individualized work cultures like gaming, is possible and already happening (Woodcock, 2019). The focus of activism needs to extend beyond ensuring basic rights such as a living wage to radical demands like state planning, employee's cooperatives, state and sectoral planning, and the devolution of decision-making powers. The workplace is seen in socialist politics as a critical site for imagining alternatives and generating mass popular support for shifting the balance of power from capital to labour (Fromm, 1961).

Second, human rights activism highlights the importance of identity-based vulnerabilities while obscuring shared experiences of exploitative working conditions and common destiny under neoliberalism. Certainly, inequalities in employment are compounded by memberships in various categories like gender, sexuality, caste, and religion. A socialist vision brings class back into focus to be addressed simultaneously with identity-specific vulnerabilities (Polychorniou, 2019).

Attention to specific categorical deprivations should be given so that solidarities built on the primary identities as individuals devoid of agency under capitalist control can also be fostered. Reorganization of the production practices to make them more democratic is a more fundamental means to eradicate identity-based discrimination. The presence of working-class-based movements gives oppressed castes a means to express their opposition and fight for justice.

Third, a socialist society will demand investments in public education of science and protect publicly funded scientific establishments. The focus of scientific research can then be redirected from facilitating profits to corporates to understanding and alleviating the causes of exploitation and suffering ordinary citizens. For this era where conspiracy theories compete with truth, public investments that foster critical thinking are essential for democracy to survive.

Certainly, indigenous organizations in India like the People's Science Movements and the Andhashraddha Nirmoolan Samiti (Committee for the Eradication of Superstition) have long recognized that social emancipation in India cannot be disentangled from the fight against superstitions and the damage caused by Hindu supremacist policies on science education and research (All India People's Science Network [AIPSN], 2018; Dhabholkar, 2018). However, the role of wealth concentration in the systematic injection of irrationality and unscientific attitudes into Indian policymaking remains ignored. The increasing concentration of wealth has allowed the corporate classes to indulge in ostentatious displays of obscurantism and make superstitions acceptable in the public sphere (Nanda, 2011). Socialist sensibilities will allow these organizations to trace the blame for increasingly militant forms of obscurantism to the hegemonic plutocracy.

Recent events have revealed the contrasting consequences for societies run on sectarian plutocratic or democratic socialist principles. When the pandemic struck in early 2020, the central government, driven by sectarian plutocracy, first delayed its response to topple regional governments it deemed hostile, and then abruptly imposed a brutal lockdown, without considering the plight of millions of poor and informal migrant workers (Ellis-Peterson and Rahman, 2020). It sought to blame religious gatherings by minority groups for spreading the virus while allowing those of Hindus to proceed (Jagannathan and Rai, 2021). When the lockdown was at its peak, the government circumvented parliamentary procedures to bulldoze policies that scuttled labour rights, removed environmental protections, opened up the agriculture sector to big businesses, and further constrained the functioning of civil society organizations (*EPW*, 2020; Vaishnav, 2020).

Key functionaries of the government promoted quackery and superstitions – including medicines made of cow urine and excreta – as treatments for the coronavirus (Chopra, 2021; Dore, 2020). In its obsession to impose itself nationally, the government spent most of its attention on crowd-gathering spectacles and ignored the warnings from scientists and doctors of an impending surge in demand for oxygen (Ghoshal and Das, 2021). When local and global criticisms became unavoidable, instead of accepting failure, the government sought to intimidate and suppress information by intimidating journalists and social media companies (Recchia and Vijayan, 2021).

In contrast, the government of Kerala (southwest India) was led by the Left-Democratic Front constituted by political parties with roots in socialism. As one of the earliest places to detect the virus, the health department moved quickly to create a frontline network of healthcare professionals to tackle the spread of the virus (Government of Kerala, 2020, Chandrashekhar, 2020; Faleiro, 2020). Its agencies acted with urgency to set up community kitchens and distribution networks that brought food to individual houses – an intervention that ensured that children from poor families, daily wage earners, the elderly, and inter-state migrants did not go hungry (Heller, 2020).

The local health ministry strictly followed the science, bringing in laws against the spread of pseudoscientific claims and misinformation causing vaccine hesitancy (*Economic Times*, 2021). Senior ministers held daily press conferences to update the public and field questions from journalists to provide an unusual level of transparency to the government's policy decisions

(Ramachandran, 2020). The government invested in oxygen plants leading to a state ready with a surplus when the second wave hit (Mathoor, 2021). To arrest profiteering by the corporate hospitals, the government created a ceiling on medical costs for essential treatment (Biju, 2021)

The heart-rending scenes witnessed in India of patients gasping for air as cities and hospitals run out of oxygen, long queues forming outside crematoriums, funeral pyres crammed into every available corner, and the bodies being pushed into rivers by relatives unable to bear the costs of cremation are consequences of callousness that can be traced to the sectarian plutocracy in power (Haig, 2021; Jagannathan and Rai, 2021; Roy, 2021). At the same time, a regional government (in Kerala) with comparatively minuscule economic resources, but with a commitment to democratic socialism, ensured a robust, humane, egalitarian, and scientific response to dampen the impact of the pandemic on the most vulnerable sections of the population (Heller, 2020; Narayanan and Poruthiyil, 2021).

NEXT STEPS AND CHALLENGES

In countries where the neoliberal project has run aground, 'socialism' no longer attracts the widespread derision it did barely a decade ago – socialist ideas have re-entered public imagination, particularly among the youth, even in the United States, the supposed bastion of capitalism (Stockman, 2018). Socialism in India, in contrast, remains in the margins, not least because of the current hegemony of the sectarian plutocracy. The challenges for popularizing democratic socialism in India are, therefore, admittedly steep (Guha, 2013; Prashad, 2015).

First, in societies with structural inequalities, even a precarious job (as in the gig economy) created through the dismantling of labour protections creates an illusion of social mobility, especially when provided with gizmos of modernity like smartphones and when referred to as entrepreneurs (Salve and Paliath, 2019; Surie, 2018). This promise of neoliberalism, coupled with the belief that Hindutva is best positioned for its realization, will form hurdles in convincing the middle classes and subaltern, particularly among the youth, of the genuine protections that socialism provides.

Second, the inability to distinguish neoliberal economic policies from cultural nationalism prevents the acknowledgement of the pernicious effects of neoliberalism even by the exploited groups (Frank, 2004, Pierson, 2017). Since any rejection of the economic policies espoused would also entail the rejection of identity, support for pro-elite policies that worsen the standard of living of the entire class of poor, including their own, can be difficult to dislodge (Metzl, 2019). The support for sectarian plutocrats may be difficult to dislodge given the current upsurge of polarization, driven by social media and the resulting breakdown of shared realities (Sunstein, 2014).

Third, Indian socialist movements are losing national relevance through an inability to respond to the sharpening of identity politics (Prashad, 2015). They are stymied by the politics of identity, a serious hurdle in generating mass support against neoliberal capitalism. Even the religious minorities and caste groups adversely affected by sectarianism may be unwilling to subsume religious identities to class-based solidarities if they retain trust in neoliberalism's promise of upward mobility. They may not accept a socialist alternative involving the redistribution of wealth.

In spite of these challenges, human rights organizations, to avoid irrelevance or remain in the status as a bystander as this sectarian plutocracy further entrenches itself in India, have to rediscover its socialist foundations and strive towards achieving material equality. 'Resignation,' Polanyi had argued in bleaker times, 'was ever the fount of ... strength and new hope ... life springs from ultimate resignation' (Polanyi, 1944: 268). As a legitimate human rights movement must transform itself into a socialist movement, sufficiency is not enough; equality must be the goal. The vicious processes that sustain the sectarian plutocracy – concentration of wealth, polarization, and the uncritical acceptance of supremacist propaganda – can only be disrupted by adherence to the basic tenets of democratic socialism such as the dismantling of labour markets, creating solidarities based on vulnerability to economic exploitation, and adopting a scientific temper. The initial arguments for this reorientation have been given here, together with the strikingly different policy responses to the pandemic that give a vivid illustration of the contrasting priorities of sectarian plutocracies and socialist governments. A tragedy of epic proportions has inadvertently offered striking proof for the viability and need for democratic socialism.

ACKNOWLEDGEMENTS

The author would like to thank Rohit Varman, Srinath Jagannathan, and Anupam Guha for their close reading and comments on earlier drafts, Linda McPhee for the language editing, and Sarah Nazamuddin Harniswala for the meticulous work on references. All errors are mine.

REFERENCES

Agarwala, R. (2019). The politics of India's reformed labor model. In *Business and Politics in India*, ed. C. Jaffrelot, A. Kohli and K. Murali. Oxford University Press, 95–123.

All India People's Science Network. (2018). On scientific temper. Accessed on 30 December 2020: http://resources.aipsn.net/sites/default/files/2019-04/On-Scientific-Temper-NSTD-WS-June-2018.doc.

Amnesty International. (2018). *Amnesty International Report 2017/18*. Accessed on 30 December 2020: https://www.amnesty.org/en/documents/pol10/6700/2018/en/.

Bal, H. S. (2019). The *Hindutva* nation and its discontents. *Caravan Magazine*, 24 May.

Biju, R. M. (2021). Kerala High Court approves State govt decision to cap Covid treatment price, reserve 50% beds in private hospitals for Covid patients. *Bar and Bench*, 10 May.

Bijukumar, V. (2019). Pungent irrationality and troubled modernity in Kerala. *History and Sociology of South Asia* 13(1): 19–35.

Broad, W. J. (2014). 'Billionaires with big ideas are privatizing American science'. *New York Times*, 15 March.

Bruff, I. (2014). The rise of authoritarian neoliberalism. *Rethinking Marxism* 26(1): 113–129.

Brown, W. (2019). *In the Ruins of Neoliberalism: The Rise of Antidemocratic Politics in the West*. Columbia University Press.

Center for Media Studies. 2019. Poll expenditure, The 2019 elections. Accessed on 25 November 2019: https://cmsindia.org/sites/default/files/2019-05/Poll-Expenditure-the-2019-elections-cms-report.pdf.

Chacko, P. (2019). Marketising Hindutva: The state, society and markets in Hindu nationalism. *Modern Asian Studies* 53(2): 377–410.

Chandrashekhar, V. (2020). How a communist physics teacher flattened the COVID-19 curve in southern India. *Science* 9 (November). Accessed on 24 December 2020: https://www.science.org/content/article/how-communist-physics-teacher-flattened-covid-19-curve-southern-india.

Chatterji, A. P., T. B. Hansen, and C. Jaffrelot. (2019). *Majoritarian State: How Hindu Nationalism Is Changing India*. Noida: HarperCollins.

Mander, H., N. Badhwar, and J. Dayal. (2018). *Reconciliation*. New Delhi: Westland Publications.

Chandhoke, N. (2018). The crackdown on civil society. *The Hindu*, 30 August.

Chopra, R. (2021). The catastrophic cost of junk science, bogus information and the Hindutva inferiority complex. *Scroll.in*, 1 May. Accessed on 3 May 2021: https://scroll.in/article/993255/the-catastrophic-cost-of-junk-science-bogus-information-and-the-hindutva-inferiority-complex.

Crabtree, J. (2018). *The Billionaire Raj*. Noida: HarperCollins.

Day, M. (2019). Bernie has opened the door for democratic socialism. *Jacobin*, 12 June. Accessed on 7 December 2019: https://www.jacobinmag.com/2019/06/bernie-sanders-democratic-socialism-speech-fdr.

Desan, M., and M. McCarthy (2018). A time to be bold. *Jacobin*, 31 July. Accessed on 3 October 2018: https://jacobinmag.com/2018/07/socialism-democrats-alexandria-ocasio-cortez.

Desai, S. (2019). New elite vs liberals: The rift widens after Modi's win. *Economic Times*, 24 May.

Dore, B. (2020). Hindu nationalists are pushing magical remedies for the Coronavirus. *Foreign Policy*, 9 March.

Ghoshal D. and K. Das (2021). Scientists say India government ignored warnings amid coronavirus surge. Reuters, 1 May.

Dhabholkar, N. (2018). *The Case for Reason*, vol. I: *Understanding the Anti-superstition Movement*. New Delhi: Westland.

Economic Times (2021). COVID-19: Kerala police launches 'cyber patrol' to nab those spreading fake news. 25 April.

EPW (2020). Bills of contention (editorial). *Economic and Political Weekly* 55(39). Accessed on 5 October 2020: https://www.epw.in/journal/2020/39/editorials/bills-contention.html.

Ellis-Petersen, H. and S. A. Rahman (2020). 'I just want to go home': The desperate millions hit by Modi's brutal lockdown. *The Guardian*, 4 April.

Fromm, E. (1961). *Marx's Concept of Man*. New York: Frederick Ungar Publishing.

Faleiro, S. (2020). 'What the world can learn from Kerala about how to fight covid-19'. *MIT Technology Review*, 13 April.

Frank, A. G. (1976). Economic genocide in Chile: Open letter to Milton Friedman and Arnold Harberger. *Economic and Political Weekly* 11(24): 880–888.

Frank, T. (2004). *What's the Matter with Kansas*. New York: Picador.

Fraser, N. (2020). What should socialism mean in the 21st century. *Socialist Register 2020: Beyond Market Distopia*, ed. L. Panitch, L and G. Alba,. Noida: Aakar Books, 282–294.

Giridharadas, A. (2018). *Winner Take All: The Elite Charade of Changing the World*. New York: Knopf.

Gopalakrishnan, S. (2008). Neoliberalism and Hindutva: Fascism, free markets, and the restructuring of Indian capitalism. *Monthly Review*, 14 November.

Government of Kerala (2020). Corona guidelines, Department of Health and Family Welfare, Government of Kerala. 26 January 2020.

Gopalakrishnan, R. and K. R. S. Sundar (2018). 'Who cares for labour, anyway?' *Hindu Business Line*, 23 January.

Guha, R. (2013). *The Past and the Future of the Indian Left*. New Delhi: Penguin.

Guerin, D. (1939/1973). *Fascism and Big Business*, trans. F. & M. Merr. London: Monad/Pathfinder Press.

Gupta, R. (2019). Liberals completely misreading public mood is the election's real shocker. *The Wire*, 3 June.

Hacker, J. S. and P. Pierson (2020). *Let Them Eat Tweets: How the Right Rules in an Age of Extreme Inequality*. New York: Liveright Publishing.

Harvey, D. (2007). *A Brief History of Neoliberalism*. Oxford: Oxford University Press.

——— (2014). *Seventeen Contradictions and the End of Capitalism*. Oxford: Oxford University Press.

Heller, P. A virus, social democracy, and dividends for Kerala. *The Hindu*, 18 April.

Human Rights Watch. (2019). Violent cow protection in India. Human Rights Watch, 18 February. Accessed on 3 May 2019: https://www.hrw.org/report/2019/02/18/violent-cow-protection-india/vigilante-groups-attack-minorities.

Iber, P. (2016). The path to democratic socialism: Lessons from Latin America. *Dissent* 63(2): 115–120.

Jackson, M., and D. B. Grusky (2018). A post-liberal theory of stratification. *The British Journal of Sociology* 69(4): 1096–1133.

Jaffrelot, C. (2017). India's democracy at 70: Toward a Hindu state? *Journal of Democracy*, 28(3): 51–63.

———— (2019) Losing by religion. *Caravan Magazine*, 1 March.

Jagannathan, S. and R. Rai (2021). The necropolitics of neoliberalstate response to the Covid-19 pandemic in India. *Organization*, 1–23. doi: doi:10.1177/13505084211020195.

James, D. (2017). The compatibility of freedom and necessity in Marx's Idea of communist society. *European Journal of Philosophy* 25(2): 270–293.

Jenkins, R. (2004). Labor policy and the second generation of economic reform in India. *India Review* 3(4): 333–363.

Jodhka, S. S. (2016). Ascriptive hierarchies: Caste and its reproduction in contemporary India. *Current Sociology* 64(2): 228–243.

Joshi, S. and D. Malghan (2017). IIMs have a dismal diversity record – and the new bill isn't going to fix that. *The Wire*, 16 March.

Kelly, A. H., and L. McGoey (2018). Facts, power and global evidence: A new empire of truth. *Economy and Society* 47(1): 1–26.

Khan, S. (2019). The casteist underbelly of the Indian private sector. *The Wire*, 15 March.

Klagge, J .C. (1986). Marx's realms of 'freedom' and 'necessity'. *Canadian Journal of Philosophy* 16(4): 769–777.

Kumar S. and P. Gupta. (2019). Where did the BJP get its votes from in 2019? *Mint*, 5 June. Accessed on 4 July 2019: https:// www.livemint.com/politics/news/ where-did-the-bjp-get-its-votes-from-in-2019-1559547933995.html.

Lam, B. (2017). Trump's promises to corporate leaders: Lower taxes and fewer regulations. *The Atlantic*, 24 January.

Letelier, O. (1976). Economic 'freedom's' awful toll: The 'Chicago Boys' in Chile. *Review of Radical Political Economics* 8(3): 44–52.

Lilla, M. (2016). *The Shipwrecked Mind: On Political Reaction*. New York Review of Books.

Marx, K. (1959). Estranged Labour. Trans. Martin Milligan. Moscow: Progress Publishers, Marxist Internet Archive, 1844.

Mathew, B., and C. Jain (2018). Reviewing the labour code on Industrial Relations Bill, 2015. *Economic and Political Weekly* 53(21): 17.

Mathur, N. (2018). The low politics of higher education: Saffron branded neoliberalism and the assault on Indian universities. *Critical Policy Studies* 12(1): 121–125.

McGoey, L. (2014). The philanthropic state: Market–state hybrids in the philanthrocapitalist turn. *Third World Quarterly* 35(1): 109–125.

Mahaprashasta, A. A. (2019). BJP experimented with its brand of caste and religion-based politics in 2014 and cemented it in 2019. *The Wire*, 23 May. Accessed on 1 June 2019: https://thewire.in/politics/bjp-experimented-with-identity-politics-in-2014-and-cemented-it-in-2019.

Mathoor, V. (2021). 'Political lessons from Kerala: People's response to the communist welfare system. *Modern Diplomacy*, 10 May.

McCarthy, M. (2018). Democratic socialism isn't social democracy. *Jacobin*, 7 August. Accessed on 1 June 2019: https://jacobinmag. com/2018/08/democratic-socialism-social-democracy-nordic-countries.

Meyer, N. (2018). What is democratic socialism? *Jacobin*, 20 June. Accessed on 25 July 2018: https://jacobinmag.com/2018/07/democratic-socialism-bernie-sanders-social-democracy-alexandria-ocasio-cortez.

Metzl, J. M. (2019). *Dying of Whiteness: How the Politics of Racial Resentment Is Killing America's Heartland*. London: Hachette.

Mounk, Y. (2018). *The People vs. Democracy: Why Our Freedom Is in Danger and How to Save It*. London: Harvard University Press.

Moyn, S. (2014). *Human Rights and the Uses of History*. New York: Verso Books.

———. (2018a). *Not Enough: Human Rights in an Unequal World*. Cambridge, MA: Harvard University Press.

——— (2018b). Are human rights enough? *New Humanist*, 9 July.

Narayanan, N. C. and P. V. Poruthiyil (2021). India, Kerala and Covid-19. In *Covid-19 and Governance: Crisis Reveals*, ed. J. N. Pieterse, H. Lim and H. Khodker. Abingdon, UK: Routledge, 47–57.

Nanda, M. (2011). *The God Market: How Globalization Is Making India more Hindu*. New York: NYU Press.

Newman, M. (2005). *Socialism: A Very Short Introduction*. Oxford: Oxford University Press.

Oreskes, N. (2019). *Why Trust Science*. New Jersey: Princeton.

Oxfam (2018). *India Inequality Report 2018: Widening Gaps.* New Delhi: Oxfam.

Palshikar, S. (2017). India's second dominant party system. *Economic and Political Weekly* 52(11): 1–10.

Passmore, K. (2014). *Fascism.* Oxford: Oxford University Press.

Patnaik, P. (1993). The fascism of our times. *Social Scientist* 21(3/4): 69–77.

Paul, K. T., and C. Haddad (2019). Beyond evidence versus truthiness: Toward a symmetrical approach to knowledge and ignorance in policy studies. *Policy Sciences* 52(2): 299–314.

Paxton, R. O. (2004). *The Anatomy of Fascism.* London: Penguin.

Piketty, T. (2018). *Capital in the Twenty-first Century.* Cambridge, MA: Harvard University Press.

Pierson, P. (2017). American hybrid: Donald Trump and the strange merger of populism and plutocracy. *British Journal of Sociology* 68: S105–S119.

Polanyi, K. (1944). *The Great Transformation: The Political and Economic Origins of Our Time.* Boston: Beacon Press.

People's Union of Civil Liberties (PUCL). (2021a). PUCL statement on bail to Disha Ravi – Stop the witch hunt! Drop all false cases – respect right to free speech and dissent. Accessed on 1 March 2021: http://pucl.org/press-statements/pucl-statement-bail-disha-ravi-stop-witch-hunt-drop-all-false-cases-respect-right.

——— (2021b). Joint press statement: Appointment of Justice Arun Mishra as Chairperson, NHRC: Another move to subvert and destroy democratic institutions. Accessed on 3 June 2021: https://www.pucl.org/press-statements/joint-press-statement-appointment-justice-arun-mishra-chairperson-.nhrc-another-move.

Poruthiyil, P. V. (2019). Big business and fascism: A dangerous collusion. *Journal of Business Ethics* 168: 1–15.

Polychorniou, C. J. (2019). To be effective, socialism must adapt to 21st century needs. *Truthout*, 9 June. Accessed on 3 July 2019: https://truthout.org/?s=To+be+effective%2C+socialism+must+adapt+to+21st+century+needs.

Prashad, V. (2015). *No Free Left: The Futures of Indian Communism.* New Delhi: LeftWord Books.

Purkayastha, P. (2020). The untold story of the Left in Indian science. *Newsclick*, 17 October.

Recchia, F. and S. Vijayan (2021). 'In India, social media is a lifeline: It's being silenced. *Washington Post*, 6 May.

Rodrigues, J., Choudhary, A. and H. Dormido (2019). A murky flood of money pours into the world's largest election. *Bloomberg*, 17 March. Accessed 17 May 2019: https://www.bloombergquint.com/elections/a-murky-flood-of-money-pours-into-the-worlds-largest-election.

Salve, P. and S. Paliath (2019). India's gig workers: Overworked and underpaid. *IndiaSpend*, 4 June. Accessed on 12 July 2019: https://www.indiaspend.com/indias-gig-workers-overworked-and-underpaid/.

Stockman, F. (2018). 'Yes, I'm running as a socialist.' Why candidates are embracing the label in 2018. *New York Times*, 20 April.

Sundar, P. (2018). Using CSR funds for political gain. *The Wire*, 22 December. Accessed on 1 January 2019: https://thewire.in/business/modi-government-csr-political-gain.

Randeria, S. (2007). The state of globalization: Legal plurality, overlapping sovereignties and ambiguous alliances between civil society and the cunning state in India. *Theory, Culture and Society* 24(1): 1–33.

Ramachandran, R. (2020). Transparency has been Kerala's biggest weapon against the Coronavirus. *The Wire*, 27 March. Accessed on 30 May 2020: https://thewire.in/government/kerala-coronavirus-response-transparency.

Ramachandran, R. (2016). Of 'cowpathy' and its miracles. *Frontline*, 2 September.

Roy, A. (2021). We are witnessing a crime against humanity': Arundhati Roy on India's Covid catastrophe. *The Guardian*, 28 April.

Sarkar, S. (1993). The fascism of the Sangh Parivar. *Economic and Political Weekly* 28(5): 163–167.

Sarkar, T. (2019). How the Sangh Parivar writes and teaches history. In *Majoritarian State: How Hindu Nationalism Is Changing India*, ed. A. P. Chatterji, T. B. Hansen, and C. Jaffrelot. New Delhi: Oxford University Press, 151–174.

Sen, A. (1993). The threats to secular India. *Social Scientist* 21(3/4): 5–23.

Sardesai S., and V. Attri (2019). Post-poll survey: The 2019 verdict is a manifestation of the deepening religious divide in India. *The Hindu*, 30 May.

Shrivastava, A. and A. Kothari (2012). *Churning the Earth: The Making of Modern India*. New Delhi: Penguin.

Snyder, T. (2017). *On Tyranny: Twenty Lessons from the Twentieth Century*. London: Penguin.

Sridharan, E. (2014). Class voting in the 2014 Lok Sabha elections. *Economic and Political Weekly* 49(39): 72–76.

Stanley, J. (2018). *How Fascism Works: The Politics of Us and Them*. London: Random House.

Sundar, N. (2010). Vigilantism, culpability and moral dilemmas. *Critique of Anthropology* 30(1): 113–121.

Sunstein, C. R. (2014). *Conspiracy Theories and other Dangerous Ideas*. New York: Simon and Schuster.

Surie, A. (2018). 'Are Ola and Uber drivers entrepreneurs or exploited workers?' EPW Engage, 16 June.

Teltumbde, A. (2005). Hindutva agenda and Dalits. In *Religion, Power and Violence: Expression of Politics in Contemporary Times*, ed. R. Puniani. New Delhi: Sage, 208–224.

Udupa, S. (2018). Enterprise Hindutva and social media in urban India. *Contemporary South Asia* 26(4): 453–467.

United Nations (2018). Report of the Special Rapporteur on contemporary forms of racism, racial discrimination, xenophobia and related intolerance. Accessed on 2 February 2019: https://digitallibrary.un.org/record/1637435?ln=en.

Vaishnav, A. (2020). Central government's response to the COVID-19 pandemic (May 23–May 29, 2020). PRS India, 29 May.

Venkatramakrishnan, R. (2019). Are India's elite anti-BJP? Actually, the party drew its greatest support from upper castes, rich. *Scroll.in*, 5 June. Accessed on 6 June 2019: https://scroll.in/article/925925/are-indias-elite-anti-bjp-actually-saffron-party-got-greatest-support-from-upper-castes-rich.

Wilde, O. (1891). The soul of man under socialism. Marxist Internet Archive (privately printed 1891). Accessed on 5 May 2019: https://www.marxists.org/reference/archive/wilde-oscar/soul-man/index.htm.

Woodcock, J. (2019). *Marx at the Arcade: Consoles, Controllers, and Class Struggle*. Chicago: Haymarket Books.

4

GROUNDED IN REALITY, A RADICALLY ALTERNATIVE FUTURE

ASHISH KOTHARI

As India proceeds further into its eighth decade after independence, it is evidently deeply troubled. Every day the news channels shout out terrifying, gut-wrenching issues. Religious, racial, and caste hatred spawn a spate of killings and maiming, the state complicit in its eerie silence if not tacit encouragement. Air pollution epidemics affect millions. Plastics in rivers and lakes and cow's bellies, and pesticides in our food. No let-up in gender violence, domestic and elsewhere, with the rape and murder of little girls only the shocking tip of the iceberg. Adivasis and fishers and farmers and pastoralists, deliberately forgotten as the relics of the past, being displaced *en masse* for mines and industries and highways and amusement parks (the amusement being, of course, a prerogative of the rich). Financial scandals in which the swindling of hundreds of crores is now routine, almost boring, with how and where the swindler has escaped to becoming a point of greater interest. Species of wildlife being wiped out, and increasingly unpredictable climatic patterns. Politicians are reducing the world's largest elections (the latest in the summer of 2019) to farcical, bitter slanging matches devoid of the substance that political debates should be about. And the latest twist, the unprecedented slap in humanity's face by a tiny virus, with its own horrific consequences to the health and livelihoods of millions of Indians.[1]

It is as if all the fundamental ills of our society were converging: caste, gender, and race-based oppressions coming to us from the past, capitalist class exploitation and state-sponsored violence against communities (in the name of 'development') as more recent additions, and, underlying these, an increasing alienation from the rest of nature. These ills do not necessarily locate themselves in the same set of oppressive people, nor are the oppressed always the same. Indeed, the status of 'being oppressed' and 'being an oppressor' sometimes merges confusingly into each other in the same individual or group. Therefore, it is more meaningful to locate the structures of power domination and not just individuals who currently control those structures to understand, challenge, and find alternatives to these structures and their various manifestations.

Elsewhere, a colleague and I have critically analysed the dominant model of 'development' based on blind faith in economic growth as the engine to move people out of poverty, hunger, and deprivation (Shrivastava and Kothari, 2012). With its roots in the desire of imperial powers to find new ways of exploiting and dominating the world after the so-called Second World War, to aid in the reconstruction of their own economies, this model is based on a unilinear notion of how nations should 'progress' (farming/fishing/pastoral to industrial and post-industrial; traditional to modern, and so on), considers measures like gross domestic product (GDP) as the most important indicators of the stage and rate of development, and promotes unrestrained industrialization, commercialization, extraction of resources, and urbanization. Its impacts have been disastrous across the world, as evidenced by the way in which human activity has crossed several critical planetary thresholds, with rapid biodiversity decline, widespread water and air pollution, and potentially runaway climate change as some of the results (Deb, 2009).

In this chapter, I depart from an examination of these structures and forces of injustice, oppression, ecological unsustainability, and the fundamental faults of the 'model' of development foisted upon the country by them. Here, I focus on the kind of responses that people are giving to their manifestations in their lives. How are people in India reacting to continued deprivation and discrimination and to new forms of displacement and dispossession?

There seem to me two crucial sets of responses: one, resistance to what is perceived to be wrong (that is unjust, unequal, unsustainable, and so on) and, second, the construction of alternatives in ways that are considered right (the opposite of these 'uns'). I deal only briefly with resistance here; most of the chapter is dedicated to the alternatives.

RESISTANCE

On 22 May 2018, police firing upon protestors in Thoothukudi, Tamil Nadu, resulted in the death of 13 people. The event was not one-off but a culmination of resentment brewing over two decades of pollution impacts by factories, including Sterlite Copper, which boiled over when local demands to stop further expansion were not heeded by the government. This struggle is just one of possibly hundreds of such movements across India, some very small and very quiet, others bigger and more vocal (Shiva, 1991; S. Kothari, 2000; Sen, 2018a, 2018b).[2] They have an ancient heritage, with stories of peasant, Dalit, and Adivasi resistance against despotic rulers, oppressive castes, and the British colonial government being increasingly unearthed and written about. They have a more recent heritage too, in a large number of movements against independent India's policies and projects in the last few decades, or against the communalization of public life and discrimination against religious minorities, or against continued and new forms of patriarchy and masculinity.[3] Such resistance is invaluable in many ways. It shows as a myth the narrative that everyone is in favour of 'development' and economic growth, or okay with India becoming a 'Hindu rashtra', or accepts masculinist notions of how women should behave in order not to get molested. It puts a brake, howsoever slow and small, on the progress of the 'crush-everything-in-its-path' juggernaut that a nation aspiring to be a twenty-first-century superpower in the same image as those it is copying has become. It shows, sometimes powerfully, that there are other notions of what it is to live well as humans with each other and with the rest of nature, far from the consumerist, selfish, individualistic, and exploitative world that corporate capitalism hardsells. And by managing to sustain a diversity of worldviews, ways of living, ecologies and economies, cultures, and arts and crafts, it provides the possibility of constructing alternative pathways out of the multiple crises we face. It is to these alternative pathways that I now turn, and focus my attention on.

TRANSFORMATIONS IN FIVE SPHERES

Across India, there is an incredible churning of ideas and practices taking place, albeit still small or 'on the margins', showing alternatives to the dominant system. These include attempts at sustainable and equitable ways to meet basic material needs (food, water, energy, housing, sanitation, clothing); alternative and community-based health, learning, and education initiatives; assertions of localized decision-making and governance of villages and urban neighbourhoods; struggles for gender, caste, age, ability, and sexuality justice; livelihood security through greater control over economic processes; democratizing the media, arts, and other cultural spaces; initiatives towards peace, harmony, and non-violence in the midst of conflict situations; rebuilding a relationship of co-existence with the rest of nature, including through community-led conservation of ecosystems; exploring the complex balance between individual freedoms (including spiritual quests) and collective good; asserting basic spiritual and ethical principles to challenge the dogma of institutionalized religions; and much more. What we see in these and myriad other examples, in nascent or well-developed ways, are transformations taking place in five spheres: political, economic, social, cultural and knowledge, and ecological. These are elaborated, with examples, here.

POLITICAL TRANSFORMATIONS

Here, I explore nascent experiments in India directed at radical democracy. The first few months of 2018 witnessed a series of news items emanating from central and eastern India, of a movement labelled 'Pathalgari', of Adivasis declaring a region of autonomy though very much within the framework of the Indian Constitution (Tewary, 2018). According to several reports, the movement has arisen from the consistent failure of the Indian state to provide for the needs of Adivasis in ways that respect their distinct identity and their own worldviews and knowledge systems, and in fact, on the contrary, its proclivity to alienate Adivasis from their lands and natural resources by allowing corporations to take over. For some years before this, the Dongria Kondh Adivasis of Odisha have repeatedly rejected proposals for mining in their area, asserting that the territory belongs to their deity Niyamraja and no one had the right to do such extraction from it; their struggle reached the Supreme Court, which held up the right of their *gram sabha*s to allow or reject mining (Tatpathi, Kothari, and Mishra, 2016). In the Gadchiroli district of Maharashtra, 90 villages in the Korchi *taluka* have come together as a *maha gramsabha* to resist mining proposals but also to work out self-governance mechanisms (Broome et al., 2020). In the same district, the example of the Gond village Mendha-Lekha is well known, having declared nearly three decades back that '*our* government in Delhi and Mumbai, but in our village, *we are* the government' (Broome, 2018). In the town of Bhuj, Kachchh, some colonies have asserted their role in decision-making with regard to the planning of infrastructure and civic amenities, rather than leave it only to bureaucrats and politicians; I will refer again to this later.

In other parts of the world, parallel initiatives include the iconic movements by indigenous Zapatista communities in Mexico and the Kurdish ethnic community in west Asia to assert autonomous governance, as also the struggles for self-determination by many indigenous peoples in Latin America, North America, and Australia (Aslan and Akbulut, 2019; Esteva, 2019; Leyva-Solano, 2019). In urban situations, there is the 'municipalism' movement, where a more collaborative, solidarity-based politics is attempted to ensure the participation of local neighbourhood institutions.[4] In these, there is an attempt to broad-base decision-making to the general population, and not restrict it only to a few elected or chosen people.

These examples from different regions across the world point to a different conception of democracy than the one adopted by most countries. Time and again, the limits and perversions of representative, liberal democracy have been exposed. Political parties and politicians who fight elections promise the earth but once in power, by and large, appear to find all kinds of excuses to shy away from coming good on their commitments. Increasingly, as demonstrated by some of the examples here, people are realizing that the crucial locus of power can be themselves, as individuals and collectives. The ground-level struggle to empower *gram sabha*s and local urban bodies, beyond even what the Constitution mandates, is a manifestation of this realization. It is radical or direct democracy, flourishing in situations where people can take decisions face to face, that brings back the true meaning of the word (demos = people;

cracy = rule) and takes society closer to *swaraj* as Gandhi and others appear to have meant it (more on this later).

Meaningful power at the scale of the village or urban neighbourhood would require more than what the Indian Constitution and laws under the 73rd and 74th Amendments provide. In particular, almost nowhere in India do such local bodies have financial and legal powers that could make them truly independent. A partial exception is the power of village councils in Nagaland due to its special Constitutional status as also the extension of financial powers over several departments through its 'communitisation' law (Broome, 2014). Kerala's attempt at decentralizing planning to village bodies is another partial exception (Isaac and Franke, 2002).

Radical democracy, of course, can work best in small populations; at larger scales, it can work in limited situations such as with referendums for very important decisions, but otherwise, there will still be a need for representative or delegated institutions of decision-making at those larger levels. Processes of making such institutions accountable then become crucial; these could include the right to recall, public charters, the right to information, the responsibility to report back, frequent rotation of representatives or delegates, regular public hearings, full transparency of budgets, plans, and decisions, and so on. Even the few of these put into place in India already show the potential of making larger-scale institutions of decision-making more accountable, as, for instance, in the case of the Right to Information (RTI) law.

Radical democracy will work best where at least four features are met. First, people must have the *right to participate* in decision-making in all matters that affect their lives. Second, they must have the *capacity to participate* meaningfully (including access to relevant information and knowledge), something that will need time to build, given that a couple of centuries or more of centralized decision-making have robbed people of the confidence and ability to participate. Third, there need to be *accessible forums* of decision-making: *gram sabha*s, neighbourhood assemblies, subsidiary bodies for various functions, and so on. Fourth, perhaps most crucial and most difficult to grasp and achieve, there needs to be a certain *maturity, or wisdom*, of decision-making processes – for instance, a sense of responsibility among the majority towards the minority so that decisions do not get reduced to the politics of majoritarianism. This is not to say that *only* when these four features are in place should radical democracy be tried out, but rather that in exploring it on the ground, as is happening in some examples cited earlier, these features need to be introduced, strengthened, and evolved, including through appropriate policy changes. Without this, radical democracy can also go horribly wrong, as when local elites capture or retain power or when referendums go haywire based on public perception manipulation. Clearly, the move towards radical democracy is no overnight magic wand but a difficult, very possible, long-term process.

Another important and complex issue with moving towards radical democracy is the need to review decision-making boundaries based on ecological and cultural links and contiguities. Nation-state boundaries across the world are often the result of arbitrary decisions. In the case of India, the South Asian boundaries make little ecological and cultural sense; they have divided up the Sundarbans and fisher communities between India and Bangladesh, unique deserts and nomadic populations between southern Pakistan and India, contiguous mountain ecosystems and peoples between northern Pakistan and India, the trans-Himalayan plateau and nomadic peoples between Tibet and India, and so on. At this historical juncture, the idea of dissolving or making porous these boundaries seems rather remote, but at least one can begin with some transboundary cooperation to sustain the ecological and livelihood security of these regions, even establish 'peace parks' where there is a history of conflict, and take other such steps that can bring down the fences and walls.

There are not too many examples of ecoregional or bioregional political boundaries, but lessons can be learned from attempts within India or outside. For about a decade, 60-plus villages in the Arvari river basin in Rajasthan, for instance, governed the area through a people's parliament ('Arvari Sansad'), putting the river at the centre and ignoring *tehsil* or district boundaries (Hasnat, 2005[5]). In Australia, there has been an initiative to plan for the Great Eastern Range cutting across conventional political boundaries, for integrated planning. Transboundary protected areas in several regions of the world are another example; while they do not challenge nation-state boundaries, they prioritize the ecological (and sometimes cultural) contiguities across these boundaries. A broader approach of this kind is called 'connectivity conservation' (Pulsford et al., 2015; Sandwith et al., 2001). An initiative to conceive of the Ecuadorian and Peruvian Amazon as one bioregion, centred around visions and planning by resident indigenous nations, began in 2018 as the Sacred Headwaters Initiative.[6] And perhaps the boldest initiative is that of the Kurds, attempting an autonomous region run on direct democracy principles in a region cutting across Syria, Turkey, and Iraq (Flach et al., 2016).

Building on the kind of examples given here, essays in a recent book, *Alternative Futures*, lay out what India's political future could be. They posit a 'radical democracy' or a 'socialism freed of the state', where people and collectives are at the centre of decision-making (including on laws and policies), and ecological contiguities and flows are respected. These are resulting partly from the emergence and spread of mass movements demanding transparency, accountability, wages, and community rights (such as those that brought RTI legislation) and a 'rainbow coalition of grassroots social movements' (Das, 2017; Kodiveri, 2017; Nigam, 2017; Patankar, 2017; Roy et al., 2017). Such a system, liberated from historical contestations, could integrate many ideals of Gandhi, Ambedkar, M. N. Roy, Iqbal, Tagore, Phule, Marx, and Kosambi, especially those focused on achieving social justice, direct democracy, and ecological sustainability, which in various different ways these activist-thinkers espoused (Nigam, 2017; Patankar, 2017). In any case, social movements and those practising radical grassroots alternatives do not divide themselves into these ideological boxes and combine several elements across these boxes (A. Kothari, 2018). India could then also play a significant role in a new, dynamic, and democratic multilateral governance at global levels (Dubey, 2017).

ECONOMIC TRANSFORMATIONS

In this section, I explore experiments anchored around food and livelihood sovereignty, reorganizing economics around the local, greater producer control, and alternative organizational forms. In some of the examples of attempted self-governance and autonomy mentioned earlier, one of the central motivating factors is the desire to take greater control over the economy. The Gadchiroli examples are some among many across India, asserting that forests belong to the community, and their use and conservation will be governed according to its rules. Corporates exploiting these forests, usually with the permission and assistance of the Forest Department, have been told to leave. Instead, the villages are building the capacity to do sustainable harvesting and trade in forest produce. This process does not necessarily challenge the larger capitalist or statist economic structures (the produce is, after all, sold to contractors from outside), but it makes a dent in them by asserting collective control and greater ability to determine prices and other terms by trying to make sure benefits are equitably shared among the producers, and in many cases building in ecological sustainability principles.

Similar processes are seen in examples of producer companies and self-governed cooperatives established by farmers, fishers, craftspersons, pastoralists, service providers like waste-pickers and hawkers, and others. Examples include Nowgong Agriculture Producer Company Ltd (NAPCL) in Madhya Pradesh, the Aharam Traditional Crop Producer Company (ATCPC) in Tamil Nadu, and the Dharani Farming and Marketing Cooperative Ltd in Andhra Pradesh, all examples of farmer-run companies encompassing several settlements that enable producers to directly reach their markets; Qasab – Kutch Craftswomen's Producer Co. Ltd in Kachchh does the same for women working on embroidery, appliqué, and patchwork.[7] In not-so-common situations, the state too has helped in the process, as in the case of Kudumbashree's production units covering about 5 million women in Kerala and Jharcraft's craftsperson collectives in Jharkhand that have provided sustained or better livelihoods for over 300,000 families (though reportedly of late this has faltered due to change in leadership).[8]

Movements towards sovereignty over the means of meeting basic needs are also spreading. An example is that of food sovereignty, asserted by some farmer movements such as the Deccan Development Society (DDS[9]) and the Food Sovereignty Alliance[10] in southern India, or the Beej Bachao Andolan (Save the Seed Movement) in the north. For about three decades now, the Dalit women farmers of DDS have shown how dryland, local biodiversity, and knowledge-based agriculture can provide not only full food security to thousands of households but also complete control (hence not only *security* but *sovereignty*) over the means of food production and consumption. Based on these and many other examples, Mansatta et al. (2017) posit an agricultural future with community-based food sovereignty and agroecological approaches as its basis. To this is added a perspective on pastoral futures, advocating an enabling environment that can integrate pastoral production with nature conservation, ensure space for pastoralists in the landscape, and develop combined livestock production and environmental protection as an attractive 'career' option for young people (Köhler-Rollefson and Rathore, 2017).

Several initiatives at localized generation, governance, and management of water exist across India; an increasing number are also focusing on energy, housing, and other such basic needs. In Kachchh, for instance, the group Arid Communities and Technologies (ACT) has enabled water self-sufficiency using the meagre rainfall of the region in several dozen villages and in some colonies of Bhuj town; the group Hunnarshala has provided new respect to traditional mud-building techniques and trained over 100 youths to become architects using both traditional and modern knowledge; groups like Khamir, Qasab, Kalakshetra, and others have helped revive local crafts to the level where thousands of people are deriving decent livelihoods.[11] The social enterprise SELCO has enhanced the livelihood and social conditions of over 150,000 families through decentralized solar power, provided by ensuring financial linkages that help the families ultimately pay for it themselves (SELCO, n.d.). These and other initiatives provide fodder for the envisioning of a more sustainable, equitable future for water and energy governance and for livelihoods (Dharmadhikary and Thakkar, 2017; Hande et al., 2017; Uzramma, 2017).

Of crucial importance is a reorganizing of economics to be centred around the local. This includes trade and exchange conducted on the principles of democracy and fairness. Groups of villages, or villages and towns, could form units to further such economic democracy. For instance, in Tamil Nadu state, the former Dalit *panchayat* head of Kuthambakkam village, Elango Rangasamy, envisages organizing a cluster of between 7–8 and 15–16 villages to form a 'regional network economy', in which they will trade goods and services with each other (on mutually beneficial terms) to reduce dependence on the outside market and government; Ela Bhatt, social worker and founder of one of India's largest women's cooperatives, Self Employed Women's Association (SEWA), calls for a 100-mile radius approach to self-reliance. This and other examples are generalizable to posit localization and regionalization of economies that are ecologically stable and renewable, with substantial use of biomass for various needs (Bhatt, 2015; Joy, 2017; Kajka, 2018; Shrivastava and Rangasamy, 2017). This way, the money stays back in the area for reinvestment in local development, and relations among villages become stronger. In the Nilgiris of Tamil Nadu, the initiative Just Change has attempted to bring together producers, consumers, and investors to form a single cooperative, enhancing the localization of exchanges that are benefiting several hundred families.[12]

There are vibrant examples of alternative organizational forms that depart from the dominant corporate form. While examples of non-profit retail or social enterprises whose main motive is not profit are uncommon,[13] the ones that exist show the potential. One that celebrated its tenth anniversary in early 2018 is reStore, the non-profit store in Chennai that enables organic farmers, craftspersons, and others to reach consumers without claiming any profit from their transactions; it has inspired several dozen more such stores in Chennai, confederated under the banner of Organic Farmers Market.[14] Millet Mama is a low-priced restaurant specializing in millet-based food that a young person interested in promoting healthy cuisine runs and where profits are not one of the motives.[15] The Shaheed Hospital in Chhattisgarh was established by workers, does not rely on corporate or governmental funding, and is run on principles of reaching the neediest first and foremost.[16]

Crafts (India's second-biggest employer after agriculture) provide an opportunity for India to bypass the option of high-energy industrialization, which benefits only a few, in favour of low-energy, dispersed craft industries, which could usher in democracy in production, a basic building block for true social equity (Uzramma, 2017). This sector is only one of many where ownership of the means of the production is or could be in the hands of the producer and away from capitalist owners. As Roy (2017) has argued, the future of industrial work lies in a radical change of two crucial determinants of capitalist society, that is, competition and profit. Some of this has been attempted by movements in India, but they need to go beyond a politics and theorization that can go change all structures of exploitation, inequality, and injustice. In India, initiatives that challenge corporate capitalism, such as worker takeover of industrial production facilities and their subsequent running on democratic, equal-pay principles, and alternative currencies or exchange systems that enable some freedom from centralized monetary systems, are absent or rare. But there are examples of these in many other countries that we can learn from (Meira, 2014; Karyotis, 2019; Labour Party, undated; Vio.Me, 2019; Workerscontrol.net, 2020). Though still marginal to the dominant systems, these show the potential of non-capitalist, non-statist economies.

Another major shift has to be a radically different vision for the nature of urban areas. Currently characterized by unsustainability and inequity both within themselves and in their relationship with rural areas, cities in India have to undergo drastic transformations. Kapoor (2017) envisages dispersed urbanization with small towns as development and skilling hubs, innovative mechanisms for financing, public authorities at multiple levels to regulate the uses of land and water, empowering urban local bodies or governments for decentralized governance, and low carbon pathways. The 'Homes in the City' programme initiated by several civil society groups in Bhuj contains several of these elements, with its focus on empowering marginalized populations to self-govern and self-provision basic needs, and make the town authorities more accountable (Bajpai and Kothari, 2020).[17] Patwardhan (2017), based on several decades of activism and research, proposes people-centric sustainable transport that can make a city pleasant and safe, where people can walk, cycle, and reach destinations without dependence on automobiles. Pune's cycle plan,[18] made after substantial public consultation, is a good example of what can be done, though its actual implementation appears to be faltering.

Overall, the initiatives mentioned here point to a very different economic system than the one dominant today. Its main elements would be mindfulness to ecological limits, local to global; a primary focus on meeting human needs, and in particular those of historically or presently marginalized people; localized self-reliance for basic material and non-material needs; producers having control over means of production and consumers over the conditions of consumption, the two overlapping as prosumers by realizing the full potential of meaningful and diversified work; dissolution of the hard divide between 'work' and 'leisure', and the revitalization of livelihoods that combine labour, enjoyment, dignity and meaningfulness in place of deadening and mechanical jobs ('deadlihoods'[19]); a mutually beneficial relationship and indeed a continuum rather than a sharp break between the rural and the urban; bringing back to centre stage the relations of caring, sharing, and affect in the economy, including recognition of the enormous and currently invisibilized contribution of women in production and reproduction.

SOCIAL TRANSFORMATIONS

Localized governance systems can also go horribly wrong in enabling or encouraging elite capture, continued social oppression, and exploitation. A series of recent examples in parts of India, where local *panchayat*s or customary community institutions have given regressive judgements in cases of inter-caste or inter-religious partnerships, are manifestations of this. Economic localization can also be counterproductive to those who are historically weak, such as the landless. Trends in Europe and the United States or, for that matter, north-east India, where migrants and 'refugees' are being denied basic human rights and livelihood opportunities in the name of 'nationalism' or localization, are further indications of these dangers. Hence the crucial importance of simultaneous struggles towards greater social justice and equality or equity, and of bringing to bear on such situations globally accepted norms, such as the Universal Declaration on Human Rights and the Declaration on the Rights of Indigenous Peoples (A. Kothari, 2019).

While explicit resistance and social movements such as those of many strands of feminism, anti-racism, Dalits, LGBTQ (lesbian, gay, bisexual, transgender, and queer), and others have their very legitimate role in this, there are also fascinating examples of quieter, somewhat indirect routes towards social justice. The Dalit women of DDS, mentioned earlier, have not only achieved food sovereignty for their households but also, through this and through some remarkable work in alternative media, education, and other sectors, transformed the gender and caste relations in several dozen villages. As Dalits, women, and small farmers, their members were previously triple disprivileged; they now stand tall and proud, with other castes, men, and large farmers having to treat them with respect. The revival of handloom weaving in Kachchh, western India, mentioned earlier, has helped remove the most regressive manifestations of casteism towards the Dalit weavers (though it must be mentioned that this revival is based on elite markets, and thus a crucial part of the macro-economic system remains unchallenged in this) (Kothari et al., 2020). In Tamil Nadu, the former Dalit sarpanch Elango Rangasamy, also mentioned earlier, made good use of a government scheme to persuade a few hundred families of Dalits and other castes to move into a mixed housing society, resulting in a gradual reduction of casteism (Kajka, 2018). The activist musician T. M. Krishna's initiative to combine his classical Carnatic singing with the music of the transgender community in southern India attempts to break down traditional social attitudes against this community.[20] Various initiatives at using sports to empower the girl child, such as football in Uttar Pradesh,[21] are some other interesting approaches.

In none of these examples has the transformation been complete. Given the deep historical roots of many injustices, the complete removal of the structures of gender, caste, sexual orientation, and other inequities is a long-term process. Teltumbde (2017) has argued that the Dalit movement needs to recognize its class consciousness and move beyond the focus on political reservations towards economic empowerment, adoption of a proportional representation system, and outlawing castes altogether. On gender relations, Gupte (2017) envisions an India without gender binaries and patriarchy, one that will refute sexual interactions as power-laden transactions; people will have reproductive and sexual rights; women will have open and safe access to private and public spaces and inequalities related to caste, class, and religion would be abolished. Dealing with the problems of religious minorities, Engineer (2017) draws on the example of a mohalla (neighbourhood) committee in Bhiwandi to propose the building of local social networks and groups of diverse communities to tackle communal tensions. Narrain (2017), dealing with the stigmatization of multiple sexualities, advocates the recognition of the notion of love in a wider sense, which can be characterized as the love of justice or empathy for the suffering other. And Dungdung (2017), bringing out the plight of Adivasis for many of whom independence never seems to have arrived, argues for a future in which they can determine their own paths of well-being, based on territorial autonomy and their own cultural, ecological, intellectual roots.

Contemporary India even seems to be going through a worsening of hostilities and conflicts around these inequities, encouraged or at least not actively discouraged by the right-wing state; but paradoxically this may be a manifestation of the entrenched system trying desperately to retain its domination against an up-swell of justice-based movements.

Social transformations are also about achieving well-being as a whole. This includes rescuing the concept of 'wealth', 'prosperity', and 'happiness' from the materialist distortions that modern capitalism has trapped them into, and reviving their non-material sources, including family and friendship relations, relaxed modes of learning, forums for expressing one's creativity and innovation, vibrant cultural spaces, means of spiritual deepening, and connecting with the rest of nature.

CULTURAL AND KNOWLEDGE TRANSFORMATIONS

This section explores initiatives at reviving and sustaining cultural and knowledge diversity, integrating various forms of knowledge for transformation, and promoting the knowledge commons.

India's enormous cultural and knowledge diversity is celebrated in many ways, such as in the thousands of festivals dotting the entire country. But it is also under threat, both from the forces of homogenization (not least of which is the uniform, top-down, dulling education imparted in most schools) and from those who portray and use this diversity for their own divisive ends (such as religious 'superficialists'[22] and hyper-nationalists).

Take, for instance, language. Not so long ago India may have had well upwards of 1,000 languages (not counting dialects within them); even now, it has at least 780 living languages, according to the remarkable People's Linguistic Survey of India (PLSI) initiated in 2010.[23] Each of these languages is a library of knowledge, and when any is lost, we lose a storehouse of information, experience, and wisdom. India's school system mostly imparts education in the official state language, ignoring the diversity of mother tongues that the students come from, and, within a generation or two, causing the loss of languages (or a substantial part of them) that may have sustained for centuries before this. Added to this is the politics of divisiveness that has made language a tool of conflict between states or regions within states. But a breath of fresh air in this dismal scenario are the attempts by groups like Bhasha, which coordinated the PLSI, helps revive and popularize languages being otherwise lost, creates dictionaries and literature for children to continue using their mother tongues while also learning state and 'national' languages, and organizes *sangams* (confluences) for speakers of various languages to come together. Its founder, Ganesh Devy, has struggled to also promote recognition of 'forgotten' or marginalized groups of Adivasi and nomadic communities, and leads a movement to create communal harmony and counter inter-community hatred. In an essay on the future of languages in India, Devy (2017) advocates support for languages that are not popular or in the mainstream or have not reached the cities, maintaining e-libraries and literary societies, and initiating magazines of and for indigenous languages.

Perhaps the most important agenda in all this is the transformation of the education system, away from the stultifying homogeneity and poor quality of public schools and universities as also the elitism of private institutions. An increasing number of alternative learning centres are showing how education can be fun, creative, and meaningful, bringing back the original meaning of school ('skhole' = learning with leisure!), providing avenues for more holistic development of the child (head, hands, heart … and feet!), and enabling youth to grow up as innovative, responsible adults who will question dogmas of capitalism, statism, casteism and patriarchy. Examples include the *jeevan shalas* ('life schools') of the Narmada Bachao Andolan, Marudam in Tamil Nadu, Adharshila Learning Centre in Madhya Pradesh, and Imlee-Mahua in Chhattisgarh; colleges like the Adivasi Academy at Tejgadh, Gujarat; and open-learning institutions like the Bija Vidyapeeth in Dehradun in Uttarakhand, Bhoomi College in Bengaluru, and Swaraj University in Udaipur.[24]

Another strand of the movement includes people who reject institutional learning altogether, preferring to do home or community-based 'schooling'. Even more important than these alternative initiatives, though, are attempts to transform the formal system, especially of government institutions; for instance, Students' Educational and Cultural Movement of Ladakh (SECMOL) and others in Ladakh led a movement to introduce mother-tongue-based education in its schools, the Krishnamurthy Foundation has facilitated new, mixed-age self-learning methods in some schools in Karnataka,[25] and so on. Based on these and other examples, Tultul Biswas and Rajesh Khindri of Eklavya argue for a vision and practice of education that can open up opportunities and unleash the potential towards the development of a balanced, just, and responsive students and teachers (Biswas and Khindri, 2017).

Many of the examples of alternative initiatives given in this chapter (such as Arid Communities and Technologies, Hunnarshala, DDS, and Bhasha) have as one of their core elements the use of diverse knowledge systems. This is increasingly seen in the health sector also. The central government's programme on traditional health systems, supporting Ayurveda, yoga, Unani, Siddha, homoeopathy, and naturopathy, is positive but very partial and often half-hearted. For instance, it does not ensure that all public health institutions like village and urban ward-level clinics have multiple health systems available. Allopathy still gets the lion's share of attention. It also does not pay much attention to folk systems that are not necessarily codified like the ones named earlier, even though they are widespread and often very effective (though also rapidly eroding as relevant knowledge and skills disappear with each passing generation). Additionally, the privatization of health services and increasing control by the corporate sector has meant a horrendous loss of access to the poor, and increasing financial burden on the household economy. This has been especially sharply exposed by COVID-19.

Here too several initiatives are noteworthy, such as the promotion of alternative health systems by the Foundation for Revitalisation of Local Health Traditions, enabling access to reliable, accountable, community-based health services by constituents of the national network, Jan Swasthya Andolan, and groups like Tribal Health Initiative, devolution of some financial control over official health services to village councils through the 'communitization' scheme of Nagaland, and worker-led facilities like the Shaheed Hospital mentioned earlier and others. These initiatives form the basis for some futuristic thinking by health activists Abhay Shukla and Rakhal Gaitonde, with a stress on the democratization of health centred on a Universal Health Care (UHC) approach that will bring in the vast majority of public and private healthcare providers under a single integrated system, including multiple systems of health (Shukla and Gaitonde, 2017). Robust community health systems have been key to communities being able to cope with the COVID-19 pandemic, such as in Sittilingi *panchayat* of Tamil Nadu and Kunariya *panchayat* of Kachchh, Gujarat.[26]

As important as all the aforementioned is the struggle to keep knowledge and information in the public sphere, as a common good. Over the last century or so, and especially in the last two–three decades, there has been a significant thrust towards privatization, such as through intellectual property rights. This is not to say that all knowledge in the past was in the public domain or democratically available; *vaids* could hold crucial medicinal knowledge to themselves, dominant castes dictated what kind of knowledge could be accessed and generated by whom, and so on. But knowledge for everyday use, knowledge that was crucial for survival and livelihoods and basic needs, was freely shared (Posey, 1996). This may have been the base for the enormous diversification of plants and animals in agriculture. For instance, one species of rice domesticated long back spread from farmer to farmer into various ecoregions of India, where it was bred through successive generations of trial and error into over 50,000 varieties; or countless home remedies using commonly available plants like *neem* or turmeric became common knowledge for millions of people. Countering the trend towards privatization, especially into the hands of the corporate sector, is therefore very much part of the alternative movement; this includes initiatives for open-source software, copyleft and creative commons, deliberate acts of putting IPR (intellectual property rights)-protected materials into the public domain, and other initiatives that could democratize knowledge (see Raina, 2017, for a futuristic look into what this would entail; for more global trends, De Angelis, 2019, and Halpin, 2019).

This also becomes important in the fields of media and arts. Corporatization of the economy and society in general has also captured these arenas; nothing better illustrates this better than the grip that private corporations have over much of the mainstream media (Guha Thakurta, 2017), and how some of the 'social' media platforms have allowed themselves to be used for distorting national elections and spreading hatred. The arts too have become commodities for private (mostly elite) consumption, adding to the older trend of the artificial division between classical (accessible to the elite) and folk (accessible to others). Countering these trends are some remarkable initiatives such as alternative media, for example, online portals like *Scroll.in* and *The Wire*, community radio, decentralized cellphone-based communication initiatives like CGNetSwara, and the continuation or revival of folk and street theatre; or the use of music for social transformation such as Justice Rocks, the example of T. M. Krishna and transgender collaboration mentioned earlier, and Bangla Natak in West Bengal.[27] These and other examples are used by Paranjoy Guha Thakurta (2017) and Sudha Gopalakrishnan (2017) to posit a future in which media and the arts, respectively, are democratized by and also contribute much more to the struggles for justice and sustainability.

What all this means is that a crucial part of the transformation towards justice and sustainability is the sustenance of cultural and knowledge diversity, the maintenance of knowledge, arts, and media as a public commons, and the enabling of democratic pathways of generating, transmitting, storing, and evolving knowledge. This applies to modern science and technology as well (see, for instance, Abrol, 2017). A crucial part of all this is the decolonization of knowledge (and of tools like maps) and building equitable collaborations between different forms of knowledge.[28]

ECOLOGICAL TRANSFORMATIONS

In this section, I examine initiatives across India of rebuilding a harmonious relationship with the rest of nature, ecological regeneration and community-led conservation, and transformations in environmental governance, especially in relation to 'development' decisions.

There is much to be done to repair humanity's very troubled relationship with the earth and its various constituents. The global impact of our war on the rest of nature, whether through the COVID-19 pandemic or through the climate crisis, is very much visible now. As a counter-trend, several initiatives by governments, civil society, communities, and individuals have enabled some threatened species and ecosystems to sustain and revive in the midst of an otherwise dismal loss of biodiversity. Unfortunately, many of these, especially those implemented by governments and civil society and corporations based on the dominant exclusionary, Western models of conservation have alienated and dispossessed millions of people in the Global South. A vibrant alternative to this is the phenomenon of community-driven initiatives at governing and managing ecosystems in ways that help conserve them and their constituent species and functions; termed Indigenous Peoples' and Community Conserved Territories and Areas (ICCAs) or Territories of Life, these have been recognized in global policy, cover a vast part of the globe, and have significant potential to help in the repair of the earth. But they are also severely under-recognized in most countries, and many are threatened with extractive activities and other factors.[29] Elsewhere, shifts in global paradigms of conservation are also leading to more co-governance approaches with governments, communities, and others as equal partners. As Shanker, Oommen, and Rai (2017) point out in an essay on the future of conservation in India, there is a need for a holistic approach that integrates conservation ideals with social and environmental justice. Any conservation approach has to embrace community and traditional knowledge as an ethical and moral imperative to distributive justice so that it can address a variety of issues ranging from inequalities to oppression.

An exciting recent development is the spread of the notion of nature having rights, not necessarily because it is of use to humans but in itself.[30] In 2006, Tamaqua Borough in the United States banned the dumping of toxic sewage sludge as a violation of Rights of Nature. Very soon after that, in 2008, Ecuador became the first country in the world to recognize Rights of Nature in its Constitution. In 2009, the United Nations General Assembly adopted a resolution proclaiming 22 April as International Mother Earth Day. Later, in the same year, it adopted a resolution on Harmony with Nature. In 2010, Bolivia held a *World People's Conference on Climate Change and the Rights of Mother Earth*, where the '*Universal Declaration on the Rights of Mother Earth*' was issued. It has been submitted to the United Nations for consideration. In 2012, Bolivia also passed a law of Mother Earth and Holistic development for living well. In 2015, alongside the United Nations Climate Change Conference in Paris, a manifesto was adopted highlighting co-violations of nature's rights and human rights around the world. In 2017, New Zealand adopted the Te Awa Tupua Act granting the Whanganui river legal rights (prior to and subsequently, it also recognized such rights of a national park and a mountain). Colombia, the United States, Mexico, Scotland, Canada, Chile, and other countries have also adopted national or local policies and legislation recognizing the rights of nature. In several places, such declarations are being used to stop extractive or other ecologically destructive proposals.

In India, there has been a flurry of judicial activism on this front, with the Uttarakhand High Court declaring that Ganga and Yamuna rivers have rights of 'personhood' and appointing 'parents' to secure these rights. The order (subsequently put on stay by the Supreme Court) does not have much clarity on what specifically the rights mean, what constitutes violation, how action will be taken on these violations, and so on; and it has some problematic social implications in prioritizing the Hindu reverence of the river (Kothari and Bajpai, 2017).

The same high court also gave an astounding order in late 2018, declaring that the 'entire animal kingdom' has similar rights of personhood. Again, the court does not go into the nitty-gritty of what such rights could entail, how they would be actualized in situations of violation, and how such orders would not be misused by class, caste, or religious interests (for example, discriminating against people eating meat as part of their cultural traditions).

Moreover, giving legal rights to nature has its own pitfalls and limitations, not the least of which is that in most cases this is happening by giving it 'personhood', thereby conferring it the same rights as people would enjoy. This retains anthropocentrism of sorts. Could the movement towards recognizing legal rights of nature lead to what indigenous peoples and many religions have recognized for long, that the rest of nature needs to be treated as equals, with respect, and with full consciousness of the restraints that come necessarily from such treatment?

Any attempt at giving nature its space also requires a questioning of the overall model of environmental governance in India. Lele and Sahu (2017) point to four major issues: regulatory failure, limits to judicial activism, domination of neo-liberal growth ideas, and the assumption that conservatism is environmentalism. They argue that environmentalism has to be embraced as a way of life, that is, quality of life, sustainability, and environmental justice. This leads us to the issue of ethical transformations in the next section.

In summary, ecological transformations require re-healing our relations with the rest of nature, regenerating degraded ecosystems and reviving declining species, recognizing the rights and responsibilities of communities living closest to or most dependent on nature, re-commoning privatized spaces, putting the environment squarely into the centre of all human (including economic) activities, and democratizing decision-making on processes and projects that affect the environment.

ETHICAL TRANSFORMATIONS

At the foundation of alternative initiatives is a set of ethical principles and values, often unstated and implicit, sometimes explicitly articulated. These are very different from the principles underlying today's capitalist or state-dominated economic and political systems (including their 'green economy' and 'green growth' narratives, which remain trapped within the status quo).[31]

- Respecting the functional *integrity and resilience of ecological processes and biological diversity*, enshrining the *right of nature* and all species to thrive in conditions in which they have evolved.
- *Equitable and inclusive access* of all people, in current and future generations, to the conditions needed for human well-being (*sarvodaya*).
- The *right of each person and community to participate* meaningfully in decision-making and the *responsibility* to ensure this is based on ecological integrity and socio-economic equity.
- Autonomy and self-determination, individual to community, while ensuring that this does not undermine the autonomy of others (*swashasan, swaraj*).
- Self-reliance for basic needs, material and non-material (*swavalamban*).
- Respect for the *diversity* of environments and ecologies, species and genes, cultures, ways of living, knowledge systems, values, economies and livelihoods, and polities.
- *Collective and cooperative thinking and working* founded on the commons, respecting individual freedoms and innovations within such collectivities.
- Social and human *resilience* in the face of external and internal forces of change.
- Mindfulness towards *interconnectedness* and *reciprocity* among humans, and between humans and the rest of nature.
- *Simplicity* and *enoughness*, with *satisfaction* and *happiness* derived from the quality of relationships (*aparigraha*).
- Respect for the *dignity and creativity of labour and work*, with no occupation or work being inherently superior to another, and the need

for work to be dignified, safe, free from exploitation, and enjoyable as a livelihood (*aajivika*).

- *Non-violence, harmony, peace (ahimsa).*

This is not an exhaustive list, and many of the values have diverse meanings and interpretations. These values will continue to evolve as frameworks like *eco-swaraj* or Radical Ecological Democracy (which I describe later) are explored, modified, and adapted for different sociocultural, economic, and political conditions.

A similar (if varying) set of values is seen in many other alternative initiatives around the world. Anti-mining or indigenous autonomy movements in South America, for instance, invoke ancient indigenous worldviews like *buen vivir, sumak kawsay, sumak allpa, suma qamana, allin kawsay,* and *kametsa asaike* which posit a 'good life' based on harmonious relation with each other and with the rest of nature (Caruso and Barletti, 2019; Chuji et al., 2019; Gualinga, 2019). Many of these, or others like *sentipensar*, challenge modernity's separation 'between mind and body, reason and emotion, humans and nature, secular and sacred, life and death' (Gomez, 2019). Minobimaatisiiwin and other worldviews of the native peoples of North America offer similar alternatives to extractivist modernity (McGregor, 2019). In Africa, *ubuntu* and its various equivalents across the continent refer to the belief in collective life, the commons; *agaciro* from Rwanda as a belief in dignity and self-worth is invoked for arguments to define one's own model of well-being and development (Le Grange, 2019; Ndushabandi and Rutazibwa, 2019). In Asia too several such concepts and worldviews continue to exist or are being revived. *Hurai* is about the relationship of people with the rest of nature, guiding the lives of the Tuva people in China; so is the Tao worldview of indigenous people in Taiwan; in Japan, *kyosei* refers to conviviality or symbiosis; in Bangladesh, *sohoj* means an intuitively simple, non-hierarchical, bio-spiritual way of life and is invoked in the Nayakrishi (new agriculture) movement (Fuse, 2019; Hou, 2019; Hugu, 2019; Mazhar, 2019). Several initiatives and movements from the Global North also embed the ethics of responsibility, equality, and harmony. Eco-feminism (in its many variants across the globe), degrowth in Europe, conviviality as powerfully described by Ivan Illich, the transition and ecovillage movements, and pacifism are examples (Barkin, 2019; Chaves, 2019; Demaria and Latouche, 2019; Deriu, 2019; Hopkins, 2019; Illich 1973; Kin Chi, 2019; Terreblanche, 2019; Underhill-Sem 2019). Struggles of autonomy such as that of the Zapatista in Mexico and of the Kurds in western Asia, referred to earlier, are also heavily based on such ethics. A recent publication contains descriptions of over 90 such radical alternatives, including socially relevant interpretations of the world's religions (Kothari et al., 2019).

PUTTING IT ALL TOGETHER: *ECO-SWARAJ* OR RADICAL ECOLOGICAL DEMOCRACY

Across the world, people and communities are exploring sustainable and equitable ways of achieving well-being in one or more sectors of life. These initiatives are a complex mix: of creating further spaces within the existing system and fundamentally challenging it, of retaining or regaining the best of tradition while discarding its worst, of synergizing old and new knowledge. Most of them point to a different set of principles and values than the ones on which the currently dominant economic and political structures are based. None is perfect; all have issues that need resolution, and many even have internal contradictions, but they show the potential for a different future for India. They point to a paradigm or vision of the future that can be called Radical Ecological Democracy (RED) or *eco-swaraj: a socio-cultural, political, and economic arrangement in which all people and communities have the right and full opportunity to participate in decision-making, based on the twin fulcrums of ecological sustainability and human equity.*[32]

The term *swaraj* is ancient and has been variously used by prominent figures of Indian history, including by Radhakrishnan, Tagore, and Gandhi. It was made most popular by Gandhi during the independence struggle, but he was careful to point out that it did not simply mean freedom from colonial rule. It is a combination of both internal and external rule by the self, the rights of autonomy coupled with restraint in thought and behaviour, and responsibility towards others (Shrivastava, 2019). Extending the 'others' to include non-human species and all of the rest of nature, one can consider *eco-swaraj* as being a paradigm that combines direct democracy, socio-economic justice, and ecological sustainability with a foundation of ethical and spiritual values.

Importantly, such a paradigm has emerged more from the lived experiences of grassroots movements and initiatives (such as those mentioned in various sections earlier), though they do not use the term *RED* or *eco-swaraj* (some do use variants of *swaraj*, especially those with explicit or implicit roots in Gandhian thought and practice). This is not to deny the influence key ideologues, activists, and figures from Indian and global history have had on many of these initiatives, including of Buddha, Gandhi, Marx, Ambedkar, Tagore, and tribal, Dalit, feminist, or other traditional revolutionaries and rebels. RED or *eco-swaraj* is an eclectic mix of all these, plus strands of deep and social ecology from Western thought and action. An elaboration of this has emerged from a process of countrywide gatherings of people working on initiatives in various sectors, called Vikalp Sangam or Alternatives Confluence.[33]

Utopian visions are crucial; they give us a sense of direction, even if we know we may never reach an ideal state. But end-goals too are of little point unless we can generate pathways of trying to head to them. To some extent the many examples in India and elsewhere are already showing pathways and the potential for larger transformation. But they are scattered, mostly too small to change the macro picture. Much greater networking among initiatives from different sectors, collaboration with resistance movements (where they are not already part of such movements), and joint forums for greater political mass are crucial. Greater documentation and publicity of these initiatives (if their actors consent), using all possible media, will help inspire others to try their own transformations. Using this documentation as material for learning in educational institutions would create a generation of youth more exposed to ways of thinking, acting and behaving that is different from the usual rat-race. Influencing, enabling, and networking key figures in *gram sabhas*, *panchayats*, district planning bodies, urban wards and area *sabhas*, and other such institutions of governance is crucial. Continued advocacy for policy changes can create greater space for grassroots initiatives or at least remove the hurdles in their way. These are only some of the pathways, all worth trying out, none individually capable of making sustained transformation happen.

VIKALP SANGAM, OR ALTERNATIVES CONFLUENCE

One small and humble attempt at networking multiple emergent alternatives is the Vikalp Sangam, or Alternatives Confluence. Initiated in 2014 by the civil society group Kalpavriksh in partnership with several other groups, this process attempts to bring together movements and organizations working on the entire range of alternatives, for greater documentation and public exposure of initiatives, cross-learning across sectors, collaborations to make each other's work more holistic, critical collective thinking, and joint visioning of alternative futures. As of 2021, over 20 *sangams* have been held at regional and thematic levels, the Vikalp Sangam website[34] has collected over 1,500 stories of hope and inspiration, over 100 films have been made and several case studies for deeper analysis have been generated, and a continuously evolving framework note of an alternative society, mentioned earlier, has been created.[35] The Sangam process can be considered one of collective visioning and dreaming about an ideal society, rooted in grassroots practice (Kothari, 2019).

Vikalp Sangam is not a formal organization, but a platform that anyone interested in alternatives can use to convene gatherings, do documentation and outreach, or take on policy advocacy, as long as they are agreeable to its core principles as laid out in the document mentioned earlier. But while this informal non-structure is crucial for encouraging inclusive, non-hierarchical, and non-threatening relations within the process, the enormity of the initiative also necessitates some level of structure. For this purpose, there is a national core group of over 80 organizations, networks, and movements (as of late 2021) that acts as an advisory body, or helps convene specific activities.[36] One organization (currently Kalpavriksh) acts as the overall coordinator, which is envisaged to be a rotating function. A larger facilitation team, chosen from the core group, helps in this.

While the Sangam's objectives of bringing people from diverse sectors and enabling exchange of views and information, facilitating collaborations, and jointly conceiving a vision of the future are being met to some degree or the other (much more is needed, of course!), what had until recently not happened was the objective of also making it a forum for macro-change. In early 2019 it took its first collective step towards advocacy, by drafting a 'People's Manifesto for a Just, Equitable and Sustainable India'.[37] This was oriented towards the mid-2019 national elections in India but was also meant to help constituent groups orient their own work and help with advocacy at various other levels. Another was produced for the Western Himalayan region, with similar objectives (Singh, 2019).

The Vikalp Sangam process has also inspired a move towards a worldwide confluence, the Global Tapestry of Alternatives[38] launched in May 2019.

While one can see glimpses of the radical transformation underway in many parts of the world, the challenges and hurdles in arriving at the vision of RED (or any others mentioned earlier) are humungous. RED calls for big mind-shifts and changes in human behaviour, away from complacency and an increased ability to learn from mistakes. It needs a continuously enhanced understanding of the impacts of human activities on the environment and of the workings of nature. It has to contend with the continued power of capitalism (including its ability to constantly reinvent itself) and patriarchy or masculinity, the ecological illiteracy and centralizing tendency of the state, the hegemony of modernity and the continuing tension between various knowledge systems, corruption of various kinds, the awesome power of the military, and a feeling of 'helplessness' among the general public. Organizations frozen in their orthodox, un-evolving ideological positions, including from within Leftist, Gandhian, Ambedkarite, feminist, or other such persuasions, are also hurdles, as they refuse to acknowledge that the walls they build around themselves do not enable even a recognition that they hold the goal of justice in common with others. And then there is the old bugbear of Indian civil society, a lack of maturity to let go of personal egos and 'territorial' behaviour, as repeatedly encountered by this author in various networking initiatives.

These challenges cannot be a reason for giving up. The most oppressed and marginalized of society have shown us that even in what seemed to be hopeless situations, they have created a revolution. Those of us who have the luxury of reading and writing about such things, who most likely do not have the worry of where the next meal is coming from, simply do not have any right to throw up our hands and say it is all pointless. We must continue to dream and envision our collective utopias, and co-learn and co-generate the paths of progressing towards such visions along with the most marginalized of peoples and the rest of nature.

POSTSCRIPT

The COVID-19 pandemic affecting most of 2020 and continuing to affect the world in 2021 has thrown up an unprecedented challenge to humanity. Either we learn the hard lessons it teaches us – especially the perils of destroying and exploiting nature in the name of 'development', and the nature of precariousness that much of the world lives in due to shameful levels of inequality and socio-economic exploitation – and radically restructure our economy and polity or we try to go back to 'normal' and lurch through crises after crises. Most governments and mega-corporations not only appear to not be wanting to learn the lessons but in fact have used the opportunity to become more authoritarian and profit-seeking. On the other hand, communities and collectives, and some governments, have also shown alternative pathways that provide hope. In India we have documented several dozen stories of food, health, and livelihood resilience by communities, which have crucial lessons for public policy and collective action.[39] As of the time of finalizing this, though, the Indian government continues to stumble along the worn path of unsustainable development; it is up to its people to build stronger and stronger countertrends that may help avert future such crises.

NOTES

1. This chapter was written before the COVID-19 hit, and while it has been possible to introduce some elements of the 2020–21 period at the final stage of going to press, the kind of restructuring I would have liked to do of the chapter to take into account lessons of this period has not been possible.
2. A useful resource for movements, brought out annually, is the Kriti Team's diary, see https://krititeam.blogspot.com/search/label/annual%20movement%20diary, accessed on 21 December 2021.
3. Even as this chapter was undergoing final revision for publication, farmers had been on protest for several months, starting late 2020, against three farm laws that further corporatize agriculture and remove essential state guarantees for minimum prices to their produce. Finally in December 2021 they won a significant victory as the central government announced withdrawal of the

laws, as also agreeing to a number of other demands. This is widely seen as one of the most significant mobilisations of farmers, with support from a cross-section of society including other workers, environmentalists, feminists, and Adivasi and Dalit groups, since independence.

4. See https://www.opendemocracy.net/en/can-europe-make-it/which-municipal ism-lets-be-choosy/, accessed on 21 December 2021.

5. See also http://tarunbharatsangh.in/river-arvari-parliament/, accessed on 21 December 2021.

6. See www.sacredheadwaters.org.

7. Avani Mohan Singh, NAPCL Board, pers. comm., 2009; http://www. timbaktu-organic.org/aboutdharani.html; http://www.facebook.com/pages/ Qasab-Kutch-Craftswomen-Producer-Co-Ltd/120970047978656, accessed on 21 December 2021.

8. See Devika (2014); see also www.kudumbashree.org.

9. See www.ddsindia.com.

10. See https://foodsovereigntyalliance.wordpress.com/, accessed on 21 December 2021.

11. For a detailed study of one remarkable revival of a craft, handloom weaving in Kachchh, see https://vikalpsangam.org/article/sandhani-weaving-transformations-in-kachchh-india-key-findings-and-analysis/, accessed on 21 December 2021.

12. See www.justchangeindia.com.

13. There are many initiatives in the name of 'social enterprise' in India now, but it is not clear whether the majority of them are motivated more by social and less by profit-making motivations.

14. See https://www.ofmtn.in.

15. See https://www.facebook.com/milletmama.bengaluru/.

16. See http://shaheedhospital.org; http://vikalpsangam.org/article/shaheed-hospital/; see also film at http://vikalpsangam.org/article/more-videos-for-vikalp-sangam-by-video-volunteers/#.XPOQrS2B1E4, accessed on 21 December 2021.

17. See also http://homesinthecity.org/en/.

18. See https://punecycleplan.wordpress.com, accessed on 21 December 2021.

19. See https://vikalpsangam.org/article/why-do-we-wait-so-restlessly-for-the-workday-to-end-and-for-the-weekend-to-come/, accessed on 21 December 2021.

20. See the film *Ode to Equality*, http://www.vikalpsangam.org/article/videos-for-vikalp-sangam-by-srishti-school-of-art/#.XPPSFC2B1E4, accessed on 21 December 2021.

21. See the film *Football As a Tool to Advance Sexual and Reproductive Health of Women*, http://www.vikalpsangam.org/article/videos-by-video-volunteers/#.XPPSuS2B1E4, accessed on 21 December 2021.

22. I prefer using this term rather than the more popular 'fundamentalists', which I believe is a distortion, for the fundamentals of all religions are about ethical behaviour, love, caring, solidarity, respect, and other such values that the superficialists suppress to spread their message of hatred and 'otherness'.

23. See http://www.peopleslinguisticsurvey.org.

24. See www.narmada.org/ALTERNATIVES/jeevanshalas.html; www.marudam farmschool.org; http://adharshilask.tripod.com/aboutadh.html; Coelho and Padmanabhan (2018); www.Adivasiacademy.org; www.navdanya.org/earth-university; http://bhoomicollege.org/; www.swarajuniversity.org.

25. See www.secmol.org; www.kfionline.org/education-centres/.

26. See https://vikalpsangam.org/article/extraordinary-work-of-ordinary-people-in-multi-language-translation/, accessed on 21 December 2021.

27. See https://www.youtube.com/watch?v=rmVgyOUggsA, accessed on 21 December 2021.

28. See for instance, https://decolonialatlas.wordpress.com and https://www.arcticbiodiversity.is; see also Santos (2014).

29. See www.iccaconsortium.org; see also Borrini-Feyerabend and Farvar (2019).

30. For a global overview and regular updates of developments, see https://www.therightsofnature.org.

31. For more details, see https://vikalpsangam.org/about/the-search-for-alternatives-key-aspects-and-principles/, accessed on 21 December 2021.

32. An early treatment of this concept is in A. Kothari (2009); subsequent development is in Shrivastava and Kothari (2012); A. Kothari (2014a, 2014b).

33. See http://www.vikalpsangam.org/about/ accessed on 21 December 2021.

34. See www.vikalpsangam.org.

35. See https://vikalpsangam.org/about/the-search-for-alternatives-key-aspects-and-principles/, accessed on 21 December 2021.

36. The full list of members and their profiles are at https://vikalpsangam.org/members/, accessed on 21 December 2021.

37. See http://vikalpsangam.org/article/peoples-manifesto-for-a-just-equitable-and-sustainable-india-2019/#.X41Gty1h1hE, accessed on 21 December 2021.
38. See https://globaltapestryofalternatives.org.
39. See series of reports called 'Extraordinary Work of 'Ordinary' People: Beyond Pandemics and Lockdowns', at www.vikalpsangam.org; see also https://www.thehindu.com/opinion/op-ed/india-needs-a-rainbow-recovery-plan/article32776442.ece, accessed on 21 December 2021.

REFERENCES

Aslan, A., and B. Akbulut (2019). Democratic economy in Kurdistan. In *Pluriverse: A Post-Development Dictionary*, ed. A. Kothari, A. Salleh, A. Escobar, F. Demaria, and A. Acosta. Delhi: Tulika and Authors Upfront, 151–153.

Bajpai, S. and A. Kothari. (2020). Towards decentralised urban governance: The case of Bhuj city, Kachchh, India. Kalpavriksh, Pune. Accessed on 10 September 2021: https://vikalpsangam.org/article/towards-decentralised-urban-governance-the-case-of-bhuj-city-kachchh-india/.

Barkin, D. (2019). Conviviality. In *Pluriverse: A Post-Development Dictionary*, ed. A. Kothari, A. Salleh, A. Escobar, F. Demaria, and A. Acosta. Delhi: Tulika and Authors Upfront, 136–138.

Bhatt, E. (2015). *Anubandh: Building 100-Mile Communities*. Ahmedabad: Navajivan Trust.

Borrini-Feyerabend, G., and T. Farvar. (2019). ICCAs – territories of life. In *Pluriverse: A Post-Development Dictionary*, ed. A. Kothari, A. Salleh, A. Escobar, F. Demaria, and A. Acosta. Delhi: Tulika and Authors Upfront, 208–211.

Broome, N. P. (2014). Communitisation of public services in Nagaland. Vikalp Sangam. Accessed on 21 December 2021: http://www.vikalpsangam.org/static/media/uploads/Resources/nagaland_communitisation_neema.pdf.

—— (2018). Mendha-Lekha: Forest rights and self-empowerment. In *Alternatives in a World of Crisis*, ed. M. Lang, C.-D. Konig, and A.-C. Regelmann. Global Working Group Beyond Development. Brussels: Rosa Luxemburg Stiftung, 134–179.

Broome, N. P., S. Bajpai, and M. Shende. (2020). On the cust: Reframing democracy and well-being in Korchi, India. Beyond Development. Accessed on 21 December 2021: https://beyonddevelopment.net/on-the-cusp-reframing-democracy-and-well-being-in-korchi-india/.

Caruso, E., and J. P. S. Barletti (2019). Kametsa asaike. In *Pluriverse: A Post-Development Dictionary*, ed. A. Kothari, A. Salleh, A. Escobar, F. Demaria, and A. Acosta. Delhi: Tulika and Authors Upfront, 220–222.

Chaves, M. (2019). Ecovillages. In *Pluriverse: A Post-Development Dictionary*, ed. A. Kothari, A. Salleh, A. Escobar, F. Demaria, and A. Acosta. Delhi: Tulika and Authors Upfront, 175–177.

Chuji, M., G. Rengifo, and E. Gudynas. (2019). Buen vivir. In *Pluriverse: A Post-Development Dictionary*, ed. A. Kothari, A. Salleh, A. Escobar, F. Demaria, and A. Acosta. Delhi: Tulika and Authors Upfront, 111–113.

Coelho, N., and S. Padmanabhan (2018). Imlee Mahuaa: Learning in freedom the democratic way. In *Ecologies of Hope and Transformation: Post-Development Alternatives in India*, ed. N. Singh, S. Kulkarni, and N. P. Broome. Pune: Kalpavriksh and SOPPECOM.

Das, P. (2017). 'The power equation and India's future'. In *Alternative Futures: India Unshackled*, ed. A. Kothari and K. J. Joy. Delhi: Authors Upfront, 103–119.

De Angelis, M. (2019). Commons. In *Pluriverse: A Post-Development Dictionary*, ed. A. Kothari, A. Salleh, A. Escobar, F. Demaria, and A. Acosta. Delhi: Tulika and Authors Upfront, 124–127.

Santos, de S. B. (2014). *Epistemologies of the South. Justice against Epistemicide.* Boulder, CO: Paradigm Publishers.

Deb, D. (2009). *Beyond Developmentality: Constructing Inclusive Freedom and Sustainability.* London: Earthscan.

Demaria, F. and S. Latouche. (2019). Degrowth. In *Pluriverse: A Post-Development Dictionary*, ed. A. Kothari, A. Salleh, A. Escobar, F. Demaria, and A. Acosta. Delhi: Tulika and Authors Upfront, 148–151.

Deriu, M. (2019). Pacifism. In *Pluriverse: A Post-Development Dictionary*, ed. A. Kothari, A. Salleh, A. Escobar, F. Demaria, and A. Acosta. Delhi: Tulika and Authors Upfront, 265–267.

Devika (2014). Don't let the magic fade: Thoughts on Kudumbashree's sixteenth anniversary. *Kafila*, 16 August. Accessed in November 2014. http://kafila.

org/2014/08/16/dont-let-the-magic-fade-thoughts-on-kudumbashrees-sixteenth-anniversary/.

Devy, G. (2017). Between diversity and aphasia: The future of languages in India. In *Alternative Futures: India Unshackled*, ed. A. Kothari and K. J. Joy. Delhi: Authors Upfront, 411–424.

Dharmadhikary, S. and H. Thakkar. (2017). The future of water in India. In *Alternative Futures: India Unshackled*, ed. A. Kothari and K. J. Joy. Delhi: Authors Upfront, 63–79.

Dubey, M. (2017). The future world order and India's role in shaping it. In *Alternative Futures: India Unshackled*, ed. A. Kothari and K. J. Joy. Delhi: Authors Upfront, 192–212.

Dungdung, G. (2017). A vision for Adivasis. In *Alternative Futures: India Unshackled*, ed. A. Kothari and K. J. Joy. Delhi: Authors Upfront, 594–614.

Engineer, A. (2017). Future of religious minorities in India. In *Alternative Futures: India Unshackled*, ed. A. Kothari and K. J. Joy. Delhi: Authors Upfront, 574–593.

Esteva, G. (2019). Autonomy. In *Pluriverse: A Post-Development Dictionary*, ed. A. Kothari, A. Salleh, A. Escobar, F. Demaria, and A. Acosta. Delhi: Tulika and Authors Upfront, 99–101.

Flach, A, E. Ayboğa, and M. Knapp (2016). *Revolution in Rojava*. London: Pluto Press.

Fuse, M. (2019). Kyosei. In *Pluriverse: A Post-Development Dictionary*, ed. A. Kothari, A. Salleh, A. Escobar, F. Demaria, and A. Acosta. Delhi: Tulika and Authors Upfront, 226–227.

Gomez, P. B. (2019). Sentipensar. In *Pluriverse: A Post-Development Dictionary*, ed. A. Kothari, A. Salleh, A. Escobar, F. Demaria, and A. Acosta. Delhi: Tulika and Authors Upfront, 302–-303.

Gopalakrishnan, S. (2017). The future of arts in India: Challenges and opportunities towards revitalization and sustainability. In *Alternative Futures: India Unshackled*, ed. A. Kothari and K. J. Joy. Delhi: Authors Upfront, 441–459.

Gualinga, P. (2019). Kawsak sacha. In *Pluriverse: A Post-Development Dictionary*, ed. A. Kothari, A. Salleh, A. Escobar, F. Demaria, and A. Acosta. Delhi: Tulika and Authors Upfront, 223–225.

Guha Thakurta, P. (2017). Future of alternative media in India. In *Alternative Futures: India Unshackled*, ed. A. Kothari and K. J. Joy (eds.). Delhi: Authors Upfront, 460–479.

Gupte, M. (2017). Envisioning India without gender and patriarchy? Why not? In *Alternative Futures: India Unshackled*, ed. A. Kothari and K. J. Joy. Delhi: Authors Upfront, 555–573.

Halpin, H. (2019). Free software. In *Pluriverse: A Post-Development Dictionary* ed. A. Kothari, A. Salleh, A. Escobar, F. Demaria, and A. Acosta. Delhi: Tulika and Authors Upfront, 188–190.

Hande, H., V. Sastry, and R. Misra. (2017). Energy futures in India. In *Alternative Futures: India Unshackled*, ed. A. Kothari and K. J. Joy. Delhi: Authors Upfront, 80–102.

Hasnat, S. N. (2005). Arvari Sansad: The farmers' parliament. *LEISA: Magazine on Low External and Input and Sustainable Agriculture* 21(4): 14.

Hopkins, R. (2019). Transition movement. In *Pluriverse: A Post-Development Dictionary*, ed. A. Kothari, A. Salleh, A. Escobar, F. Demaria, and A. Acosta. Delhi: Tulika and Authors Upfront, 317–319.

Hou, Y. (2019). Hurai. In *Pluriverse: A Post-Development Dictionary*, ed. A. Kothari, A. Salleh, A. Escobar, F. Demaria, and A. Acosta. Delhi: Tulika and Authors Upfront, 203–205.

Hugu, S. (2019). Tao worldview. In *Pluriverse: A Post-Development Dictionary*, ed. A. Kothari, A. Salleh, A. Escobar, F. Demaria, and A. Acosta. Delhi: Tulika and Authors Upfront, 314–316.

Illich, I. (1973). *Tools for Conviviality*. London: Calder and Bacon.

Isaac, T. T., and R. W. Franke (2002). *Local Democracy and Development: The Kerala People's Campaign for Decentralized Planning*. Washington: Rowman & Littlefield.

Joy, K. J. (2017). Biomass-based rural revitalization in future India. In *Alternative Futures: India Unshackled*, ed. A. Kothari and K. J. Joy. Delhi: Authors Upfront, 304–325.

Kajka, A. (2018). Kuthambakkam: Re-embedding economy in society. In *Ecologies of Hope and Transformation: Post-Development Alternatives in India*, ed. N. Singh, S. Kulkarni, and N. Pathak Broome. Pune: Kalpavriksh and SOPPECOM.

Kapoor, R. (2017). Reimagining India's urban future. In *Alternative Futures: India Unshackled*, ed. A. Kothari and K. J. Joy. Delhi: Authors Upfront.

Karyotis, T. (2019). Worker-led production. In *Pluriverse: A Post-Development Dictionary*, ed. A. Kothari, A. Salleh, A. Escobar, F. Demaria, and A. Acosta. Delhi: Tulika and Authors Upfront, 332–334.

Khindri, R. and T. Biswas. (2017). Future of learning in Indian schools. In *Alternative Futures: India Unshackled*, ed. A. Kothari and K. J. Joy. Delhi: Authors Upfront, 425–440.

Kin Chi, L. (2019). Peacewomen. In *Pluriverse: A Post-Development Dictionary*, ed. A. Kothari, A. Salleh, A. Escobar, F. Demaria, and A. Acosta. Delhi: Tulika and Authors Upfront, 268–270.

Kodiveri, A. (2017). Legal futures for India. In *Alternative Futures: India Unshackled*, ed. A. Kothari and K. J. Joy. Delhi: Authors Upfront, 138–154.

Köhler-Rollefson, I. and H. S. Rathore (2017). Pastoral futures in India. In *Alternative Futures: India Unshackled*, ed. A. Kothari and K. J. Joy. Delhi: Authors Upfront, 213–227.

Kothari, A. (2009). Radical ecological democracy: Escaping India's globalization trap. *Development* 52(3): 401–409.

—— (2014a). India 2100: Towards radical ecological democracy. *Futures* 56: 62–72. Accessed on 21 December 2021: https://doi.org/10.1016/j.futures.2013.10.010.

—— (2014b). Radical ecological democracy: A path forward for India and beyond. *Development* 57(1): 36–45.

—— (2018). Legacies crucial for the commons. *The Hindu*, 17 November. Accessed on 10 September 2021: https://www.thehindu.com/opinion/op-ed/legacies-crucial-for-the-commons/article25600040.ece.

—— (2019). Collective dreaming: Democratic visioning in the Vikalp Sangam process. *Economic and Political Weekly* 54(34): 70–76.

Kothari, A., and S. Bajpai (2017). We are the river, the river is us. *Economic and Political Weekly* 52(37): 103–109.

Kothari, A., and K. J. Joy, eds. (2017). *Alternative Futures: India Unshackled*. Delhi: Authors Upfront.

Kothari, A., A. Salleh, A. Escobar, F. Demaria, and A. Acosta, eds. (2019). *Pluriverse: A Post-Development Dictionary*. Delhi: Tulika and Authors Upfront.

Kothari, A., D. Venkataswamy, G. Laheru, A. Dixit, K. Trivedi, and R. Mulay (2020). *Sandhani: Weaving Transformations in Kachchh, India*. Pune: Kalpavriksh; Bhuj: Khamir and Vankars of Kachchh. Accessed on 21 December 2021: https://vikalpsangam.org/article/sandhani-weaving-transformations-in-kachchh-india-key-findings-and-analysis/.

Kothari, M. (2019). Human rights. In *Pluriverse: A Post-Development Dictionary*, ed. A. Kothari, A. Salleh, A. Escobar, F. Demaria, and A. Acosta, eds. Delhi: Tulika and Authors Upfront, 200–202.

Kothari, S. (2000). A million mutinies now: Lesser-known environmental movements in India. *Humanscape*, 5–9 October.

Labour Party. Undated. *Alternative Models of Ownership*. Report to the Shadow Chancellor of the Exchequer and Shadow Secretary of State for Business, Energy and Industrial Strategy. Accessed on 10 September 2021: http://labour. org.uk/wp-content/uploads/2017/10/Alternative-Models-of-Ownership.pdf.

Le Grange, L. (2019). Ubuntu. In *Pluriverse: A Post-Development Dictionary*, ed. A. Kothari, A. Salleh, A. Escobar, F. Demaria, and A. Acosta. Delhi: Tulika and Authors Upfront, 323–325.

Lele, S., and G. Sahu. (2017). Environmental governance in future India: Principles, structures, and pathways. In *Alternative Futures: India Unshackled*, ed. A. Kothari and K. J. Joy. Delhi: Authors Upfront, 46–62.

Leyva-Solano, X. (2019). Zapatista autonomy. In *Pluriverse: A Post-Development Dictionary*, ed. A. Kothari, A. Salleh, A. Escobar, F. Demaria, and A. Acosta. Delhi: Tulika and Authors Upfront, 335–338.

Mansatta, B, K. Kuruganti, V. Jardhari, and V. Futane (2017). Anna swaraj: A vision for food sovereignty and agro-ecological resurgence. In *Alternative Futures: India Unshackled*, ed. A. Kothari and K. J. Joy. Delhi: Authors Upfront, 228–249.

Mazhar, F. (2019). Nayakrishi Andolan. In *Pluriverse: A Post-Development Dictionary*, ed. A. Kothari, A. Salleh, A. Escobar, F. Demaria, and A. Acosta. Delhi: Tulika and Authors Upfront, 247–249.

McGregor, D. (2019). Minobimaatisiiwin. In *Pluriverse: A Post-Development Dictionary*, ed. A. Kothari, A. Salleh, A. Escobar, F. Demaria, and A. Acosta. Delhi: Tulika and Authors Upfront, 240–242.

Meira, F. B. (2014). Liminal organization: Organizational emergence within solidary economy in Brazil. *Organization* 21(5): 713–729.

Narrain, A. (2017) Imagining utopia: The importance of love, dissent, and radical empathy. In *Alternative Futures: India Unshackled*, ed. A. Kothari and K. J. Joy. Delhi: Authors Upfront, 411–424.

Ndushabandi, E. N. S., and O. U. Rutazibwa (2019). Agaciro. In *Pluriverse: A Post-Development Dictionary*, ed. A. Kothari, A. Salleh, A. Escobar, F. Demaria, and A. Acosta. Delhi: Tulika and Authors Upfront, 79–81.

Nigam, A. (2017). For a radical social democracy: Imagining possible Indian future/s. In *Alternative Futures: India Unshackled*, ed. A. Kothari and K. J. Joy. Delhi: Authors Upfront, 155–173.

Patankar, B. (2017). Multilinear critical theory: For a society of liberated humanity. In *Alternative Futures: India Unshackled*, ed. A. Kothari and K. J. Joy. Delhi: Authors Upfront, 174–192.

Patwardhan, S. (2017). Alternative transportation in future India. In *Alternative Futures: India Unshackled*, ed. A. Kothari and K. J. Joy. Delhi: Authors Upfront, 379–389.

Posey, D. (1996). *Traditional Resource Rights: International Instruments for the Protection and Compensation for Indigenous People and Local Communities.* Gland, Switzerland, and Cambridge, UK: IUCN.

Pulsford, I, G. L. Worboys, and G. Howling (2010). Australian Alps to Atherton connectivity conservation corridor. In *Connectivity Conservation Management: A Global Guide*, ed. G. L. Worboys, W. L. Francis and M. Lockwood. London: Earthscan, 96–105.

Pulsford, I, D. Lindemayer, C. Wyborn, B. Lausche, M. Vasilijevic, and G. L. Worboys. (2015). Connectivity conservation management. In *Protected Area Governance and Management*, ed. G. L. Worboys, M. Lockwood, A. Kothari, S. Feary, and I. Pulsford. Canberra: ANU Press, 851–888.

Raina, R. (2017). Knowledge futures: Democratic values and learning capacities for sustainability. In *Alternative Futures: India Unshackled*, ed. A. Kothari and K. J. Joy. Delhi: Authors Upfront, 480–496.

Roy, A, N. Dey, and P. Kashyap (2017). Allowing people to shape our democratic future. In *Alternative Futures: India Unshackled*, ed. A. Kothari and K. J. Joy. Delhi: Authors Upfront, 120–137.

Roy, D. (2017). Industry, workers, and nation: Dreaming the good dream. In *Alternative Futures: India Unshackled*, ed. A. Kothari and K. J. Joy. Delhi: Authors Upfront, 266–284.

Sandwith, T., C. Shine, L. Hamilton, and D. Sheppard. (2001). *Transboundary Protected Areas for Peace and Co-operation.* Gland, Switzerland, and Cambridge, UK: IUCN.

SELCO (no date). *Access to Sustainable Energy Services via Innovative Financing: 7 Case Studies.* Bengaluru: SELCO.

Sen, J., ed. (2018a). *The Movements of Movements*, Part 2: *Rethinking Our Dance*. New Delhi: OpenWord and Oakland, CA: PM Press.

———, ed. (2018b). *The Movements of Movements*, Part 1: *What Makes Us Move?* New Delhi: Authors Upfront, in collaboration with OpenWord and PM Press.

Shanker, K., M. A. Oommen, and N. Rai. (2017). Changing natures: A democratic and dynamic approach to biodiversity conservation. In *Alternative Futures: India Unshackled*, ed. A. Kothari and K. J. Joy. Delhi: Authors Upfront, 25–45.

Shiva, V. (1991). *Ecology and the Politics of Survival: Conflicts over Natural Resources in India*. New Delhi: Sage.

Shrivastava, A. (2019). Prakritik swaraj. In *Pluriverse: A Post-Development Dictionary*, ed. A. Kothari, A. Salleh, A. Escobar, F. Demaria, and A. Acosta. Delhi: Tulika and Authors Upfront, 283–285.

Shrivastava, A., and A. Kothari (2012). *Churning the Earth: The Making of Global India*. Delhi: Viking/Penguin.

Shrivastava, A., and E. Rangasamy (2017). Regionalization and localization of economies: A preliminary sketch for an ecological imperative. In *Alternative Futures: India Unshackled*, ed. A. Kothari and K. J. Joy. Delhi: Authors Upfront, 285–303.

Shukla, A., and R. Gaitonde (2017). Health systems in future India. In *Alternative Futures: India Unshackled*, ed. A. Kothari and K. J. Joy. Delhi: Authors Upfront, 411–424.

Singh, A. (2019). A people's manifesto for the Western Himalayas Mountain Region. Vikalp Sangam, April 2019. Accessed on 10 September 2021: http://www.vikalpsangam.org/article/a-peoples-manifesto-for-the-western-himalayas-mountain-region-april-2019/#.XPOMyi2B1E4.

Tatpathi, M., A. Kothari, and R. Mishra (2016). The Niyamgiri story. Vikalp Sangam. Accessed on 21 December 2021: https://vikalpsangam.org/wp-content/uploads/migrate/Resources/niyamgiricasestudyjan2018.pdf.

Teltumbde, A. (2017). Envisioning Dalit futures. In *Alternative Futures: India Unshackled*, ed. A. Kothari and K. J. Joy. Delhi: Authors Upfront, 536–554.

Terreblanche, C. (2019). Ecofeminism. In *Pluriverse: A Post-Development Dictionary*, ed. A. Kothari, A. Salleh, A. Escobar, F. Demaria, and A. Acosta. Delhi: Tulika and Authors Upfront, 163–165.

Tewary, A. (2018). The Pathalgadi rebellion. *The Hindu*, 14 April. Accessed on 10 September 2021: https://www.thehindu.com/news/national/other-states/the-pathalgadi-rebellion/article23530998.ece.

Underhill-Sem, Y. (2019). Pacific feminisms. In *Pluriverse: A Post-Development Dictionary*, ed. A. Kothari, A. Salleh, A. Escobar, F. Demaria, and A. Acosta. Delhi: Tulika and Authors Upfront, 262–264.

Uzramma (2017). Crafts show the way for Indian industrialization. In *Alternative Futures: India Unshackled*, ed. A. Kothari and K. J. Joy. Delhi: Authors Upfront, 250–265.

Vio.Me (2019). Occupy, resist, produce. Accessed on 10 September 2021: www.viome.org/search/label/English.

Workerscontrol.net (2020). Archive of workers' struggle. Accessed on 10 September 2021: www.workerscontrol.net.

PART II

ALTERNATIVE VISIONS OF RIGHTS AND REPRESENTATIONS

5

HARNESSING CONSTITUTIONAL AND POLICY SPACES FOR ORGANIZED RESISTANCE

MOVEMENT TO SAVE HASDEO ARANYA FORESTS

PRIYANSHU GUPTA

Accompanying the announcement of the largest-ever round of auctioning of coal blocks in India in June 2020 were stories of resistance from a relatively nondescript region of central India: the Hasdeo Aranya forests. The media outlets – regional, national, and even global – were replete with news of letters from *sarpanchs*[1] (Alam, 2020; Kaiser, 2020), petitions from the *gram sabhas*[2] (Mishra, 2020b), reports of organized community resistance (Dasgupta, 2020; MS, 2020), and even interventions from the state government of Chhattisgarh (Drolia and John, 2020; P. Singh, 2020) and the political elites like the former Union Environment Minister Jairam Ramesh (*The Wire*, 2020). The community resistance of 20 villages of one of the most impoverished states of India threatened to put a spanner into the prime minister's plans of 'Atmanirbhar Bharat' (a self-reliant India) and dreams of becoming the world's largest exporter of coal (Gupta and Regan, 2020; PTI, 2020). The *Guardian* characterized Hasdeo Aranya as the 'battleground' where the 'war' for coal pitted 'indigenous people, ancient trees, elephants and sloth bears against the might of bulldozers, trucks and hydraulic jacks' (Ellis-Petersen, 2020).

However, descriptors such as war, battleground, and conflict are perhaps the least likely to be associated with the area based on traveller accounts. As one travels on NH130 around 300 kilometres from the state capital of Raipur, one is greeted by the relative calm and the resplendent beauty of the expansive

Hasdeo-Bango reservoir (one of the longest, widest, and oldest multipurpose irrigation projects in Chhattisgarh, irrigating approximately 300,000 hectares of agricultural farms downstream) at the beginning of Hasdeo Aranya forests. For another ~40 kilometres on the highway that skirts the Hasdeo Aranya forests' periphery, the dense forest canopy that almost entirely blocks sunlight appears as a welcome relief to weary travellers. However, regular signboards indicating the need to be careful of 'elephants' and 'sloth bears' discourage casual tourists from stepping out to bask in the beauty of the surroundings. It is almost entirely possible to miss any signs of habitation at the first visit beyond the occasional wooden huts by the roadside, a couple of teashops, and the forest range office with its green signboards camouflaged with the surroundings. Only a purposive visit to one of the villages a few kilometres from the highway on one of the often muddy, arterial roads would reveal a warm and welcoming human populace that is eager to share stories of the forest, their encounters with wildlife, and their peaceful quiet and happy existence since ages. What is striking are the slogans written on the walls of almost every hut regarding the various legal and constitutional provisions. These include the Panchayat Extension to Scheduled Areas Act (PESA Act, 1996), the Scheduled Tribes and Other Traditional Forest Dwellers (Recognition of Forest Rights) Act, 2006 (hereafter Forest Rights Act or FRA 2006), Schedule 5 of the Indian Constitution, and others. It requires one to dig deeper and ask questions about these slogans to find stories of gloom, worries, and insecurities stemming from the impending threat of displacement and of resolve to resist it. Perhaps, the more likely characterization of the Hasdeo Aranya region would be of remoteness, calm, beauty, and a socio-economically marginalized, relatively sparse Adivasi (indigenous tribes, literally 'first/original residents') population (Image 5.1).

The difference in this characterization of the region as one of the most critical battlegrounds across India's energy-conservation debate vis-à-vis a picture of remoteness and calm in traveller accounts throws up a series of questions. How does a remote, peaceful, subaltern, and supposedly powerless population capture the national (and international) imagination dominating media stories and the policy debate to challenge the State narrative on the most significant coal liberalization policy action in recent times? What are the strategies and tools underlying the local community's struggle to resist

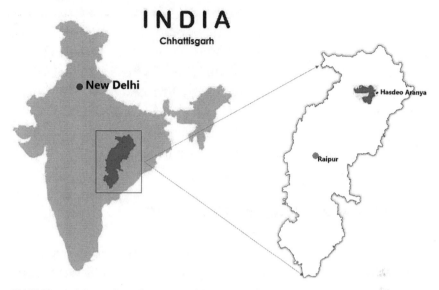

IMAGE 5.1   Location of Hasdeo Aranya forests

Source: Author.

Note: Map not to scale and does not represent authentic international boundaries.

displacement and protect their densely forested and biodiversity-rich regions? And what are the prospects of their eventual success?

This chapter analyses the decade-long journey of the Hasdeo Aranya Bachao Sangharsh Samiti (HABSS) – the local Adivasi community-led resistance movement to investigate these questions. We find the key to this movement's relative success in capturing the policy attention lies in its ability to harness constitutional and policy spaces to launch and sustain organized resistance. The *gram sabha* resolutions, reliance on legal provisions like PESA and FRA, and dialogues across scales of governance (local to state and central government) have emerged as valuable tools to bridge the tyranny of distance from the seats of political power and media influence. The consequent framing and advocacy strategies allow for successful scaling and amplification of local voices. However, we also note the limits and challenges of sustaining this approach over the long run. The analysis is based on the author's extensive fieldwork in the region between 2014 and 2020 and comprises conversations with community members, movement leaders, and references to documents maintained by HABSS.

In the next section, we outline the legal provisions and policy spaces offered by India's forest governance framework. Subsequently, we trace the social movement trajectory of HABSS to analyse its strategies and tools of resistance. Thereafter, we explore the interim successes and failures of the movement to highlight the existing legal framework's challenges and limitations in giving space to the local community resistance. Finally, we conclude by analysing the long-term implications of the HABSS's movement on building alternative organizations for resisting capitalist expansion.

CONSTITUTIONAL AND POLICY SPACES FOR RESISTANCE

Hasdeo Aranya (literally the forests over the Hasdeo river) region represents a microcosm of forest-governance-related conflicts due to its vast mineral potential, strong environmental considerations, and the habitat of the Adivasi population. It is one of the largest intact forest regions in central India to remain outside of the protected area system and, therefore, not yet protected from non-forest activities. The region comprises around 1,900 square kilometres, 80 per cent of which has dense forests, with an average forest cover density of over 40 per cent, crossing even 70 per cent in some parts[3] (HABSS, 2014; Sivalingam, 2014). As per the official working plan of the forest department, the region has a rich biodiversity with over 300 species of flora and fauna, including some of the rare and endangered species of flora and Schedule 1 protected mammals like elephant, leopard, and sloth bear, among others (HABSS, 2014; National Green Tribunal, 2014).[4] It is also believed to be a part of a large contiguous elephant corridor with a high annual seasonal presence and regular visits during other parts of the year. At the same time, it is one of the largest coalfields in India, with estimated coal reserves of 5.2 billion tonnes and at least 20 identified coal mining blocks at different stages of allocation and commencement of mining operations (HABSS, 2014). It is also home to a population of around 15,000, approximately 80 per cent of which comprises Scheduled Tribes (Census, 2011). The Gond constitutes the majority of the tribal population, interspersed with Majhwar and Kawar tribes, and other communities. Minor forest produce, especially *tendu* (scientific name *Diospyros Melanoxylon*) and *mahua* (scientific name *Madhuca longifolia*),

IMAGE 5.2 The Hasdeo Aranya forest region
Source: Photograph by Alok Shukla.

constitutes a significant share in the livelihood of the local population. Nearly 90 per cent of households (both tribals and non-tribals) are involved in its collection, and close to 30–50 per cent of the total income of the household (Janabhivyakti, 2015) is derived from it (Image 5.2).

Owing to the inherently contested nature of the resource, Hasdeo Aranya also emerges as a test case for the multitude of policies and constitutional provisions designed to account for the distinct considerations associated with India's governance of forest resources. As we shall see in the next section, these policy spaces and legal provisions emerge as critical tools for organizing the resistance movement. It is important to recognize the trajectory of the evolution of these policy spaces for local communities, especially since they remained essentially absent in the colonial and much of the post-colonial era.

A BRIEF HISTORY OF FOREST GOVERNANCE IN INDIA

The traditional pre-colonial forest governance framework in India comprised a plethora of local customary rights, which, though subordinated to the local kings and rulers, were respected as primarily a domain of traditional community-led governance institutions. The advent of British rule brought radical changes wherein the colonial administration through the forest department asserted absolute authority over forests without recognizing the customary rights of the forest dwellers (Guha, 1983; Sivaramakrishnan, 1995). The colonial forest policy based on 'scientific forestry' principles focused primarily on commercial exploitation of forest resources with limited recognition of other forest-based resource uses (Guha, 1983; Sivaramakrishnan, 2009). The early post-colonial policies, formalized as Forest Policy in 1952, largely followed the framework of colonial policies. However, the post-colonial administration shifted its focus on industrialization, resulting in large-scale clearance of forests for mining and other industrial projects, often with limited resettlement or compensation to the forest dwellers. As a result, over 60 million people were displaced in India during 1951–2004 for various kinds of developmental projects, of which; a disproportionate 40 per cent were tribals and forest dwellers (W. Fernandes, 2009). Although the Constitution of post-independence India recognized the unique status of tribals and provided for various socio-economic policies for the so-called Scheduled Tribes, including provisions of self-governance in Schedule 5 and Schedule 6 areas, such provisions did not get harmonized with the forestry policies. Thus, contentious issues of land rights or tenurial reforms remained unaddressed (Rights and Resources Initiative, 2012; Chemmencheri, 2015). In official parlance, the forest dwellers remained mere 'encroachers' with limited rights.

Growing environmental consciousness and a realization that State-led forest policy was unable to prevent massive degradation and diversion of forests for non-forest uses brought a plethora of policy changes in the 1980s and 1990s (Ramesh, 2017). These included the Environment (Protection) Act, 1986 (for all aspects of environment protection), the Forest Conservation Act, 1980 (focused on forests), and the Wildlife Protection Act, 1972 (for ensuring wildlife conservation). These laws provide a veto right to the Ministry of Environment, Forest and Climate Change (MoEFCC) through the clearances processes for forest diversion (P. J. D. Kumar, 2015). As part of this framework, elaborate procedures and guidelines were developed to harmonize and streamline the environment and forest clearance processes, including the introduction of a public hearing with affected communities.

The other key change was decentralization through the Joint Forest Management (JFM) programme in 1988. The programme was supported by international agencies and in line with global changes that saw community resource governance as an efficient alternative to the State-led command and control approach to forest conservation (Agrawal, Chhatre, and Hardin, 2008; Larson and Dahal, 2012). The JFM programme involved collaboration between forest officials and local community members for managing the forest resources. However, there was limited participation of communities in the planning process that was effectively controlled by the forest departments (Sarin, Singh, and Bhogal, 2003; P. Bose, 2012; Kashwan, 2013; Joshi, 2016). As Purabi Bose (2012) puts it, the essential idea of JFM seemed to be that 'we decide (the Forest Department) and you participate (the forest people)', and the forest dwellers were often reduced to mere labourers hired to plant trees (P. Bose, 2012; Kashwan, 2013).

The growing marginalization and tenurial insecurity of forest dwellers, coupled with limited recognition of the community self-governance provisions guaranteed by the constitution, led to increasing resistance and mobilization of Adivasis. It culminated in the implementation of the PESA Act in 1996. Further, growing discursive legitimacy of forest conservation objectives and increased frustration with poor government initiatives to stop forest degradation combined to determine the next phase of transition in the Indian forest governance regime. A series of litigations in India's Supreme Court sought to check rampant, often illegal, and unsustainable commercial exploitation of forests by various State and non-State stakeholders. In a series of orders, the Supreme Court banned all kinds of forest encroachments. It stayed and even reversed the process of regularization of forest dwellers' rights. A court order to frame a time-bound action plan to evict all forest encroachers became the pretext for the government to carry out a large-scale eviction of forest dwellers from the forests. The forcible evictions met with spontaneous and large-scale protests and an organized social movement to recognize forest dwellers' long-pending tenurial and property rights, bringing the issue to the forefront of political agenda (Bijoy, 2008; I. Bose, 2010; Kumar and Kerr, 2012). Mass resistance in Adivasi areas, an effective social movement campaign, and a supportive newly elected UPA government eventually culminated in the enactment of FRA in 2006.

OVERVIEW OF THE CURRENT POLICY FRAMEWORK

In the context of Hasdeo Aranya, the following policies and laws have emerged as the most significant:

(i) Schedule 5 of the Constitution and PESA Act 1996 – the entire region being a majority Adivasi habitation is deemed a Scheduled Area where the local communities can exercise self-governance through their *gram sabhas*. The PESA Act 1996 has empowered *gram sabhas* with powers to make local plans and manage resources, prevent alienation of land, and the right to be consulted in all matters of land acquisition and mineral exploitation (Upadhyay, 2001; Dandekar and Choudhury, 2010). Before enacting PESA in 1996, the State had absolutist eminent domain powers to acquire land in 'public interest' without any consultation with the affected communities. This provision was rampantly abused to ostensibly facilitate industrial and infrastructure development with little consideration to the rights and interests of communities (Sampat, 2013). In several cases, it also became a pretext for the accumulation of real estate for speculative gains (Levien, 2015). While the PESA Act empowered the Adivasi population in scheduled areas, subsequent laws like FRA and the Right to Fair Compensation and Transparency in Land Acquisition, Rehabilitation and Resettlement Act, 2013 (LARR 2013) extended the consultative process to other communities and regions.

(ii) Forest Rights Act, 2006 – FRA provides for a bouquet of tenurial land rights including (*a*) community forest rights (CR) guaranteeing access to common property resources (sections 3[1] [b]–[f], [j]–[m]), (*b*) a set of individual rights (IFR) that are exercised by participants in their individual capacities (section 3[1][a]), and (*c*) community forest resource rights (CFR) that seek to legitimize traditional forest governance practices and acknowledge the community leadership in protecting, conserving, managing, and regenerating forest resources (section 3[1][i]) while giving them exclusive ownership over all non-timber forest produce (section 3[1][c]) (GOI, 2007). Recognizing the vital issue of marginalization of forest dwellers' rights due to forest diversion for various kinds of mining and developmental projects, the FRA framework (outlined explicitly in an August 2009 circular from the Ministry of Environment and Forests [MoEF]) provides for free prior

and informed consent of local communities for such diversion (MoEF, 2009; MoTA, 2012). The requirement of consent from all associated *gram sabhas* before any forest diversion (including for mining) is undertaken was further reaffirmed in the famous Niyamgiri judgment of the Supreme Court. Using the consent provisions, local communities thwarted bauxite mining plans of a large conglomerate (K. Kumar, 2014; Borde, 2017).

(iii) Go/No-Go or Inviolate area policy – initiated in 2009 as a joint exercise between India's environment and coal ministries, this policy sought to 'objectively demarcate' India's forests across mining and conservation end-uses (PIB, 2009; P. J. D. Kumar, 2015). As per the initial criteria formulated in 2010, the entire Hasdeo Aranya region was declared 'no-go' for mining owing to its high forest density – the only coalfield declared entirely as 'no-go' among all the surveyed coalfields. It is pertinent to note that such regions represented only 8.11 per cent of India's potential coal-bearing area and 11.50 per cent of its total explored coal-bearing areas (MoEF, 2011; Ramesh, 2015). However, the policy was subsequently withdrawn in 2011 and revisited in the form of 'inviolate' areas that sought to include a more comprehensive set of environmental parameters to determine those areas that needed to be conserved at all costs (Chakraborty and Sethi, 2015). While the new policy remains work-in-progress and therefore not in force, the latest drafts confirm that Hasdeo Aranya has the maximum share of 'inviolate blocks', and 18 of the 20 identified coal blocks would be deemed out of bounds for mining.[5]

(iv) Various processes under the Environment and Forest Clearance processes, particularly the 'public hearing' provisions – prior to any diversion of land for mining projects, an elaborate approval process is needed to ascertain and mitigate the environmental impacts. It involves consultations with the local community in the form of a 'public hearing', a certification that the forest rights have been recognized and settled, and various appraisal stages by expert bodies where public stakeholders can share their comments (Chaturvedi et al., 2014).

With such an elaborate rights schema and constitutional and legal safeguards, it would prima facie appear that ecologically important areas like Hasdeo Aranya would remain protected. Further, the local communities have sufficient powers to articulate their opposition (if they so wish to) and exercise their rights to thwart any displacement. However, the experience from implementation and forest-diversion processes across India belie such suppositions. Scholars have often lamented the 'pro-business' nature of the Indian State (A. Kohli, 2009). It has meant that marginalized communities have found it extremely difficult to assert their rights or participate in policy processes that remain tied with business interests (Kohli and Menon, 2016b). This calls for a critical assessment of the potential and prospects of harnessing policy spaces within the framework of capitalist democracy.

PROSPECTS OF UTILIZING POLICY SPACES FOR RESISTING CAPITALIST EXPANSION

It is imperative to note that these policy spaces have been created at specific conjunctures due to coordinated civil society action, a supportive political opportunity structure, and democratic imperatives faced by ruling governments in a constitutional democracy (Chakrabarti and Sanyal, 2017). For instance, a favourable political climate where the Adivasi vote was becoming increasingly crucial for electoral success, its consolidation around issues of forest rights, and a supportive political dispensation[6] is believed to have been critical for the enactment of FRA (Kumar and Kerr, 2012). Similarly, the personal initiative and impetus of the then Environment Minister Jairam Ramesh are credited with the formulation of the No-Go policy (P. J. D. Kumar, 2015; Ramesh, 2015). Yet an alignment of ruling elites with business interests has often thwarted the potential of these policies to provide real redistribution of powers or effective rights to the hitherto marginalized communities (Kohli and Menon, 2016b). Further, subsequent governments, especially the BJP-led government post-2014, seen as more business-friendly, have been less supportive of such laws and policies. They have actively attempted to either dilute the key provisions or circumvent them altogether (Sethi, 2015b; Aggarwal, 2019; K. Kohli, 2019). Even as the path dependency of policy evolution ensures some resistance to any subsequent policy changes, there are limits and constraints on the prospects of policy spaces reliant on parliamentary democracy within the broader framework of a capitalist economy.

Even when the policy spaces do not get foreclosed by subsequent policy changes, the implementation dynamics can thwart their radical potential.

There remains a significant gap between policy design and its implementation across several policy arenas in India. In an attempt to explain the wide divergence between the policy framework and its implementation outcomes in India, scholars have commented that India represents a 'Cunning State'. It capitalizes on its 'perceived weakness' in State capacity to render itself unaccountable to select ideas and interest groups even while notionally recognizing their concerns and interests within the policy framework (Randeria, 2003b, 2003a). Therefore, despite a robust policy framework that accommodates the rights of communities in design (or de jure), the implementation processes tend to subvert these guaranteed rights, making them *de facto* inapplicable in several cases. For instance, multiple studies have shown how 'the experience of PESA has been tragically stilted' and no real autonomy or power has been devolved to the *gram sabha*s (Dandekar and Choudhury, 2010: 6). Further, FRA's most radical provisions have either not been implemented or been implemented in only a few regions (Chemmencheri, 2015; Broome, Rai, and Tatpati, 2017; Kumar, Singh, and Rao, 2017). The consent provisions that require *gram sabha* approval before forest diversions are thwarted as consent is 'manufactured' through the various power-laden bureaucratic processes such that 'all documents lead to consent' (Choudhury and Aga, 2020). The inviolate policy, in any case, remains inoperative, and clearances are customarily accorded in such areas despite official recognition of their ecological importance (India Environment Portal, 2011; Chellam, 2016). Similarly, the environment and forest clearances yield limited meaningful participation as public hearing comments are wilfully ignored and clearances accorded in most cases despite strong grounds to the contrary (K. Kohli, 2015; Menon and Kohli, 2015).

Thus, despite offering policy spaces to resist capitalist expansion on the grounds of ensuring social and environmental justice, there is little actual room for sustained and effective opposition. It is crucial to remember that such policy spaces arise and get negotiated within the framework of a capitalist State. To that extent, it is not a revolutionary space for confronting capitalism. Consequently, the civil society space largely remains bereft of success stories. Even a decade after the local Kondh community's victory in protecting their forests from destruction by global capitalist forces, the Niyamgiri example continues to get cited as the poster child of social movement success in India.

The Niyamgiri example, in many ways, remains an exception rather than the norm. In this context of few success stories and constrained policy spaces available in a capitalist State, it is remarkable to understand how communities of Hasdeo Aranya were able to harness these constitutional and policy spaces to mount sustained resistance and achieve their relative successes, howsoever provisional they may be.

THE MOVEMENT STRATEGY AND TRAJECTORY

The movement was forged after the bitter experiences and frustrations from initial mine operationalization processes for two coal mines – Chotia (owned initially by Prakash Industries until 2015 and later by Balco, a Vedanta group company) and Parsa East Kete Basen (operated by Adani on behalf of Rajasthan Rajya Utpadan Nigam Ltd). In fact, most villagers reported having no understanding of the constitutional and legal provisions. A Forest Advisory Committee (FAC)[7] report dated 15 May 2011 affirms the same by noting:

> Interaction with villagers, who are likely to be affected if the projects become operational, revealed inadequate knowledge about the R&R [Relief and Rehabilitation] policy/measures ... the process for settlement of community rights, in accordance with the provisions of the Scheduled Tribes and other Traditional Forest Dwellers (Recognition of Forest Rights) Act, 2006, on the forest land proposed for diversion have not been completed, so far. There is a lack of basic awareness of such provisions in this very important Union legislation on the matter of forest and community rights.[8]

Consequently, the local communities could not have any say or organize much resistance for the initial projects. Also, they remained largely unaware of whether their consent was needed and reported not having participated in any *gram sabha* where they accorded their consent to the mining project. Further, the experiences with resettlement and compensation remained poor. Over time, it also became clear that the threat of displacement and living with adverse impacts of mining projects was not just limited to these projects. As more mines continued to get allocated, it became clear that the entire region was sitting over coal. All the villages of the region were implicated in the struggle to save the forests. Realizing the need for a jointly organized resistance, all the region's villages – that span several tribal and non-tribal groups – covering a substantially large area came together to organize themselves under a common banner. Thus, Hasdeo Aranya Bachao Sangharsh Samiti (literally, a collective to resist and save the Hasdeo Aranya forests) was formed with the aim of saving the region and their lifestyle from imminent devastation. A monthly meeting was instituted to ensure effective coordination across this vast region, wherein representatives of all the villages in the area regularly participate.

SUSTAINED CAPACITY-BUILDING AND AWARENESS GENERATION

It was clear that the biggest challenge was the community's lack of awareness of their rights and entitlements and their role in the various consultative processes that underpin India's mining and forest-diversion processes. Further, decades of tenurial insecurity before FRA and the adverse power relationships with the forest bureaucracy meant that the local community remained underconfident and unwilling to articulate or assert their rights even when they became aware. As Umeshwar Singh Armo, convenor of HABSS and an elected peoples' representative[9] from the region, highlighted:

> Before the early 2000s [before the enactment of FRA], we were just users of forest produce whose access and use of forest resources was carefully regulated by the forest department. We could not bring back too much forest produce to our homes without the fear of being beaten and fined. After FRA, even though our legal position changed, it is difficult to convince people to shed their fear and insecurities. *From user to owner is a big cultural shift* that requires a change in mindset. (Interview notes, emphasis added)

The problem required HABSS to approach various non-governmental organizations (NGOs) for technical inputs and capacity-building support. This, however, brought with it the risk of a shift in power from the community to these NGOs. To ensure that the movement remained disciplined and community-driven and did not deviate from its core aims, the HABSS adopted a five-point principle – community issue, community decision, community struggle, community resources, and community leadership. Simply speaking, the community is responsible for identifying the problem, making decisions, and raising resources to support and lead the movement. However, the extent to which they have been able to imbibe these principles in their movement strategy is crucially predicated on the community's abilities and access to the critical sources of power in their chosen terrain of conflict. For instance, a reliance on the written documents as the mode of protest (letters, petitions, and written submissions) is bound to tilt the powers in favour of the more 'lettered'[10] among the community. Similarly, an intervention in the environmental clearance processes requires a detailed understanding of environmental processes, impacts, and technical language that is often only accessible to local communities through focused environmental groups and NGOs. Thus, the movement principles are bound to get tested over time as the members encounter newer forms of information and power asymmetry in their encounters with the mining companies and the State (Image 5.3).

IMAGE 5.3   Community awareness and training by Janabhivyakti (NGO)

Source: Photograph by Alok Shukla, Chhattisgarh Bachao Andolan.

With the help of Janabhivyakti (NGO working in north Chhattisgarh on FRA implementation and environmental justice issues), and several invited experts on FRA, PESA, Environmental Justice, Local Governance, HABSS conducted many training and workshops on the various constitutional and legal provisions. Some of the key legal provisions were converted to easily accessible and catchy slogans painted across the houses to reinforce the messages and serve as a constant reminder to the local population. These include slogans like 'Vanon ke maalik hum, hum se van, van se hum' (We are the owners of the forest, the existence of forest is dependent on us, and we exist because of the forest) and 'Na Lok Sabha na Vidhaan Sabha, sabse oonchi Gram Sabha' (Neither state assembly nor national parliament, most important is the local *gram sabha*). Such slogans have been derived from interpreting PESA and FRA provisions, specifically section 3(1)(i). Further, various signboards were also put up at several places that indicated that the village was a Schedule 5 area where *gram sabha* had powers to settle all issues under PESA provisions. Partly, these measures also helped the community gradually alter their power relationships with the forest bureaucracy. As Bajrang, a community leader from Gidhmudi village, commented, 'now forest officials treat us with respect, they even come to our *gram sabha*s for informing us of regular forest management activities' (interview notes).

OVERCOMING THE TYRANNY OF DISTANCE BY USING THE FORMAL AUTHORITY OF 'LOCAL GOVERNANCE' STRUCTURES

The training and awareness campaigns helped the community better understand and articulate their local interests and alter local power asymmetries. However, the resistance to mining required effective articulation at a larger scale – district, state, and national levels in addition to the local level. There remained two critical challenges – (*a*) the tyranny of distance where the mere remoteness of the region from seats of power and influence (the state and national capital) meant that it was difficult to attract and sustain media or policymakers' attention to any local protests and (*b*) the challenges and high costs of organizing any large-scale mass protests in Raipur or Delhi for sustained periods, especially given the relatively lower population density. It was likely that the local protest sites would be completely ignored while the protests in centres of power would get lost in the din of urban city-centric issues.

A formal *gram sabha*[11] resolution became the primary tool for articulation, which partially overcame these challenges and complemented the more conventional forms of protest. Vested with PESA powers, the *gram sabha*s have a legitimate and legally recognized role in articulating community opinions, decisions, and prevention of land and resource alienation. Thus, a *gram sabha* resolution can be seen as a decision of one government level (local) vis-à-vis the other levels of government (centre and state levels). Also, a formal resolution from *gram sabha*s is believed to have constitutional standing, especially after the Niyamgiri judgment recognized the primacy of *gram sabha*s in forest-diversion decisions. Further, by its very nature, a formal *gram sabha* resolution represents the will of a 'majority' of local residents, thereby bridging the crisis of legitimacy that most social movements face as their various protests get questioned on the grounds of being determined by a small, motivated group of individuals. Thus, a *gram sabha* resolution's legal sanctity can serve to elicit formal State and policymakers' response, bridging the tyranny of distance and breaking through the clutter of informal urban-centric protests (Image 5.4).

The use of *gram sabha* as the primary mode of articulation of community issues also ensured broad community-wide participation in the resistance struggle, including cross-sections. There was adequate space for women's leadership in the movement, and often, the *gram sabha*s were chaired by women leaders, including several elected women's representatives. The youth, more well-versed with the language of official government correspondence, were at the forefront of drafting the community's resolutions and engaging with the formal processes. HABSS regularly ensured that all associated *gram sabha*s periodically (often every three–six months) passed formal resolutions (with compliance of all due processes) opposing mining in their region. Further, most village-level meetings started being called *gram sabha* meetings – some backed by formal processes and some informal. When a joint meeting is organized involving more than one village, it is often termed a *mahagramsabha* (meeting of *gram sabha*s) rather than a simple community event. For instance, when HABSS invited the Minister for Tribal Affairs of the state government in February 2019, the event was termed *gramsabhaon ka*

IMAGE 5.4 *Gram sabha*
Source: Author.

mahasammelan (a conference of *gram sabhas*). These *gram sabha* resolutions became the focal point of their advocacy strategy in their various letters and petitions to the various ministries and statements to the media (Gupta and Roy-Chowdhury, 2017). It does not mean that HABSS shelved the regular protests like *dharna*s, strikes, protest marches, sit-downs at district and state headquarters, and so on. These protest tactics were typically complemented with *gram sabha* resolutions. The banners and posters at their protest sites referred to these duly passed *gram sabha* resolutions, citing the legally vested powers under PESA and FRA.

'PROACTIVE' RATHER THAN 'REACTIVE' ENGAGEMENT WITH THE POLICY PROCESSES

One of the key challenges of relying on *gram sabha*'s rights and powers is the late stage in the forest-diversion process at which such community consultations are formally required to be conducted, and consent from *gram sabha* is sought. Instead of a meaningful exercise of rights to 'free, prior and informed consent' that would require community involvement from the early stages of project conceptualization, the process of *gram sabha* consultations seems to almost appear as an afterthought to the forest-diversion decision, a mere compliance requirement (Choudhury and Aga, 2020). It can take up to three–seven years before the community is first consulted after the decision to allocate a coal block has been taken, and the pre-mining processes are started (IDFC, 2010). Even a committee constituted by the central government admitted that community consultations are treated merely as a compensation and rehabilitation problem rather than a process of ascertaining the community's opinions (MoTA, 2014: 258–298). However, even when seeking consent and No Objection Certificates (NOC) for mining operations, there is no discussion on the actual compensation and rehabilitation package; this is announced later at the time of land acquisition based on a pre-determined policy. As such, there is no genuine consultation envisaged under the current policy processes.

While the environment clearance process also provides for community consultations in the form of a public hearing, it gets treated as a one-off event. The entire process is ridden with a significant conflict of interest favouring project proponents like mining companies. The Environment Impact Assessment (EIA) Report, which forms the basis of such community consultations, is prepared by a consultant hired by the project proponent (Menon and Kohli, 2007). The public hearing process, including the preparation of minutes, is often led by the project proponent itself, even though the government is responsible for the conduct of such hearings (K. Kohli, 2014b). Further, the project proponent is not legally bound to address the issues raised therein (Lahiri-Dutt, Balakrishnan, and Ahmad, 2012). The experience with governments' role in public hearings has also been disappointing as they are often marred by intimidation, violence, and procedural irregularities (K. Kohli, 2014a; Menon and Kohli, 2015). Moreover, there have been instances of the MoEF grant of clearance despite justifiably adverse public hearings and EIAs, such as the Parsa mining project in Hasdeo Aranya (Menon and Kohli, 2007; K. Kohli, 2014b).

HABSS has attempted to follow a 'proactive' approach to engaging with the policy processes to partially address the challenge. Instead of waiting for their turn to answer the question of consent when formally asked by the project proponents (and the higher levels of government), HABSS has tried to intervene at the early stages of the decisions to allocate or auction a coal block. This proactive engagement is sustained at every stage of the subsequent policy processes – for instance, every step of the environment and forest clearance processes – through letters, petitions, representations, and meetings. This strategy allows for a more prolonged engagement with formal policy spaces, thereby offering greater temporal space for articulating the resistance. It also keeps the local communities meaningfully engaged, collectivized, and committed to the movement principles of following constitutionally mandated democratic spaces.

In one of their key campaigns in the winter of 2014–2015, 20 *gram sabhas* of Hasdeo Aranya tried to influence the allocation of coal blocks itself by taking their resolutions against mining to the concerned ministries (coal, environment, tribal affairs, and the prime minister). They argued that since they were unlikely to give their consent as required to start mining operations, the central government should not go ahead with allocation itself (Chhattisgarh Bachao Andolan, 2015; Choudhury, 2015). In many ways, this was a unique framing of the situation wherein the local-level government vested with its powers under PESA and FRA tried to influence the allocation process, which is the exclusive domain of the central government (Gupta and Roy-Chowdhury, 2017). The elected and formally recognized leaders (*sarpanchs*) played a lead role in representing the *gram sabhas* in communicating with the other government functionaries. This campaign was repeated at every subsequent allocation of a new coal block in the region, most recently in June 2020 (Alam, 2020; Mishra, 2020b). While the government has disregarded these *gram sabha* resolutions and went ahead with allocating blocks, this strategy has allowed HABSS to capitalize on other political spaces – media, political leaders, and government officials. The allocation (or auction) of coal blocks is usually done with much fanfare – launched by the prime minister himself or the senior-most minister on most occasions. Therefore, a proactive strategy to engage at the very instance when the public attention is high has allowed HABSS to access and exploit media and policy spaces that open up around such events (Aggarwal, 2015; Sethi, 2015a; Wal, 2015) (Image 5.5).

IMAGE 5.5   Meeting of HABSS

Source: Author.

CAREFUL FRAMING THAT AMALGAMATES ENVIRONMENTAL AND SOCIAL DIMENSIONS

The Hasdeo Aranya region offers possibilities of resistance on both environmental and social grounds, given the region's particular facts. However, too often, movements tend to emphasize only one of these dimensions, thereby foregoing possibilities of engagement across the entire policy spectrum. The social movement literature is also replete with examples of tensions and conflicts between the social and environmental movements, popularly referred to as 'blue–green conflicts' (Satheesh, 2020). The schism between environmental and social dimensions of a resource conflict becomes particularly stark in the context of India's forest governance. The forest bureaucracy sees local communities as a challenge to forest conservation efforts, thereby adopting a hostile approach to the issue of rights of forest dwellers (B. K. Singh, 2021) (Image 5.6).

IMAGE 5.6 Community protest march

Source: Photograph by Alok Shukla, Chhattisgarh Bachao Andolan.

In the case of Hasdeo Aranya, there was the added challenge of overcoming the community's hostility and fear of wildlife in the wake of rising human–elephant conflict (Gopalakrishnan and Selvaraj, 2017; WTI, 2017). Due to the extensive crop losses, house damages, and even loss of life from elephant conflicts every year, it is not easy to sustain the communities' narrative of a quest for both environmental and social justice. However, faced with the more significant threat of displacement and disruption to their way of life, HABSS amalgamated environmental and social dimensions into their movement strategy.

The master frame for HABSS emerged from the community's own socio-historical experiences – the communities' peaceful and harmonious co-existence with nature since ancient periods. To the forest dwellers of Hasdeo Aranya, the forest was a way of life. There was no visualization of an alternate lifestyle that did not involve co-partaking from nature's bounty along with other species. The movement for FRA by the umbrella coalition of forest-based movements in the early 2000s and FRA's enactment had already provided recognition and legitimacy to this frame (Kumar and Kerr, 2012). The powers granted to *gram sabha* to 'protect, conserve, and manage forests and resources' in their CFR areas and legal recognition of their historical role in this function further provided a useful frame to articulate the community's interests (MoTA, 2012; Kumar, Singh, and Kerr., 2015). The roots of the growing human–wildlife conflict were traced to the pressure faced by large mammals due to disruption of their habitat by the expansion of mining and industrial activities in nearby areas (A. Fernandes, 2012; Sivalingam, 2014). This issue was also carefully documented and analysed in a report by Greenpeace that claimed that the real 'Elephant in the Room' was the threat of coal mining (Sivalingam, 2014). The Hasdeo Aranya area's notification as a 'no-go' area based on the governments' internal bureaucratic exercise further provided grounds for HABSS to exploit the political space offered by the region's vital environmental and ecological parameters.

This framing allowed HABSS to ensure a credible and consistent intervention across all policy arenas – FRA implementation processes, *gram sabha* consent processes, as well as environmental and forest clearance processes. Thus, all letters, petitions, and even *gram sabha* resolutions included a consistent message which included (*a*) the role and powers as per constitutional and legal provisions, (*b*) the ecological importance of the region, including it being deemed a 'no-go' or 'inviolate' areas, and (*c*) the historical relationship of the community with forests that make it essential for the communities to protect forests at all costs to conserve their life, livelihood, and identity.

LEVERAGING A BROADER CIVIL SOCIETY NETWORK WHILE RETAINING COMMUNITY'S IDENTITY

It was evident that despite strategies that sought to leverage the available policy spaces, Hasdeo Aranya is still a localized movement representing a relatively small and remotely located population. Thus, it could not expect to capture attention on a stand-alone basis without building solidarities and alliances with other civil society actors. The importance of national and transnational advocacy networks in extending influence spheres of influence with decision-makers had already been outlined by the Niyamgiri movement's case (Macdonald, Marshall, and Balaton-Chrimes, 2017). However, the Niyamgiri case had also presented insights into the challenges of navigating the heterogeneity of interests of different actors in these networks and highlighted the need for caution by local movements in such interactions (Kraemer, Whiteman, and Banerjee, 2013). Thus, the importance of close alignment of interests and the need for deeper relationships with the associated advocacy networks remained crucial for HABSS.

At the outset, HABSS joined the Chhattisgarh Bachao Andolan (Save Chhattisgarh Movement, hereafter called CBA), a state-level alliance of peoples' movements working on similar issues across various parts of Chhattisgarh (Gupta and Roy-Chowdhury, 2017). Being a relatively small and closely aligned group of movements enabled HABSS to retain its core identity and interests even with the presence of an alliance. Due to the geographical proximity, the members of individual movements associated with CBA could also actively participate in each other's resistance sites and forge effective solidarities and relationships. At the same time, being a state-level civil society platform, CBA offered access to the regional and state-level policy circles and networks. It also allowed HABSS to pool resources and technical and legal expertise from other member groups and their leaders.

To traverse policy scales, HABSS, however, needed to extend its presence to the national level. Again, CBA could channel its collective strength and legitimacy to gain access to the NGOs, media personnel, and national-level advocacy coalitions. These often helped amplify local community voices to the national-level policy scale. HABSS also joined newer civil society alliance networks like the Bhoomi Adhikar Andolan to raise broader land alienation issues. However, the challenge before HABSS remained its limited ability to influence larger national networks given the tyranny of distance that we discussed earlier. Therefore, HABSS relied on its tactical strength of leveraging *gram sabha* resolutions to retain distinct community articulation of its core interests even while participating in the broader alliances and networks.

A CRITICAL APPRAISAL OF THE MOVEMENTS' ACHIEVEMENTS

The high point for HABSS came in September 2020, when five coal blocks were eventually withdrawn from the list of mines put up for auctions (Trivedi, 2020). The decision was taken after a sustained campaign surrounding the first-ever commercial coal block auctions announced by the prime minister in June 2020 (PTI, 2020). Based on *gram sabha* resolutions (Mishra, 2020b), all the region's elected *sarpanchs* had written a letter to the prime minister and other associated ministries expressing their continued opposition to mining in the region (Alam, 2020; Kaiser, 2020). Directly attacking the prime minister's speech on the need for auctioning coal blocks in the quest for 'Atmanirbhar Bharat' (self-sufficient India), the *sarpanchs* had argued that these auctions ran contrary to the *atmanirbharta* of these villages. In their letter subsequently released to the media, they mentioned:

> On the one hand, you speak of atmanirbharta; on the other, you talk of destroying the livelihood, lifestyle, and culture of Adivasis and forest-dwelling communities through this auction.... In the region, the gram sabhas have already built a model of 'atmnirbhar' local self-governance under the provisions of PESA and FRA. (Letter by *sarpanchs* to the prime minister dated 18 June 2020)

The local resistance found resonance and support from several quarters and was widely covered across the media outlets. The local resistance to coal in Hasdeo Aranya also became the focal point of a global debate on issues of India's tryst with decarbonization and climate change, as reported by CNN and *The Guardian* (Ellis-Petersen, 2020; Gupta and Regan, 2020).

Remarkably, the issue of 'no-go' areas also took centre stage as several political leaders and the state-level governments intervened to protect high-conservation zones from the list of mines to be auctioned in the current list (Jamwal, 2020; *The Wire*, 2020). The most crucial intervention came from the state government of Chhattisgarh, which is run by the Congress party that is politically opposed to the BJP-led government at the centre. The Chhattisgarh state forest minister referred to the state government's intentions to create an elephant reserve project (called Lemru) in the region (Mishra, 2019, 2020a) and requested his counterpart in the central government to withdraw coal blocks from auctions. He wrote:

> [T]he jungles around the coal blocks have been reserved for the Lemru elephant reserve.... It will not be right to ever create coal blocks in these areas, with regards to environmental safety. So, kindly remove the coal blocks falling in Hasdeo Aranya, and the catchment areas of Mand river should be removed from the current and any future list of available coal blocks. (Verma, 2020)

The support from the state government and political elites can be seen as an outcome of the series of advocacy campaigns over the years and meetings with political leaders across the political spectrum. These included visits by some of the seniormost leaders of the Congress party, including its vice president, Rahul Gandhi (R. K. Das, 2015). This was followed by multiple rounds of meetings and discussions with the state's current chief minister, including when he was in opposition.[12]

The removal of Hasdeo Aranya blocks from the auctions list appears to mark the culmination of the decade-long protests by HABSS to gain policy attention for their issues. It also represents a remarkable success story amidst the chequered history of civil society struggles in India. However, by no means does it mark the end of the community's struggle, as became evident within months of this success.

A CAUTIONARY NOTE

In January 2021, the central government announced its intention to acquire land for the Madanpur South coal block, which lay adjacent to and sandwiched between the five coal blocks that had just been withdrawn from the auction list (A. Das, 2021). Like six other coal blocks of the region, this block had already been allocated between 2015 and 2020. However, clearance processes had not been undertaken thus far owing to stern community resistance. It is important to note that these blocks had been allocated to various mining companies despite prior opposition and repeated *gram sabha* resolutions from the associated *gram sabha*s (Aggarwal, 2015; Wal, 2015). The fact that the government was also willing to ignore its classification as a 'no-go' or 'inviolate' area while allocating these blocks points to the inherent limits offered by the policy spaces for a resistance movement's success.

Even though these new mining projects would continue to require consent from the local *gram sabha*s, the communities remain worried about the forcible processes that could be followed to obtain, or as Choudhury and Aga (2020) articulate, 'manufacture' this consent. The Parsa coal block experience in Hasdeo Aranya documents communities' bitter experience navigating formal consent processes (MS, 2020). The very design of the process of community consultations is loaded against the communities wherein the consent can be sought any number of times. However, the community has to consent only once to have an irretrievable decision. If the community does not provide consent, it can be asked repeatedly until it relents. Further, the *gram sabha* is not empowered to invalidate such consent with a subsequent resolution. Jainandan Singh Porte of Ghatbarra village, a community leader affected by the Parsa project, explained the inherent injustice in the system:

> We have been opposing mining through several gram sabha resolutions, but the government didn't listen ... then in 2017, the government conducted 4–5 gram sabha meetings over a span of 6 months to pressurize us to give consent ... however, when even that failed, it forged the consent and took NOC to process the clearance. We have subsequently passed a fresh resolution opposing mining, but that is held as invalid. (Interview notes)

HABSS also needs to worry about the long and arduous legal processes if a project manages to get clearance despite any irregularities or even blatant violations of the legal procedures. For instance, the forest clearance for Parsa East Kete Basen (operational) mining project was invalidated on multiple grounds by the National Green Tribunal (National Green Tribunal, 2014). Yet the mine continues to remain operational and continues to seek expansion as the case remains pending in the Supreme Court (Nandi, 2021). Further, the villagers of Ghatbarra also continue to struggle in courts to regain their community forest rights after their CFR title was invalidated by administrative fiat in what remains the only such exercise across the country (K. Kohli, 2016; Sethi, 2016). It is important to note that success in the legal arena requires an altogether different set of capabilities than in the social and political arenas. Local indigenous communities are often ill-equipped to navigate the legal challenges.

While the example of HABSS represents a moment of success in India's experience of social movements, it also throws up the challenges and limitations of following such a strategy. Despite remarkable achievements in capturing popular imagination and gaining the policymakers' attention, there is a limited guarantee that the movements' core aims will be met in the long run. Even as the HABSS carefully navigated and exploited the constitutional and policy spaces, their case also throws up newer questions on the scope of these spaces to offer meaningful environmental and social justice.

Even the ability to explore and raise these newer legal and constitutional questions, which remain pending before the courts and the policy-making bodies, can partly be seen as a success of the essentially local social movement (Gupta and Roy-Chowdhury, 2017; Choudhury and Aga, 2020; K. Kohli, 2019). In essence, HABSS has managed to expose and highlight the inherent asymmetric design of policy processes and contemporary policy dilemmas – auction before consent and clearance, asymmetric design of consent provisions, limits of powers under CFR and FRA recognition processes. Thus, HABSS's movement strategy can be seen to have been successful in traversing the scales of policy design and policy implementation.

LESSONS FOR THE FUTURE

Scholars have elaborately commented on the inadequacies of the institutional and policy spaces for organized resistance in India – inadequate devolution of powers under PESA (Dandekar and Choudhury, 2010), the abysmal implementation, and disregard to the substantive provisions of FRA (CFR-LA, 2016; Kumar, Singh, and Rao, 2017), the inadequate consultation and 'free, prior, informed, consent' framework for local-level consultations regarding displacement projects (Choudhury and Aga, 2020), and an ineffective environmental clearance framework (Menon and Kohli, 2015). Despite these shortcomings, the success of HABSS in harnessing these spaces, as available in any constitutional democracy, can serve as a model for organized resistance to the capitalistic expansion project.

HABSS's methods represent a valuable experiment in utilizing the *gram sabha* not only for local self-governance – as envisaged in policy – but also as a valuable tool to articulate the community views and negotiate with the central and state tiers of government. The successful framing of the issue as a conflict between the local government, that is, the *gram sabhas* pitted against the collective might of the powerful central and state-level government tiers, managed to capture policy attention and expose the fault-lines in the decentralization and democratic framework of the constitution. Interestingly, the movement primarily targeted policy spaces where the State is the dominant actor and consequently the primary target for the resistance struggle. While HABSS mentioned the corporates in most of the letters, petitions, and documents, they remained in the background of the formal conflict. The policy processes seek to negotiate clearances and consent for a project, ostensibly as an independent arbiter between the communities and the project proponents or the corporates. However, the State–corporate nexus ensures that the corporate interests get reflected in the formal policy positions adopted by the central and state governments, thereby assigning a semblance of legitimacy to the corporate interests. Thus, the corporates often recede to the background as the State is often at the centre stage of the conflict (A. Kohli, 2009; Kohli and Menon, 2016a). In this context, the HABSS's strategy of pitting one level of government (local) against the other levels (centre and state) could help expose this State–corporate nexus and bridge the legitimacy gap typically faced by social movements across the country.

The movement's ability to resist any expansion of mining operations over the last nine years in the face of some of the most powerful corporate groups of the country remains laudable and a testament to the collective resolve of the local communities. Yet, in the wake of an ever-expanding capitalist project, any momentary success remains provisional and vulnerable to reversals. There are limits to such strategies of using *gram sabha* as the focal point for a social movement amid the asymmetric distribution of real powers between different tiers of government. Further, a movement's strategies and variegated responses remain embedded within the broader structures of power in the society that operate differently in each context and even in the same context over different points of time. It is neither guaranteed that HABSS would be able to achieve its objectives over the long run nor that another movement could expect to achieve similar results with such strategies.

One must also recognize the inherent pitfalls of using the strategies adopted by HABSS. As multiple scholars have warned, as 'the rule of law' became the central focus of the movement, the communities were forced to enter into 'political and legal negotiations already constituted as certain kinds of legal subjects, which constrains their imagination in certain ways' (Sundar, 2011: 419). The very choice of focusing on institutional and policy spaces offered by a constitutional democracy forces the communities to adapt and respond to the knowledge systems privileged by the State and subject themselves to the asymmetric power balances represented therein. In the long run, such strategies reliant on legal rights and constitutional guarantees run the risk of falling into the trap of becoming unwilling participants in newer modes of 'neo-liberal governance'. By disembedding the tribal society from their intimate connection with nature, rights-based legislation like PESA and FRA, and the knowledge systems that produce and manage these laws, force such communities to encounter and respond to the modernity and capitalist expansion project on inherently unfamiliar terms (Bhattacharya, Bhattacharya and Gill, 2017). Addressing this challenge would require conceptualization of radical spaces and alternate development models across levels of governance – national, regional, and local. Even as such alternatives are emerging in select regions across the country, they remain marginalized in the broader public discourse (Kothari and Joy, 2017). In the absence of such radical spaces, the formal policy spaces embedded within the current constitutional framework of a capitalist democracy would remain a significant challenge to the long-term success of any movement like HABSS.

Regardless of the current achievements, or the potential and prospects of the strategies adopted by the HABSS, the movement needs to be celebrated for its remarkable resilience in the face of adverse power structures. The forest-dwelling communities of Hasdeo Aranya have shown how even a remote, peace-loving, and powerless populace can wage an effective 'war' (Ellis-Petersen, 2020) against the powerful elites and the State in their quest to protect and conserve their union with nature. The movement by Hasdeo Aranya captures the indomitable spirit and the age-old Adivasi traditions and their struggle for rights and dignity as captured by this poem by the late Adivasi rights activist Abhay Xaxa:

> Among the doom and gloom they smile,
> Mistaken for idiots by the mad rational world.
> The Adivasis, beautifully damaged people!
> On the treasures of iron, gold and diamond they sit,
> Poor and powerless, holding the curse of nature.
> The curse of loving their land, water, forest,
> where they prefer to die as mad lover
> beautifully damaged people!
> With stars in their eyes, n moon in their minds,
> Thoughts flowing like an undammed river
> with hearts unadulterated with twisted philosophies,
> Religions, ideologies, lust and greed.
> Their vision misunderstood as juvenility,
> On the face of violence, loot and hopelessness they remain,
> Dreamy, defiant and deviant,
> Beautifully damaged people!
> —excerpts from the poem titled
> 'Beautiful Damaged People'
> by Abhay Xaxa (Xaxa, 2017)

POSTSCRIPT

Over the last few months, the government has issued a notification for land acquisition for four new coal blocks in Hasdeo Aranya – Parsa, Kete Extension, Gidhmudi Paturia, and Madanpur South. In each of these cases, no prior *gram sabha* consent was taken. The government has held that land acquisition under an earlier Act called Coal Bearing Areas Acquisition and Development Act, 1957, does not attract PESA and FRA consent provisions. Further, the initial forest clearance (Stage-1) for the Parsa coal block was processed based on what the communities have alleged is a fake NOC based on forged *gram sabha* resolution. The proposed boundaries of Lemru Elephant reserve were amended to 450 square kilometres in June 2021 from the initial 3,827 square kilometres for which *gram sabhas* had been consulted only nine months ago in October 2020. To resist these developments, hundreds of villagers from the region marched on foot (Hasdeo Bachao Padyatra, or the Save Hasdeo Foot-Rally) from Surguja to Raipur – a 330-kilometre journey over ten days from 4 to 13 October. This delegation met the chief minister and governor, who assured them of looking into their demands and ordering an enquiry into the allegations of forged *gram sabha* resolutions. The event and protest also received widespread coverage in regional and national media.

The resistance of Hasdeo Aranya communities received partial success as the Lemru Elephant reserve boundaries were again amended to a 1,995 square kilometre area to include parts of the region while still excluding a large number of coal blocks. Further, in his meeting with the communities on 14 October 2014, the chief minister of Chhattisgarh assured of his intention to protect Gidhmudi Paturia and Madanpur South coal blocks by including them in the elephant reserve project. At the same time, on 21 October 2014, the final forest clearance (Stage-2) for the Parsa coal block was processed within a week of this meeting despite the clear assurance from the chief minister and governor for an investigation into the allegations of forged *gram sabha* consent. These developments and the partial and provisional successes further highlight the prospects and challenges of relying on constitutional and policy spaces for organized resistance to capitalist expansion.

ACKNOWLEDGEMENTS

The author would like to express gratitude towards the HABSS members for their active support and open discussions that led to this chapter. They warmly welcomed me and openly shared their stories – both old and new, of misery and joy, of losses and gains, of freedom and tradition. They also taught me how to find joy and hope amidst the most trying circumstances. I am grateful to Alok Shukla, convenor of Chhattisgarh Bachao Andolan, for his sharp insights and feedback on the contents of this chapter. I would also like to thank Rohit Varman, Devi Vijay, and the reviewers for their insightful comments and detailed feedback on earlier drafts of the manuscript.

NOTES

1. Elected head of the local governance unit, the 'panchayat'.
2. *Gram sabha* refers to a constitutionally recognized village assembly that comprises of all the eligible voters of the village.
3. Under the Indian forest classification system, forests with canopy cover of 40–70 per cent are classified as moderately dense forests, and those above 70 per cent are classified as very dense forests.
4. The National Green Tribunal is a quasi-judicial institution set-up by the Ministry of Environment, Forest and Climate Change (MoEFCC) for effective and expeditious resolution of legal disputes relating to issues of environment protection, conservation of forests, and other natural resources.
5. Drafts of policy documents reviewed by the author through information obtained under RTI.
6. United Progressive Alliance (UPA) formed as an alliance of left-liberal Congress, other socialist parties and Left political parties came to power in 2004. It is credited with enactment of a number of people-centric legislations like the FRA, National Rural Employment Guarantee Act, Right to Education, LARR, among others.
7. This committee is responsible for advising the ministry on issue of forest clearances. It often submits reports based on site inspections by a team or sub-committee.
8. Observations of the sub-committee of Forest Advisory Committee (National Green Tribunal, 2014)
9. Block Development Council representative elected by a group of approximately 20 villages.

10. I use 'lettered' instead of learned or educated to indicate the privileging of the homogenized forms of knowledge and the language of the State, as opposed to the traditional forms of knowledge and articulation.

11. The *gram sabha* comprises of all elected voters of the village, and a formal resolution can only be passed by a majority of all members present and voting. Further there are quorum requirements (33 per cent of total voters of the village) for passing such resolutions, although in the case of Hasdeo Aranya, *gram sabha* meetings are attended by over 50–60 per cent of the members. Therefore, a *gram sabha* resolution can be seen as a formal, legitimate, and a representative articulation of the village. In the case of opposition to mining projects or assertion of rights under FRA, such resolutions were passed by consensus.

12. Between 2014 and 2019, both the centre (national-level) and the state (provincial) governments were ruled by the BJP. Motivated by the strong resistance from HABSS, the opposition Congress party periodically used the issues of conservation of Hasdeo Aranya region, protection of rights of communities under PESA and FRA, and the need for elephant reserve. In 2019, the Congress came into power in the state with the promise of Lemru Elephant reserve in their manifesto. However, since coming to power, the Congress-led state government has adopted an ambivalent stance to the issue – sometimes supporting the local resistance and creation of elephant reserve, at other times continuing to expand mining clearance processes in the same areas.

REFERENCES

Aggarwal, M. (2015). 20 gram sabhas in Chhattisgarh pass resolutions against auction of coal mines. *Livemint*, 15 January. Accessed on 22 December 2021: http://www.livemint.com/Politics/9ReivDrAjzdvv7d6Hw8NGL/20-gram-sabhas-in-Chhattisgarh-pass-resolutions-against-auct.html.

———(2019). With forest rights in focus ahead of elections, proposed changes to Forest Act draw attention. *Mongabay*, 27 March. Accessed on 22 December 2021: https://india.mongabay.com/2019/03/with-forest-rights-in-focus-ahead-of-elections-proposed-changes-to-forest-act-draw-attention/.

Agrawal, A., A. Chhatre, and R. Hardin (2008). Changing governance of the world's forests. *Science* 320(5882): 1460–1462.

Alam, M. (2020). Chhattisgarh: 9 sarpanchs write to PM to stop mining auction at Hasdeo Arand. *The Wire*, 16 June. Accessed on 22 December 2021: https://thewire.in/rights/chhattisgarh-sarpanchs-modi-hasdeo-arand-atmanirbhar.

Bhattacharya, R., S. Bhattacharya, and K. Gill (2017) The Adivasi land question in the neoliberal era. In *The Land Question in India: State, Dispossession, and Capitalist Transition*, ed. A. P. D'Costa and A. Chakraborty. Oxford: Oxford University Press, pp. 177–198.

Bijoy, C. R. (2008). Forest rights struggle: The Adivasis now await a settlement. *American Behavioral Scientist* 51(12): 1755–1773.

Borde, R. (2017). Differential subalterns in the Niyamgiri Movement in India. *International Journal of Postcolonial Studies* 19(4): 566–582.

Bose, I. (2010). How did the Indian Forest Rights Act, 2006, emerge. Institutions for Pro-Poor Growth Discussion Papers, 39.

Bose, P. (2012) *Forest Rights: The Micro-politics of Decentralisation and Forest Tenure Reform in Tribal India*. Wageningen: Wageningen University.

Broome, N. P., N. D. Rai, and M. Tatpati (2017). Biodiversity conservation and Forest Rights Act. *Economic and Political Weekly* 52(25 & 26): 51–54.

Census (2011). *Houselisting and Housing Census Data – 2011, Census of India*. Accessed on 27 July 2016: http://www.censusindia.gov.in/2011census/hlo/HLO_Tables.html.

CFR-LA (2016). *Promise and Performance: 10 Years of Forest Rights Act in India*. Delhi: Community Forest Rights–Learning and Advocacy Process.

Chakrabarti, R. and K. Sanyal (2017). *Shaping Policy in India: Alliance, Advocacy, Activism*. New Delhi: Oxford University Press.

Chakraborty, S. and N. Sethi (2015) Final number of inviolate coal blocks down from 206 to less than 35. *Business Standard*, 2 September. Accessed on 22 December 2021: http://www.business-standard.com/article/economy-policy/final-number-of-inviolate-coal-blocks-down-from-206-to-less-than-35-115090200004_1.html.

Chaturvedi, V., V. Gupta, N. Choudhury, S. Mittra, A. Ghosh, and R. Sugam (2014). *State of Environmental Clearances in India: Procedures, Timelines and Delays across Sectors and States*. New Delhi: Council on Energy, Environment and Water.

Chellam, R. (2016). Violating the inviolate forests. Greenpeace, 21 March. Accessed on 22 December 2021: http://www.greenpeace.org/india/en/Blog/ Campaign_blogs/the-green-blindfold-over-our-forest/blog/55949/.

Chemmencheri, S. R. (2015). State, social policy and subaltern citizens in Adivasi India. *Citizenship Studies* 19(3–4): 436–449.

Chhattisgarh Bachao Andolan (2015). Press Release: Twenty gram sabhas (village assemblies) pass resolutions, urge government to safeguard of constitutional rights and restrict coal mining. 14 January. Accessed on 22 December 2021: https://indiaresists.com/chhattisgarh-20-gram-sabhas-pass-resolutions-demand-protection-of-constitutional-rights-of-adivasis-restrict-coal-mining-in-hasdeo-arand-and-dharamjaigarh-forests.

Choudhury, C. (2015). Not just a coal block. People's Archive of Rural India, 2 January. Accessed on 22 December 2021: https://ruralindiaonline.org/ articles/not-just-a-coal-block-hasdeo-arand/.

Choudhury, C. and A. Aga (2020). Manufacturing consent: Mining, bureaucratic sabotage and the Forest Rights Act in India'. *Capitalism Nature Socialism* 31(2): 70–90.

Dandekar, A. and C. Choudhury (2010). *PESA, Left-Wing Extremism and Governance: Concerns and Challenges in India's Tribal Districts, Report of a Study Commissioned by Ministry of Panchayati Raj, Government of India.* Anand: Government of India.

Das, A. (2021). Is centre violating peoples' rights for acquiring coal-bearing land in Chhattisgarh? *Newsclick*, 8 January. Accessed on 22 December 2021: https://www.newsclick.in/is-centre-violating-peoples-rights-acquiring-coal-bearing-land-chhattisgarh%3F.

Das, R. K. (2015). Chhattisgarh coal mines protest gets Rahul Gandhi's stamp. *Business Standard*, 15 June. Accessed on 22 December 2021: https://www. business-standard.com/article/politics/chhattisgarh-coal-mines-protest-gets-rahul-gandhi-s-stamp-115061500885_1.html.

Dasgupta, A. (2020). Adani and the elephants of the Hasdeo Aranya forest. *Newsclick*, 26 June. Accessed on 22 December 2021: https://www.newsclick. in/Adani-Elephants-Hasdeo-Aranya-Forest.

Drolia, R. and J. John (2020). Exclude coal blocks in ecologically sensitive areas from e-auction, Chhattisgarh govt tells centre. *Times of India*, 21 June. Accessed on 22 December 2021: https://timesofindia.indiatimes.com/

india/exclude-coal-blocks-in-ecologically-sensitive-areas-from-e-auction-chhattisgarh-govt-tells-centre/articleshow/76487073.cms.

Ellis-Petersen, H. (2020). India plans to fell ancient forest to create 40 new coalfields. *The Guardian*, 8 August. Accessed on 22 December 2021: https://www.theguardian.com/world/2020/aug/08/india-prime-minister-narendra-modi-plans-to-fell-ancient-forest-to-create-40-new-coal-fields.

Fernandes, A. (2012). *How Coal Mining Is Trashing Tigerland*. Delhi: Greenpeace. Accessed on 22 December 2021: http://www.greenpeace.org/india/Global/india/report/How-Coal-mining-is-Trashing-Tigerland.pdf.

Fernandes, W. (2009). India's half century search for a resettlement policy and the right to livelihood. In *Beyond Relocation: The Imperative of Sustainable Resettlement*, ed. R. Modi. New Delhi: SAGE Publications India, 102–126.

GOI (2007). *The Scheduled Tribes and Other Traditional Forest Dwellers (Recognition of Forest Rights) Act, 2006*. New Delhi.

Gopalakrishnan, S. T. S. C. and M. S. Selvaraj (2017). It is not just about fences. *Economic and Political Weekly* 52(52): 97–104.

Guha, R. (1983). Forestry in British and Post-British India: A historical analysis. *Economic and Political Weekly* 18(44): 1882–1896.

Gupta, P. and A. Roy-Chowdhury (2017). Harnessing gram sabhas to challenge state profligacy in Chhattisgarh. *Economic and Political Weekly* 52(48): 58–63.

Gupta, S. and H. Regan (2020). India's plans for a coal-fuelled recovery are threatening this ancient forest. CNN, September. Accessed on 22 December 2021: https://edition.cnn.com/interactive/2020/09/world/climate-covid-money-intl/.

HABSS (2014). *Perspective Document on Coal Mining in Hasdeo Arand Region*. Raipur: Hasdeo Arand Bachao Sangharsh Samiti. Accessed on 22 December 2021: https://global-uploads.webflow.com/5d70c9269b8d7bd25d8b1696/5dbffdbed8384f399e321e58_Implications-of-Mining-in-Hasdeo-Arand-coloured.pdf.

IDFC (2010). *Captive Coal Mining by Private Power Developers: Issues and Road Ahead*. Mumbai.

India Environment Portal (2011). Go, no go and all go. 13 April. Accessed on 22 December 2021: http://www.indiaenvironmentportal.org.in/content/326817/go-no-go-and-all-go/.

Jamwal, N. (2020). After Jharkhand, Chhattisgarh and Maharashtra oppose the Centre's auction of 41 coal blocks for commercial mining. *GaonConnection*, 22 June. Accessed on 22 December 2021: https://en.gaonconnection.com/after-jharkhand-chhattisgarh-and-maharashtra-oppose-the-centres-auction-of-41-coal-blocks-for-commercial-mining/.

Janabhivyakti (2015). *Development Imperatives for Udaypur Block, South Surguja: Issues and Challenges with Recognition of Land & Forest Titles and Implementation of various Government Schemes*. Raipur.

Joshi, S. (2016). Tribes, land and forests: Emerging legal implications with reference to PESA and FRA. National Seminar on 'Governance, Resources and Livelihoods of Adivasis in India: Implementation of PESA and FRA', NIRDPR, Hyderabad, 18–19 November.

Kaiser, E. (2020). Coal mining: Sarpanchs urge PM Narendra Modi to stop auction of blocks. *New Indian Express*, 18 June. Accessed on 22 December 2021: https://www.newindianexpress.com/nation/2020/jun/18/coal-mining-sarpanchs-urge-pm-narendra-modi-to-stop-auction-of-blocks-2158059.html.

Kashwan, P. (2013). The politics of rights-based approaches in conservation. *Land Use Policy* 31(March): 613–626.

Kohli, A. (2009). *Democracy and Development in India: From Socialism to Pro-business*. New Delhi: Oxford University Press.

Kohli, K. (2014a). Environmental impact assessment: The problem with public hearings. mylaw.net, 16 June. Accessed on 22 December 2021: http://blog.mylaw.net/environmental-impact-assessment-the-problem-with-public-hearings/.

——— (2014a). (2014b). Ignoring the 'public' at a public hearing. *India Together*, 28 May. Accessed on 22 December 2021: https://indiatogether.org/irregularities-in-parsa-coal-bock-public-hearing-environment.

——— (2016). Mining is in the way of Adivasi forest rights, not the other way round. *The Wire*, 7 June. Accessed on 22 December 2021: http://thewire.in/40405/mining-is-in-the-way-of-adivasi-forest-rights-and-not-the-other-way-round/.

——— (2019). Historical injustice and 'bogus' claims: Large infrastructure, conservation and forest rights in India. Heinrich Böll Stiftung India. Accessed on 22 December 2021: https://in.boell.org/sites/default/files/uploads/2019/06/historical_injustice_and_bogus_claims_large_infrastructure_conservation_and_forest_rights_in_india.pdf.

Kohli, K., and M. Menon (2016a). *Business Interests and the Environmental Crisis*. New Delhi: SAGE Publications India.

——— (2016b). Introduction: Green and pink. in *Business Interests and the Environmental Crisis*, ed. K. Kohli and M. Menon. New Delhi: SAGE Publications India Pvt Ltd.

Kothari, A., and K. J. Joy (2017). *Alternative Futures: India Unshackled*. New Delhi: AuthorsUpFront.

Kraemer, R., Whiteman, G., and B. Banerjee (2013). Conflict and astroturfing in Niyamgiri: The importance of national advocacy networks in anti-corporate social movements. *Organization Studies* 34(5–6): 823–852.

Kumar, K. (2014). The sacred mountain: Confronting global capital at Niyamgiri. *Geoforum* 54(July): 196–206.

Kumar, K., and J. M. Kerr (2012). Democratic assertions: The making of India's recognition of Forest Rights Act. *Development and Change* 43(3): 751–771.

Kumar, K., N. M. Singh, and J. M. Kerr (2015). Decentralisation and democratic forest reforms in India: Moving to a rights-based approach. *Forest Policy and Economics* 51(February): 1–8.

Kumar, K., N. M. Singh, and Y. G. Rao (2017). Promise and performance of the Forest Rights Act: A ten-year review. *Economic and Political Weekly* 52(25 & 26): 40–43.

Kumar, P. J. D. (2015). *Defending the Green Realm: The Forest Conservation Act 1980 of India in Theory and Practice*. Bengaluru: Institute for Social and Economic Change.

Lahiri-Dutt, K., R. Balakrishnan, and N. Ahmad (2012). Land acquisition and dispossession: Private coal companies in Jharkhand. *Economic and Political Weekly* 47(6): 39–45.

Larson, A. M., and G. R. Dahal (2012). Forest tenure reform: New resource rights for forest-based communities? *Conservation and Society* 10(2): 77–90.

Levien, M. (2015). From primitive accumulation to regimes of dispossession: Six theses on India's land question. *Economic and Political Weekly* 50(22): 146–157.

Macdonald, K., S. Marshall, and S. Balaton-Chrimes (2017). Demanding rights in company-community resource extraction conflicts: Examining the cases of Vedanta and POSCO in Odisha, India. In *Demanding Justice in the Global*

South, ed. J. Grugel, J. N. Singh, L. Fontana, and A. Uhlin. Cham: Palgrave Macmillan, 43–67.

Menon, M., and K. Kohli (2007). Environmental decision-making: Whose agenda? *Economic and Political Weekly* 42(26): 2490–2494.

—— (2015). Environmental regulation in India: Moving 'forward' in the old direction. *Economic and Political Weekly* 50(50): 20–23.

Mishra, R. (2019). Hasdeo Arand forest to be declared elephant reserve. *Hindustan Times*, 23 August. Accessed on 22 December 2021: https://www.pressreader. com/india/hindustan-times-ranchi/20190823/281831465390428.

—— (2020a) Chhattisgarh govt considering extending area of proposed Lemru Elephant Reserve. *Hindustan Times*, 18 June. Accessed on 22 December 2021: https://www.hindustantimes.com/india-news/chhattisgarh-govt-considering-extending-area-of-proposed-lemru-elephant-reserve/story-TDYYe1FgSFfANsjHUu8MYN.html.

—— (2020b). Gram sabhas of Hasdeo Arand area write to PM to stop coal block auction. *Hindustan Times*, 16 June. Accessed on 22 December 2021: https://www.hindustantimes.com/india-news/gram-sabhas-of-hasdeo-arand-area-write-to-pm-to-stop-coal-block-auction/story-W2hn3GGWJh Ioedt4W3PHcN.html.

MoEF (2009). Circular F.No. 11-9/1998-FC: Diversion of forest land for non-forest purposes under the Forest (Conservation) Act, 1980 – ensuring compliance of the Scheduled Tribes and Other Traditional Forest Dwellers (Recognition of Forest Rights) Act, 2006. New Delhi.

—— (2011). Comments of MoEF on draft note for Cabinet Committee on infrastructure regarding making available more coal bearing areas for coal production. New Delhi.

MoTA (2012). *The Scheduled Tribes and Other Traditional Forest Dwellers (Recognition of Forest Rights) Amendment Rules, 2012.* New Delhi.

—— (2014) *Report of the High Level Committee on Socio-Economic, Health and Educational Status of Tribal Communities of India.* New Delhi.

MS, N. (2020). The long battle of Hasdeo Arand residents against the Parsa coal project in Chhattisgarh. *The Caravan*, 24 June. Accessed on 22 December 2021: https://caravanmagazine.in/communities/long-battle-of-hasdeo-arand-residents-against-parsa-coal-project-chhattisgarh.

Nandi, J. (2021). Reserves exhausted early, Chhattisgarh coal mine seeks larger forest area. *Hindustan Times*, 5 March. Accessed on 22 December 2021: https://www.hindustantimes.com/india-news/reserves-exhausted-early-chhattisgarh-coal-mine-seeks-larger-forest-area-101614919495021.html.

National Green Tribunal (2014). *Appeal no. 73/2012*. New Delhi: National Green Tribunal, Government of India.

PIB (2009). Ministries of Coal and Environment & Forests finalise action plan for expediting coal mining project clearance. Press Information Bureau, New Delhi.

PTI (2020). Atma Nirbhar Bharat: PM Modi launches auction process for 41 coal blocks. *Business Today*, 18 June. Accessed on 22 December 2021: https://www.businesstoday.in/sectors/energy/atma-nirbhar-bharat-pm-modi-launches-auction-process-for-41-coal-blocks/story/407290.html.

Ramesh, J. (2015). *Green Signals: Ecology, Growth, and Democracy in India*. New Delhi: Oxford University Press.

———— (2017). *Indira Gandhi: A Life in Nature*. New Delhi: Simon & Schuster.

Randeria, S. (2003a). Cunning states and unaccountable international institutions: Legal plurality, social movements and rights of local communities to common property resources. *European Journal of Sociology* 44(1): 27–60.

———— (2003b). Glocalization of law: Environmental justice, World Bank, NGOs and the cunning state in India. *Current Sociology* 51(3/4): 305–328.

Rights and Resources Initiative (2012) *Deeper Roots of Historical Injustice: Trends and Challenges in the Forests of India*. Washington, DC: Rights and Resources Initiative.

Sampat, P. (2013). Limits to absolute power: Eminent domain and the right to land in India. *Economic and Political Weekly* 48(19): 40–52.

Sarin, M., N. Singh, and R. K. Bhogal (2003). *Devolution as a Threat to Democratic Decision-making in Forestry? Findings from Three States in India*. London: Overseas Development Institute.

Satheesh, S. (2020). Moving beyond class: A critical review of labor-environmental conflicts from the global south. *Sociology Compass* 14(7): 1–14.

Sethi, N. (2015a). Five coal blocks in Chhattisgarh might see land conflict. *Business Standard*, 15 January. Accessed on 22 December 2021: http://www.business-standard.com/article/economy-policy/five-coal-blocks-in-chhattisgarh-might-see-land-conflict-115011500019_1.html.

——— (2015b). PMO ordered 60 changes to green clearances, environment ministry delivered on most. *Business Standard*, 20 January. Accessed on 22 December 2021: https://www.business-standard.com/article/economy-policy/pmo-ordered-60-changes-to-green-clearances-environment-ministry-delivered-on-most-115012001495_1.html.

——— (2016). Chhattisgarh govt cancels tribal rights over forest lands. *Business Standard*, 18 February. Accessed on 22 December 2021: http://www.business-standard.com/article/current-affairs/chhattisgarh-govt-cancels-tribal-rights-over-forest-lands-116021601327_1.html.

Singh, B. K. (2021). *Forest Rights Act: Accelerated Deforestation*. Chennai: Notion Press.

Singh, P. (2020). Chhattisgarh opposes Modi govt on coal block auction, says move to hit elephant reserve plan. *ThePrint*, 23 June. Accessed on 22 December 2021: https://theprint.in/india/chhattisgarh-opposes-modi-govt-on-coal-block-auction-says-move-to-hit-elephant-reserve-plan/447155/.

Sivalingam, N. (2014). *Elephant in the Room*. New Delhi: Greenpeace. Accessed on 22 December 2021: http://www.greenpeace.org/india/Global/india/docs/Elephant report_Final6oct14.pdf.

Sivaramakrishnan, K. (1995). Colonialism and forestry in India: Imagining the past in present politics. *Comparative Studies in Society and History* 37(1): 3–40.

——— (2009). Forests and the environmental history of modern India. *Journal of Peasant Studies* 36(2): 299–324.

Sundar, N. (2011). The rule of law and citizenship in central India: Post-colonial dilemmas. *Citizenship Studies* 15(3–4): 419–432.

The Wire (2020). Allowing coal auction in very dense forest areas will be 'triple disaster': Jairam Ramesh. 20 June. Accessed on 22 December 2021: https://thewire.in/politics/allowing-coal-auction-in-very-dense-forest-areas-will-be-triple-disaster-jairam-ramesh.

Trivedi, V. (2020). Five coal blocks falling in dense forests of Chhattisgarh removed from auction list, 3 new added. News18.com, 7 September. Accessed on 22 December 2021: https://www.news18.com/news/india/five-coal-blocks-falling-in-dense-forests-of-chhattisgarh-removed-from-auction-list-3-new-added-2857457.html.

Upadhyay, V. (2001). Forests, people and courts: Utilising legal space. *Economic and Political Weekly* 36(24): 2131–2134. Accessed on 22 December 2021: http://www.jstor.org/stable/4410744.

Verma, G. (2020). Chhattisgarh minister writes to Centre, seeks removal of 5 coal blocks from auction list. *Indian Express*, 22 June. Accessed on 22 December 2021: https://indianexpress.com/article/india/chhattisgarh-minister-writes-to-centre-seeks-removal-of-5-coal-blocks-from-auction-list-6470278/.

Wal, A. (2015). Chhattisgarh tribals in Delhi with pleas to save their land. *DNA*, 13 January. Accessed on 22 December 2021: http://www.dnaindia.com/india/report-chhattisgarh-tribals-in-delhi-with-pleas-to-save-their-land-2052206.

WTI (2017). *Right of Passage: Elephant Corridors of India*. Edited by V. Menon, S. K. Tiwari, K. Ramkumar, S. Kyarong, U. Ganguly, and R. Sukumar. New Delhi: WIldlife Trust of India.

Xaxa, A. (2017). Beautiful damaged people. *CJP: Defending Human Rights in the Courts and Beyond*, 30 November. Accessed on 22 December 2021: https://cjp.org.in/beautiful-damaged-people.

6

THE WIRE AND CIRCUITS OF RESISTANCE

IMMERSIONS IN THE SLOWNESS OF DEMOCRATIC TIME AND DE-NATURALIZING THE PRESENT

SRINATH JAGANNATHAN
RAJNISH RAI

Jawaharlal Nehru University (JNU) is one of the most important public universities in India and is a site for nurturing critical thought and scholarship. On 9 February 2016, some students had organized a meeting in JNU to protest against the hanging of Afzal Guru, a Kashmiri separatist (*The Hindu*, 2016). Afzal Guru was a Kashmiri who was awarded the death sentence after being convicted of conspiracy to attack the Indian Parliament on 13 December 2001 (Tripathi, 2013). The Indian Supreme Court upheld his death sentence, and he was subsequently hanged on 9 February 2013. Several human rights organizations, activists, and lawyers alleged that Afzal Guru was denied a fair trial, and the police extracted his confessions under duress and torture (Roy, 2013). On the third death anniversary of Afzal Guru, a group of students in JNU had organized a cultural program to voice their dissent against his judicial killing and express their solidarity with the struggle of Kashmiri people (*The Hindu*, 2016). Akhil Bharatiya Vidyarthi Parishad (ABVP), the student wing of the ruling Hindu nationalist political formation, the Bharatiya Janata Party (BJP), protested against the programme organized by the JNU students (Sen, 2016).

Some news channels with leanings towards the BJP's Hindu nationalist politics whipped up a frenzy by repeatedly telecasting the ABVP's allegation that JNU students had shouted anti-national slogans during the protests on 9 February 2016 (Varadarajan, 2016). Rajnath Singh, the Home Minister of

India, tweeted that the students who organized the protest on 9 February 2016 had connections with terror organizations in Pakistan (Sen, 2016). Later, forensic evidence raised serious questions about the veracity of the video footage showing JNU students shouting anti-national slogans and the basis of the Home Minister's tweet. The Home Minister had relied on a parody Twitter account, which resembled the name of a Pakistani terrorist, Hafiz Saeed (Varadarajan, 2016). Despite lack of concrete evidence, the Delhi Police, which functions under the administrative control of the Union Home Ministry, arrested Kanhaiya Kumar, the president of the JNU Student's Union and charged him with sedition (*The Hindu*, 2016).

JNU students, academics from all over the world, civil society organizations, and opposition political parties protested against Kanhaiya Kumar's arrest, even as Kumar himself denied raising any anti-national slogans (Varadarajan, 2016). A few lawyers and a BJP legislator assaulted Kumar when the police were escorting him to the court (Kaushika and Janwalkar, 2016). Serious concerns were raised about the action taken by the state against Kumar (Padmanabhan, 2016). Later, the Delhi Police arrested two more JNU students, Umar Khalid and Anirban Bhattacharya, who were also booked on charges of sedition (*India Today*, 2016). As the protests against the arrests mounted and the police failed to produce evidence against the arrested students, the case against them weakened. In March 2016, the three students arrested for sedition got bail (Mathur, 2016; Sheriff, 2016).

Drawing upon this context, where the state orchestrated the crisis in JNU, we reflect on how the media can offer resistance by questioning violent Hindu nationalism. Chatterjee (2019) contends that the media often channelize questions of justice from the realm of politics to the space of law and end up narrowing the opportunities for the pursuit of justice in the wake of nationalist violence. Chatterjee argues that Hindu nationalism mobilizes law as a space for asserting Hindu supremacy and subordinates law to majoritarian orientations. From a feminist perspective, Bumiller (2009) argues that legal processes of testimony often engender a politics of re-victimization and arrest the possibility of law repairing the injustice and harm caused by the violence inflicted on subjects. As legal processes mobilize the unreliability of the testimonies of witnesses, it may become necessary to re-politicize theatres of law.

Friedland (2002) outlines how gendered metaphors are a part of religious nationalism. Religious nationalist politics draws on images of the womanly materiality of the nation; for instance, Hindu nationalism projects India as Bharat Mata, or Mother India, who needs to be protected from being dishonoured by those who stand against her (Bacchetta, 1999). At the same time, in the name of protecting the womanly materiality of the nation, Hindu nationalists seek to exercise gendered control over women's bodies. Golden (2002) argues that the articulation of the nation as a motherly figure constructs a temporal order, where citizens are constructed as belonging to the time of childhood, who have yet to learn about their relationship with the nation.

Nationalism is also connected to the politics of the present as the nationalist is searching for issues and angsts through which she can enact her presence (Friedland, 2002). An imagination of evil helps the nationalist establish her presence, as the nationalist's energetic violence directed against evil becomes proof of her existence. Derrida (1981) argues that the politics of the present operates within the premise of immediacy and performances that do not immediately appear less authentic. Derrida observes that the present is contingent on that which is absent, which in turn threatens the identity of the present. In this sense, the nationalist figure is contingent on the anti-national figure for her presence and requires the constant reincarnation of the anti-national figure to articulate her own presence.

The Wire is an alternative media organization founded by journalists who have worked for several years within mainstream media spaces (Varadarajan, Bhatia, and Venu, 2015). These journalists felt the need to structure a media organization that breaks free from the traditional models of family-owned, corporate-funded, or advertisement-driven media outlets (Varadarajan, Bhatia, and Venu, n.d.). In 2015, these journalists felt that India was taking a political turn where the dissenting voices were increasingly curbed. They structured a not-for-profit internet-based media platform dependent on voluntary contributions from readers and other public-spirited individuals (*The Wire*, n.d.). *The Wire* is organized around the premise of enabling professional journalistic judgement to overcome censorship from proprietors, politicians, bureaucrats, and market actors. The Foundation for Independent Journalism (FIJ) is a non-profit company that publishes *The Wire*. The bulk of the funding for the functioning of *The Wire* comes from voluntary contributions made by individuals and trusts. As the FIJ is a non-profit company, Indian law mandates that only Indian citizens can make contributions to it. One of the public charitable trusts that have provided large donations for the functioning of *The Wire* is the Independent and Public-Spirited Media Foundation.

Since its inception in 2015, *The Wire* has been constantly dragged into legal battles for its reportage by influential figures connected with Hindu nationalism. To illustrate, Rajeev Chandrashekhar, a Bharatiya Janata Party (BJP) Member of Parliament (MP), filed a defamation suit against *The Wire* for publishing articles questioning his conflict of interest in being a member of the parliamentary committee on defence and investing in private defence manufacturing (*Scroll.in*, 2017). Similarly, Jay Shah, son of Amit Shah, the Union Home Minister, also filed a defamation suit against *The Wire* for publishing an investigative story alleging exponential growth of about 16,000 times of a company co-owned by him after the BJP came to power at the center in 2014 (*Outlook*, 2017). *The Wire* has been a dissenting voice against transgressions of the ruling establishment, and it consistently broke stories of wrongdoings of the ruling dispensation and its sympathizers. Thus, it is useful to examine how *The Wire* covered the JNU episode while advancing public discourse surrounding this crisis.

Given the immersion of JNU students and *The Wire* in acts of dissent, we want to understand two aspects of the JNU crisis in order to outline the possibilities of resistance. First, as Hindu nationalism is embedded in the gendered imagination of articulating the woman's body as always needing protection, we ask whether the politics of resistance adopts alternative discourses of gender and time. Second, as Hindu nationalism is embedded in the politics of the present, we ask whether resistance is articulated through narratives that problematize the imagination of presence. We believe that we can examine these two issues in the context of media coverage of the JNU crisis, as media are spaces filled with the curation of discourses that both hegemonize and outline the possibility of contesting hegemonies (King and de Young, 2008). As mainstream media are often incorporated in the production of hegemonic discourses, we explore whether alternative media can nurture a discursive project of resistance to critique violence produced by the crisis of nationalism.

In this study, we enquire into *The Wire*'s coverage of the JNU crisis and compare it with the coverage of some other media sources. In opening up subversive imaginations, *The Wire* can enable democratic enactments of citizenship that resist the trappings of Hindu nationalism. This study makes two significant contributions, which outline the construction of public spaces that contest nationalist hegemonies. First, we attempt to understand how media-based circuits of resistance can move away from the tropes of consumption to tropes of citizenship and critique Hindu nationalist politics, which produces gendered subordination. Second, we explore how media-based circuits of resistance can problematize imaginations of presence by outlining how presence is a fiction stitched together by intertextual narratives enacted by the state, media, and political actors.

While making these two contributions, we believe that organizational theorists can draw some implications about the possibility of dissent from the organizational practice of *The Wire*. Since *The Wire* is not rooted in proprietorial or other market-based forms of ownership, it enables it to craft reportage that contests majoritarian consensus. The organizational practice of *The Wire* ensures that it is not chasing the aims of state patronage or market hegemony. Consequently, its reportage takes the form of structures of lament, which contain the possibility of awakening a sense of public conscience against majoritarian consensus.

Through our two contributions in this study, we add to conversations in the realm of critical management studies about the intersection of state, citizenship, and violence (Barratt, 2014; Jagannathan and Rai, 2017). Through our analysis of *The Wire*, we indicate that alternative forms of media and witnessing are required to build cultures of democratic attentiveness and hold the state accountable for the majoritarian violences it enacts. These alternative organizational practices of media and witnessing deepen the process of democratic reflection by counteracting hegemonic constructions of gender that are implicit in the violence of majoritarian nationalism.

THEORETICAL FRAMEWORK: NATIONALIST TEMPORALITIES AND THE POLITICS OF PRESENCE

Chatterjee (2019) describes how victims of majoritarian violence in India are often denied justice, as their voices are marginalized in political and legal spaces. In the face of muscular discourses of Hindu nationalism, the media channelize struggles for justice inside the courtroom. Chatterjee contends that the quest for justice has many political angsts, and the displacement of justice to the courtroom transforms the victim's testimony into a narrow, technical inquisition. The victim waits for an extended period to appear in court to narrate the violence that she has witnessed and experienced. The victim's act of bearing witness in the courtroom is punctuated by a sense of loneliness where the defence lawyers confuse and intimidate her.

Within a short span of time, the victim's testimony as a witness is complete, and the court holds her testimony to be unreliable in the face of narrow technical requirements, which frame the facticity of testimony (Chatterjee 2019). Against this inattentive temporality, we argue for the need for a slow, immersed temporality that gives democracy a polyvocal texture. Attentiveness transcends calls for citizen participation in state-making, as managerial frames of state-making circumscribe citizen participation within tropes of appropriate enactments of citizenship (Barratt 2014). Imaginations of the appropriate citizen are mobilized to restrict the dialogical possibility of citizenship, and the citizen is imagined within managerially determined roles that citizens can take (Foucault, 1982). Citizen's participation becomes embedded in the temporalities of democratic inattentiveness as the state's agendas are legitimized by invoking formal mechanisms of participation without the possibility of extended dialogue (Burchell 1996).

Golden (2002) states that the enactment of the nation through inattentive temporalities marginalizes the personal experiences of citizens, and they are inserted into nationalist projects through vertical frames of comradeship. These vertical frames of comradeship imply that some citizens are described as inhabiting an older time and an authentic claim of belonging to the nation (Hasan, 2006). In order to become appropriate citizens, others are required to fashion themselves according to these older and authentic modes of belonging to the nation (Drexler, 2008). In the context of Hindu nationalism, being a Hindu is fashioned as the older and authentic claim of belonging to the nation, and other religious claims of belonging to the nation are violently marginalized. Chopra and Jha (2014) outline how the Hindu nationalist claims have structured violent riots against religious minorities to establish the supremacy of Hindu belonging to the nation. Hindu nationalist presence becomes a project of domination that is impossibly trying to escape the instability of having to rely on religious enemies to define itself (Norris 1987).

Derrida (1981) problematizes the politics of presence by arguing how reality is constituted by contaminations rather than claims of authenticity. According to Derrida, a politics of reality that recognizes contaminations is open to possibilities of reinterpretation and contestation. Such a politics of reality does not rely on pre-decided logics of belonging, and claims of belonging to the nation are no longer the outcome of majoritarian temporalities, which reinvent the glorious past of the nation (Jagannathan and Rai, 2017). Instead, the politics of reinterpretation and contestation implies attentiveness to multiple temporalities, an imagination of cultural times, which are in dialogue with each other, and an openness to the remaking of meanings (Gildersleeve and Kuntz, 2010). The dialogical texture of cultural times rests on practices of the time that transgress the rhythms of modern or nationalist time (May and Thrift, 2001). If the rhythms of nationalist time involve the invocation of enemies, cultural time involves the embracement of difference. India's syncretic culture involving multiple traditions of mysticism, reform, rationality, love, and performative craft and the different imaginations of time inhering in these cultures contain the possibilities of considering India as a lyrical space of difference (Flood, 2009).

Lyricality draws from literary moments of re-imagining social relations, interrupting presence, and raising questions of justice, which refashion social existence (Abbott 2007). It embodies the democratic slowness of time, where the poetry of cultural dialogue provides for layered identities and entanglements to exist (Hope, 2009). The democratic slowness of time provides opportunities for recognizing gender as a site of justice (Turcotte, 2014). Within accelerated experiences of time, where processes of law are seen as being distinct from the process of politics and culture, adequate opportunity does not exist to engage with difference and the specific ways in which women experience violence and justice. Women's experiences of violence are classified under broader categories of violence, which lead to many constraints in women accessing justice (Turcotte, 2014). The democratic slowness of time subverts nationalist temporalities, which repress women's agency. Within nationalist temporalities, the repression of women's agency is articulated as a consequence of the corruption of national culture and the erosion of nationalist consciousness (Bacchetta, 1999).

The nationalist road to gender justice requires the recognition of the time of foreign invasion and culturally undoing the consequences of invasion to regain national consciousness (Bacchetta, 1999). The regaining of nationalist consciousness restores the rights of women and rescues the feminine image of the motherland from cultural decay (Friedland, 2002). In contrast to nationalist temporalities of recognizing and undoing cultural invasion, democratic temporalities call for attention to the deliberate deployment of slowness as a subversion of the dominance of speed (Parkins, 2004). Nationalist consciousness relies on metaphors of natural recognition of hostile figures enabled by media-produced discourses of the nation being under threat (Holzberg, Kolbe, and Zabarowski, 2018). Holzberg and colleagues point out that processes of nationalist consciousness rely on imaginations of national stability being threatened and do not allow time for contemplating on conditions in the political economy that may create tensions for national projects.

The slowness and attentiveness of democratic temporalities subvert the speed of nationalist consciousness by engaging with events in the spirit of dialogue than privileging any imagination of natural interpretations (Parkins, 2004). Within the spirit of dialogue, facts are understood as discursive productions that normalize some social categories as being meaningful (Gildersleeve and Kuntz, 2010). In the sense of dialogue, events are deeply entangled with tropes that seek to order the irrational and the unreasonable (Gildersleeve and Kuntz, 2013). Gildersleeve and Kuntz contend that events do not lend themselves to any authentic or singular imagination of facts but contain multiple meanings and invoke multiple references spread across time and space.

Nationalist interpretations of events run into several paradoxes as they involve the intersection of tropes of abuse and redemption (Jiwani, 2016). Jiwani outlines how several institutions of the nation-state inflict violence on marginalized women, and yet the nation-state claims to give meaning, purpose, and resilience to these women. The nationalist imagination embedded in notions of progress and development fails to notice how facts are not organic artefacts but are generated through discursive effort (Granzow and Dean 2016). In claiming to provide authentic meaning to women's lives, the nationalist imagination seeks to restore the imagination of an authentic culture from the past and structures violence against cultural minorities who are seen as pollutants damaging the nation (Bacchetta, 1999).

METHODS

In this chapter, we situate *The Wire* as a possible site of resistance that awakens a re-imagination of citizenship in a polity where majoritarianism is becoming normal. We adopt the methodological strategy of looking at textual fragments of *The Wire* to understand how *The Wire* narratively inserts itself into contesting the production of the anti-national figure. Besteman (2013) argues that literary fragments move away from straightforward meaning-making processes and outline complex and ambiguous meaning-making processes. Besteman contends that fragments outline the need to respect local stories and problematize any straightforward association between local stories and the historical context in which they are embedded. Jackson (2002) indicates that stories are not merely repositories of individual and social meaning; instead, they contain the negotiation of subjectivities between private and public worlds.

Jackson (2002) contends that the enactment of stories in the public realm is related to conditions through which some plots are rendered as real and recognizable. In this context, we focus on stories published in *The Wire* and contrast them with stories published in other media outlets to understand plays of recognition and themes that connect private and public realms. While these stories occur in the context of the JNU crisis, they are interventions, which are momentary fragments of the crisis. They are not a part of the linear narrative of the crisis, where the state frames some subjects as anti-national actors, several people come out to protest against the state's framing, and, finally, the state grants bail to students whom it had framed. Instead, we focus on narrative fragments that enable us to engage with tensions of recognition, such as themes of gender and presence, which provide us with insights into the contested meaning-making processes.

We read several stories published in *The Wire* and other media outlets between 10 February 2016 and 20 March 2016, where several elements of the JNU crisis played out in the media. In all, we read 1,371 pages of media data while engaging with textual artefacts of the JNU crisis. We decided to engage with a greater focus on some narrative fragments of media data based on two theoretical interests. First, we were interested in fragments, which showed conversations between the private and public realms and how cultural fields of gender and time were implicated in the subjectivities of actors during the JNU crisis. Second, we were interested in fragments, which showed how some versions of reality were more readily accepted and how the media, political actors, and the police collaborated to make some tropes more recognizable than others.

In working with narrative fragments of the JNU crisis, we engage with ten media stories in this study. Six of these stories are from *The Wire*, and four are from other media outlets. We engage in a literary analysis of these stories, where we consider the imaginations they evoke and other imaginations they foreclose. The literary analysis presents possibilities of understanding how texts are embedded in moral imaginations, which signal tropes of redemption and decay (Doyle, 2015). The themes of redemption and decay permeated the JNU crisis and structured numerous social tensions as the state and Hindu nationalist actors contended that JNU students were contributing to the decadence of the nation through seditious acts and the nation could only be redeemed by putting them in their place.

We wrote detailed memos on each of the 10 media stories we had picked up to undertake a literary analysis of these texts. In our memos, we contemplated how each of these stories either pushed the boundaries of the imaginable or foreclosed possibilities of imagination. Through our memos, we wanted to understand the moral universes that the stories constructed to embed them within larger tropes of state action and the journey of the nation. We also wanted to understand whether some stories could subvert tropes of Hindu nationalism and advance alternative imaginations about the nation and citizenship. In our memos, we wrote about the implied imaginations of gender, time, and the politics of the present that the stories hinted at.

In order to reflect on our analytical memos, we engaged in conversations with some journalists, activists, and lawyers. In all, we engaged in conversations with seven journalists, six lawyers, and six activists between January and August 2018. In our conversations, we focused on making sense of the narrative fragments that we were analysing and other aspects of *The Wire*'s coverage of the JNU crisis that could outline possibilities of resistance. We reached out to these 19 informants after reading their public interventions in the JNU crisis and felt that their insights could enable us to make sense of *The Wire*'s coverage of the JNU crisis. Over a period of eight months, we had informal conversations with our informants, where we discussed various aspects of *The Wire*'s coverage of the JNU crisis.

Each of our conversations lasted for nearly an hour. We had at least two to three conversations with each informant. We explained the purpose of our study to them and promised them confidentiality. We have anonymized the details of our informants. We also assured them that they could withdraw from our research at any juncture and we would not use the data provided by them. Our conversations revolved around questions of the nature of public space and media, the possibilities of resistance in the aftermath of the JNU crisis, the ability of *The Wire* to provide solidarity to resistance in its coverage of the JNU crisis, and the capacity of *The Wire* to engage in collective conversations with other media figures to deepen discourses of critique. After these conversations, we again wrote detailed memos reflecting on various issues and themes.

Our informants saw us as individuals who had taken up critical positions against Hindu nationalism in our research and understood us as people who were interested in possibilities of resistance. While one of the authors of this study is an academic working in a public management institute, the other is an erstwhile police officer who has recently transited to academia. Both of us became friends while pursuing our doctoral studies, and we have collaborated on a range of themes, which stand at the intersection of public discourse, state action, organizational enactments of the police, and violence.

While we interviewed 19 informants, we present data provided by 10 informants in this study. The insights provided by these 10 informants are not representative of the data gathered by us, but they embody significant possibilities of *The Wire*'s coverage of the JNU crisis. In engaging with narrative fragments, we are not undertaking an exercise of uncovering objective, neutral or exhaustive knowledge. Instead, we engage in a partial and political reading of events to contest and problematize linear media narratives. Linear media narratives usually comprise tropes of majoritarian violence, political struggle, legal challenge, and some institutional relief. We hope to uncover themes that show how resistance may need to depart from the linearity of these themes to draw from imaginations that deepen practices of citizenship, dissent, public space, and time.

NARRATIVES OF THE ANTI-NATIONAL

We pay attention to two themes to contrast *The Wire*'s coverage of the JNU crisis with the coverage provided by other media outlets. First, we pay attention to questions of gender in *The Wire*'s coverage of the JNU crisis and point out how stories published in *The Wire* unravelled women's political agencies as a part of the struggle against Hindu nationalism and the authoritarianism of the state. We explore the role played by *The Wire*'s coverage in creating a discursive space, where Hindu nationalism's abusive characterization of women could be resisted. Second, we pay attention to how *The Wire*'s coverage contested the politics of presence in which nationalist imaginaries are invested. We explore *The Wire*'s role in outlining that the state's production of the anti-national figure relies on tropes of recognition and believability that are nurtured by mainstream media and Hindu nationalist politics.

GENDER AND THE SLOWNESS OF DEMOCRATIC TIME

The slowness of democratic time is embedded in social capacities to occupy time attentively. Democratic attentiveness involves deliberation and multiple perspectives rather than being guided by nationalism or majoritarianism in arriving at quick political positions. In foregrounding gender as a frame for witnessing the entanglement of authority with democratic processes, the media can slow down the frame of authority. By slowing down the frame of authority, we imply ways in which political and cultural processes can question authority structures, force authority structures to respond to issues, and prevent authority structures from leveraging conditions of crisis to claim the need for enforcing emergency actions. Gendered forms of witnessing can focus on questions of love, solidarity, and resistance, which are not bound by state authority. Women often experience the state as a regulatory force that is antithetical to their concerns and can form bonds of solidarity with others who resist the state. In contrast to the gendered figure poetically contesting injustice, state authority can become bound up with the trope of moral horror about nationalism being under siege and the need to purge anti-national traitors immediately.

In the immediate aftermath of the crackdown on JNU, Jahnavi Sen (2016), a reporter with *The Wire*, gave space to women's concerns in leading the protest against state crackdown:

Women's organisations, including the All India Democratic Women's Association, the All India Progressive Women's Associations, ANHAD, and the Pragatisheel Mahila Sangathan, have also issued a statement in support of the JNU students and teachers.

We in no uncertain terms register our strong protest against the highly derogatory observations made by senior Haryana Government functionary Jawahar Yadav, a close associate of the Chief Minister and former OSD and current chairperson of Haryana Housing Board against women students of JNU who are involved in political protests.

Yadav had earlier tweeted that women protestors were worse than prostitutes.

Sen paid attention to women's concerns while reporting the abuses hurled against them. Sen's attentiveness extended a deliberative space that was not trapped in the language of panic and fear that the BJP government wanted to produce. The attentiveness to gender implied imaginations of critique that could break away from nationalist rhetoric and advance an insistence for re-imagining the nation as a site of gendered democracy.

An academic who had followed the JNU crisis remarked on the importance of Sen's attentiveness to gender:

In Sen's reporting, you will find several elements that outline the stillness of time. There are several photographs in black and white. The use of black and white slows downtime in contrast to the modernist velocity of colour. There are pasts and futures, which are being invoked. In addition, most of Shome Basu's photographs that accompany Sen's reportage show the bodies of protestors from close proximity. The proximity produces an intimacy filled with hope and solidarity for the idea of citizenship. There is a particularly striking photograph where women protestors are holding their hands even as they are walking ahead. The presence of so many women holding their hands gives courage and shows that the police action has miserably failed in producing any sense of fear. The women's faces are calm, resilient, and cheerful, in contrast to the men who are leading nationalist mobs. (Interview, Mumbai, 10 February 2018)

The academic's analysis indicates how attentiveness to women's participation in political protests in the public sphere counteracted the political atmosphere of fear that the BJP government wanted to create. Fear operates within tropes of suddenness and the inability to think and collectively reflect on the poetry of social life. *The Wire*'s witnessing of the collective mobilization of the female body produces a sense of calm, safety, and the reclamation of public space as a deliberative sphere.

On the same day of 14 February 2016, when Jahnavi Sen's reportage was published in *The Wire*, the *Indian Express*, which was regarded by many as having carried reasonably liberal and critical coverage of government actions during the JNU crisis, carried three reports about JNU in its front page. One of these reports focused on conveying the police version of the crisis and resorted to quoting police sources to convey official interpretations of the events at JNU.

Alok Singh (2016) conveyed these tropes of national security by quoting uncritically from a letter written by the Deputy Commissioner of Police (DCP):

'The matter needs probe regarding the links between the JNU students and terrorist Afzal Guru as the students were against the sentence of Afzal Guru', the DCP's letter stated.

In contrast to Sen's reportage, which focused on reflection and created an atmosphere of deliberation around the JNU incidents, Singh's reporting advances the trope of nationalist crisis. In adopting a police lens towards reporting, Singh creates the imagery of national crisis as he presents how students might be complicit in terror. While adopting the mask of neutrality in merely conveying the contents of a police document, Singh fails to refer to any actors who might have been critical of the police version of events.

The *Indian Express* carried another report on 14 February 2016, which, while outlining statements of opposition leaders condemning the government action, used language to characterize the government action as being energetic (*Indian Express*, 2016):

> Minister of State for Home Kiren Rijiju too took a firm stand: 'We can't allow JNU to be a hub of anti-national activities…. This was an unfortunate incident. But these are not small kids who don't know what they do. In the name of freedom of speech, you can't abuse the nation.'

In describing Rijiju's stand as being firm, the report characterizes government action as having a strong sense of conviction. Rather than reporting the opposition's protest as advancing a deliberative sphere, such a position reduces the opposition leaders' voices to a discourse that fails to measure up to the solidity of governmental action. The 'firmness' of Rijiju's stand adds weight to the nationalist horror of the decay of the university and the transformation of students into anti-national elements.

In contrast to the other two reports, the third report of the *Indian Express* appeared to take a more critical stance, as it documented the humble roots of Kanhaiya's family (S. Singh 2016):

> Kanhaiya's mother, Meena Devi, puts on a brave face. 'This phase will pass…. Nothing shall happen to my son because he can never say or do anything against the country…. There is a court. I have full faith in my son and God.' An anganwadi worker, she supports the family with her earnings of Rs. 3,000 a month – the eldest of three sons also works.

The report describes the vulnerable conditions in which Kanhaiya's family lives. In describing the vulnerable conditions, the report creates a picture of victimhood and equates vulnerability with innocence and belongingness to the nation.

An activist lawyer described the differences between the reportage of *The Wire* and a mainstream outlet such as the *Indian Express*:

> When the *Indian Express* presented issues of gender, such as the vulnerability of Kanhaiya's mother, rather than showing the agency of women, it painted them as weak and helpless victims. Whereas when *The Wire* documented women's role in the JNU protests, it showed them as active agents who raised their voice against the government. Weakness, fear, and anxiety show the vulnerability of civil society. On the other hand, resistance and struggle show hope, possibility, and the creative direction of energies. There were other differences as well. While the *Indian Express* merely reported the police version, such as there being a terror angle, *The Wire* raised questions about the nature of evidence. While the *Indian Express* reported the assertions of government ministers without questioning them, *The Wire* raised important questions about ministers' claims. By raising questions, *The Wire* expanded the scope of civil society. (Interview, Delhi, 9 April 2018)

As the activist points out, the role played by *The Wire* expanded the public sphere and challenged the government's position. In challenging the government's position, *The Wire* slowed down the processes through which the government wanted to acquire legitimacy for its actions. In discursively advancing women's voices throughout its coverage of the JNU crisis, *The Wire* structured a counterpoint to nationalist hysteria by outlining how such hysteria was complicit in gendered forms of abuse and humiliation.

In order to contest cultures of abuse and humiliation, *The Wire* also published articles of people who reflected on their experiences in JNU. Anupam Pandey (2016), an academic teaching in Canada and a JNU alumna, reflected on her experiences in JNU in an article published in *The Wire*:

Sometime in the late 1990s, violence and sexual harassment against women increased significantly, not on campus but on the deserted roads and in the woods encircling it, where we would go for walks and jogs. I myself was involved in one of several such instances when a drunken motorbike rider sexually assaulted me.

In keeping with the issue of safety and security of women students on campus, the matter was taken to the VC by the political parties on campus. I was also asked to present my story as a critical case in point to the VC. He was deeply sympathetic and stated in no uncertain terms that he would ask for greater police protection along the deserted ring road for the safety of women students. I approved of the VC's promise. But it came as a rude shock to me that the female political party members and activists who had taken me with them to spearhead their campaign reprimanded me for supporting the VC's decision. They were unequivocal that I had greatly jeopardised women's security by inviting more uniformed personnel on campus. This would have severe long-term consequences that I had not considered. I countered the argument by asking whether they felt that women's security would be beefed up by putting up posters and writing slogans along the ring road. When I look back now, at my stand of 20 years ago and theirs, I see the urgency of my youthful 'problem-solving' approach clashing with the wisdom of their caution.

Pandey's article shows the tension between gender dilemmas, the urgency of problem-solving, and state intervention. It outlines how state interventions quicken the response to urgent situations but create long-term climates of surveillance, censorship, and the erosion of deliberative spaces. Particularly, while responding to gendered violence, it becomes necessary to move away from the urgency and participate in slow practices of time, as urgency obscures more profound questions of politics and agency.

A journalist commented on *The Wire*'s coverage of the JNU crisis:

I liked the Wire because it gave voice to commentaries about people and their memories of JNU. These memories took us away from the pace of everyday events and revealed what JNU meant to women's experiences and their voices. This significantly counteracted the stereotype of alcohol, drugs, and sex used to drown women's voices into silence. (Interview, Delhi, 11 April 2018)

The journalist outlines how *The Wire*'s coverage helped in transporting public discourse to an alternative time. JNU was not articulated merely as a space caught in the warps of an immediate crisis. On the contrary, JNU was described as space and experience that grew slowly with time, allowing multiple and contradictory reflections on voice and politics.

Another academic pointed out elements of *The Wire*'s coverage that were important:

The Wire also covered acts of violence inflicted on people protesting against government action in other parts of the country. Lawyers in Allahabad had disrupted protests by people. These lawyers also beat women protestors and threatened them with rape. If the meaning of nationalism is to rape women who protest against some political ideas and government action, what is the use of such nationalism? (Interview, Mumbai, 3 May 2018)

Amid the JNU crisis, the street had become a space where Hindu nationalist forces invoked violence to marginalize the possibility of protest and dissent. The threats of rape outlined the willingness of Hindu nationalists to materialize anti-national fantasies in women's bodies and transform their bodies into objects of anger and hate. *The Wire* constructed public discourses of the street becoming a space of gendered violence by uncovering these violent discourses.

An activist who worked on women's issues pointed out how *The Wire*'s coverage of different events during the JNU crisis foregrounded issues of gender:

Several news agencies merely covered events as they were occurring during the JNU crisis. Events have a speed of their own. People can become unthinkingly lost at this speed. For instance, Umar Khalid, one of the students who had been accused of sedition, had gone away for more than a week. He then returned after some time to JNU and made himself available to the probe that the police had instituted. Almost all media houses covered Khalid's return to JNU. However, *The Wire* contextualized Khalid's return in the backdrop of threats of violence that had been made against his family, particularly threats of sexual violence against his sisters. We must remember that Khalid had only been accused of sedition; he had not been charged with terrorism. Even if Khalid had committed a terrorist act, what kind of a nation would want to rape the sisters of a man who had done wrong? A nation that needs to rape a woman is clearly a nation that is formed by hatred against women at its core. (Interview, Delhi, 10 April 2018)

By foregrounding questions of gender associated with the turn of events in the JNU crisis, *The Wire* created narrative idioms that transgressed the sheer speed of events. *The Wire* compelled readers to see connections about the ease with which nationalist righteousness co-habited with the language of gendered violence. *The Wire* contributed to building a layered narrative of the JNU crisis where questions of democracy and justice were not overwhelmed by the velocities of nationalist anger and police action.

INTERRUPTING DISCOURSES OF PRESENCE

On the one hand, the media can denaturalize presence in imagining radical futures. These radical futures can draw from understanding the past as a field of conflicts. They can also cast presence as fiction, which binds actors to plots structured by authoritarian discourses.

In an interview with Shehla Rashid, one of the student leaders who led the student movement, Akhil Kumar, the multimedia editor at *The Wire* and a correspondent, asked (A. Kumar 2016), 'How has the response of your family been? Are your persons supportive of your struggle here at JNU?'

Akhil Kumar's questions interrupt the imagination of the family as a supportive presence. They privilege the idea of struggle as being necessary for imagining a society premised on justice. In this context, Akhil Kumar is trying to understand the family's role in sustaining the politics of struggle. Rashid's response to Akhil Kumar's question opens up a reflective conversation about the role of the family (A. Kumar 2016):

> In the initial days that this issue came up, the students in this university from across the country started getting calls from their parents asking why they were conducting such anti-national events. This happened because of the biased media coverage. All parents have been advising their children to stay away from students' politics, but defying their parents' advice, students have come out in huge numbers to participate in this movement. I am dealing with a similar situation at home.

In her interview with *The Wire*, Rashid points out how students rebel against their parents' advice of becoming apolitical actors. In becoming political actors against their parents' advice, students demonstrate the necessity of rebelling against intimate forms of authority. They interrupt the imagination of love as parental presence and imagine a new form of love that is based on the solidarity of citizenship.

There were voices in the mainstream media, which were pursuing a similar project of interrupting presence. Ravish Kumar, who works with NDTV India, played an iconic role in covering the JNU protests. In one of the episodes in his primetime show, Ravish Kumar (2016) speaks to a woman student participating in a protest and asks her, 'So when you speak to people in your home, what do they tell you? Many problems emerge from home. We should discuss these issues more.'

Ravish Kumar chronicles the participation of a woman student in the JNU struggle and interrupts the presence of parental anxieties about their children's involvement in the political struggle. We argue that the political activist is a situated figure who mobilizes a civic space that weaves angsts against multiple absences, such as that of justice, romance, equality, and militant citizenship. In Ravish Kumar's (2016) coverage of the protest, the woman student replied to him and said, 'Apparently, people in my home don't want me to participate in the struggle. They want me to focus on my studies.' Ravish Kumar (2016) persisted, 'And, what is their opinion about the entire controversy? What do they advise you?' The woman student replied, 'They say that they are with us. What is happening is wrong. Our sympathies are with you. But don't go to the protests.' Ravish Kumar's exchange with the students chronicles how the presence of the family shapes conformist practices of citizenship. Ravish Kumar's conversations show how students escape the conformist presence of the family to enact a new imagination of citizenship. The students enact citizenship as a culture of collective protest against nationalist hegemonies being structured by the state.

The Wire provided an opportunity to transform journalistic practice into a civic space of solidarity by chronicling subversive journalistic narratives that actors like Ravish Kumar were building. Chitra Padmanabhan (2016) published an interview with Ravish Kumar in *The Wire*, outlining how media coverage of the JNU crisis was eroding the practice of citizenship. She wrote about how Ravish Kumar's journalism offered an opportunity to witness the transformation of the citizen into a subject of hate:

> And then the anchor vanished from the screen, asking viewers to listen and reflect on whether they wanted to be part of the terrible world that he and his fraternity create day after day.... Released from the snare of the image, one could finally hear with a sense of mounting horror the ugly reality of hatred and violence dripping from the voices – anchors as well as speakers.

Padmanabhan builds elements of reflection in her piece. Through her reflection, she attempts to distance journalistic practice from being entrapped in the imagination of presence. We believe that reflection offers a critical romantic gesture in mourning and lamenting presence and making a call for alternative futures.

An academic commented on the nature of the JNU crisis and *The Wire*'s role in covering it:

> The government needed the label of sedition. The personalisation of the seditionist serves a specific purpose. It is not the purpose of the nation being in crisis. It is the horror of ungratefulness. If you look at a journalist like Arnab Goswami and the hostile way in which he engaged with a student like Umer Khalid on national television, Goswami is essentially telling Khalid that he is an ungrateful figure. The

Indian state has subsidised Khalid's higher education, and yet Khalid has no gratitude for the state. In many ways, the Wire's coverage paid attention to this politics of gratitude. The Wire paid attention to the micro-realities of the family and power relations that govern our lives. (Interview, Mumbai, 25 May 2018)

We believe that journalism premised around the culture of gratitude erases the possibility of questions from the realm of public space. The imagination of public space is contingent on people's abilities to break free from reciprocities of gratitude. Public space outlines social relations of courage and angst, which question the legitimacy of gratitude and the possibility of asking questions that can unsettle prevailing contracts of gratitude.

A journalist pointed out how *The Wire*'s coverage built references between journalists and infused the coverage of the JNU crisis with the energy of craft culture:

When you read the interview between Chitra Padmanabhan and Ravish Kumar, you get a scent of a craft. In their discussion about patriarchy, they ask how anchors are speaking in patriarchal tones to produce a passive audience. They wonder how Indian men can relate to these anchors and how Indian men talk to women in their families mirror how anchors speak to the audience. Through these discussions, the Wire produces journalistic craft as conversations that challenge how state and masculine authority are enmeshed in each other. (Interview, Mumbai, 12 March 2018)

We contend that reflective conversations such as the one between Padmanabhan and Kumar outline the possibility of craft to complicate questions of presence. The mainstream media produced discourses of the seditious and ungrateful subject who was guilty of not understanding memories of sacrifice that went into building the nationalist imagination of India. Through their conversation, Padmanabhan and Kumar moved away from being trapped within the presence of seditious guilt and outlined ways in which the discourse was anchored around the imagination of masculine authority.

The imagination of presence is centred around the idea of rational choice. The media coverage of an incident in the JNU crisis outlines how rationalization of personhood leads to privileging presence as a factual anchor of life. Amidst the JNU crisis, a journalist resigned from a media outlet, Zee News, accusing it of manufacturing hatred by distorting the role played by JNU students. The *Hindustan Times* (2016), a leading Indian newspaper, carried a story with the headline 'Journalist resigns from news channel over JNU coverage' (*Hindustan Times*, 2016). The *Hindustan Times* headline presents the journalist as exercising a professional choice emerging from his disagreement with the editorial policies of Zee News.

On the other hand, *The Wire* (2016) published the entire letter the journalist had written to Zee News under the headline 'Zee News journalist quits in disgust over JNU coverage, tells all in letter'. *The Wire's* headline de-emphasizes the frame of rational choice, and professional disagreement emphasizes a discourse of affective angst. Within boundaries of rational choice, actors make a reasoned choice of the action they want to pursue. *The Wire* describes the journalist as being overwhelmed by the sense of disgust, a situation where the journalist's self overflows with dissent, and the journalist quits Zee News as an act of protest, not knowing where the protest is going to lead him. *The Wire* does not describe the protest as a premeditated act in the hope of some tangible outcome but as an act of dissent anchored in the ethical responsibility of citizenship. In the caption following the headline, the article in *The Wire* describes the resignation in the following terms: 'In a moving letter of resignation from Zee News, journalist Vishwa Deepak accuses the channel of "toeing the government's line" on JNU and "pushing towards ruin the careers, dreams, and families of several students."' *The Wire's* referencing of the resignation as a moving document transforms the textuality of the journalist's letter into an act of affective dissent. In publishing the full letter and unravelling the themes of 'bias in the newsroom', 'wilful distortion of JNU story', and 'unleashing the mob', *The Wire* outlines how resistance may be embedded in lyrical angsts that are committed to radical futures. Later, in line with Vishwa Deepak's assertion, a committee of forensic experts commissioned by the Delhi government found that videos purportedly carrying anti-national slogans raised by JNU students had been doctored and fabricated (Deshmane and Vishnoi, 2016).

An academic outlined how *The Wire*'s coverage embodied a lament about the degeneration of social spaces:

> In the JNU crisis, *The Wire* offered a space where we could lament the erosion of citizenship. *The Wire* made us feel that these were young students, and the state was ruining their lives by labelling them as villains to satisfy the quest for power of the Prime Minister and the BJP. *The Wire* made us reflect on what was missing in our politics and society. We lacked any sense of empathy for young people, their pursuit of scholarship, and a politics of justice. (Interview, Delhi, 12 April 2018)

The academic points out how *The Wire* moved away from a politics of presence to literary textuality of lament, mourning of the many absences that constitute social life. The reproduction of Vishwa Deepak's entire resignation letter is a part of this literary textuality, which urges readers to reflect with a sense of conscience while engaging with the turn of events in JNU. The act of reproducing is an invitation to readers to pay attention to acts of conscience in un-annotated and unabridged ways.

One of the founder editors of *The Wire*, Siddharth Varadarajan (2016), interrupted the toxic ways in which the mainstream media was articulating the presence of JNU students as anti-national figures by highlighting how several media houses had been broadcasting doctored video clips of a JNU student leader, Kanhaiya Kumar. Varadarajan wrote in his article:

> Those of us who tried to look for evidence of these grave charges against him, instead, discovered a vibrant young man who is anything but the 'anti-national' of the Home Minister's description ... he has the wisdom and political skill to ... channel their demand for azadi into the wider struggles for dignity of the people of India. His azadi is the freedom for which all of India's people yearn: azadi from hunger, azadi from feudalism, azadi from communalism.
>
> Goswami [the then editor of Times Now, a prominent news channel] can clearly be heard repeatedly asking Patra [a BJP spokesperson] (from 22:50' onwards) to 'show the video, show the video.' When Patra shows it, he orders the Times Now camera to zoom in on it. 'Show the video

close by,' says Goswami. After the forgery is aired, Goswami declares triumphantly, 'I can clearly hear him say, if that is indeed him in the video, I can clearly hear him say "leke rahenge aazadi".' He then turns to a guest, Anand Kumar from JNU, and says, 'If this video is correct, what are you going to say now?'

As ABP News pointed out on Thursday, this clip is an edited version of the original clip we saw at the beginning of this article. Kanhaiya's call for azadi from *bhukhmari, samantvad, sanghvad,* etc. has been cleverly converted into a call for Kashmir's azadi – something he never said.

Varadarajan chronicles how a mainstream news channel, Times Now, and its editor, Arnab Goswami, resorted to fabricating evidence to stir up hate against JNU students. One of the spokespersons of the BJP, Sambit Patra, played a key role in purveying the fabrication as Times Now used him as a narrative device to show the distorted clips of Kanhaiya Kumar. Varadarajan's article shows how images of presence, articulated as unchallenged facts, are carefully curated works of fiction, co-produced by politicians, media, and the state.

A lawyer articulated the importance of positions taken by *The Wire*:

When I first heard about the incident in JNU and saw television reports, I believed them. I thought that the students were chanting these slogans for the dismemberment of India. Of course, I did not feel that any legal action was warranted against them. These were just slogans, and the students were entitled to air their political opinions. I tried to reason with people around me. I told a rickshaw driver what is wrong with what the students said. You look at the way police harass poor people. The military and the police similarly harass people in Kashmir. What is wrong with raising slogans? It was only when other news channels and the Wire pointed out the fabrication that I began to question how our beliefs and truths are shaped by forgery, fiction, and deceit. All this while, I had been defending something which had not even occurred. (Interview, Delhi, 21 May 2018)

The lawyer's statement outlines how presence is not embedded in any claims of authentic reality but is an outcome of the politics of believability. The media as a deliberative space, which produces the conditions of believability and presence, emerges as complex stitching together of political positions that produce hegemonic realities. Presence is an imagined form of reality that appears to be the only plausible explanation of events due to the consolidation of hegemonic positions.

In his article, Varadarajan (2016) carries forward the tradition of lament, as he mourns the degeneration of journalism into a practice that nurtures the politics of hate:

> There is no criminal law that readily applies to the journalists who for the past ten days have engaged in the character-assassination of Kanhaiya Kumar, putting his very life in danger. Some of them have sons and daughters who are Kanhaiya's age, and yet felt not a twinge of guilt in feeding a young man to rabid dogs. Let our contempt for them be their punishment. They are a disgrace to journalism – and to India.

Varadarajan's anger against journalists militates against the presentation of Kanhaiya Kumar as an anti-national figure in public space. Varadarajan contends that the production of the anti-national figure involves a loss of intimacy with the subject, an act of distancing, where even the subject's loss of life is no longer considered to be an important issue. The act of distancing is immersed in producing the presence of the anti-national figure as a fantasy, as an image of evil, which nationalist politics is pitted against.

An activist working with riot victims and police encounter victims pointed out these elements of fantasy that *The Wire* was contesting:

> The attack against JNU was the attack against the thinking citizen. The citizen's ability to think and the question was being destroyed. The BJP attacked JNU because it wanted to label the very idea of scholarship as anti-national. It wanted to label sociology, literature, history, philosophy, and political science as anti-national. The BJP created a fantasy that if you became invested in such scholarship, you became anti-national. In reality, the anti-national figure did not exist. I mourn the fact that the anti-national figure did not exist. What is the nation? A nation where the Babri Masjid is demolished in 1992, where riots frequently occur

against Muslims, where terrible riots occurred against Sikhs in 1984, such a nation needs to be rebelled against. But such a rebellion and the anti-national figure do not exist. So the BJP had to invent a fantasy to pursue its politics of hate. (Interview, Delhi, 20 May 2018)

In several ways, presence is a fantasy anchored around making some illusions look so real that people find it uncomfortable to question its premise. The Wire's journalism of lament provided an opportunity to question the demonization of university students. We believe that the students were labelled as 'anti-nationals' to advance the fantasy of Hindu nationalism as a noble idea. Hindu nationalism could be validated within a politics of presence only by perpetually presenting a few as hostile figures. By presenting the intellectual as an anti-national figure, Hindu nationalism's popular muscularity aimed to curb any practice of dissent and critique and bind the intellectual to a culture of celebratory majoritarianism.

DISCUSSION: DEEPENING THE PRACTICE OF WITNESSING

We discuss The Wire's coverage of the JNU crisis to explore the themes of gendered temporalities and the problematization of the politics of presence. In its coverage of the JNU crisis, we find that The Wire focuses on women's protests against the abuse and the humiliation heaped on them by actors speaking in the name of Hindu nationalism (Sen, 2016). Hindu nationalist discourse is immersed in producing anxieties about the nation passing through temporalities of decay, and the sexualities of women are shown to be diseases that threaten the moral order of the nation (Bacchetta, 1999). In the Derridean (1981) sense of presence, majoritarian nationalism is contingent on articulating crisis and anxieties for justifying its relevance. The articulation of women's sexualities as nationalist decay encodes women's bodies as sites for observing the preserving nationalist culture (Friedland 2002). The horror of nationalist decay is used to produce the insertion of women's bodies into predictable temporalities and signify the production of future sexualities as the continuation of a regulated and cherished past (Zhang, 2015).

The Wire's coverage of women's protests resists incorporating women as cultural symbols who signify the reproduction of a cherished past into the future. We argue that gender is an important site for resisting Hindu nationalism, and when the media pay attention to questions of gender, they enable the possibility of resistance by advancing subversive conjectures about temporality and the project of the nation. One of the ways in which Hindu nationalism operates is to narrow the frames through which people witness majoritarian violence (Chatterjee 2019). Media coverage of women's collective protests against abusive forms of Hindu nationalism interrupts the common sense of Hindu nationalism being a discourse of cultural pride and nationalist resilience (Bacchetta, 1999).

Interrupting the sensibility of Hindu nationalism's association with cultural pride evokes discourses of cultural lament, where tropes of mourning are activated against discourses of nationalist violence (Jagannathan and Rai 2017). Lament structures the agency of the marginalized in raising subversive questions about the status quo and provides space for the articulation of dissent in resisting regimes of injustice (Zidjaly, 2017). We contend that lament deepens cultural possibilities of witnessing by framing experiences of events within intertextual imaginations of time. Kristeva (1980) describes intertextuality as the process through which all texts can be understood as dialogues between previous texts and anticipated future usages. In this sense, texts do not have any sovereignty of their own.

Texts are temporal dialogues between previous contexts and the political futures they encode (Kristeva 1980). The imagination of intertextuality helps problematize the solidity of presence, as presence is contingent on selective invocations of pasts and futures and has no truth claim by itself (Derrida, 1981). As Chatterjee (2019) points out, people's capacities for witnessing and bearing testimony are classified as unreliable when witnessing is understood merely as a legal act that re-narrates an event that occurred in a specific time and place, without paying heed to the intertextuality of specificity itself. *The Wire*'s coverage of gendered protests in the context of the JNU crisis provides a template for going beyond the legal imagination of witnessing and situates witnessing as a temporal dialogue that slows down the velocity of nationalist and authoritarian interpretations.

The Wire builds a complex network of dialogical textualities in its coverage of the JNU crisis. The coverage of women's protests (Sen, 2016) is supplemented by a JNU alumna's memories of the need to subvert the speed of urgent problem-solving (Pandey, 2016). *The Wire* also published interviews with women leaders of the student's movement in JNU (A. Kumar 2016) and referenced the work of other journalists (Padmanabhan, 2016) who were interrogating social structures that informed the unconscious of the mainstream media's willingness to become the propaganda machinery of Hindu nationalism. *The Wire* also published the dissenting resignation of a journalist who quit from a television channel after being disturbed by the slant in its coverage in declaring students to be anti-national figures (*The Wire*, 2016). It also intervened in calling out television channels and journalists who were purveying fabricated videos and mourned the lack of empathy for young students whose lives were being endangered by portraying them as anti-national figures (Varadarajan, 2016).

We argue that these aspects of *The Wire*'s coverage build the possibility of reflective citizenship and slow, democratic temporality (Hope, 2009; Parkins, 2004) that moves away from the velocity of mainstream media. *The Wire*'s coverage of women's protests (Sen, 2016) traces the genealogy of Hindu nationalism as being steeped in the past and future that merely frames women's bodies as objects of nationalist piety and consequently imagines women's political agency within the texture of the contaminable (Bacchetta, 1999). *The Wire*'s act of publishing Pandey's (2016) memories of her existence in JNU and the need to avoid frames of urgent problem-solving deepen the gaze of witnessing by building an intertextual reference to memories, which outline tensions between agencies of the police and citizenship. The weakening of social capacities of resistance is also shown in the tensions between the family structures and the possibility of resistance that a student leader articulates in an interview published in *The Wire* (A. Kumar, 2016). Chitra Padmanabhan's (2016) interview with Ravish Kumar adds another layer of witnessing by situating conversations as a craft critique of the media's production of sound and image.

Craft critique produces witnessing as an act of solidarity and conversational solace between craftspeople who are disturbed by the entrapment of the media in the velocity of industrial rhythms and profits

(Ghimire and Upreti, 2014). Both Vishwa Deepak's (*The Wire*, 2016) letter of resignation and Varadarajan's (2016) calling out of media fabrications advance the culture of lament, which situates witnessing within the contours of public expressions of grief and mourning. These expressions of lament question the tragic consequences of the politics of presence within which nationalist hysteria plays out (Friedland, 2002). We argue that *The Wire* shifts the practice of witnessing from the frame of legal reliability to feminist practices of life that question the articulation of women's bodies within the imagination of the contaminable; the feminist questioning of the politics of urgency and tensions with prevailing family structures; the craft politics of discontent with the aesthetics of nationalist hysteria and populism; and the politics of lament which mourns the coercive and fictional production of the anti-national figure. We contend that such a politics of witnessing transforms acts of viewing and interpreting events away from the fiction of honest truths (Chatterjee, 2019) to layered explorations of gender, subversion of urgency, building spaces for discontent, and cultures of lament.

We argue that the politics of witnessing based on nuanced lenses of gender, craft, and lament embed witnessing as a reflective act that deepens the possibilities of citizenship, hope, solidarity, and justice. We believe that by explicating themes of gendered temporalities and subversion of the politics of presence that permeate *The Wire*'s coverage of the JNU crisis, we are outlining two ways in which media texts can embed themselves in circuits of resistance. First, the attention to gendered temporalities can explicate inter-temporal dialogue that deepens the witnessing of events and prevents events from being signified solely in terms of fear and hate that constitute the tropes of majoritarian nationalism. Second, the subversion of the politics of presence invokes the imagination of citizenship as encompassing subjectivities of grief, discontent, and lament and posits the citizen as a questioning and grieving figure in search of justice.

CONCLUSION

In this study, we have relied on narrative fragments of *The Wire*'s coverage of the JNU crisis to outline the possibilities of resistance. We have shown that reading events from a gendered lens has the potential to problematize the normality of the temporal experience of majoritarian nationalism. *The Wire*'s focus on gendered narratives of the JNU crisis interrupts the experience of nationalist time as a process of inquisition. Similar to other majoritarian nationalisms, Hindu nationalism is embedded in the politics of constructing women's bodies as a site of virginal piety.

In this study, we have argued that there are deep linkages between the marginalization of gender and the legitimacy of Hindu nationalism. In imagining women's sexual agency as the premise of nationalist decay, Hindu nationalism inserts itself into a temporality of arresting decay. The temporality of inquisition then collapses into an inquisition of the woman's body. In drawing on these gendered nuances in its coverage of the JNU crisis, *The Wire* problematizes the velocity of inquisition and provides energy to a temporality of witnessing.

The Wire's coverage of the JNU crisis alludes to the possibility of a multi-layered, intertextual sensibility of witnessing. Witnessing emerges as a slow, democratic act of reflection that pays attention to the construction of gender and departs from the fictionality of presence. The witnessing of an event spans layers of gendered imagination, memory, craft, discontent, critique of social structures, and lament. Such a multilayered act of witnessing resists tropes of reliability as an index of truth claims and instead produces a discursive scape informed by a sense of grief and craft-based discontent.

REFERENCES

Abbott, A. (2007). Against narrative: A preface to lyrical sociology. *Sociological Theory* 25(1): 67–99.

Bacchetta, P. (1999). Militant Hindu nationalist women reimagine themselves. *Journal of Women's History* 10(4): 125–147.

Barratt, E. (2014). Bureaucracy, citizenship, governmentality: Towards a re-evaluation of new labour. *Ephemera* 14(2): 263–280.

Besteman, C. (2014). Refuge fragments, fragmentary refuge. *Ethnography* 15(4): 426–445.

Bumiller, K. (2009). *In an Abusive State: How Neoliberalism Appropriated the Feminist Movement against Sexual Violence*. Durham: Duke University Press.

Burchell, G. (1996). Liberal government and the techniques of the self. In *Foucault and Political Reason*, ed. A. Barry, T. Osborne, and N. Rose. London: UCL Press, 267–282.

Chatterjee, M. (2019). Against the witness: Hindu nationalism and the law in India. *Law, Culture and the Humanities* 15(1): 172–189.

Chopra, S. and P. Jha (2014). *On Their Watch: Mass Violence and State Apathy in India*. New Delhi: Three Essays.

Derrida, J. (1981). *Dissemination*. Trans. Barbara Johnson. Chicago: University of Chicago Press.

Deshmane, A. and A. Vishnoi (2016). JNU videos doctored: Forensic report; Smriti Irani's aide Shilpi Tiwari under lens. *Economic Times*, 3 March. Accessed on 9 November 2018: https://economictimes.indiatimes.com/news/ politics-and-nation/jnu-videos-doctored-forensic-report-smriti-iranis-aide- shilpi-tewari-under-lens/articleshow/51232360.cms.

Doyle, B. (2015). The postapocalyptic imagination. *Thesis Eleven* 131(1): 99–113.

Drexler, E. F. (2008). *Aceh, Indonesia: Securing the Insecure State*. Philadelphia: University of Pennsylvania State.

Flood, F. B. (2009). *Objects of Translation: Material Culture and Medieval Hindu– Muslim Encounter*. Princeton: Princeton University Press.

Friedland, R. (2002). Money, sex, and god: The erotic logic of religious nationalism. *Sociological Theory* 20(3): 381–425.

Foucault, M. (1982). The subject and power. In *Michel Foucault: Beyond Structuralism and Hermeneutics*, ed. H. L. Dreyfus and P. Rainbow. Hemel Hempstead: Harvester, 208–226.

Ghimire, S. and B. R. Upreti (2014). Wavering between profit-making and change-making: Private media companies in conflicts in Nepal. *Media, War and Conflict* 7(2): 187–200.

Gildersleeve, R. E and A. Kuntz (2013). Dialogue as a requiem for analysis. *Cultural Studies ↔ Critical Methodologies* 13(4): 263–266.

—— (2010). A dialogue on space and method in qualitative research on education. *Qualitative Inquiry* 17(1): 15–22.

Golden, D. (2002). Belonging through time: Nurturing national identity among newcomers to Israel from the former Soviet Union. *Time and Society* 11(1): 5–24.

Granzow, K. and A. Dean (2016). Ghosts and their analysts: Writing and reading toward something like justice for murdered or missing indigenous women. *Cultural Studies ↔ Critical Methodologies* 16(1): 83–94.

Hasan, Z. (2006). Mass violence and the wheels of Indian (in)justice. In *Violence and Democracy in India* ed. Amrita Basu and Srirupa Roy. London: Seagull Books, 198–222.

Hindustan Times (2016). Journalist resigns from news channel over JNU coverage. 22 February. Accessed on 27 October 2018: https://www.hindustantimes. com/india/journalist-vishwa-deepak-resigns-from-zee-news-channel- over-jnu-coverage/story-OvlToVEl7DiSOZ3vYb3LIL.html.

Hope, W. (2009). Conflicting temporalities: State, nation, economy and democracy under global capitalism. *Time and Society* 18(1): 62–85.

Holzberg, B., K. Kolbe, and R. Zaborowski (2018). Figures of crisis: The delineation of (un)deserving refugees in the German media. *Sociology* 52(3): 534–550.

India Today (2016). Midnight surrender: A timeline of Umar Khalid and Anirban Bhattacharya's surrender. 24 February. Accessed on 30 October 2018: https://www.indiatoday.in/india/story/midnightsurrender-a-timeline- 310219-2016-02-24.

Indian Express. 2016. It's now govt vs oppn: Cong, Left join protests, Centre firm. 13 February. Accessed on 30 June 2018: http://epaper.indianexpress. com/m/721482/Indian-Express/14-February-2016#issue/3/1

Jagannathan, S. and R. K. Rai (2017). Organizational wrongs, moral anger and the temporality of crisis. *Journal of Business Ethics* 141(4): 709–730.

Jiwani, Y. (2016). Obituaries as markers of memory: Grievability and visibility in representations of aboriginal women in the national Canadian imaginary. *Cultural Studies ↔ Critical Methodologies* 16(4): 387–399.

Kaushika, P. and M. Janwalkar (2016). Day after Patiala court assault: BJP MLA OP Sharma defiant, party backs him, police drag their feet. *Indian Express*. Accessed on 3 May 2019: https://indianexpress.com/article/india/ india-news-india/day-after-patiala-court-assault-bjp-mla-op-sharma- defiant-party-backs-him-police-drag-their-feet/.

King, E. G. and M. de Young (2008). Imag(in)ing September 11: Ward Churchill, frame contestation and media hegemony. *Journal of Communication Inquiry* 32(2): 123–139.

Kristeva, J. (1980). Word, dialogue and novel. In *Desire in Language: A Semiotic Approach to Literature and Art*, ed. L. S. S. Roudiez (trans. T. Gora, A. Jardine and L. S. Rouddiz). New York: Columbia University Press, 64–91.

Kumar, A. (2016). Interview: Shehla Rashid on the attack on JNU, Left–Dalit solidarity and more. *The Wire*, 14 March. Accessed on 8 July 2018: https://thewire.in/politics/interview-shehla-rashid-on-the-attack-on-jnu-left-dalit-solidarity-and-more.

Kumar, R. (2016). Prime time by Ravish Kumar on JNU. NDTV India, 24 February. Accessed on 8 July 2018: https://www.youtube.com/watch?v=UFKhFIa3ofo.

Mathur, A. (2016). JNU row: Kanhaiya Kumar gets bail and a lesson on thoughts that 'infect (like) gangrene …' *Indian Express*, 3 March. Accessed on 30 October 2018: https://indianexpress.com/article/india/india-news-india/kanhaiya-kumar-bail-jnu-delhi-high-court/.

May, J. and N. Thrift (2001). *Timespace: Geographies of Temporality*. London: Routledge.

Norris, C. (1987). *Derrida*. London: Fontana Press.

Outlook (2017). Amit Shah's son Jay Shah files defamation case against seven people over The Wire's report. 9 October. Accessed on 30 October 2018: https://www.outlookindia.com/website/story/amit-shahs-son-jay-shah-files-defamation-case-against-seven-people-over-the-wire/302811.

Padmanabhan, C. (2016). NDTV's Ravish on the dark world of news television. *The Wire*, 21 February. Accessed on 26 October 2018: https://thewire.in/media/ndtvs-ravish-on-the-dark-world-of-news-television.

Pandey, A. (2016). What I learned during my days at JNU. *The Wire*, 28 February. Accessed on 28 October 2018: https://thewire.in/education/what-i-learned-during-my-days-at-jnu.

Parkins, W. (2004). Out of time: Fast subjects and slow living. *Time and Society* 13(2/3): 363–382.

Roy, A. (2013). The hanging of Afzal Guru is a stain on India's democracy. *The Guardian*, 10 February. Accessed on 30 October 2018: https://www.theguardian.com/commentisfree/2013/feb/10/hanging-afzal-guru-india-democracy.

Scroll.in (2017). In highly unusual move, Bengaluru court orders The Wire to remove articles on Rajeev Chandrashekhar. 7 March. Accessed on 30 October 2018: https://scroll.in/article/831159/in-highly-unusual-move-bengaluru-court-orders-the-wire-to-remove-articles-on-rajeev-chandrasekhar.

Sen, J. (2016). As Rajnath sees Lashkar hand, support for arrested JNUSU president mounts. *The Wire*, 14 February. Accessed on 30 June 2018: https://thewire.in/education/as-rajnath-sees-lashkar-hand-support-for-arrested-jnusu-president-mounts.

Sheriff, M. K. (2016). JNU students Umar Khalid, Anirban Bhattacharya get bail: 'Educated, have no criminal record,' says judge. *Indian Express*, 19 March. Accessed on 30 October 2018: https://indianexpress.com/article/india/india-news-india/umar-khalid-anirban-bhattacharya-jnu-sedition-patiala-house-court/.

Singh, A. (2016). Sedition arrest later, police want NIA and special cell to come in. *Indian Express*, 13 February. Accessed on 30 June 2018: http://epaper.indianexpress.com/m/721482/Indian-Express/14-February-2016#issue/3/1.

Singh, S. (2016). Meet the family of the student who is 'a danger to Mother India'. *Indian Express*, 13 February. Accessed on 30 June 2018: http://epaper.indianexpress.com/m/721482/Indian-Express/14-February-2016#issue/3/1.

The Hindu (2016). JNU row: What is the outrage all about? 16 February. Accessed on 30 October 2018: https://www.thehindu.com/specials/in-depth/JNU-row-What-is-the-outrage-all-about/article14479799.ece.

The Wire (2016). Zee News journalist quits in disgust over JNU coverage, tells all in letter. 22 February. Accessed on 27 October 2018: https://thewire.in/media/zee-news-reporter-quits-over-jnu-coverage-tells-all-in-letter.

—— (no date). How we are funded. Accessed on 3 May 2019: https://thewire.in/about-us.

Tripathi, R. (2013). Afzal Guru hanged, buried in Tihar. *Indian Express*, 10 February. Accessed on 30 October 2018: http://epaper.indianexpress.com/88721/Delhi/10-February-2013#page/1/2.

Turcotte, H. M. (2014). Feminist asylums and acts of dreaming. *Feminist Theory* 15(2): 141–160.

Varadarajan, S. (2016). On Kanhaiya: It is time to stand up and be counted. *The Wire*, 19 February. Accessed on 28 October 2018: https://thewire.in/politics/on-kanhaiya-it-is-time-to-stand-up-and-be-counted.

Varadarajan, S., S. Bhatia, and M. K. Venu (2015). Note from the founding editors. *The Wire*. Accessed on 30 October 2018: https://thewire.in/about-us.

Zhang, Q. (2015). Sexuality and the official construction of Occidentalism in Maoist and early post-Mao China. *European Journal of Cultural Studies* 18(1): 86–107.

Zidjaly, N. (2017). Memes as reasonably hostile laments: A discourse analysis of political dissent in Oman. *Discourse and Society* 28(6): 573–594.

7

PEOPLE'S ARCHIVE OF RURAL INDIA (PARI) AS AN ALTERNATIVE TO CORPORATIZED MEDIA

THE PUBLIC SPHERE AND RURAL SILENCING IN INDIA

APOORV KHARE
RAM MANOHAR VIKAS

This chapter discusses People's Archive of Rural India (PARI), an open-source digital archive and a living journal dedicated to rural India. We situate PARI within the broader canvas of transformations in Indian media, especially since the 1990s. This transformation, marked by corporatization and commodification of media houses, has had a pronounced degrading effect on representations of the rural poor. Indeed, any meaningful representation of rural India is erased from the press and from deliberative democratic spaces in India. We trace how PARI attends to this gaping wound in Indian democracy by enabling rich and plural representations of and by the subaltern. In so doing, PARI partially resurrects this crumbling fourth pillar of democracy and creates an alternative imagination.

Several scholars have discussed the perverse effects of neoliberal tendencies on the structure and logic of media and journalism in India (Guha Thakurta, 2014; Guha Thakurta and Chaturvedi, 2012; Mudgal, 2011, 2015). While there is consensus among the experts and researchers working on rural India that the majority of the population is going through prolonged and severe distress (Chandra, 2010; Patnaik, 2013; Sainath, 2011), the crises, issues, and challenges of rural India are almost absent in India's leading newspapers (Mudgal, 2011). Moreover, media houses have removed or reduced the number of rural correspondents. In its present neoliberal logic, the media is more interested in covering breaking news to increase its viewership than covering underlying structural processes of inequality and poverty. Consider how Tamil Nadu's farmers travelled to New Delhi and adopted extreme measures, such as carrying skulls of farmers who had committed suicide, in order to draw some attention to their plight from the ruling classes. Similarly, the 165-kilometre 'Long March' by Maharashtra's farmers remained unreported until it reached Mumbai. These instances provide a glimpse of the extraordinary crises in large swathes of India (see also Khare and Varman, 2016, 2017; Varman and Vikas, 2007). The vast majority of those residing in rural India are silenced and excluded in the already shrinking democratic sphere.

In this chapter, we discuss the role of media in a democracy and the repercussions when the media, an important institution of democracy, is driven by the neoliberal agenda. To understand the role of media in deciding the agenda of deliberations in a democracy and its transformation under neoliberalism, we draw upon Jürgen Habermas's (1989) idea of the public sphere. The concept of the public sphere focuses on political participation by private people based on the strength of their argument, not their status. As a normative ideal, the public sphere strives to engage in debates that concern various publics in a democracy. Discussions in the public sphere presuppose non-interference from the state, and the debates are often critical of the state (Habermas, 1989). A well-functioning democratic public sphere is an important institutional mechanism to ensure the political participation of its people. It is an institutionalized arena for critical debate where the press is an important institution (Calhoun, 1992). The idea of the public sphere provides a critical theoretical lens to highlight the media's role in democracy.

A critical revision of Habermas's public sphere also enables us to understand how an alternative media initiative can create conditions for the inclusion of rural India in democratic debates. Alternative organizations bring into being a different world, emphasizing human emancipation, equity, and justice (Vijay and Varman, 2018; Khare and Varman, 2018). We explore how PARI, as an alternative organization, challenges normalized assumptions of corporate media and commodification of the public sphere. In so doing, PARI creates emancipatory possibilities that are repressed, silenced, or annihilated by the dominant elite.

The chapter is structured as follows: First, we explain the idea of the public sphere, its transformation, and the role of media in it, as discussed by Habermas. We also discuss the limitations of Habermas's idea of the public sphere to critically understand the role of media in the Global South. Next, we discuss the legacy of media in Indian democracy and its transformation leading to the PARI initiative. Finally, we discuss how PARI is (re) transforming the democratic public sphere by creating conditions to bring back rural India into key democratic debates.

THE PUBLIC SPHERE AND ITS TRANSFORMATION

Habermas (1989) discussed the bourgeois public sphere, a particular historical category in eighteenth- and nineteenth-century Europe, as a sphere where private people addressed matters of general public interest through rational critical debate. Of particular interest is the role of the press and media in the development of the public sphere. With the advent of technology, the press played an important part in the development of capitalism and the bourgeois public sphere.

Habermas (1989: 27) conceptualized the bourgeois public sphere as a 'sphere of private people come together as a public ... to engage ... [the public authorities] in a debate over the general rules governing relations in the basically privatized but publicly relevant sphere of commodity exchange and social labor'. What was unprecedented about this public sphere was the use of reason by private people in the critical debates. In other words, participation in the public sphere was based on the strength of the rational argument, not on the socio-economic status of participants.

Press, along with salons and coffee houses, was one of the critical institutions of the public sphere. It played an essential role in shifting key debates in the public sphere from 'political tasks ... to the more properly civic tasks of a society engaged in critical public debate' (Habermas, 1989: 52). As an institution of the public sphere, the press played an essential role as the fourth estate. To the general public, it provided access to parliamentary deliberations. The public sphere also provided space for the issues and concerns of those, including minorities, who were underrepresented in the parliament. Thus, the public sphere played a vital role in a Western democracy in the eighteenth and nineteenth centuries.

Habermas explained the role of the media not only in the creation of the bourgeois public sphere but also in its transformation. An essential condition of the bourgeois public sphere was the clear separation between the state and civil society. With rising neomercantilism and a protectionist state, the separation between state and society was challenged, resulting in the transformation of this bourgeois public sphere (Habermas, 1989). The state and the society interlaced with each other with the emergence of the welfare state. The media played an essential role in transforming the bourgeois public sphere from a sphere of culture debate 'into a sphere of culture consumption' (Habermas, 1989: 162). This transformation was achieved through the commodification of culture where rational critical debate became a commodity in media, as 'one of the production numbers of the stars in radio and television, a sal[e]able package ready for the box office' (Habermas, 1989: 164). Discussing the press's role in the degeneration of the bourgeois public sphere, Habermas explained the new logic of the mass press. Rather than enabling rational critical debate, the media 'was based on the commercialization of the participation in the public sphere' (Habermas, 1989: 169). Such mass media was 'a public sphere in appearance only' (Habermas, 1989: 171). A commercialized media transformed the public sphere's critical debates into a commodity and its readers into customers.

Though Habermas presented a particular historical account of how the bourgeois public sphere developed and then transformed during the eighteenth and nineteenth centuries in Europe, the idea has normative importance for our understanding of democracy (Calhoun, 1992). Habermas highlighted the primacy of rational critical debate by private individuals in public discourse over their status and the importance of institutional mechanisms to ensure the rational critical debate on important matters in a meaningful and well-functioning democracy. For Habermas, the public sphere holds great potential to coordinate human life in a democracy. The public sphere is a better mode of coordination and political participation than state or market economy, which are exclusionary and are more prone to 'domination and reification' (Calhoun, 1992: 6).

While the public sphere is an important idea having theoretical and political importance, it is not without its limitations. An essential criticism is about the participatory potential of the public sphere. Habermas contended that it is reason, not status, that was the criterion for participation in the bourgeois public sphere. However, such a formulation elides significant exclusions such as gender, class, and other hierarchies. A drawback of such a simplistic and idealized version of the public sphere is the omission of non-bourgeois and other forms of public spheres, including the conflictual conditions (Fraser, 1990). The relation between various forms of public spheres should also constitute democratic debates in a well-functioning democracy. In other words, Habermas failed to incorporate the multiplicity of the public in favour of the bourgeois nature of publicness. These other forms of publics remain silenced or excluded in the bourgeois version of public debates. Additionally, openness and disclosure, key conditions for the rational critical debate in the bourgeois public sphere, do not apply to political or social deliberations in many contexts. For example, investigating popular politics in India, Piliavsky (2013: 117–118) notes that in rural Rajasthan, 'full disclosure is neither the precondition for discussion nor its aim. Instead, disclosure is a carefully managed process ... [and] discussions are very far from Habermasian zero-gravity zones of rational thought'.

Thus, a more effective conceptualization of the public sphere may not necessarily be focused on a site where participation is guaranteed only by rationality and arguments. Rethinking the public sphere as a site highlighted by cultural and political contestations and negotiations by various publics is more apt. Another criticism of Habermas's conceptualization of the public sphere is the issue of access. In the bourgeois public sphere, status inequality is thought to be 'bracketed', not eliminated, for the rational critical debate (Fraser, 1990: 63). Such a conceptualization masks the unequal power relations that are responsible for the non-participation of subaltern publics through silencing and exclusion.

In her critique of Habermas, Mouffe (2000: 13) questioned the idea of 'the free and unconstrained public deliberation' and consensus as an outcome. Using the concepts of antagonism and plurality, Mouffe (2000) argued that the ideal speech situation is ontologically not possible due to the incommensurability of different (and competing) public spheres. Any agreement or totality thus arrived would be a result of power politics and not simply a result of rational critical debate. There is a danger of concealing cultural hegemony in arriving at consensus through rational critical debate.

Despite the aforementioned limitations, we agree with Kapoor (2002) that there is merit in Habermas's idea of deliberative democracy as it strives to achieve an ideal speech situation through the institutional mechanism of empowerment. However, Habermas's theorization lacks engagement with the difference in the material conditions of the Global South from those in the West. Similarly, the role of the state in a Global South democratic order is critical and cannot be overlooked for achieving the ideal public sphere (Kapoor, 2002). Digital media is transforming the media landscape in India and elsewhere. It is now an important constituent of the public sphere. While it has democratized access and expanded the public sphere, it has also structurally transformed the public sphere, creating new challenges for political decision-making and public opinion (Rasmussen, 2013). Thus, there is a need to incorporate these realities and account for the shortcomings discussed earlier in Habermas's conceptualization of the public sphere before using it to analyse the alternative media initiative in India.

CONTEXT AND METHODOLOGY

P. Sainath, founder and a trustee of PARI, launched the PARI in 2014. Sainath is a widely cited expert on rural India, and his book titled *Everybody Loves a Good Drought* (Sainath, 2012a) is considered a classic. The book is a collection of cases of rural distress. Sainath is a recipient of the 2007 Magsaysay Award and worked as a rural correspondent. In 2014, he resigned from the post of journalist and rural-affairs editor of *The Hindu*, one of the oldest and largest-circulating English-language newspapers, and founded PARI.

Around the period of PARI's inception, a spurt of media groups commenced internet-based multimedia news portals that were considered as 'anti-establishment'. For example, *The Wire, Scroll.in, Newslaundry,*

Lallantop, and others came up. These portals were founded by some eminent journalists and claimed to follow different capital structures compared to the existing large capital-based equity-owning media business houses. The latter are often categorized as pro-establishment with allegations of receiving favours from the government through advertisements. Sainath, known for his critical stance of the government in his writings, is also perceived as 'anti-establishment'.

Our professional experience of working with a rural management institute and of conducting ethnographic research in rural sites drew our attention to the erasure of rural India in the mainstream media such as print media, television, and internet-based news portals. There is considerable rhetoric around villages in policies and programmes of the Parliament of India and the Government of India (see also Gupta, 2012). Yet we repeatedly found that the leading newspapers and mainstream media did not offer adequate space for village-specific stories. It is in this milieu that we situate the case of PARI as an alternative organization.

We collected data for our study from four sources: an in-depth interview of PARI's founder, contents of the PARI website, Sainath's writings, and other writings on PARI and Sainath. We interviewed Sainath in his office in Mumbai in a naturalistic setting (Belk et al., 1988; McCracken, 1988). We also observed and interacted with volunteers working in the office. With Sainath's permission, the interview was recorded. The focus of the interview was on the founder's life history and organizational understanding of PARI, which included organization structure, source of finance, operating procedures, and continuity plan. PARI uses internet and multiple media content. PARI is not a political news portal, and its content has a longer shelf-life compared to the other 'anti-establishment' news portals. PARI's focus is on rural areas across India. We analysed the content of the PARI website, which included reports and videos grouped according to themes such as Things We Do, Things We Make, Farming and its Crisis, Foot-Soldier of Freedom, The Rural in the Urban, and Musafir. There were 176 videos. The section titled 'Library' contains reports prepared by various agencies and Acts relevant to PARI's focus areas. A few details are summarized in Tables 7.1–7.3. We did an interpretive analysis of the data. In the next section, we present our findings.

TABLE 7.1 Number of reports on PARI website during the COVID-19 pandemic (March–November 2020)

States	COVID-19 reports
Haryana	1
MP	2
Gujarat	4
Delhi	1
Karnataka	5
Odisha	1
UP	4
Chhattisgarh	7
Telangana	7
Kerala	2
Bihar	2
Punjab	1
J&K	4
WB	11
AP	7
TN	7
Maharashtra	39
Rajasthan	2
Total	107

TABLE 7.2 Month-wise number of reports on PARI website on COVID-19

Month (2020)	COVID-19 reports
March	10
April	27
May	27
June	16
July	7
Aug	9
Sept	4
Oct	7

RECLAIMING THE PUBLIC SPHERE: A CASE STUDY OF PARI

We present our findings under two themes. First, we describe conditions leading to the introduction of the PARI initiative. Specifically, we trace the

TABLE 7.3 Theme-wise reports on PARI website

Themes	Number of reports
Agriculture	6
Culture	14
Vocation	23
Nomadic	3
Entrepreneurship	11
Health	6
Education	2
Food Security	7
Climate Change	3
Migrants	13
Ritual	1
Homeless	2
Frontline Workers	4
Dairy	1
Domestic Violence	2
Law	1
Market	1
Debt	1
Craftsmen	1
General	1
Public Policy	1
Community	1
Total	105

transformation of news reporting in India as media became corporatized and steadily silenced the concerns of rural India. Second, we explain how PARI provides an alternative to the mainstream profit-oriented media. We also discuss the challenges faced by PARI in providing the alternative media space.

CORPORATIZATION OF INDIAN MEDIA: THE NEED FOR PARI

The logic of journalism in India has changed since the 1980s and dramatically after the 1990s. Sainath elaborates, 'Good journalism is a society in conversation with itself, a nation in an argument with itself'. This ethos disappears when 'journalism is meant to maximize the profit to the owner and acts as blackmail and coercion lobby for the government to get concessions and benefits from it'. He pointed towards the transformation in Indian media, reducing journalism to revenue stream (see Sainath, 2012b).

Operating under a neoliberal logic, media houses such as Bennett and Coleman (owner of the *Times of India*) in the mid-1980s introduced a contract system of 11 months for journalists. The journalists are now at the mercy and volition of their masters. Sainath argues, '[T]he contract system is morally reprehensible. The editor will tell a journalist at the end of contract tenure to publish a report written by a PR [public relations] agency in his name.'

Technological developments such as mechanization and automation further exacerbated the situation. It made many jobs redundant. For example, the proofreaders disappeared. He continues:

> You might have noticed in NDTV that it uses Samsung [mobile phones] for producing news. The correspondent is also the cameraman. The contract arrangement by media houses further diluted the power of journalist unions as membership decreased, and when many positions became obsolete, the membership decreased further. Many correspondents working in domains that are not popular among middle-class readers were also removed.

This apathy of corporatized media became more evident in the past two decades when amidst growing farmers' suicides, the mass media clearly and deliberately overlooked the rural distress in India. In an interview, Sainath (2012b) chided the media:

> At the time of the Lakme Fashion Week in Mumbai in 2006, one of the worst years ever for the farmers' suicides, there were six journalists covering Vidarbha, all outsiders, while 512 accredited journalists covered the Fashion Week for the full seven days and another 100 did it on daily passes.

A direct consequence of this corporatization is the underrepresentation of rural India in media, both print and television. The transformation of media, from its role as 'society in conversation with itself' to a neoliberal institution meant to maximize profit, has led to a dangerous information vacuum.

Commenting on the most restricted, limited, and concentrated media environment in India, Sainath wondered, '[W]hy would newspapers cover rural India? Today no newspaper has a dedicated labour correspondent. No newspaper now has a dedicated rural correspondent.' Sainath clarified that although many newspapers claim to have agriculture correspondents, they cover the agriculture ministry and agriculture business, not the farmers.

A personal point of inflection for Sainath came in the year 1991–1992. In 1991 towards the end of the year, 29 tribal children died due to hunger in Mokhada in Thane district of Maharashtra state. The media was blaming the government. Sainath was convinced that the journalism that the media was doing was inadequate. While covering the drought in the 1980s and while covering this incident in Thane, Sainath realized that the issue was not as much about water shortage. Rather, it had more to do with power relations and inequality. In Thane, before the deaths, there were a few marches of the Adivasis (indigenous people of India, mentioned as Scheduled Tribes, or ST, in the Constitution of India) to Mumbai. Sainath elaborated, remembering the last march in 1991:

> They had all gathered from Flora Fountain all the way to Dalal street. And we were all thrilled about the Sensex for the first time, crossing some 2500 or 3000 points. Below were thousands of Adivasis saying our children are dying. Newspapers put one photograph saying, 'Farmers demand remunerative process.' They [Adivasis] came there to tell us our children are dying. We were too busy looking at the Sensex to see the people below.

The Indian press covered the event, but they did not cover the process. Sainath said, 'Had they covered the process, the children might have been healthy, grown adults with productive lives.' This trend continues today. The press continues to cover the events. They covered events such as when thousands of farmers marched to Delhi or Mumbai. The press does not cover the reasons leading to such a march, that is, prolonged rural distress.

An important trend in Indian media is the silencing of the subaltern and excluding their concerns from debates in the public sphere. Theorists from the Frankfurt school have discussed the role of mass media and advertising in perpetuating hegemonic relations and in reducing the person into a 'one-dimensional man' (Marcuse, 1964). This is also true about the Indian middle class, which has grown to be more consumerist and less concerned about the political aspects of civil life (Fernandes, 2004). Such a civil society, shaped by consumerism and bourgeois ideals, is less concerned about the inequalities in society.

Another trend in Indian mass media is the phenomenon of paid news. Sainath first exposed the practice of paid news – that is, charging a fee for presenting biased news as routine news (2009). This practice is akin to deceiving the people in a democracy and undermining the crucial role of the press as the fourth pillar of democracy (Mudgal, 2015). The marketized media has legalized the practice of paid news through supplements such as city editions. For example, city supplements (*Trichy Times, Delhi Times,* and so on) published by the *Times of India* are a form of legalized paid news. These supplements are published as advertorial, entertainment, or promotional features (interview excerpt, also see Mudgal, 2015). Paid news is another reason behind the lack of rural coverage in the Indian press.

It is no surprise then that this consumerist focus has created an entire generation in India, which is media-saturated but primarily by representations of the commercial media. Mudgal (2011) reported that leading mainstream English and Hindi dailies devote only 2 per cent of space to rural India. Out of this, only 15 per cent of themes are on rural poverty, underdevelopment, and distress. In effect, the Indian middle-class reader-consumer base of mainstream media remains oblivious to rural and agrarian issues. This is particularly dangerous because contemporary politics in the name of the poor does not include the poor and their concerns. Rather, it is a politics of and by the middle classes that has significantly shored up economic privileges in the post-liberalization period (Baviskar and Ray, 2011).

In sum, we have discussed the corporatization of Indian media that has systematically shrunk democratic spaces for rural India. It is against this backdrop that we understand PARI as an alternative media platform that diverges from corporatized media practices and creates space for rural India.

PARI: AN ALTERNATIVE TO CORPORATIZED MEDIA

PARI is a free-to-access alternative media platform that serves as both a 'living journal and an archive' (for more details, visit PARI: www.ruralindiaonline. org). It generates and hosts reports from rural India. PARI is also an archive for such reports in various forms such as videos, stories, audios, and reports.

It sets itself apart on many counts in comparison with corporate mainstream media. Sainath shared with us, 'We cover what the daily newspapers do not do, which the channels cannot do; we cover that ... telling stories of everyday life of everyday people and covering every aspect of the countryside.'

PARI emphasizes process over events. Covering the aspects of everyday life and everyday stories of ordinary people is critical to shift this focus from events to the process. As a case in point, 19 November 2020 was World Toilet Day. PARI created a slider – that is, a content area on the page where contents keep changing with various slides of visuals/information – titled 'November 19, World Toilet Day'. Here, all existing content on the PARI website related to toilets was compiled in the form of slides. The slides included topics on law (for example, the prohibition of employment of manual scavengers and their rehabilitation act 2013), policy (for example, articles on the efficiency of the Government of India's ambitious Swachh Bharat Mission), people affected by the 'act' of toilet (for example, deaths due to scavenging in Mumbai during COVID-19, daily lives of sanitation workers of Chennai during COVID-19), discrimination and extreme forms of subjugation (for example 'Visible work, invisible women – cleaning up!').

A media focused on breaking news, an extreme and commodified form of event, would not focus on the process. Breaking news, by design, is focused on increasing viewership and presenting viewers to advertisers to increase profits. By focusing on the everyday life of everyday people and by choosing not to be a daily news website, PARI is different from the mainstream media and is in a better position to focus on the process.

Sainath stated that PARI's organizing philosophy is 'wholly dedicated to ordinary people, [it is] not celebrity-driven ... not profit-seeking'. It encourages people to download and use its material for free. PARI deliberately does not carry any advertisements. Sainath elaborates further, 'I am dead against selling products. This is not the role of media. The big change in the 70s and 80s came when the fundamental role of the media changed … [from] deliver[ing] information and knowledge to audience … to deliver[ing] audiences to advertisers.'

Subverting the consumerist logic, PARI focuses on covering not what people want but what readers should read as informed citizens. Habermas (1989) pointed to this transformation in the bourgeois public sphere when media shifted from treating news as a mode for rational debate to packaging rational debate itself as a commodity. Bhushan (2015) describes this process of media expansion since the 1990s in India. A negative fallout of this expansion based on the market logic is the shift of control from journalists to marketing managers. This resulted in making editorial content more 'palatable' to new target markets. Readership now morphs into a customer base to attract advertisers of consumer goods (Bhushan, 2015).

PARI does not seek any direct grant from the government. It does not take foreign contributions under Foreign Contribution Regulation Act (FCRA). As a policy, it does not solicit funds from corporations or venture capitalists. PARI does not want to compromise its journalistic freedom and ethos. Journalistic quality and independence in digital news organizations tend to be compromised due to the exigencies of profit. An advisement revenue-based business model often results in digital news organizations 'bowing down to the advertisers' wishes' (Sibal, 2019: 1). Also, the subscription-based business models, especially the ones which do not provide open access to their content, runs the risk of dividing the public sphere and may undermine democratic politics by masking the issues of 'non-paying' subscribers or readers (Sibal, 2019). PARI does not charge any subscription fee. It is an advertisement-free website. Sainath clarified that PARI is willing to work with the government or universities on research projects. They are also willing to work on documentaries and films for the government or corporations as long as journalistic and creative freedom is ensured. Sainath clarified, 'I'll do the film, made on my terms, on Indian labour by Ministry of labour on a transactional basis if the creative independence remains intact.' PARI takes unconditional donations. Every PARI film, article, photograph, or video is made along stringent guidelines to ensure high-quality criteria. For example, one of the protocols is that no

PARI article or film shall carry anything that is incendiary or inflammatory in nature based on communal or caste lines.

PARI is a multilingual site. It has content not just in English and Hindi but in 12 languages. The translations follow a review process to ensure the quality of translations. The volunteers are paid a token honorarium of 500 rupees for one piece of nearly 1,500 words. At PARI, Urdu is the second largest language after English. It is important to note that, unlike the general perception that Urdu is the preferred language of Muslims from north India, Urdu is a pan-Indian language spoken by millions of people in many Indian states such as Punjab, West Bengal, Jharkhand, and Tamil Nadu (Alavi, 2018). Contents in Marathi, Hindi, and Kannada come next. Sainath mentioned that school-teachers particularly appreciate the high-quality translations and use the website's content frequently. By providing high-quality content in 12 languages, PARI is making rural India accessible to not only English-speaking readers and researchers but also to a larger vernacular population. In these ways, PARI challenges the hierarchies of English-based knowledge production in English and creates different sources and forms of knowledge. In so doing, PARI also addresses the problem of accessibility, a key limitation of the bourgeois public sphere (Fraser 1990).

PARI is run by Countermedia trust, a nonprofit organization. There are six trustees. None of the trustees, except one who is a technical editor, seeks any remuneration from the organization. They do other work to subsidize PARI and do not seek travel reimbursements from the trust. At PARI, the remuneration process follows an inverted logic. 'The junior-most staffs do more work, and they have more needs as they have to start a family life. Hence, they are paid more', said Sainath. He elaborated that since senior people in the organization are already in a better financial position, the young journalists' needs are prioritized and are reflected in the inverted remuneration policy.

The organization consists of a core group, active volunteers, and PARI fellows. PARI's aim is to appoint 100 fellows. The organization has divided India into 95 geographical regions and strives to cover the entire country. Additionally, there are five trans-regional fellows. PARI aims to engage 50 women, 16 Dalits, 8 Adivasis, and 15 minorities as its fellows. All fellows get a one-year fellowship. They need not be professional journalists. The fellows get 200,000 rupees. An additional expenditure of nearly 50,000 rupees is incurred on training, orientation, equipment, and so on. At the end of the fellowship, the equipment is gifted to the fellows. Twenty-five million rupees in a year are required to engage 100 fellows, but PARI faces resource constraints. Presently, PARI has 45 fellows. Sainath said that a typical media organization covers 8 to 10 regions. Thus, even with resource constraints, PARI does a better job of representing the country.

The PARI fellowship programme aims to create journalism within the community. For example, Adivasis have been consciously discriminated against and excluded from media (*The Telegraph*, 2019). Sainath exhorts, 'Show me one Dalit chief editor/sub-editor in a newspaper.' PARI attempts to overcome this structural challenge by promoting journalism among Adivasis. PARI covers not only marginalized communities but also assists marginalized communities in doing journalism. For example, the photo essay 'Book of Bandipur' (see www.ruralindiaonline.org/articles/book-of-bandipur/), showcases the images from the Bandipur National Park in Karnataka. The stories in this photo essay are told not by professional photographers but by the Adivasi residents who live around Bandipur forest. As local residents, they know the forest better than anyone, and with the training they took distinctive photographs. The photographers were paid 10,000 rupees for the photo essay.

A fellow must have a three-month residence in the region and can cover any aspect of the region assigned to her, be it culture, daily livelihood, resource conflicts, the healthcare environment, and so on. This diverse range of content is reflected in a wide variety of categories of stories available at PARI (see www.ruralindiaonline.org/categories/).

(RE)CREATING A PARTICIPATIVE PUBLIC SPHERE

In this section, we analyse PARI's content and highlight how PARI covers 'multiple publics' of rural India. It is important to provide space and voice to these multiple and varied 'publics' to imagine a participative democracy.

A unique project undertaken by PARI is called the Grindmill Songs Project (GSP), launched on Women's Day, 8 March 2017. The project is a 'collection of over 100,000 folk songs composed and sung by the women of Maharashtra over generations while toiling at the jāte (English: grind

mill, IPA: zɑːʈə) at home and performing other household tasks' (see www.
ruralindiaonline.org/articles/the-grindmill-songs-recording-a-national-
treasure/). According to PARI, '[s]ome 3,302 performers across more than
1,000 villages were involved in this phenomenal recording of a poetic-musical
legacy'. The practice of grindmill songs is disappearing as the hand-operated
grindmill is replaced by motorized grindmills. These songs provide valuable
insights on issues of culture, gender, religion, caste, everyday life, and so
on, from the vantage point of the subaltern. Writing about South India's
folksongs, Grover (1871: 1) stated, '[T]here is no better way of discovering the
real feelings and ideas of a people than that afforded by the songs.' In this
specific form of folk music, the sound of the grinding stone is the music.
The singers are women as they traditionally performed the work of grinding
flour. Similarly, Grierson (1886: 210) mentioned that 'every mill-song must be
sung to the melody'. There are 17 videos under this category uploaded on the
YouTube page of PARI with English subtitles. The 'Grindmill Project' page
description mentions that more than 100,000 songs have been collected from
various districts of Maharashtra (also refer to Chanda-Vaz, 2017). PARI's
effort is also crucial as it offers space and visibility to Maharashtra's grindmill
songs collected by the Centre for Cooperative Research in Social Sciences
(CCRSS, Pune) (Bacci, 1997).

The grindmill songs are expressions of feminine emotion for various
aspects of life (Freitag, 1989). However, these are no ordinary expressions of
women. In a song titled 'Gangu Bai: Village Voice, Marathi Soul', the elderly
Gangu Bai perceives herself as Sita, a lonely Sita, in the forest without the
presence and support of her husband. As no one is around her to listen to her
woes of life, Gangu Bai is narrating the pain and agony of daily life difficulties
to *bori* (jujube) and *babhali* (acacia). Both *bori* and *babhali* are thorny
trees. Ubhe (2020: 222) says, 'This is not a millstone, but a hermit from the
mountain; I tell you, woman, open your heart to him.' This genre and form
of folk songs have almost vanished from the rural cultural landscape, partly
due to mechanization. PARI's effort is special because grindmill songs, called
'jatsar' by G. A. Grierson, have a recorded reference in the late nineteenth
century (1884, 1886) from the Bihar region. In PARI's collection 'Songs of
Love for the Migrant Away from Home', the women sing, 'O Woman, my
husband has gone to a faraway place; he has gone away leaving me alone;

There is no one to care for him'. Thus, this oral repository provides unique sociological insights into affective elements of migration, separation, kinship, and intimacies.

The collection of Grindmill songs also engages with expressions beyond personal pain and agony. Consider the references to Baba Saheb Bhim Rao Ambedkar, the author of the Constitution of India: 'Jai Bhim, Jai Bhim' (Hail Bhim, Hail Bhim), 'Bhimraya moved heaven on earth', 'Ambedkar lives on in rural women's songs', and 'Fighting for Water is Fighting Inequality'. The presence of photographs of Buddha and Ambedkar in the videos indicates that the singers are Dalits. Since the grindmill songs are sung collectively, they represent the singers' collective expression (Vikas, 2015). Thus, the Grindmill Project provides a collective voice to the marginalized and is a repository of 'orature', literature in oral form (Maid et al., 2005). In these ways, PARI's Grindmill Project not only provides insights into the rural culture of the marginalized women of Maharashtra but also serves as a medium to reclaim the public sphere by propagating the ideas of equality and democratic rights among the marginalized (Poitevin and Rairkar, 1993).

Moreover, PARI extensively covers the farming and agrarian crises. From challenges of farming in big cities such as Delhi to dilemmas of farmers in small villages, to how BT cotton monoculture creates disruptions and deep distress in Odisha, PARI provides valuable researched articles on a wide range and aspects of the rural crisis. PARI also contains freely downloadable articles, bills, reports, and documents in its library.

Though PARI is dedicated to rural India, it also has a section on migrant workers in urban areas titled 'The Rural in the Urban'. This section has covered myriad issues such as migrant workers' challenges due to the country-wide lockdown during COVID-19, the struggles of migrant workers' children to learn a new language, and stay on in school when their parents migrate, and garbage workers' life stories and trysts in metropolitan cities. In these ways, PARI ensures that silenced voices get a representation in media that can be accessed by anyone, anywhere for free.

Another unique feature of PARI is the section on 'Foot-soldier of Freedom: The Last Living Freedom fighters' (see www.ruralindiaonline.org/stories/categories/foot-soldiers-of-freedom/). Noting that in a few years, the last living freedom fighters would not be with us, PARI features the stories of these freedom fighters. These are the stories that have not found mention in the grand historical narratives but are equally important for a better understanding of India's fight for independence. This section creates an archive of such accounts that, if not covered now, shall be lost forever.

The nationwide COVID-19 lockdown that started on 25 March 2020 triggered distress for millions of ordinary Indians – stranded migrant workers, farmers, sugarcane cutters, Adivasis, Dalits, sanitation workers, construction workers, cancer patients staying on city pavements, brick kiln workers, pastoral nomads, and others. While many are on the brink of survival with no work, income, or food, several continue to work amid extremely hazardous conditions. PARI has a special section on COVID-19 in which there are 107 reports from 18 states. Even though the highest number of reports (# 38) is from Maharashtra, the coverage is across the length and breadth of India – from Jammu and Kashmir to Tamil Nadu and from Gujarat to West Bengal. However, there are no reports on COVID from North-East India.

We read the COVID reports filed between 23 March and 29 October 2020. These reports cover various issues, such as agriculture, climate change, food security, culture, health, and education. The reports cover affected groups of people ranging from primary school children, elderly people, Adivasi kiln workers, nomadic pastoralists, sanitary workers, and front-line health workers. The reports focus on multiple intersectionalities (Crenshaw, 1991). For example, 'Seeing the world through touch in pandemic' is about an elderly visually impaired couple who sell handkerchiefs in Mumbai local trains. The couple belongs to the Adivasi Gond Gowari community. The report surfaces the compounded precarities surfacing from intersecting vectors of tribe, disability, and age. Similarly, the latest report, 'In Kashmir, no migrants to reap rice harvest', explores the lives of elderly paddy farmers and migrant workers in Jammu and Kashmir after the Government of India abrogated the special provisions of Article 370 to maintain peace and order.

The number of reports filed in the COVID section varies. There are more reports from the lockdown period. April and May account for 54 reports. In these two months, there was a complete lockdown, and many migrant workers left cities for their respective native places. Migration stories find significant space among these PARI reports. The stories of migration have been depicted using various media – prose, poetry, painting, songs, and videos.

The reports also include people who are invisible to the mainstream media. For example, there are two reports on the homeless cancer patients sleeping on the footpath near the Tata Cancer Hospital, Mumbai. One report describes the plight of Geeta, a homeless cancer patient who is exposed to multiple vulnerabilities during the COVID lockdown. Another important aspect of the COVID reports is the grey line between the worker and an entrepreneur as the stories filed come from the large informal sector that is neglected by the mainstream media. For example, reports document the lives and trysts of the scrap collectors, tailors, watch repairers, and potters from various regions.

Summing up, PARI enables the rational critical debate in India by providing voices to multiple overlooked publics such as Dalits, Adivasis, and rural women. As a free resource, PARI also enables scholars interested in rural India to use the rich information and articles available on its website.

CHALLENGES TO CREATING AN ALTERNATIVE PUBLIC SPHERE

PARI requires 800,000 to 1 million rupees per month to run its operation in the present capacity. If it wants to achieve its aim of covering the entire country with 100 fellows, it will require nearly 30 million rupees in a year. Sainath stated that this money is required only for content generation, fellowship, editing, and so on. PARI articles are multimedia products in the form of text, still photographs, audios, and videos, which require significant production expenditure. Presently, nearly 30 per cent of its revenue comes from individual small donations. Twenty-nine per cent of the revenue is contributed by the trustees. PARI also receives donations from small foundations and individual bigger donors without affecting their agenda. The organization strictly follows the protocol of non-interference by the donors in its agenda. Sainath further told us,

> Our protocol is that we cannot take money which will affect our agenda. We really hope there will be three thousand human beings in this country who, looking at the value of what we are doing for Indian society, will give us ten thousand rupees a year. If that happens, we are ok.

There are three more ways in which PARI receives its support. Many people provide free labour. This has been the biggest source of PARI's success in Sainath's views.

> Techies, in the age group of 23 to 28 years, have put in more than rupees two crores [20 million rupees] to build this sophisticated technology platform called PARI. People, who are working for various companies, have contributed voluntary labor. Many people have gifted PARI with old or new hardware and software. For example, video editing software is very expensive. People have given PARI subscriptions for such software, cameras, laptops to the extent of lakhs of rupees.

In addition to this, PARI has won major 16 national and international awards. Sainath also got a few personal awards, such as the Tilak award and the Justice Ranade award. Nearly 1.5 million rupees in total came from the awards.

Sainath informed that in 2018 there were 900,000 page views, which is considerable for a non-news website. Therefore, while PARI has a significant readership base, this remains circumscribed mainly due to severe resource constraints. Sainath shared that it feels 'unfair' that they have to struggle despite their efforts. He said,

> An average newspaper spends more in a day than we spend in a year. Other websites spend more in a month than what we spend in a year. Last year in 2018, PARI spent more than one crore [rupees]. People working for PARI get less than what they would get in the market outside. They are idealism-driven people, not revenue-driven.

PARI operates from a residential apartment in Mumbai and through people's laptops. The office is used primarily for editing work and internships. Otherwise, people work from their homes to minimize the cost of operation. The minimally furnished PARI office is unlike an embellished corporate workplace. The setting is home-like, with a bed for workers to sleep if they need a break. Many workers do not come to the office, and they work from their own location. The content is prepared both by full-timers and freelancers. There is an emphasis to encourage and induct a community insider to organize content. The formal procedure of college-based qualification certificates for recruitment is not followed.

Sainath accepts that they are not good at fund-raising. It is one of the reasons why PARI is struggling. In a marketized society, PARI struggles to get 10,000 rupees from 3,000 individuals in a year to run its operations. Though short on funds, PARI is not short of idealism-driven people who work for it. Covering rural India is a mammoth task and is probably beyond the capability of one initiative. But, in its rich content, its struggle, and in the recognition that it has received, PARI is certainly proof that an alternative to the current order is possible.

DISCUSSION AND CONCLUSION

The media plays a vital role in democracy by enabling rational critical debate. In this chapter, we paid attention to the role of media in Indian democracy. Specifically, we traced the media's transformation from an organic link between the public and the state to a corporate entity focused on profits. In this corporatization, media silences subaltern voices. Drawing upon Habermasian idea of the public sphere, we investigated how PARI provides an alternative to mainstream neoliberal media.

First, we highlight how PARI creates conditions for the inclusion of subaltern voices in spaces colonized by the corporate class. By keeping the content as open access and providing the content in 12 vernacular languages, PARI opens up participation for a vernacular public. It also strives for high-quality translations, thus expanding the circulation of vernacular content. Unique projects undertaken by PARI, such as the Grindmill Project, Rural in the Urban, and India's Last Living Freedom Fighters, are important steps to rupture the hegemonic discourses of bourgeois publics (Fraser, 1990). PARI's rich and nuanced documentation of rural India also creates high-quality archival database for researchers. Finally, PARI also brings journalism to subaltern publics through its fellowship programme.

Second, we highlight how PARI, as an alternative organization, resists the market logic. It does not allow advertisements on the website and does not seek corporate sponsorship or donation. A subscription-based digital news media may create information inequality by providing differentiated access to its content to paying versus non-paying readers (Sibal, 2019). Such business models may seriously compromise the media's role in participative democracy. By keeping its content open-source, PARI practices journalism driven by ideals wherein the role of media is to create conditions for a well-functioning democracy by fostering rational critical debates on issues pertaining to its various publics, including non-bourgeois publics.

Third, our findings suggest that PARI has both inverted and adapted elements of mainstream media. Specifically, PARI challenges the mainstream media by inverting structural elements in the domain of financial management, human resources management, and operations management. PARI's financial management strategy is not a profit-seeking one but does include the idea of surplus. PARI does not advertise, which is the most important source of revenue in the mainstream media. It seeks small donations from individuals. An important inversion is paying more to PARI's junior-most workers. This is counterintuitive, as pay cheques are instruments of status and indicators of position in any conventional organization's hierarchy. The idea of need-based remuneration is seldom practiced in modern organizations.

PARI has also adapted a few elements from mainstream media to suit its structure. Its content collectors are stipend-based field correspondents. They are not permanent staff, which is a strategy adopted by the mainstream media as a cost-cutting measure. While PARI is not profit-seeking, it needs such efforts to minimize costs in order to remain alive. PARI also adopts other methods to keep content preparation costs low by encouraging freelancers to upload content. In some cases, they also pay freelancers, but the payment is low compared to the payments made by the mainstream media. Further, there is no liability for paying monthly remuneration to the freelancers.

Finally, we learn that alternative forms can craft new cultural genres. PARI has crafted a new genre of reporting, and its model of media reporting is being followed by other emerging media platforms. For example, Alt news (www.altnews.in) that 'monitors social media and mainstream media for incorrect and/or dubious information' does not include any advertisement on its page. It meets its expenses from grants and small donations from individuals. Students and researchers working in the development sector actively seek PARI's content. PARI also visits schools and colleges to promote the use of its content in training and lectures. Its content follows neither the conventional academic journal style nor journalistic style. Unlike journalists, the volunteers spend a significant amount of time on research to prepare reports. Similarly, PARI's reports are not only about villagers' problems and suffering but also celebrate various cultural elements. As Overdorf (2016) notes, PARI 'lies somewhere between these dystopian and utopian visions'. In these ways, PARI has created an alternative organization by creating spaces for those otherwise silenced, resisting the capitalist market logic, and inverting and adapting elements of mainstream media. PARI's importance is evidenced in crafting a new and visible genre of media reporting.

In this chapter, we highlighted the importance of media as an important democratic institution in a democracy. A marketized media hollows out and perverts democracy for its subaltern population. As Habermas (1989) discussed, when the news became a commodity, it created conditions for the emergence of the bourgeois public sphere. An essential and critical point is that when market logic is extended to treat rational critical debates as a commodity, it leads to the degradation of the public sphere. A corporatized media functioning by the profit logic has failed as the fourth pillar and institution of democracy in India.

We see PARI as an alternative to corporate-controlled media. A limitation of our work is that we could not interview the field correspondents and observe their work. How do field correspondents select any site or community or any incident to study? How much time do they take to file a report, what problems do they face, and what techniques do they adopt to get access to the community? Attention to these questions would provide a more nuanced understanding of the processes of alternative organizing. Our chapter poses further avenues to explore work practices in such alternative organizations. With concentrated media ownership and the changing logic of media business, how would small initiatives, as an alternative to capitalist media, sustain themselves when it becomes increasingly difficult to work outside the market logic? When people are consuming sensational and breaking news, how would media focus on critical and process-oriented journalism? Answers to these questions are essential for reimagining and creating a democratic public sphere.

REFERENCES

Alavi, S. (2018). Census data on language reveals a surprise about Urdu. *The Wire.* 6 July. Accessed on 30 July 2021: https://thewire.in/culture/urdu-census-language-2011-north-india.

Bacci, V. (1997). Grindmill songs in Maharashtra: A musical-anthropological study. Accessed on 5 May 2021: https://ccrss.org/baccproj.htm.

Baviskar, A. and R. Ray (2011). *Elite and Everyman: The Cultural Politics of the Indian Middle Classes.* New Delhi: Routledge.

Belk, R. W., J. F. Sherry, and M. Wallendorf (1988). A naturalistic inquiry into buyer and seller behavior at a swap meet. *Journal of Consumer Research* 14(4): 449–470.

Bhushan, B. (2015). The Changing structure of media and ethics in India. In *Media Ethics and Justice in the Age of Globalization,* ed. S. Rao and H. Wasserman. Hampshire: Palgrave Macmillan, 194–209.

Calhoun, C. (1992). Introduction: Habermas and the public sphere. In. *Habermas and the Public Sphere,* ed. C. Calhoun. Cambridge, MA: The MIT Press, 1–50.

Chanda-Vaz, U. (2017). *Grindmill Songs: Listen to the World's Largest Archive of Folk Songs.* Accessed on 5 May 2021: https://scroll.in/magazine/833884/grindmill-songs-listen-to-the-worlds-largest-archive-of-folk-songs.

Chandra, N. K. (2010). Inclusive growth in neoliberal India: A facade? *Economic and Political Weekly* 45(8): 43–56.

Crenshaw, K. (1991). Mapping the margins: Intersectionality, identity politics, and violence against women of color. *Stanford Law Review* 43(6): 1241–1299.

Fayol, H. (1949). *General and Industrial Management.* Accessed on 27 April 2020: https://archive.org/details/in.ernet.dli.2015.13518/page/n5/mode/2up.

Fernandes, L (2004). The politics of forgetting: Class politics, state power and the restructuring of urban space in India. *Urban Studies* 41(12): 2415–2430.

Fraser, N. (1990). Rethinking the public sphere: A contribution to the critique of actually existing democracy. *Social Text* 26(25/26): 56–80.

Freitag, S. (1989). *Culture and Power in Banaras: Community, Performance, and Environment, 1800-1980.* Berkeley: University of California Press.

Grierson, G. A. (1884). Some Bihari folk songs. *Journal of the Royal Asiatic Society* 16(2): 196–246.

────── (1886). Some Bhojpuri folk songs. *Journal of the Royal Asiatic Society* 18(2): 207–267.

Grover, C. E. (1871). *The Folk Songs of Southern India.* Madras: Higginbotham & CO. Accessed on 5 May 2021: https://ia800209.us.archive.org/26/items/ TheFolkSongsOfSouthernIndia/The-folk-Songs-of-southern-india.pdf.

Guha Thakurta, P. (2014). What future for the media in India? *Economic and Political Weekly* (June). Accessed on 27 March 2020: http://www.epw.in/ journal/2014/24/web-exclusives/what-future-media-india.html.

Guha Thakurta, P., and Chaturvedi, S. (2012) Corporatisation of the media. *Economic and Political Weekly* 47(7): 10–13.

Gupta, A (2012). *Red Tape: Bureaucracy, Structural Violence, and Poverty in India.* New Delhi: Duke University Press.

Habermas, J. (1989). *The Structural Transformation of the Public Sphere: An Inquiry into a Category of Bourgeois Society.* Cambridge, MA: The MIT Press.

Kapoor, I. (2002). Deliberative democracy or agonistic pluralism? The relevance of the Habermas-Mouffe debate for Third World politics. *Alternatives* 27(4): 459–487.

Khare, A., and R. Varman (2016). Kafkaesque institutions at the base of the pyramid. *Journal of Marketing Management* 32(17–18): 1619–1646.

────── (2017). Subalterns, empowerment and the failed imagination of markets. *Journal of Marketing Management* 33(17–18): 1593–1602.

────── (2018). Shaheed hospital: Alternative organisation, ideology and social movement. In *Alternative Organisations in India: Undoing Boundaries,* ed. D. Vijay and R. Varman. New Delhi: Cambridge University Press, 152–182.

Maid, J., P. Pdalghare, and G. Poitevin (2005). Communication for socio-cultural action: 'Is the discourse "on", "for" or "of"?' In *Media and Mediation,* ed. B. Bel, J. Brouwer, B. Das, et al. New Delhi: Sage Publications, 371–404.

Marcuse, H. (1964) *One-Dimensional Man: Studies in the Ideology of Advanced Industrial Society.* Massachusetts: Beacon Press.

McCracken, G. (1988). *The Long Interview.* New Delhi: Sage Publications.

Mouffe, C. (2000). *Deliberative Democracy or Agonistic Pluralism.* 72 Political Science Series, Vienna: Institute for Advanced Studies. Accessed on 15 January 2022:https://www.ihs.ac.at/publications/pol/pw_72.pdf.

Mudgal, V. (2011). Rural coverage in the Hindi and English dailies. *Economic and Political Weekly* 46(35): 92–97.

—— (2015) News for sale: 'Paid news', media ethics, and India's democratic public sphere. In *Media Ethics and Justice in the Age of Globalization*, ed. S. Rao and H. Wasserman. Hampshire: Palgrave Macmillan, 100–120.

Overdorf, J. (2016). Documenting Indian villages before they vanish. *The Atlantic*, 16 April. Accessed on 27 April 2020: https://www.theatlantic. com/international/archive/2015/04/india-villages-digital-archive-rural-sainath/390630/.

Patnaik, U. (2013). Poverty trends in India 2004–05 to 2009–10. *Economic and Political Weekly* 48(40): 43–58.

Piliavsky, A. (2013). Where is the public sphere? Political communications and the morality of disclosure in rural Rajasthan. *Cambridge Journal of Anthropology* 31(2): 104–122.

Poitevin, G., and H. Rairkar (1993). *Indian Peasant Women Speak Up*. Hyderabad: Orientman Longman.

Rasmussen, T. (2013) Internet-based media, Europe and the political public sphere. *Media, Culture and Society* 35(1): 97–104.

Sainath, P. (2009). The medium, message and the money. *The Hindu*, 26 October. Accessed on 1 August 2017: http://www.thehindu.com/opinion/columns/ sainath/The-medium-message-and-the-money/article13666073.ece.

—— (2011). Census findings point to decade of rural distress. *The Hindu*. Accessed on 21 August 2017: http://www.thehindu.com/opinion/columns/ sainath/census-findings-point-to-decade-of-rural-distress/article2484996.ece.

—— (2012a). *Everybody Loves a Good Drought: Stories from India's Poorest Districts*. New Delhi: Penguin Books.

—— (2012b). Media more keen on Fashion Weeks than farmers suicides. *Sunday Indian*, September. Accessed on 3 August 2017: http://www. thesundayindian.com/en/story/media-more-keen-on-fashion-weeks-than-farmers-suicides/77/40281/.

Sibal, P. (2019). Can independent journalism thrive under paywalls? EPW Engage, 26 January. Accessed on 9 May 2021: https://www.epw.in/engage/ article/can-independent-journalism-thrive-under/.

The Telegraph (2019). Study finds SC and ST journalists missing from Indian media. 4 August, New Delhi. Accessed on 29 March 2020: https://www. telegraphindia.com/india/study-finds-sc-and-st-journalists-missing-from-indian-news-media/cid/1695824.

Ubhe, T. (2010). From grindmill songs to cultural action. In *Communication, Culture and Confrontation*, ed. B. Bel, J. Brouwer, B. Das, et al. London: SAGE, 219–227.

Varman, R., and R. M. Vikas (2007). Rising markets and failing health: An inquiry into subaltern health care consumption under neoliberalism. *Journal of Macromarketing* 27(2), 162–172.

Vikas, R. M. (2015) 'I will give gold, silver and gold coins', says bride's mother: Ethnomusicology of consumer culture in the ritual songs in India. *Asia-Pacific Advances in Consumer Research* 11: 85–89.

Vijay, D., and R. Varman (2018). Introduction: Undoing boundaries. In *Alternative Organisations in India: Undoing Boundaries*, ed. D. Vijay and R. Varman. New Delhi: Cambridge University Press, 1–25.

8

LEFTWORD

A HETEROTOPIC SPACE IN POST-DEMOCRATIC INDIA

ROHIT VARMAN
DEVI VIJAY

And when the enthusiastic
story of our time
is told,
who are yet to be born
but announce themselves
with more generous face,
we will come out ahead
– those who have suffered most from it.

And that
being ahead of your time
means much suffering from it.
But it's beautiful to love the world
with eyes
that have not yet
been born.

And splendid
to know yourself victorious
when all around you

it's all still so cold,
so dark.
— 'Before the Scales, Tomorrow'
by Otto Rene Castillo

You can disembark at the Shadipur Metro station in West Delhi and walk down or take a rickshaw through the bustling Shadi Khampur bazaar. At the end of the main bazaar road, you will find a cycle rickshaw stand. In this nook of a predominantly working-class neighbourhood is the building housing the May Day Bookstore-cum-LeftWord Office. Walk in through the bookstore's bright yellow painted doors stencilled with '8 hours of work, 8 hours of sleep, and 8 hours for books and coffee' (see Image 8.1) to lose yourselves in rows of bookshelves. As the name suggests, LeftWord publishes and distributes books on a range of subjects broadly aligned with the left ideology, issues concerning working lives, and Marxist writings. You will also find books from other independent publishing houses such as Tulika, Zubaan, Kali, and Navayana. It is a space that hopes to impel people to act against tyranny, imagine another future. A space that chronicles another time, as Castillo inscribes – *Before the scales, tomorrow.*

If you run into Sudhanva Deshpande, managing editor of LeftWord, he will generously offer you a cup of coffee at the bookstore's coffee corner – a brief encounter with him and you sense his deep commitment to left politics. If you are lucky, you might be able to time your visit with a play staged next door at Studio Safdar, an independent art space established by the legendary political street theatre group Jana Natya Manch (Janam). If you head to the May Day Bookstore on 1 May, you will find a room full of artists, academics, students, a lot of music, and poetry. If words can conjure the multiple textures and tonalities juxtaposed, opposed, interconnected, or scattered within this bookstore, think of a space with old and new books, strums of a guitar, bright posters of workers' struggles and solidarities, sounds of a play next door, the smell of freshly brewed coffee, poetry, the sounds of the bazaar....

Not far from the bookstore, about 7 kilometres away, is the shiny high-rise granite structure of DLF Centre in Connaught Place that houses Bank of America, Citibank, Standard Chartered Bank, and other sites of predatory finance. In this vicinity is the ongoing construction work for the Central

IMAGE 8.1   LeftWord office and May Day Bookstore (outside)
Source: Rohit Varman.

Vista redevelopment, which houses the Rashtrapati Bhawan, the parliament building, and other historically significant monuments. Activists and writers have challenged the conceptualization and execution of the Central Vista project as a fascist attempt to re-sculpt Delhi along the contours of the majoritarian Hindutva historiography (Appadurai, 2021; Roy, 2021). About

20 kilometres from the bookstore is Shaheen Bagh, the site of a political sit-in that lasted 101 days, led by Muslim women against the draconian Citizenship (Amendment) Act (CAA) and the proposed National Register of Citizens (NRC). About 22 and 30 kilometres away are the Tikri and Singhu borders, key sites of the ongoing farmers' movement for the last ten months (November 2020–August 2021). The farmers' movement challenges the pro-corporate, anti-farmer bases of three farm acts introduced by the current Indian government. If you were to create a map of these pulsing working lives and subterranean movements, you might see a network that weaves these seemingly disparate and yet interconnected spaces of displacement and emplacement – the shiny structures of robber-bankers, the fascist Central Vista Project, Shaheen Bagh, Tikri and Singhu Borders, and LeftWord.

In this chapter, we examine LeftWord as an alternative space of organizing located in this historical moment of India's shift towards post-democracy. In the last three decades, the country has taken a sharp rightward turn with the deepening of neoliberalism and the financialization of the economy (Patnaik, 2019). The interconnectedness of neoliberalism and fascism is evident in contemporary India. Over the last few decades, successive regimes have closely aligned with domestic and international capital and corroded the ideals of the welfare state and political liberalism that marked the imagination of independent India. These realignments of the state have been accompanied by the rise of fascist political forces such as the current government of the Bhartiya Janata Party (BJP) and Narendra Modi. Aijaz Ahmad (2020) terms this particular configuration of the state, which combines the two classic forms of the capitalist state – the liberal and the fascist – as a post-democratic state. Ahmad notes,

> This type of state keeps intact many of the institutional features of the liberal state (elections, freedom of press and assembly, etc.) but, in fact, signals the decay of the Lockean frames of political liberalism while authoritarian political parties with a Far Right agenda come to dominate the formally liberal structures, modifying them but not abolishing them altogether.... This second innings [of Narendra Modi] may even witness a gradual shift from the merely authoritarian to the

post-democratic, that is, dimming of the liberal colours, sharpening of the fascist methods.

A post-democratic state is characterized by the dominance of a small elite and weak or emasculated democratic institutions (Crouch, 2004; Rancière, 1999). In such a society, the state controls and sanctions debates, largely at the behest of large corporations. Contentious politics are concerted, counterhegemonic social and political actions that require differently positioned participants to challenge dominant systems of authority and emplace alternative imaginaries (Khare and Varman, 2018; Leitner, Sheppard and Sziarto, 2008).

We look at LeftWord as a heterotopia that allows for the performative staging of contentious politics. A heterotopia inverts, resists, and often subverts dominant social relations (Lefebvre, 2003). Spaces produce politics due to their physical and relational characteristics and are central to contentious politics (Kwok and Chan, 2020; Lefebvre, 1984). As Massey (1994: 251) reminds us, space is 'one of the axes along which we experience and conceptualize the world'. Space is not just a container of politics; it constitutes and structures relationships and political actions.

In the next section, we review the literature on post-democracy and heterotopia. We follow it up with the description of our methodology. Subsequently, we describe our key findings and close the chapter with a discussion of the implications of our analysis of LeftWord as a space of resistance.

THEORETICAL CONSIDERATIONS

In his seminal work on post-democracy, Crouch (2004) foregrounds the roles of neoliberalism, globalization, and finance capital in weakening democratic orders and observes that the political systems are increasingly controlled by small elites of politicians and the corporate rich. Accordingly, while elections may continue to elect governments, public debates are tightly controlled spectacles managed by professional experts and confined to a small range of issues selected by these experts. As a result, citizens largely play a quiescent, apathetic part. Crouch notes that in the current dystopian world, democracy is used for the legitimation of corporate neoliberalism and its power to exploit people.

Adding to this understanding, Rancière (1999) interprets post-democracy as a process of depoliticization that is furthered by neoliberal control of different spheres of our lives. Accordingly, in the historical construction of most societies, there are always some who are made visible and have the ability to speak, while most others are excluded. Such an order is maintained by the police in liberal and social democratic states. The police is used to create hegemony, suture social spaces, and saturate them in a way that different groups perform their pre-assigned functions. The police includes the formal repressive institution of the police, and it encompasses all state and non-state activities (such as the provision of healthcare, state administration, and food allocation) that shape the continuation of life. For Rancière, politics interrupt the police and, as 'dissensus' confronts the blindness of those who do not see and what is not allowed to be spoken. Politics are emancipatory when actors refuse to be restricted to the spaces, speech acts, and visions distributed to them in the police order.

Such a post-democratic order reduces the spaces available for politics. In a post-democracy, politics become increasingly difficult to imagine, if not completely eliminated, because of the control exercised by the ruling elite. As Rancière (1999: 102) notes,

[p]ostdemocracy is the government practice and conceptual legitimization of a democracy after the demos, a democracy that has eliminated the appearance, miscount, and dispute of the people and is thereby reducible to the sole interplay of state mechanisms and combination of social energies and interests. Postdemocracy is not a democracy that has found the truth of institutional forms in the interplay of social energies. It is an identifying mode, among institutional mechanisms and the allocation of the society's appropriate parts and shares, for making the subject and democracy's own specific action disappear.

Thus, post-democracy destroys the ideals of politics. In such a state of a post-democratic society, as is true in contemporary India, there is a rise of fragmenting forces that often revolve around the resurgence of the 'ethnic' evil, i.e., identity politics as the cause that disrupts the consensually established order. While identitarian politics is loudly acclaimed, xenophobic or nationalist movements arise, whereby 'incorrect' outsiders are violently excluded often through erecting all manner of new material, legal or other geographical barriers, walls, and camps. (Swyngedouw, 2011: 372)

In today's India, in the name of ultra-nationalism, we witness the BJP pushing forward its majoritarian Hindutva agenda. As Desai (2017) reminds us, '[i]n this toxic, lumpenised, communal atmosphere, the suppression of all other rights too has become so much easier for the ruling classes'.

While Indian democracy before 2014 was fraught with the contradictions of inequality and the quality of government was always uneven, it did allow for some politicization and creation of institutions that furthered people's participation in their governance (Kohli, 2001). Any such claim to democracy must be carefully qualified because upper-caste elites have long constrained the political participation of India's oppressed castes, Adivasis, and landless peasants. However, as Kohli (2001, 2012) points out, India did create a complex democratic order. This democratic order has come under increasing strain in the last seven years of the current BJP regime.

In fact, we are not just witnessing depoliticization of the kind imagined by Crouch and Rancière, but, like Aijaz Ahmad, we foresee something far more dangerous in India's post-democracy – the rise of fascism. Here fascism is not just about depoliticization or totalitarian control by making populations passive. It involves mobilizing populations and converting them into instruments of violence against clearly marked enemies (such as Muslims, Dalits, activists, and socialists). As Paxton (2005: 217) emphasizes, '[a]uthoritarians would rather leave the population demobilized and passive, while fascists want to engage and excite the public. Authoritarians want a strong but limited state…. They cling to the status quo rather than proclaim a new way'. The indoctrination and training by the Rashtriya Swayamsevak Sangh (RSS) and its affiliates, lynch mobs that we have witnessed in the last few years, and the protection and legitimacy provided by the BJP leaders to stormtroopers are pointers in the direction of fascist mobilizations

(Roy, 2020). In contemporary India, there are eerie similarities with the mobilizations of the Black Hundreds in Russia and Brown Shirts in Germany (Banaji 2016; Rosenberg 2016).

Apart from the founding of the RSS in 1925 (Basu et al., 1993), the more recent trajectory of the undoing of Indian democracy and the rise of fascism can be traced to a narrow state–business alliance that allowed for unprecedented domination of a small elite in the last few decades of neoliberalism (Patnaik, 2020; Roy, 2020). As Desai (2017) incisively notes,

> [t]he last 25 years have seen a massive expansion of foreign investment, both in the entry of foreign firms and foreign financial investors. In an attempt to make up for the narrowness of the Indian market (which narrowness itself is the result of mass poverty), the ruling classes and global capital are increasingly resorting to grabbing assets of the people, including their meagre productive assets such as land and forest (and of course the minerals underneath). In doing so, they are able to make full use of the autocratic character of the Indian state and political life. This is driving the present intensified onslaught against the peasantry, particularly the tribal peasantry, by foreign and domestic big capital.

The corporate–fascist nexus unfolds along several axes. Neoliberalism and finance capital spur inequality and crisis tendencies in a society with wealth transfer from the poor to the rich. These conditions strengthen fascistic forces in contemporary India. Patnaik (2020: 43) adds, 'the existence of a crisis, a cul-de-sac, a stasis that people would desperately like to overcome, and the utter incapacity of the traditionally powerful and established political formations to do so' contribute to the rise of fascism. As Rosenberg (2016: 90) points out, in these conditions, people are seduced by the anti-establishment and nationalist 'phrase-mongering' of fascist forces, who promise to rectify the destruction caused by liberal–capitalist policies. In the process, people support fascists, who further deepen their exploitation (Varman and Vijay, 2021). Bankers and corporations actively back fascists because of their ability to stamp out any opposition to the dispossession of people and looting of public assets (Poruthiyil, 2021). Thus, it is not surprising that corporations provide support to the BJP. Between 2016 and 2018, the party received 93 per cent of the total funding from 1,731 corporate sources and 86 per cent of the funds from trusts set up by corporations for electoral funding (Association for Democratic Reforms, 2018; Rodriques et al., 2019). Moreover, the corporate-owned media actively support the BJP and make it difficult for the people to imagine alternatives to the current regime (Poruthiyil, 2021).

In such a context, studying and learning from the heterotopia of contentious politics that challenge the ruling elite gain utmost urgency. In the following section, we unpack some key features of heterotopia.

HETEROTOPIA

In an essay in 1967, Michel Foucault delineated the role of space in constructing the world around us. The word 'heterotopia' is derived from the Greek *heteros*, or 'another', and *topos*, or 'place'. Heterotopia is originally a medical term referring to a particular tissue that develops at a place other than is usual; it is not diseased but merely placed elsewhere or a dislocation (Johnson, 2006). In the essay, Foucault differentiates between utopia and heterotopia. Accordingly, utopias are not real spaces and present the possibility of a society in a perfected form. Unlike utopias, Foucault suggests that heterotopias are real sites that act as counter-sites of inversion. Heterotopia or other space is like a mirror.

Foucault elaborates on the idea of heterotopia by pointing to six key principles that constitute it. First, every society has heterotopias. In primitive societies, Foucault suggests there were crisis heterotopias such as boarding schools and military service. These were, and in some instances still continue to be, privileged, sacred or forbidden places reserved for individuals who were in a state of crisis. He gives examples of adolescents, menstruating women, pregnant women, and the elderly. He further observes that in contemporary societies, the crisis heterotopias are persistently disappearing and are replaced by heterotopias of deviation in which individuals whose behaviours deviate from the required mean or norm are placed. A psychiatric hospital or a prison are examples of a heterotopia of deviation; those considered deviant are locked in.

Second, Foucault argues that each heterotopia has a specific function that can change over time. For instance, the cemetery as a heterotopic site of burial was originally considered a sacred site that was to be located next to a church at the centre of a city. In the nineteenth century and after, however, death was seen as an outcome of a diseased body and required dead bodies to be buried outside the boundaries of cities to avoid the spread of diseases. Hence, interpretations of cemeteries as specific settings to confine the dead and as heterotopic spaces underwent a cultural shift. Thus, heterotopias are not always stable because they have contingent characteristics, and the roles they play are constantly evolving. In her novel *The Ministry of Utmost Happiness* (2017), Arundhati Roy locates her protagonists at Jannat guesthouse, which is in a graveyard. Here, Jannat (Urdu for paradise) is in the graveyard, and it is the *duniya* (Urdu for world) that is unliveable. Roy's protagonists seek refuge in the graveyard from the necropolitics of the *duniya*. It is this graveyard that now constitutes the inverted space of collective survival.

Third, Foucault suggests that in one space, a heterotopia can contain multiple, contradictory emplacements. As a result, heterotopias allow for the connection of apparently incompatible spaces. Fourth, he argues that a heterotopia may emplace different temporalities or heterochronies. Foucault (1986: 6) observes,

Heterotopias are most often linked to slices in time – which is to say that they open onto what might be termed, for the sake of symmetry, heterochronies. The heterotopia begins to function at full capacity when men arrive at a sort of absolute break with their traditional time.

As an example of heterochrony, a cemetery emplaces both the end of time with the loss of life and endless time with the presence of a grave as a quasi-eternal marker of an individual's death.

Fifth, heterotopias presuppose specific configurations of opening and closing. While some settings may allow free access to certain spaces, other sites within these settings can remain closed. For example, while a museum may allow free access to certain sections, some other sections may remain out of bounds for the public. Moreover, a heterotopia may create an opening to close access to other spaces. Finally, Foucault suggests that heterotopias are always in relation to all other spaces around them as they create a space of either illusion or compensation. The role of a heterotopia of illusion 'is to create a space of illusion that exposes every real space, all the sites inside of which human life is partitioned, as still more illusory' (Foucault 1986: 8). He gives the example of a brothel as a heterotopia of illusion because it decouples sex from love or other forms of social control as illusory. For Foucault (1986: 8), a heterotopia of compensation is 'a space that is other, another real space, as perfect, as meticulous, as well arranged as ours is messy, ill-constructed, and jumbled'. Heterotopias can act as mirrors of other spaces, as well as new independent spaces for experimentation.

While Foucault offers a sharp analysis of heterotopia, he refuses to attribute to it transformational possibilities. A Foucauldian reading of heterotopia does not offer any particular promise of change, hope, and the possibility of resistance or liberation (Johnson, 2006). In many ways, such a reading was in line with Foucault's general ambivalence towards emancipatory politics and collective action.

As one of the most original and radical thinkers on the role of space, Henri Lefebvre (2003) offers a contrasting reading of heterotopia. In his landmark work *The Production of Space*, Lefebvre (1984) interpreted spaces as products of social action and producers of social relationships and collective social practices. Accordingly, space may be dominated by technology and power or appropriated to serve a subversive group's needs. He notes that paying attention to space allows us to understand how dominant groups produce space and the contentious politics that shape it. Lefebvre (1984), committed to emancipatory politics, notes that class struggle is inscribed in space.

Lefebvre (1984) drew attention to a tripartite division of space as material space, representation of space, and spaces of representation. Material space as perceived space draws attention to the space of experiences and perceptions that are open to physical touch and experience. Representation of space as conceived space highlights the role of representations in the form of urban plans and maps. Space of representation is the lived space of sensations and meanings based on day-to-day activities. This is a conceptual triad of conceived, perceived, and lived space that helps in the analysis of contentious politics as it draws attention to the material spatial dimensions of social life, the symbolic meanings of space, and power relations, as many aspects of social control and contention rest upon the ability to control the spaces of specific social activities.

In his book *The Urban Revolution*, Lefebvre (2003) presents two key features of a heterotopic space. First, a heterotopic site is a historical space of the other and of the marginalized. For instance, he describes marginal spaces in the sixteenth century urban areas that are populated by under-classes of semi-nomads who are viewed with suspicion by those in authority. Second, Lefebvre conceived of heterotopy in tension with isotopy. For Lefebvre (2003: 38, emphasis in original), isotopy is 'everything that makes a place the *same place*. If there is a homologous or analogous place somewhere else, it is part of that isotopy'. Isotopic spaces are hegemonic and allow the dominant ideology to function and prosper. It is the accomplished and rationalized spatial order of capitalism and the state (Harvey 2012). In a dialectical tension with isotopic space, heterotopic space is one of 'difference that marks it by situating it, situating itself with respect to the initial place. This difference can extend from a highly marked contrast all the way to conflict' (Lefebvre, 2003: 38). Moreover, heterotopy and isotopy explain how utopias dialectically emerge by uniting difference (Johnson, 2006). Therefore, a heterotopic space is pregnant with the possibilities of creating a utopia that is considered an elsewhere space of desire, power, and thought (Lefebvre, 2003). In fact, Harvey (2012: xvii) suggests that Lefebvre's concept of heterotopic spaces 'delineates liminal social spaces of possibility where "something different" is not only possible but foundational for the redefining of revolutionary trajectories'.

Unlike Foucault's reading of heterotopia that is top-down and within the realm of representation of space, Lefebvre's interpretation is more in sync with the space of representation (Sacco, Ghiradi, Tartari, and Trimarchi, 2019). In Lefebvre's analysis, there is a fundamental difference between the representation of space and the space of representation. Representation of space is space as conceived by urbanists, architects, planners, and the forces of capitalism. It is about the production of relations and the imposition of order by means of the dominant ideology (Sacco et al., 2019). In contrast, the space of representation is underground, clandestine, and rooted in the experiential dimension of practices. It is notable that Lefebvre (2003: 129) suggests that 'anomic groups construct heterotopic spaces'. As Sacco et al. (2019: 203) further note, 'here, capitalist ideology shows its intrinsic limit: its lack of awareness of the deep causes, effects, motives, and implications of the action of social forces, that it constantly attempts to embezzle, but at best with partial success'. Such a reading of heterotopic space eschews the representational trap and offers the possibility of appropriation of spaces by contentious politics. In this interpretation, heterotopia functions as a platform of empowerment of the weak and emancipatory actions.

In summary, Lefebvre's reading of heterotopic space can enable a deeper understanding of sites of resistance, contradictions, and conflicts. In this chapter, we examine LeftWord as a heterotopic space. Lefebvre's conceptualization helps to comprehend how LeftWord, with its politics, resists capitalism, the current ruling dispensation, and their project of fascism in India.

METHODOLOGY

We conducted an interpretive inquiry over three years. We make use of three forms of data. Our first data source comprises interview transcripts and field notes from 2017–2018. The first author conducted interviews with the founding managing editor and marketing manager of LeftWord. We did multiple rounds of interviews with these participants in Delhi. We also interviewed three readers who were members of the LeftWord book club. Through these interviews, we sought to understand the history of LeftWord, its current operations, and key challenges and learnings. Second, we examined books published by LeftWord to understand its publishing activity and key areas of concern and emphasis. In this way, we also went beyond the publishers' spoken words to understand how their left politics are given a material form. Third, we observed and analysed their online activities on May Day. LeftWord organizes a May Day event every year as part of their celebration of international workers' days. In the last two years, the event was organized online because of the pandemic. The first author also worked as a volunteer at the May Day celebrations in 2018 to understand how the event furthers left politics.

Our interpretation of the texts in the database was through a hermeneutical process that involved continuous movement between transcripts and field notes and the emergent understanding of the data (Gadamer, 2004). The theoretical understanding presented in this chapter reflects a stage of analysis in which it is possible to establish linkages between meanings expressed by participants and the broader issue of heterotopic space.

THE HETEROTOPIC SPACE OF LEFTWORD

Interpreting LeftWord as a heterotopic site, we first describe its *emancipatory futures, inversions and contradictions*, and *marginality*. We then describe *performative staging of resistance* and *copresence, scales, and solidarity* in this heterotopic space.

EMANCIPATORY FUTURES

Prakash Karat of the Communist Party of India-Marxist (CPI-M) registered Naya Rasta Publishers as a non-government organization on 15 June 1993. The idea behind Naya Rasta (meaning new road in Hindi) was to create space for left writings, ideological debates, and movements at a time when Marxist thought was on a decline with the fall of the Soviet Union and India's economic liberalization in 1991. In December 1998, Sudhanva Deshpande, who had been working with Tulika, another independent publishing house, joined hands with Prakash Karat to launch LeftWord, as a publishing arm of Naya Rasta. Currently, Sudhanva Deshpande is the managing editor, Vijay Prashad is the editor, and Sanjay Kundan is an editorial consultant for Hindi books published by Vaam Prakashan (another imprint of Naya Rasta focusing on Hindi publications).

LeftWord's objective of furthering Marxist thought makes emancipation of exploited classes and oppressed social groups central to its politics. Such a commitment is reflected in LeftWord's very first book published in 1999 – *A World to Win: Essays on the Communist Manifesto*. This edited volume included the *Communist Manifesto* and essays by Aijaz Ahmad, Irfan Habib, and Prabhat Patnaik – three leading Marxist scholars. In his essay, Patnaik (1999: 159–160) wrote,

> Globalized finance capital has undermined the possibility, not only of Keynesian demand management but indeed of any form of significant state intervention. It is not just Keynesianism that is in retreat today but social democracy, welfare capitalism, Third World nationalism, planning in all its different varieties, and all 'isms' that seek to use the state to overcome the problems of spontaneous capitalism.

With close attention to the destructive role of finance capital, Patnaik anticipated the coming of post-democracy in India. Patnaik (1999: 265) added, 'Third World economies caught in the vortex of globalized finance experience a combination of economic crisis, social strife along lines that divide the people, as well as an erosion of sovereignty and democracy.'

Sudhanva Deshpande's myriad activities and deep commitment to left politics shape the LeftWord space. Apart from his role as a managing editor, Deshpande is also a theatre director, actor, and writer. He has been a member and organizer of the left-wing street theatre group, Jana Natya Manch (Janam), since 1987. The legendary theatre artist Safdar Hashmi co-founded Janam in 1973. Over the years, Janam has staged numerous iconic plays that focus on working-class struggles. Goons fatally attacked Safdar Hashmi in the midst of a street play in 1989. In his recent book titled *Halla Bol* (published by LeftWord in 2019), Deshpande chronicles an account of the life and death of Safdar Hashmi. Deshpande was among those performing the play *Halla Bol* on that fateful day. The book *Halla Bol* sheds light on the life and work of a popular, much loved progressive artist from a comrade's personal voice. *Halla Bol* also serves as a text on the sociopolitical context that produced left activists like Deshpande. In one of the passages, Deshpande discusses the prevailing political climate in Delhi University in the 1970s,

> Young activists on the left would have raging debates on the character of the Indian ruling class. Was it the national bourgeoisie, or an alliance of the monopoly capitalists and the big landlords, or the comprador bourgeoisie that ruled India? Those who argued the national bourgeoisie line wanted to see a National Democratic Revolution in India; those who argued the monopoly capitalists–big landlord line wanted to see a People's Democratic Revolution; and those who argued the comprador bourgeoisie line felt that a socialist revolution was imminent and that one spark would light the prairie fire.

Consistent with LeftWord's mission of taking emancipatory politics to the different pockets of the country, the book, *Halla Bol*, has been subsequently translated to Hindi, Kannada, and Tamil, while the Marathi, Telugu, and Malayalam translations are in the works.

Meanwhile, Deshpande has also co-created a riveting 20-episode podcast, which deftly infuses the textures and tonalities of theatre into the digital audio form. The space of LeftWord must be understood through these numerous emplacements that artists, activists, and writers gift in terms of form, language, and cultural practices.

With India's neoliberal turn, the 1990s was a period of decline for left movements and trade unions. Long-standing pillars of left literature in India, such as the People's Publishing House (PPH), had also weakened. Deshpande further shared,

> There is a tradition of readers groups, study groups within the left. And outside of the left, but certainly within the left. I am afraid that we are losing some of that. There used to be study groups that I used to be part of when I was growing up. I don't necessarily see Student Federation of India kids or whatever-is-comparable students being part of study groups anymore. In Delhi, at least, there are random groups of people. They are not political at all, but they are people who are nuts about books, and they have used the studio space occasionally because they go to different places and have their meetings. I am just thinking, why have we lost it on the left? Why don't we have that capability anymore? Why are we not interested anymore?

Deshpande emphasizes politics with the purpose of, as Lefebvre (2003: 29) notes, removing 'blind spots'. To reveal blind spots that are ideologically cultivated, alternative ways of seeing have to be encouraged and facilitated. Deshpande believes that LeftWord attempts to create these emancipatory possibilities by disseminating Marxist literature and writings that critically engage with India's capitalist landscape.

For a heterotopic site to offer emancipatory possibilities, it needs to give space a specific meaning and create linkages with several sites that serve the same function of challenging the powerful (Lefebvre, 2003). The creation of the current physical space of the May Day Bookstore in 2012 is at the heart of this heterotopic site. In certain ways, this heterotopic space is constituted through the life and times of Safdar Hashmi – a haunting that is alive and present and refuses to be murdered or repressed (Gordon, 2008). In *Halla Bol*,

Deshpande recounts how Safdar Hashmi had shared his dream of a cultural centre for multiple art forms in a working-class area. Deshpande writes that this dream was posthumously fulfilled when Janam created Studio Safdar in Shadipur, West Delhi. Deshpande writes (2019: 255), 'Today, it has become one of the cultural hubs in the city, alongside its next-door neighbour, the May Day Bookstore, set up by LeftWord Books.' Deshpande shared how several left-leaning artists donated their performances or shows to LeftWord to help establish the bookstore-cum-LeftWord office,

> Shabana Azmi said, 'I have a show. Let me give you that for free. You sell my show, and you get money for that.' This was Tumhari Amrita. Eventually, what worked out was that we did an eight-day festival at Prithvi Theater in Bombay where we got shows from all these people for free. So Tumhari Amrita, there were two shows in one evening. Then Nasiruddin Shah gave us a show – two performances of the same show. Swanand Kirkire gave us two shows. Shubha Mudgal gave us a concert. Sunil Shanbhag and Rajat Kapoor gave us a show, again two shows per evening. We were able to put together a festival actually of eight-ten days, something like that. What that also meant was that they were then also able to reach out to a large number of people.

LeftWord found a building to house its office and launch the May Day Bookstore because of its links with several other spaces. In 2012, LeftWord tied up with Janam, All India Democratic Women's Association (AIDWA), and the School Teachers' Federation of India to purchase a four-storeyed building in Shadipur, with each organization getting one floor. It is from here that LeftWord launched the May Day Bookstore on 1 May 2012. Thus, we see multiple times, spaces, hopes, and imaginations juxtaposed in the heterotopic space of LeftWord Books.

Apart from these juxtapositions, we witness several attempts to extend the heterotopic space of LeftWord. For instance, the opening of the May Day Bookstore allowed readers to physically visit a site that furthered emancipatory politics in numerous ways. Moreover, publishing at affordable prices compared to corporate publishing houses makes the space more accessible for those seeking Marxist writings at a low price. LeftWord also started a book club early on; book club members get discounts on publications. Well before the e-commerce tide, LeftWord had extended its space into the digital world with a website from which readers could order their books (NewsClick, 2019). Rashi, who had just finished her postgraduate degree and was discovering Marxist writings, found the LeftWord website a 'great place to start'. She found that compared to Amazon or other 'South Delhi bookstores' (a relatively upmarket residential area) where 'there is a lot of trash that you have to go through', it was convenient to find all these compilations in one place. At the time of our conversation, she was a member of the Democratic Youth Federation of India (youth wing of the CPI-M) and actively involved in their study circle. This study circle drew on LeftWord titles that they found were affordable compared to other publishers. Rashi added that she loved their bookmarks and book cover designs, which Deshpande enjoys personally crafting.

Another attempt at extending the space is by publishing diverse books. LeftWord increased its publishing from 8 to 10 titles in 2016–2017 to about 20 in 2021. Their target is to increase the number of published books each year to 50 in the next couple of years. LeftWord also aims to expand its portfolio to include more fiction and poetry. Extending the heterotopic space also demands a serious commitment to document and disseminate left writings from different parts of the country. LeftWord has translated numerous writings that were otherwise only available for a vernacular audience. For example, Vinay, an Indian Administrative Services aspirant, shared that he discovered Kerala's rich contributions to communist thought through LeftWord's English translations since he was not comfortable reading in Malayalam. More recently, Naya Rasta launched Vaam Prakashan as its Hindi publishing arm. Vaam Prakashan publishes several LeftWord publications' translations. Vaam Prakashan states, 'Ek aisey daur mein jab soch par taley laganey ki koshishein jaari hain, Vaam Prakashan jujharu aur nidar awaazon ko buland karney ka vaada karta hai' (In an era of thought control, Vaam Prakashan promises to uphold and promote contentious and fearless voices). There is a need to publish books in various Indian languages in order to reach India's vast non-elite classes and non-English groups. More recently (as mentioned earlier with *Halla Bol*'s translations), LeftWord has made a conscious attempt to achieve this goal and expand its space.

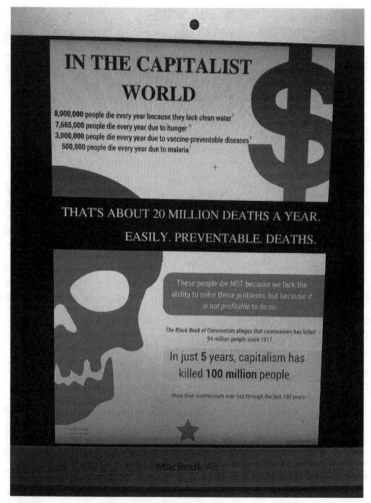

IMAGE 8.2   Posters on the LeftWord office walls
Source: Rohit Varman.

Finally, the physical space of LeftWord and the May Day Bookstore furthers emancipatory politics. As mentioned earlier, the bookstore's doors are stencilled with '8 hours of work, 8 hours of sleep, and 8 hours for books and coffee'. The bookstore is lined with Marxist titles that aim to inspire entrants into the space to imagine anti-capitalist possibilities. Challenging the post-democratic order, the bookstore's walls have posters that point to capitalist violence and revolutionary struggles (see Images 8.2 and 8.3).

IMAGE 8.3   Posters on the LeftWord office walls
Source: Sudhanva Deshpande.

These posters that call for political action and political consciousness emplace LeftWord's emancipatory politics and make it come alive for the bookstore's visitors. For instance, the poster in Image 8.2 informs visitors that capitalism is a war on people in which millions have been killed in a short span of time. It juxtaposes a skull with the dollar sign to prompt people to think about connections between deathworlds and capital. It also debunks the capitalist propaganda of communism as a violent system and instead points to the violence of profiteering.

In summary, the space of LeftWord shows that heterotopias are 'spaces of alternative ordering' (Hetherington, 1997: 41), which aim to move those who encounter them to emancipatory possibilities that challenge capitalist exploitation and fascist post-democracy.

INVERSIONS AND CONTRADICTIONS

LeftWord is a counter-site that inverts the reality around it in several ways. There is a spatial inversion that is evident in its location. The May Day

IMAGE 8.4   LeftWord office and May Day Bookstore (inside)
Source: Rohit Varman.

Bookstore is emplaced at the end of a busy bazaar and is surrounded by a wholesale tailoring shop, a milk booth, and a shop that sells rolls and *biryani*. The bookstore stands out as a site of difference in such a bazaar. Unlike the disorderly, somewhat chaotic commercial space of bazaar outside full of different sounds, colours, and people, the May Day Bookstore is serene, aesthetically decorated, and adjacent to the artistic space of Studio Safdar (see Image 8.4).

As a heterotopic space, LeftWord has a key contradiction – the idea of selling books that further Marxism and communist ideals through contemporary markets and businesses. This contradiction manifests as two nodal conflicts at LeftWord – selling books to generate revenues and ideological alignment among employees. On the one hand, LeftWord inverts the dominant capitalist ideology by publishing anti-capitalist books. Despite this ideological inversion, LeftWord has to sell books to increase its readership and generate resources as an ongoing entity. This conflict sharply surfaces in its usage of Amazon as an effective and efficient channel to sell books. Deshpande had worked at Tulika publishing for five years before starting LeftWord. He understood the conflicts of running a book business that simultaneously aimed to transcend capitalism. In our conversations, Deshpande shared how Amazon created visibility for their publications. Amazon brought in orders daily; tracked and supplied orders; gave an alert to LeftWord if products were not sold and suggested discounts. Deshpande elaborated,

> It is amazing. There are many different examples I can give.... [Amazon] will teach you how to discount, there is a fee for it. Amazon is quick with payments. You get money every fortnight or every month, which is wonderful. Which is a huge difference. The moment we started selling online, and on Amazon we have found that the cash flow is so much better.

LeftWord's attempt to create a readership of Marxist literature partially relies on selling books through monopoly capital. As a result, the heterotopic space is partially penetrated by neoliberal ideals of marketization and efficiency. Amazon's key advantage is quick payments and improved cash flows. These advantages need to be understood in the context of India's publishing business.

The publishing industry in India works on a system of credit. Since it is a small independent publisher, LeftWord pays upfront for printing books and is stuck in long credit cycles that have to be offered to its distributors and booksellers. Because of the prevailing power relations, these intermediaries delay payments and frequently return unsold books that add to LeftWord's financial burden. Amazon does not have these conditions and offers a more efficient model of selling for LeftWord. However, Amazon's effectiveness and efficiency are always tainted. LeftWord realizes that Amazon is monopoly capital, a force they are trying to overturn with the books they publish. Deshpande explained, 'As a Marxist, I have a problem with monopoly capital.' He refers to other independent publishers like Naveen Kishore of Seagull Books, Kolkata, who have refrained from using Amazon for ideological reasons. Deshpande added, 'Naveen [Kishore] – he has a different philosophy on these things. Naveen would die 1000 deaths before getting Amazon to do it. He will do his own printing. He would not let anybody else do it.' Deshpande considers Naveen Kishore a friend and appreciates his ideological commitment to left politics. However, Deshpande also points to the pragmatics of running a business that make him use Amazon to sell LeftWord books. He believes that Seagull has far greater resources that allow it to shun Amazon. Mallick, the marketing manager, further explained these compulsions,

> We get a good revenue – we are getting Rs 50,000 to 60,000 every month from Amazon. It's good for LeftWord. You have to work for one or two hours a day to regulate the price; you have to change the price daily, some days you have to increase the price, sometimes you have to decrease the price. On the LeftWord website, we get orders, but our website is not running well. That is a technical problem, but when it's working, we have got really good orders.

While some technical problems were salient at the time of our interview with Mallick in 2018, LeftWord has recently upgraded its website to address most technical glitches. As a result, sales through the website have increased. Apart from technical glitches that limited the usage of the LeftWord website in the past, there is a low awareness about the publisher. While left-leaning academics and activists are likely to be aware of the website, other readers are unlikely to know. Thus, more specialized books on the Soviet Union or the Bolshevik revolution may get sold from the website, but books of more general interest (such as the writings of Bhagat Singh or A. G. Noorani) are likely to sell easily on Amazon.

LeftWord also attempted to create an alternative distribution system. LeftWord, along with eight other like-minded publishers, created Independent Publishers Distributors Association (IPDA). However, Deshpande explained that IPDA has not been successful,

> People from our type of business are not necessarily business-minded. In local shops, they calculate every paisa. Their heads are screwed in the right way, and our heads are screwed in the wrong way. They (IPDA) choose options that make life easier for them. They have to pay for it. If IPDA sells a book that is less than INR 500, they make a loss. That is not the case with LeftWord. We can sell our books. We take a book from others and sell it for INR 250. IPDA cannot do that. Amazon figured that out. Every transaction that is happening either at the front end or back end, they are just milking it.

LeftWord was compelled to partner with Amazon because of these limitations, resulting in an ideological conflict. More recently, LeftWord has tried to address this conflict. It has tied up with a print-on-demand partner, Repro India, that uploads its titles on Amazon. Repro India also handles the publisher's Kindle sales, makes LeftWord books internationally and domestically available, and collects orders, processes, and services them. Thus, while the heterotopic space is mired in an ideological conflict of compromising with monopoly capital, there are ongoing attempts to reduce dependence on Amazon.

The second domain of inversion and conflict is that of employees. As a form of inversion, Vijay Prashad and Sudhanva Deshpande do not draw salaries. While Deshpande was paid initially and then drew a salary intermittently, he has not drawn a salary since 2016. According to Deshpande,

> [a]ny publishing house will give an arm and a leg to hire Vijay [Prashad], but even at a conservative figure, let's say if each of us were to be paid 75,000 rupees. I think it is a conservative figure. Even then, you're talking about a lakh and a half (per month). I would like a situation

where we can be in a position where we can pay a lakh and a half for salary, maybe hire one editor. If we can hire people like that, and if that means that Vijay and I don't have to do a lot of the work we are doing today, it would just help everybody.

While the editors do not draw salaries, they recognize that their employees need money for sustenance. For example, Mallick, who works as a marketing manager at LeftWord, came to it as a regular corporate employee. He had a Bachelor of Commerce and Masters in Business Administration with specializations in Marketing and Finance. Mallick explained,

> I joined marketing when I did my summer internship. I had never dealt in books. First, I dealt with insurance products. Then I dealt with Unilever FMCG products – this product is totally different. In the books industry if you say 'product,' people get angry – 'it's not a product! it's books!' The nature of selling of books and the nature of selling of any other product is different. When I saw books, I thought how could I sell books to somebody. I thought for two or three months. I did several things, I studied from the internet, and I studied Philip Kotler's book on marketing management.

Unlike Deshpande and Prashad, Mallick may not have a clear Marxist ideological affiliation. This does not mean that employees such as Mallick are not committed to LeftWord. In fact, Mallick is a core contributor to LeftWord's everyday activities. However, LeftWord's career opportunities and salaries may not be competitive. Employees who face socio-economic constraints are likely to seek conventional career paths and monetary compensation. Deshpande shared this contradiction,

> You can't have it both ways. On the one side, you can't say that we are a business and not respect the monetary value of those skills. Otherwise, you'll have to have to run it as a voluntary group, which is a totally different model. You just cannot do that. Then what do you? There's no third option that I can see.

In summary, LeftWord is a space of inversion of the capitalist ethos in terms of the books it publishes and sells. However, it is also a site that is partially penetrated by neoliberalism and monopoly capital with some emphases on markets, marketing, and remunerations.

MARGINALITY

LeftWord was created as a heterotopic space for what was rendered as a marginal ideology. Neoliberal capitalism was increasingly colonizing most sociocultural spaces and institutions in India in the 1990s. In particular, after the fall of Soviet Union in 1991, there was a belief that communist ideals were archaic, and the future could only be imagined along capitalist lines. LeftWord was founded to displace capitalist time and to create heterochrony (Foucault, 1986), so as to imagine another temporal possibility. Another time was from the margins of the prevailing hegemony of neoliberal capitalism, and yet it was, and continues to be, central to alternative imaginations. Thus, LeftWord is an attempt to alter the temporal rhythm of the present order to create a site that resurrected what was marginalized by the dominant ethos.

LeftWord is also a site of spatial marginality. It is located in Shadipur, about 7 kilometres to the West of Connaught Place, the central business district in New Delhi (see Image 8.1). The marginality of the bookstore is evident in Deshpande's account,

> We are in a tiny bookstore and one not very gentrified area. It is not in the University site, it is not in Connaught Place, not in South Extension, not in Haus Khas Village… not in a mall, none of the places that people hang out, so if anybody comes here, they come here. This is the only place. People can't come here and then say, oh okay, let me also go to this restaurant or whatever it is, right. There is nothing else here.

Shadipur was one of the several villages that the British acquired to construct New Delhi. On the one side of LeftWord office is the Pusa Institute campus – an agricultural research institute that was initially in Pusa, Bihar, and was relocated to Delhi following a devastating earthquake. Thus, the name of that place in itself contains another place in Bihar. The state acquired 500 acres of land, and those dispossessed were relocated in informal settlements in Shadipur region. In 1976, in an instance of state brutality, the police opened fire on settlements at Turkman Gate, Old Delhi. The evicted families, predominantly Muslims, were relocated to Shadipur, among other localities. As one steps outside the bookstore, it is like stepping into Old Delhi's narrow, crowded streets. The relocated lives refabricated through fragments of Old Delhi. Thus, the heterotopia of LeftWord is temporally and spatially located at the margins.

Finally, this heterotopic space is also constituted through the political margins. For instance, LeftWord reaffirmed its commitment to those at the political margins by allying with the protests against the CAA, which discriminates against Muslims and other religious minorities. LeftWord invited poet Aamir Aziz to recite his poem 'Sub kuch yaad rakha jayega' (Everything will be remembered) on May Day in 2020:

Tum raat likho hum chand likhenge,
Tum jail mein dalo hum deewar phand likhenge,
Tum FIR likho hum hain taiyar likhenge,
Tum humein qatl kar do hum banke bhoot likhenge,
Tumhare qatl ke sare saboot likhenge,
Sab yaad rakha jayega,
Sab kuch yaad rakha jayega.
Aur tum seyahiyon se jhooth likhoge,
Humein maloom hai,
Ho humare khoon se hi sahi, sach zaroor likha jayega.

You write the night, but we will write the moon.
You put us in jail, we will jump over the walls and still write.
You lodge an FIR against us, we are set to write about the injustice we suffer.
You murder us, we will come as ghosts and still write.
We will remember everything. We will remember it all.
You will ink down lies, we know it well.
May be with our blood, but plainly the truth will be written and published someday.

In summary, LeftWord as a heterotopic space is constituted by marginality – temporal, spatial, and political. However, as Lefebvre (2003) reminds us, such margins are often vibrant sites of possibilities that offer another imagination to the world.

PERFORMATIVE STAGING OF RESISTANCE

The other key element of LeftWord as a heterotopia is the performative staging of resistance through material practices. As Swyngedouw (2011: 372) suggests,

> the political arises then in the act of performatively staging equality, a procedure that simultaneously makes visible the 'wrong' of the given situation. For example, when, in 1955, Rosa Parks sat down on the 'wrong' seat on the bus in Montgomery, Alabama, she simultaneously staged equality and exposed the inegalitarian practice of a racialized instituted order, despite the latter's constitutional presentation of equality.

Performative staging of resistance in the context of LeftWord refers to material enactments that challenge the dominance of finance capital and rising fascism.

The performative staging is evident in the writings of Vijay Prashad, who joined as chief editor at LeftWord in 2015. Prashad is a historian who has written 30 books, including *The Darker Nations: A People's History of the Third World* and *The Poorer Nations: A Possible History of the Global South*. Prashad worked as a tenured professor at Trinity College (1996–2017), United States, before quitting to co-found the Tricontinental Institute. Writing the introduction to a LeftWord book titled *Lenin 150* to commemorate the 150th birth anniversary of V. I. Lenin, Prashad (2020: 13) reminds his readers,

> Revolutions do not repeat themselves in all their particulars, nor do revolutionary processes. Different historical conjunctures, the concrete

situations, require different historical revolutionary dynamics. We have Lenin over our shoulders; he is our inspiration and model.

This book includes poems by Vladimir Mayakovsky, a renowned Soviet poet, and an essay by Lenin – 'The three sources and three component parts of Marxism'. In another writing, 'Red star over the Third World', Prashad (2018: 40) described the Bolshevik revolution and the founding of the Soviet Union and observed that the October revolution inspired anti-colonial and anti-capitalist imaginations across the Global South,

> Without the October Revolution, would the people colonized by Europe have risen up in the way that they did? Would 1919 have been peppered with uprisings of the colonized against their imperial masters – from the uprising in Egypt led by Saad Zaghloul Pasha to the March First Movement in Korea to the May Fourth Movement in China; and then the next year, to the revolt in Iraq against British rule, and then in 1921 the Mongolian Revolution that created three years later the second socialist state in the world? Did they get their confidence from the October Revolution? If not for the class demands from the USSR the Indian National Congress would never have adopted in 1919 the demands of the peasantry.

Through these writings, LeftWord creates a heterotopic site that becomes a space of resistance to the current right-wing hegemony.

Performative staging of resistance and its emphasis on material practices are unmistakably noticeable at LeftWord's May Day event where, typically, there is a used books sale and artists and activists perform and speak. The event draws large crowds. In 2018, we noted that despite the summer heat and no air-conditioning, people across age groups thronged the store on 1 May. The adjacent Studio Safdar was packed with books that people had donated, and buyers jostled with each other in the small space (see Image 8.5).

In this annual event, it is common to see Delhi University historian Mukul Manglik serving coffee and several artists like Rahul Ram performing

IMAGE 8.5   May Day book sale, 2018
Source: Rohit Varman.

regularly. Ram is also part of the *Aisi Taisi Democracy* satirical/musical act, along with script-writer Varun Grover and stand-up comedian Sanjay Rajoura. Hinting at India's current state of post-democracy, Ram sang the following in his 2020 performance:

Hain re hain ye democracy!
Saap ke muh me chuchunder jaisi
Ugli jain na, nigli jain,
Aisi taisi democracy!

Oh, this lamentable democracy!
Like a muskrat in a snake's jaw
We can neither spit it nor swallow it
Our troubled democracy!

He followed it with another song in 2021, more directly criticizing India's current ruling formation by deploying 'Gobhiji' (literally a cauliflower) as a disguised reference to Narendra Modi:

Gobhiji, Gobhiji, kumbh mela, ralliyon subko on kar diya
Jab lagi oxygen ki line, apne badli apni line
Atma nirbhar hain desh, yeh announce kar diya
Gobhiji, Gobhiji kaise leader ho tum ji
Pure desh ki tumne has ke kabre khodi ji

Gobhiji, Gobhiji, you organized Kumbh Mela, election rallies
When people needed oxygen, you claimed that the country is self-sufficient
What kind of a leader are you?
You converted the country into a graveyard.

In 2020, the event included an interview with Aishi Ghosh, president of Jawaharlal Nehru University (JNU) Student Union. Ghosh discussed with Vijay Prashad the plights of workers, women, and students in light of the Indian government's recent decision to impose a draconian lockdown. Ghosh also pointed to how education had become commodified under neoliberalism. In a compelling response, Prashad observed,

It's a funny kind of democracy, Aishi, where you can have, in fact, you can celebrate the unions of the capitalist class, the federation of capitalists. They can gather, and they can have huge programmes. PM [prime minister] will address them. You know you can have all the unions that are totally acceptable, but unions of working people, unions of students are not acceptable ... it's a class attack on associations.

In 2021, another poet, Mridula Shukla, recited the poem 'Tum to gosht par hi zinda ho' (You survive on flesh):

Jab tum khode rahe hote ho khai, apne aur unke bich
Tab sir par tokra liye huye bana rahe hote hain pul
Tum ji lete ho unke hisse ki puri chaon
Bach jaati hain unke hisse mein bas dhoop...
Rotiya unke thali mein kum, bhook tumahre pet me adhik hoti hain...
Ek din jab charam pe hogi tumhari bhook aur khatam ho jayagi unki rasad
Unhi pulon se pahochenge tum tak, lekin darna mat...
Bas we utha lenge khane ka samaan...
Tumahara kyan, tum to gosht par hi zinda ho

When you are creating a chasm between you and them
They are constructing your bridges
You live their share of shade
They live their lives in the blazing sun...
They have less food on their plates,
but your greed for food is insatiable...
When your greed is at its peak,
and you have consumed all their food
They will come to you using those bridges
but you don't have to be scared...
They will only take away your food...
But so what, you anyway survive on flesh.

Unpaid young volunteers manage this performative staging of resistance on May Day. The volunteers come not only from in and around Delhi but also from other parts of the country. Deshpande elaborated,

These are just kids who are interested in things. A lot of them are kids who are interested in books, actually. They like to read; that's what draws them here. Word spreads, there is word of mouth – that is the ultimate thing.

Further emphasizing the performative element, Deshpande drew attention to the role of the bookstore café,

> People understand a left-wing bookstore, they don't understand what a left-wing cafe can be, so there was that curiosity. You know that a lot of people who came in that day were asking, 'accha, left-wing café ka kya matlab hain? How can coffee be left wing?' There is a history of politics and alternative politics that has always been part of coffee houses generally … the whole tradition of the discussion, debate, dissent, and so on.

Deshpande reminds us of the role of café as part of the public sphere that was integral to democratic politics in several parts of the world (Habermas, 1989). Indian Coffee House, a café chain, is a workers' cooperative and has a long-intertwined history with workers' movements in the country. In fact, on the founding day of the May Day Bookstore in 2012, two pictures from India Coffee House in Thrissur and Allepey were placed in the bookstore. One of the pictures showed a billing counter at the India Coffee House, with A. K. Gopalan's picture garlanded. Gopalan was a prominent communist leader who led the movement to create the India Coffee House.

In summary, performative staging of resistance that foregrounds concrete material practices is central to the heterotopic space of LeftWord. The performative staging at LeftWord takes several forms, such as the publishing of radical books, artists' performances portraying capitalist exploitation, and poetry readings that challenge India's road to fascism.

COPRESENCE, SCALES AND SOLIDARITY

Although LeftWord is located at the margins, copresence, scales, and solidarities are integral to its heterotopic essence. LeftWord has sought to create a solidarity network through its 3,000 book club members, who get discounts on books, complimentary e-books, and regular newsletters about

LeftWord events. The book club has 1,900 lifetime members and nearly 1,100 annual members. LeftWord allows people to interact with one another and brings them into each other's presence, either personally and bodily or through virtual platforms. Copresence helps to foster solidarities or commitment to collective action (Chatzidakis, McLaren, and Varman, 2021).

LeftWord creates copresence in several ways. The May Day event, and more so, the recent online version, allows people from different parts of the world to come together. For instance, in its internationalist spirit, LeftWord invited a host of international singers to participate in 2020. They included Jose Delegado from Venezuela, Tania Saleh from Lebanon, and Roger Waters from the United States. It also invites artists from different parts of India to perform (see Image 8.6). Their songs and performances contribute to contagious excitement that Durkheim (1995) called collective effervescence, and which, as he pointed out, enhances the participants' sense of solidarity with other participants.

Moreover, LeftWord creates the copresence of several social movements in the country within its space. For instance, it has published several books on caste. Many of these inclusions are not without their conflicts. Consider the example of Mythily Sivaraman's (2016: 184) writing on Periyar's role in Tamil Nadu's caste and class politics:

In the global struggle against racialism, radicals the world over have come to see the basic need of providing the oppressed black man with a sense of identity, a feeling of self-esteem which could emancipate him inside, from the impressed patterns of servility. A man has, first of all, to assert to himself his human worth before he could look the oppressor in the face and say NO. This is the case of the American Negro; this is the need of the Harijan. That Periyar sought to give such an identity to the lower caste Hindus is a social fact which appears to have escaped the serious attention of the Marxists in Tamil Nadu.

Such writing is critical of the orthodoxy on caste that has prevailed in several left movements. LeftWord tries to overcome that orthodoxy by creating a copresence of Dalit politics in a Marxist space. Vinay, a regular LeftWord reader, noted that the publisher was 'connected, and in the same space' as

IMAGE 8.6 May Day 2018 – an artist performing
Source: Rohit Varman.

independent anti-caste publishing houses like Navayana because they both 'brought forward writings that are at the margins, in an affordable way'. Vinay added that he often tied his visits to the May Day Bookstore with a play or a cultural event at Studio Safdar.

The heterotopia of LeftWord is marked by the copresence of a range of issues that move across different scales, to create broader solidarities. For example, the LeftWord website hosts over 60 allied publishers, including Navayana, Gaysi (queer publishing space), and Adivaani (publishing and archiving initiative for indigenous literature). These independent publishers provide spaces for writings that are often marginalized by corporate publishing houses. Thus, these publications create different scales in the heterotopic space. As Leitner et al. (2008: 159) note, '[s]cale is conceptualised as a relational, power-laden and contested construction that actors strategically engage with, in order to legitimise or challenge existing power relations. In the course of these struggles, new scales are constructed, and the relative importance of different scales is reconfigured'.

As another example of different scales, consider the panel discussion on May Day 2021, 'We can't breathe'. Vijay Prashad discussed the Indian state's handling of the pandemic with Tejal Kanitkar, Sathyajit Rath, and Prabir Purkayastha. Pointing to the complete failure of the state, Rath observed,

> In all of these matters – in providing acute medical care of an order that is important, in acknowledging the long-lasting consequences and hardships that are involved, and therefore the governance and politics that are necessary and in dealing with the private sector vis-à-vis the issue of vaccination in particular, India has failed itself.

Kanitkar added to this analysis,

> In the long run, if you don't vaccinate enough people fast enough, you are going to keep seeing surges. And if it is going to keep leading to economic upheavals, it's not even good for capital … it is almost as if the Modi government doesn't know how to even do capitalism properly.

This move to include the ongoing health crisis in India and to engage with experts who understand the state's failures in handling the pandemic are part of scalar strategies commonly used in left politics. The panel discussion on the pandemic makes the heterotopia of LeftWord more relevant for here and now. Instead of the more abstract capitalist relations, it raises issues of local concern – a local caught in the vortex of a devastating pandemic. The panel discussion exemplifies scale-jumping with Kanitkar moving from the Modi government's failure to protect individual citizens' health to being bad for capitalism at a broader scale. In such scale-jumping, connections are made between local, national, and global issues to expand the reach of left politics.

In a similar vein, LeftWord forges solidarities with the ongoing farmers' movement. In the May Day 2021 celebration, a session on the ongoing farmers' protest included interviews with key leaders such as Joginder Ugraha, Dharm Pal, and Rakesh Tikait. LeftWord provided the space for a copresence of farm leaders, activists, and viewers. Such copresence fosters solidarities by framing the ongoing state of post-democracy as a shared concern. As Ugraha sharply observed in his talk,

[t]his [farmers' movement] is a big battle. Don't make the mistake of under-estimating it.... This is a fight against the World Trade Organization.... This is not just about Modi government. It is a fight against the capitalist system. Nobody will be spared from the destruction [caused by the change in farm laws]. It will destroy farmers, workers, and small businesses. Everybody will get adversely affected. It's about food security and food. We all have to participate in it for our survival.

Ugraha draws attention to capitalist imperatives, whereby severely exploited workers and farmers whose lands are forcibly acquired bear the costs of corporatization and private accumulation (RUPE, 2020). Dharm Pal added to the above observations,

The government has enacted the three laws to drive farmers out of farming to hand over agriculture to large businesses. Indian agriculture was already in a state of deep crisis, and now the government is making it simpler for corporations to further drive farmers into the abyss of poverty and death.

Without naming the misdeeds of robber-bankers, corporate managers, and other agents of neoliberal capitalism, Ugraha and Pal point to the

ongoing crisis and the destruction caused by profiteering. These activities at
LeftWord foreground several scales. In such attempts to create a copresence
in the heterotopic space, there is a jump across scales – inclusion of protest
happening more locally in north India and reminders that the local is deeply
integrated in the global circuits of capital. As Sewell (2001: 67–68) notes,
'[a]lthough scale jumping is usually a matter of calling broader-scale forces
into a local struggle, it can also work in the opposite direction, with national-
scale forces seeking refuge from unequal struggles by retreating to a more
local scale where their chances are much better'.

Summing up, LeftWord is a space that resists India's descent into a
post-democratic society with rising fascist tendencies. As a heterotopic
space, LeftWord is characterized by marginality, emancipatory possibilities,
negations and contradictions, performative staging, and solidarities. Such a
space is necessary if Indian democracy has to survive the onslaught of robber-
bankers, predatory managers, and fascist collaborators.

CONCLUSIONS

In this chapter, we turned to social theories of space to reinvigorate our
imagination of alternative forms of organizing. In particular, we drew on
Lefebvre's (2003) conceptualization of heterotopic space to examine how
LeftWord resists capitalism and advancement of fascism in India. What
insights on alternative organizing may this study of LeftWord offer us?

First, this chapter highlights the significance of counter sites and another
time in organizing alternatives to the current capitalist order. Heterotopias act
as counter-sites of inversion, resistance, and often subversion. Our findings
show that LeftWord is one such site of resistance that inverts and challenges
neoliberal capitalism and fascism. Leftword as a heterotopia is a space that
is connected to various spaces around it, and yet it is at variance with it. It is
outside of hegemonic space (Lefebvre, 2003). To begin with, LeftWord was
created as a publishing house to further Marxist theorization and readership.
In a key spatial move, a bookstore and café were added to further progressive
socialization and to challenge capitalist hegemony. A heterotopia blends

displaced space (heterotopy) with displaced time (heterochrony). LeftWord is also disruptive of conventional time, and emplaces different temporalities. It is a site of heterochrony (Foucault, 1986). On the one hand, it emplaces the past in the form of communist ideals that inspired many progressive movements worldwide in the twentieth century. In these ways, LeftWord as a heterotopia stages those very historical alternatives that haunt capitalism with their subversive potential (Gordon, 2008). On the other hand, it negates the present as capitalist and emplaces a communist future that is equal, just, and fair for all. Much like Roy's graveyard (also located in New Delhi), LeftWord inverts the necropolis that is India's capital today, offering possibilities for collective engagement, thought, and struggle.

Second, this study offers an account of how a performative staging of resistance constitutes a heterotopic space with emphasis on material practices that help it to become a site of progressive and emancipatory politics (Lefebvre, 2003). If the very basis for alternatives lies in a 'profound and durable practice of thinking and being and acting toward eliminating the conditions that produce the nastiness in the first place', LeftWord squarely locates itself in the performance of these very material practices of being and acting (Gordon, 2008: xvii). As much as the rest of the world celebrates class-based hierarchies and capitalist relations, LeftWord is an attempt to be outside it and to perform a greater sense of equality. While capitalism monetizes labour and valorizes acquisitive behaviour, the managing editor and editor of LeftWord refuse to accept monetary compensation for their labour and sacrifice pecuniary gains for progressive ideals. Moreover, the left politics of LeftWord are not merely aimed at the state with some demands of inclusion in the institutional registers but to fundamentally create an alternative to capitalism. Swyngedouw (2011: 377) warns against resistance that goes on to strengthen our march towards post-democracy,

The choreographing of resistance is not any longer concerned with transgressing the boundaries of the possible, acceptable, and representable, but rather a symptom of the deepening closure of the space of the political. The problem with such tactics is not only that they leave the symbolic order intact and at best 'tickle' the police.

While dissent today gets relegated to social media likes or tweets, or at best showing up with a placard at a protest site, LeftWord's politics rooted in material practices are that of sustained organizing for transgression and transformation. It reminds people, as Harvey (2012: 6) notes, that '[t]he whole capitalist system of perpetual accumulation, along with its associated structures of exploitative class and state power, has to be overthrown and replaced'.

Third, attention to the heterotopic site of LeftWord helps to understand that alternative organizing requires copresence. As a physical and digital space, LeftWord aims to bring people together. The creation of MayDay book store and café are attempts to invite people into the heterotopic space to interact with each other in the presence of alternative ideals of Marxism, and to imagine another world. Similarly, Studio Safdar extends the space with radical theatre to enhance copresence. In addition, the recent digital organizing of the May Day event brings together people from different parts of the world, and creates wider dialogues about the diverse geographies of capitalist exploitation and anti-capitalist alternatives. Such copresence fosters solidarities and commitments to collective action (Chatzidakis et al., 2021).

Fourth, the heterotopic site of LeftWord foregrounds the significance of movement across different scales in organizing alternatives. The space of LeftWord includes issues of local, regional and global significance. As Leitner (2008, 159) observes, '[c]entral to the politics of scale is the manipulation of relations of power and authority'. These scalar strategies involve overcoming limitations of localness through scale jumping, turning local sites into regional, national and global sites to advance their causes. Such movements across scales that constitute the heterotopic site of LeftWord are central to social movements. As Leitner (2008, 159) further adds, '[l]abour unions, indigenous people's organizations, feminism, environmental justice and the living wage campaign have successfully used such strategies to advance their cause'.

Fifth, through the prism of heterotopia, we understand the inversions and contradictions that can co-exist in such alternative spaces. Lefebvre observes that a heterotopia can contain multiple emplacements that are in themselves contradictory. Although LeftWord is a space of emancipatory politics against finance capital and its neoliberal corporatization, in the distribution of books, it is partially penetrated with various capitalist concerns. For example, books have to be priced appropriately to generate revenues. The usage of Amazon to increase sales is another contradictory facet of the site. Moreover, readers may be reduced to customers in everyday practices at LeftWord. Similarly, apart from the editorial team, all employees may not be impelled by Marxist ideology and could consider LeftWord another economic opportunity. In these ways, there are connections between incompatible spaces, and creating alternatives is not free from contradictions and dysfunctions. While some heterotopias allow free access, other sites within these settings can remain closed. As a differentiated but permeable space, LeftWord provides access to people across classes. It is common to see some workers from the neighbourhood attending the May Day event. However, for most other parts, the space remains exclusive and is primarily traversed by the privileged upper and middle literate classes.

Despite these contradictions, LeftWord challenges and resists India's journey to post-democracy and descent into fascism in several ways. Leftword allows us to imagine alternative working lives and life's work in a space that is increasingly controlled by bankers, corporations, and their fascist allies. LeftWord creates an alternative space nurtured by solidarity and enables other worlds. During times when ideas are incarcerated or censored, as mainstream media serve as 'stenographers' of the ruling elite (Sainath quoted in Franklin and Shankar, 2014), and academic departments are privatized or academics partner with predatory corporate elite, spaces like LeftWord vitally enable radical intellectual expressions. LeftWord's editors, authors, and activists associated with it show the courage to speak truth to power and remind us of the banished writer in Bertolt Brecht's famous poem, 'The burning of the books':

When the Regime
commanded the unlawful books to be burned,
teams of dull oxen hauled huge cartloads to the bonfires.

Then a banished writer, one of the best,
scanning the list of excommunicated texts,
became enraged: he'd been excluded!

He rushed to his desk, full of contemptuous wrath,
to write fierce letters to the morons in power –
Burn me! he wrote with his blazing pen –
Haven't I always reported the truth?
Now here you are, treating me like a liar!
Burn me!

REFERENCES

Ahmad, A. (2020). India: Post-democratic state. Accessed on 18 June 2021: http://www.slguardian.org/2020/01/india-post-democratic-state.html.

Appadurai, A. (2021). How to kill a democracy. *Social Anthropology* 29(2): 303–310. https://doi.org/10.1111/1469-8676.13041.

Association for Democratic Reforms (2018). Analysis of donations from corporates and business houses to national parties for FY 2016–17 & 2017–18. Accessed on 11 September 2021: https://adrindia.org/content/analysis-donations-corporates-business-houses-national-parties-fy-2016-17-2017-18.

Banaji, J. (2016). *Fascism: Essays on Europe and India.* New Delhi: Three Essays Collective.

Basu, T, P. Datta, S. Sarkar, T. Sarkar, and S. Sen. (1993). *Khakhi Shorts Saffron Flags.* New Delhi: Orient Longman

Chandrashekhar, C. P. and J. Ghosh (2000). *The Market That Failed.* New Delhi: LeftWord.

Chatzidakis, A., P. Maclaran, and R. Varman (2021). The regeneration of consumer movement solidarity. *Journal of Consumer Research,* 48(2): 289–308.

Crouch, C. (2004). *Post-Democracy.* Cambridge: Polity Press.

Desai, R. (2017). The political economy of India: Democratic rights, and the democratic rights movement. Accessed on 11 September 2021: https://rupe-india.org/69/rights.html.

Deshpande, S. (2019). *Halla Bol: The Death and Life of Safdar Hashmi.* New Delhi: LeftWord.

Durkheim, É. (1995). *The Elementary Forms of Religious Life.* New York: The Free Press.

Franklin, C. G. and S. Shankar (2014). Against stenography for the powerful: An Interview with P. Sainath. *Biography* 37(1): 3001–3319.

Gadamer, H. G. (2004). *Truth and Method*. London: Continuum.

Gordon, A. F. (2008). *Ghostly Matters: Haunting and the Sociological Imagination*. Minnesota: University of Minnesota Press.

Foucault, M. (1986). Different spaces. In *Aesthetics: The Essential Works*, 2, ed. J. Faubion. London: Allen Lane, 175–185.

Gieryn, T. F. (2000). A space for place in sociology. *Annual Review of Sociology* 26(1): 463–496.

Habermas, J. (1989). *The Structural Transformation of the Public Sphere: An Inquiry into a Category of Bourgeois Society*. Cambridge, MA: The MIT Press.

Harvey, D. (2000). *Space of Hope*. Berkeley: University of California Press.

———(2012). *Rebel Cities: From the Right to the City to the Urban Revolution*. London: Verso Books.

Hetherington, K. (1997), *The Badlands of Modernity: Heterotopia and Social Ordering*. London: Routledge.

Johnson, P. (2006). Unravelling Foucault's 'different spaces'. *History of the Human Sciences* 19(4): 75–90.

Khare, A. and R. Varman (2018). Shaheed hospital: Alternative organisation, ideology and social movement. In *Alternative Organisations in India: Undoing Boundaries*, ed. D. Vijay and R. Varman. New Delhi: Cambridge University Press, 152–182.

Kohli, A., ed. (2001). *The Success of India's Democracy*. New Delhi: Cambridge University Press.

——— (2012). *Poverty Amid Plenty in the New India*. New Delhi: Cambridge University Press.

Kurien, C. T. (2012). *Wealth and Illfare: An Expedition into Real Life Economics*. Bangalore: Books for Change.

Kwok, C., and N. K. Chan (2020). The making of contentious political space: The transformation of Hong Kong's Victoria Park. *Space and Culture*. https://doi.org/10.1177/1206331220912160.

Lefebvre, H. (1984). *The Production of Space*, trans. Donald Nicholson-Smith. Oxford: Blackwell

——— (2003). *The Urban Revolution*. Twin City: University of Minnesota Press.

Leitner, H., Sheppard, E., and K. M. Sziarto (2008). The spatialities of contentious politics. *Transactions of the Institute of British Geographers*, 33(2): 157–172.

Massey, D. (1994). The geography of trade unions: Some issues. *Transactions of the Institute of British Geographers* 19(1): 95–98.

Miles, S. (2010). *Spaces for Consumption*. Los Angeles: Sage.

NewsClick (2019). The LeftWord story. Accessed on 16 June 2021: https://www.youtube.com/watch?v=0ZeBFMaF0lI

Patnaik, P. (1999). The Communist Manifesto after 150 years. In *A World to Win*, ed. Prakash Karat. Delhi: Leftword Books, 68–86.

——— (2019). Shadow of fascism. *Monthly Review*. Accessed on 9 September 2021: https://mronline.org/2019/04/08/the-modi-years/.

——— (2020). Neoliberalism and fascism. *Agrarian South: Journal of Political Economy* 9(1): 33–49.

Paxton, R. O. (2005). *The Anatomy of Fascism*. London: Vintage.

Poruthiyil, P. V. (2021). Big business and fascism: A dangerous collusion. *Journal of Business Ethics*, 168(1): 121–135.

Prashad, V. (2018). *Strongmen*. New Delhi: LeftWord.

——— (2020). *Lenin 150*. New Delhi: LeftWord.

Rancière, J. (1999). *Disagreement: Politics and Philosophy*. Minneapolis/London: University of Minnesota Press.

Rodriques, J., A. Choudhary, and H. Dormido (2019). A murky flood of money pours into the world's largest election. *Bloomberg*, 17 March. Accessed 11 September 2021: https://www.bloomberg.com/graphics/2019-india-election-funds/

Rosenberg, A. (2016). Fascism as a mass movement. In *Fascism: Essays on Europe and India*, ed. J. Banaji. New Delhi: Three Essays Collective, 19–96.

Roy, A. (2017). *The Ministry of Utmost Happiness: A Novel*. New Delhi: Vintage.

——— (2020). *Azadi: Freedom, Fascism, Fiction*. London: Penguin.

——— (2021). We are witnessing a crime against humanity. Accessed on 1 September 2021: https://www.theguardian.com/news/2021/apr/28/crime-against-humanity-arundhati-roy-india-covid-catastrophe.

RUPE (2020). *Crisis and Predation: India, COVID-19, and Global Finance*. Gurugram: Research Unit for Political Economy.

Sacco, P. L., S. Ghirardi, M. Tartari, and M. Trimarchi (2019). Two versions of heterotopia: The role of art practices in participative urban renewal processes. *Cities* 89: 199–208.

Sen, A. and Himanshu (2005). Poverty and inequality in India: Getting closer to the truth. In *Data and Dogma: The Great Indian Poverty Debate*, ed. Angus Deaton and Valerie Kozel. New Delhi: Macmillan, 306–370.

Sewell, W. (2001). Space in contentious politics. In R. Aminzade, J. Goldstone, D. McAdam, E. Perry, W. Sewell, S. Tarrow, et al. (authors), *Silence and Voice in the Study of Contentious Politics*. Cambridge: Cambridge University Press, 51–88.

Sivaraman, M. (2018). *Haunted by Fire: Essays on Caste, Class, Exploitation and Emancipation*. New Delhi: LeftWord.

Swyngedouw, E. (2011). Interrogating post-democratization: Reclaiming egalitarian political spaces. *Political Geography* 30(7): 370–380.

Varman, R. and D. Vijay (2021). The Thanatopolitics of neoliberalism and consumer precarity. In *Consumer Culture Theory in Asia: History and Contemporary Issues*, ed. Yuko Minowa and Russell Belk. London: Routledge, 179–201.

PART III

ALTERNATIVE INTERROGATIONS OF SUBALTERNITY

9

EXPLORING THE STATE WITHIN THE BOTTOM-OF-THE-PYRAMID (BOP) TERRAIN

SUPARNA CHATTERJEE

The philosopher is the spokes-person ... for a question. To insist on this means to understand what really matters, in the question, is the enchantment of the question. To insist on the question is to understand this difficult notion: that one must inhabit the question, its peculiar enchantment, without overcoming or wanting to overcome it in the answer.

—Carlos Sini (2009)

Be it multinational corporations like Unilever, S. C. Johnson and Sons, or Procter and Gamble looking for the next growth opportunity; national governments searching for solutions to the intractable issue of poverty; non-governmental organizations (NGOs) like Oxfam working with poorer communities around the world; international organizations like the United Nations Development Programme or the World Bank seeking to mitigate economic and social deprivation in the developing world – market-based solutions to poverty eradication has emerged as a viable alternative for dealing with the challenge of global poverty (Prahalad, 2006; Karnani, 2007; Hart, 2005; Roy 2010). In recent years, along with microenterprise, asset-building, social enterprise, the bottom- or base-of-the-pyramid approach has emerged at the centre of business–poverty discourses (Conney and Shanks, 2010). Propounded by C. K. Prahalad (1941–2010), management professor and consultant (along with co-author Stuart Hart, 2002), the bottom-of-the-pyramid (BOP) approach popularized the idea of large private-sector participation in poverty alleviation – a move that aimed to reconstitute the relationship between the economic calculus of profit-making with the more socially committed goals of poverty eradication. In recent years, I have engaged with the BOP proposition from a conceptual and theoretical standpoint to illuminate what has, by and large, remained undiscussed and unremarked in the BOP scholarship, that is, the dominant assumptions and presuppositions that underwrite the BOP programmatic (Chatterjee, 2014; 2016). In the present chapter, I continue my critical engagement with the BOP proposition by examining how and to what effect *the state*[1] is reimagined and reconfigured within its horizon of thinking. Where, at one level, the chapter reflects upon, clarifies, and critiques the BOP proposition insofar as the question of state is concerned, at another level, using the BOP programme as a vantage point, it offers insights into the generalized condition of the state under neoliberal capitalism.

The present chapter is based on a close reading of the BOP proposition (among others, Prahalad, 2006; Prahalad and Hart, 2002; and Hammond and Prahalad, 2004). I focus mainly on first-generation BOP scholarship as it clears the ground for apprehending the ways in which the state is perceived, represented, and reimagined within the BOP domain, in general.[2] That is to say, even as the newer iterations (second generation) of BOP scholarship refine and renew older concepts and themes, the work of the *founding* BOP scholars continues to supply the conceptual contours for locating the state within the BOP metanarratives.[3] To understand the ways in which the state is conceptualized, represented, and performed within the BOP domain, it is imperative that we take a look at the 'conditions of existence' that enabled the BOP proposition to reframe the role of the state in market-led poverty alleviation ventures, in the first place. These background conditions, primarily, have to do with the worldwide ascension of neoliberal political rationality (logics, ways of thinking), which, among other things, offers 'corporatization, commodification, and privatization' (Harvey, 2007: 35) as a veritable panacea for most of the long-standing global challenges. Of particular relevance here is one of the central features of contemporary neoliberalism, that is the tendency to capture and colonize crisis for augmenting neoliberal visions and goals. So, for instance, poverty, deprivation, joblessness, environmental degradation, and so forth, are increasingly framed as 'opportunities' calling for entrepreneurial solutions premised upon notions of efficiency, competition, and innovation. Indeed, as a technology of power, neoliberalism routinely recasts risks, burdens, and vulnerabilities across different sites as occasions for generating market-led remedial measures. On this account, the neoliberal regimes of risk management can be seen as 'a specific moment of accumulation and ... [with] ... all its entailments' (Smith, 2008: 156) led by, in most cases, one of the most 'emblematic subjects' (Sassen, 2000) of neoliberal capitalism: large multinational companies. It is this larger shifting terrain of neoliberal rationality that the BOP domain both draws on and adds to as it sets out to reimagine and redefine the mandate of the state within neoliberal-led poverty eradication schemes.

My main argument is as follows. With the rise of neoliberal political rationality, the state is no longer conceived as an active or even desirable agent in redressing societal challenges. Whether it be in the sphere of poverty eradication, employment generation, health, or education, the role of the state in our present neoliberal moment has undergone a significant shift. In its neoliberal avatar, the state is recast as a neutral overseer or facilitator of markets providing the necessary infrastructure for the survival and sustenance of what is called the 'enterprise society'[4] (Lazzarato, 2009). The BOP proposition offers an excellent jumping-off point to comprehend the ways in which neoliberal social projects construe the state as the enforcer of the rule of law, especially contractual law focused on maintaining the sanctity of contractual obligations and entitlements between large multinational corporations and poor communities. Within the BOP metanarratives, the state is explicitly positioned as secondary to markets in the fight against global poverty. What is ironic, however, is that even as the state is delegitimized, that is, generally posited as antithetical to innovation, competition, and efficiency, it is nonetheless harnessed to share the costs and burdens of market-making at the bottom of the pyramid. Indeed, the 'public' commitment and reach of the state, its symbolic and material resources, and legal mandate are drawn on strategically to create market conditions conducive to profit generation. In this sense, the state is not so much receding or waning as it is being made subservient to global capital. Even as critics (Karnani, 2006, 2007,

2009) question formulations of the state within BOP narratives, they leave unchallenged the underlying normative neoliberal rationality[5] that informs the BOP characterizations of the state. Consequently, these critical responses foreclose possibilities of rethinking the state as oppositional and resistant to the excesses, externalities, and fallacies of markets, in any meaningful way. The notion that the state might be reclaimed and revitalized (with all its contradictions and differentiations) to promote collective social emancipation and well-being based on considerations other than those sanctioned or permitted by globalizing capital remains outside the permissible BOP metanarratives.

The chapter is structured as follows. In the next section, I provide a brief sketch of neoliberalism with special attention to the question of the state within neoliberal discourses. The third section inaugurates a close examination of the BOP proposition to locate the ways in which the state is named, comprehended, and interpreted within the BOP domain and what might be the stakes involved therein. The fourth section offers a critical reading of Karnani's well-known early criticism of the state as envisaged within the BOP proposition. In the concluding section, I summarily tie up issues and concerns discussed throughout the chapter and raise some questions about locating the state within the ambit of neoliberal-led poverty alleviation efforts.

THE NEOLIBERAL CONDITION(S)

In the introduction to his widely read *A Brief History of Neoliberalism*, David Harvey (2007: 3) states that neoliberalism has become 'hegemonic as a mode of discourse', that is, its influence is so pervasive that neoliberalism has become a commonsense way of 'interpret[ing], live[ing] in, and understand[ing] the world'. In a similar vein, Bourdieu (2001: 1) talks about the 'neoliberal newspeak' as the new planetary vulgate where catchphrases like flexibility, efficiency, enterprise, responsibility, and governance, to name a few, proliferate across time and space, becoming 'commonplaces' – the 'undiscussed suppositions of discussions' structuring and shaping our horizon of thinking. What Harvey and Bourdieu seem to suggest is that neoliberalism is taken as a fait accompli, as an inevitability that requires neither explanation nor analysis about how it came to dominate our social and political worlds in the present historical moment. In this context, Stuart Hall (2010:63) writes: when a governing political philosophy (here, neoliberalism) 'becomes just how things are that [sic] it wins consent and enters common sense'. Indeed, the general acceptance of neoliberalism as 'just how things are' bespeaks its rise as a new common sense. This naturalized aura around neoliberalism, however, belies the careful, concentrated, and tenacious efforts of a transnational 'thought collective' (Mirowski and Phehwe: 2009) that promoted and popularized neoliberalism as a theory of 'political economic practices' (Harvey, 2007: 2). While tracing the historical trajectory of neoliberal thought from its enabling moments with the formation of Mount Pelerin Society in 1947 (under the guidance of Austrian philosopher Friedrich von Hayek) to its eventual rise as a globally hegemonic discourse in the 1990s (thanks to the Washington Consensus) remains outside the scope of this chapter; suffice it to say, as a political economic theory, neoliberalism has travelled a long road borrowing, transforming, and retooling many principles from its historical predecessor, eighteenth- and nineteenth-century liberalism. For the most part, neoliberalism shows greater affinity with classical liberalism or economic liberalism (Thorsen, 2009) that is associated with varying philosophies expounded by figures ranging from John Locke, Adam Smith, to Alex de Tocqueville and Fredrick von Hayek; classical liberalism, among other things, is deeply committed to individual freedom, property rights, the rule of law, laissez-faire economics, and a minimalist state whose main purpose would be to uphold law and order. What is important to note is that for classical liberalism, laissez-faire economics was held to be essential for attaining 'more freedom and real democracy' (Thorsen, 2009). On this reading, neoliberalism appears to be closer to classical liberalism than to modern liberal traditions, which, among other things, holds the state to be a significant player in the economy regulating as well as promoting competitive markets to ensure the preservation of capitalism as the dominant economic system.

Resurrecting and reinventing many of the tenets of classical liberalism, neoliberals are passionate proponents of free markets, free trade, private ownership of public goods and services, and minimal state intervention. From its first experiments in the 1970s (in Chile) to its consolidation (in advanced liberal democracies like the United Kingdom and the United States) and the eventual worldwide dispersion during 1980–1990s, neoliberalism has morphed from a political economic theory to a 'social and moral philosophy' that emphasizes market exchange as 'an ethic in itself, capable of acting as guide to all human action' (Treanor, quoted in Harvey, 2007: 3). What gives neoliberalism its distinctive character is its emphasis on market exchange, contractual transactions, and entrepreneurial freedoms as templates for organizing economic and social life. Indeed, running through all the different neoliberal scripts authored across various locations is a profound belief in market rationality guiding not only markets and commercial spheres but life in general. As Brown puts it, within neoliberalism 'all dimensions of human life are cast in terms of market rationality' (2009: 40). Not only are all aspects of human existence framed through market rationality, but neoliberalism, as Brown (2009) clarifies, is a 'constructivist project' actively promoting discourses, institutions, and policies that pursues and enacts this vision. Indeed, by performatively bringing into being conditions conducive to its own 'development, dissemination, and institutionalization' (Brown, 2009: 41), neoliberalism ensures survival even in the face of setbacks, upheavals, and crisis. In fact, as mentioned earlier, more and more, scholars are convinced that the durability and tenacity of neoliberalism is a result of its remarkable ability to process and appropriate crisis for its own self-regeneration (Adams, 2012; Schiwittay, 2001; Dean, 2014)

In recent years, scholars have recognized that as neoliberalism migrates to different sites across the world, it produces versions of itself aligning and adapting to local social and economic conditions (Ong, 2007; Peck, 2010; Peck et al., 2009). The varying neoliberal-induced outcomes, effects, entities, and embodiments suggest that rather than being a world-homogenizing system, neoliberalism is a 'mobile technology' producing 'unstable constellation shaped by interacting global forms and situated political regimes' (Ong, 2007: 5). However, notwithstanding its variegated nature (Brenner at al., 2010), there are some generic features of 'actually existing neoliberalism' that are worth mentioning. They are as follows: privatization of public services; restructuring of social provisioning; erosion of public aid; elimination of subsidies; labour deregulation; capital mobility; financialization of economic domains; dissimulation of Keynesian fiscal and monetary policies; and dismantling of the welfare state, among others. For our purposes here, it is the changing character of the state within neoliberalism that is of particular interest. Indeed, one might say that, to a large extent, the discursive and material (economic, institutional, juridical) undoing of the interventionist, regulatory welfare state under 'managed capitalism' in advanced liberal democracies and in its proximal and distant counterparts across the world has paved the road for the emergence of the *neoliberal state*.

THE STATE OF THE *NEOLIBERAL STATE*

A look at the meandering histories of neoliberal thought reveals that questions regarding the role and scope of the state were never fully settled, and, therefore, the position of the state remains rather ambiguous within the neoliberal thought collective. According to Peck (quoted in Davis, 2018: 382), 'neoliberalism's curse has been that it can live neither with, nor without the state'. Despite ambiguities surrounding the state, and contrary to the popular view that posits the state as receding or shrinking, what is noteworthy is that the state continues to be 'a central instrument for the advancement of neoliberal agenda' (Davies, 2018; 382). In this sense, it is not that the state has receded as much as it has been reconstituted and repurposed to suit the objectives and goals of neoliberal political rationality. With the caveat that there is no prototype neoliberal state, it would be worthwhile to note that, by and large, under neoliberalism, the state is positioned as the guarantor and protector of private property rights, free markets, and free trade (Harvey, 2007). The role of the state is to ensure the smooth functioning of markets by instituting legal frameworks and protocols that minimize risks and uncertainties, leading to a stable business-friendly environment. Among other things, promoting the sanctity of contractual agreements and supporting 'individual rights to freedom, action, and choice' (Harvey, 2007: 64) fall squarely within the ambit of the state. Maintaining contractual obligations, securing entrepreneurial freedoms, and promoting the rule of technocracy are central to neoliberal political regimes. Not only is the state positioned as a guarantor of the market, it is also expected to create markets in areas that have traditionally remained outside the ambit of commodification and marketization. So, for instance, water, education, health care, and environment are all areas that have been subjected to marketization with the help of the state. Even as the state is actively engaged in promoting and consolidating neoliberal policies and practices, its role is kept to the 'bare minimum' (Harvey, 2007) in relation to markets. That is to say, once the state has created the background conditions for markets to operate, it is to take a back seat, letting markets operate with minimum interference or regulation since any state intervention is invariably construed as market distortions leading to inefficiencies. What is more, apart from privileging markets, the state is expected to refashion itself 'around principles extracted from the market' (Davis, 2018: 386), imbibing qualities like competitiveness, efficiency, and flexibility. While for neoliberal advocates, the recalibration of the state along the lines of the market offsets inefficiencies and wastefulness, critics point out that ultimately it serves to 'liberate' the process of capital accumulation, leading to, among other things, the 'restoration of upper-class power' (Harvey, 2007). Indeed, under neoliberal imperatives, preservation and protection of capitalist systems (competitive markets, private property, entrepreneurial freedoms, and so on) become the 'chief business of government' (Bradly and Luxton, 2010: 8).

As mentioned earlier, notwithstanding its purported omnipresence, neoliberalism is context-driven, taking on different characteristics, roles, and aims under different historical and social formations. In this context, Fernandes (2018: 9) cautions against the tendency to 'treat the contemporary state as an after-effect of the logic of neoliberalism', since it diverts attention away from the historical continuities that mark the state under current neoliberal times. That is to say, it obfuscates the ways in which older forms of state formation, say, interventionist or developmental state, coexist alongside current restructurings of the state wrought by neoliberalism. Deemphasizing radical discontinuities, Fernandes (2018: 9) contends that the task of understanding the neoliberal state formation must attend to how modern states are reconstituted and reoriented in the face of changing perceptions of public and private, autonomy and freedom, regulation, and governance. In her discussions on neoliberalism within a global comparatist framework, Fernandes (2008:16) refocuses attention on what she calls the 'post liberalization state', which she contends better represents the ways in which different states have responded to and accommodated a variety of economic reforms and liberalization policies 'in the aftermath of the neoliberal turn'. For Fernandes (2008: 9), there are three broad contexts that are relevant to apprehending state power under neoliberalism: the changing state–capital relations in favour of capital investment and mobility; escalations in the power of the state as a security apparatus involved in surveillance and monitoring of population in the face of perceived terrorist threats; and the increasingly porous boundaries between the state and civil society helping to enliven and enforce neoliberal governmentalities in a bid to reshape subjectivities and modes of existence. These three interlocking contexts provide the backdrop for understanding the reconfiguration of the state in the contemporary neoliberal moment.

In what follows, I venture into the BOP terrain to provide a concrete instance of how the state is actively reimagined and rescaled within one particular neoliberal site. In keeping with the scholarly literature that emphasizes the need to retain the particularity and specificity of state formations under different neoliberal moments, the following section seeks to foreground the ways in which the state is articulated and bodied forth within the BOP domain.

THE STATE AND THE BOP

As a resonant terrain of neoliberal-led discourses on global poverty management, the BOP domain displays an uneasy relationship with the state. In the best-seller *Fortunes at the Bottom of the Pyramid*, Prahalad (2006: xiii) begins his reflections on market-based solutions for global poverty by acknowledging an 'implicit agreement' among the different constituencies fighting against global poverty, that is, 'the poor are wards of the state'. This declarative, which removes poverty from the larger realm of global political economy and places it squarely within the purview of state and governance, at once problematizes the state as inefficient, underperforming, and apathetic with regard to poverty. In other words, it holds the state culpable for perpetuating conditions of dependency that render the poor suppliants or wards in need of subsidies and other public provisions. The state is held to be paternalistic constraining choices and freedoms in ways that ultimately stifle individual capacities and motivations to confront the menace of poverty. This dismissive gesture that foregrounds state failures in tackling issues of poverty does two things: first, it casts the state in an unfavourable light vis-à-vis matters of poverty alleviation, relegating state efforts to redress poverty as 'solutions of the past', which, by and large, have failed; and second, it helps to situate large private-sector firms as an alternative to the state in the fight against poverty, whose resources and capacities are now held to be central to entrepreneurial solutions aimed at poverty eradication. The contrast between the inefficient and apathetic state unable to meet its obligations and priorities and the dynamic and resourceful private-sector firms, especially multinational companies, poised to lead the world towards entrepreneurial solutions is an important motif in the BOP narratives. But what is also noteworthy here is that this binary is strategically undone in moments where the state is claimed for its supportive role in engendering market ecosystems at the bottom of the pyramid. So, even as the state is maligned and marginalized, it is invoked in particular ways to facilitate BOP market-making. It is this ambivalence towards the state – a hallmark of neoliberal regimes – that is central to understanding the place of the state within the BOP domain. What comes into view, here, is that this ambivalence towards the state in the BOP narratives functions as, to put it in Omelsky's (2011: 93, emphasis original) words from a different context, a 'discursive vehicle with which to expand the contours of how we come to *think* and *imagine*' the state. Stated differently, ambivalences and indeterminations surrounding the state render it intelligible as an entity that is questionable, tentative, inauthentic, and unpredictable, and therefore in need of recovery and rehabilitation. The trope of ambiguity also performs other strategic functions. That is, it helps to mask what Marxist scholars call the central role of the state 'maintenance of the overall structural integration and social cohesion of a society "divided into classes"' (Jessop, 2012: 5). On this account, the aura of ambivalence surrounding the state distracts attention away from the state as a locus of class struggle where different classes attempt to influence and transform policies and thereby secure class domination. So, while, at one level, ambivalence helps to render the state diffused and ineffective, at another level, it mystifies the state by obscuring its class character and ideological functions 'with which the ruling class not only justifies and maintains its domination but manages to win the active consent of those over whom it rules' (Gramsci, quoted in Jessop, 2012: 9).

THE SPECTRAL STATE

At the core of the BOP proposition lies the notion that poverty alleviation can be addressed through 'large-scale and widespread entrepreneurship' (Prahalad, 2006: 4). While this turn towards entrepreneurship requires collaboration across different sites involving the poor, civil society organizations, large firms, and even governments, it is, however, to be led by 'large private sector firms and local BOP entrepreneurs' (Prahalad, 2006: 5). What this suggests is that multinational companies are the nodes around which the entire programmatic of poverty eradication unfolds; the other cast of actors play supporting roles ensuring the success of the central character (the multinational companies) involved in enacting BOP scripts. What bears mentioning is that within the BOP theatre, the state has a spectral role, present but absent; it is present because the BOP narratives demand that the state provide suitable conditions for market-making through the enforcement of laws related to contractual obligations, property rights, transparency of processes, corruption prevention, and through its overseer role maintaining law and order, in general. It is absent because the state is expected to recede or shrink in its regulative and other public responsibilities to enhance the efficient functioning of markets leading to wealth generation. This spectral quality (ambivalence, all over again) of the state within the BOP narratives is illustrative of how neoliberal regimes at once appropriates or 'privatizes' the state in the service of its own agendas, and at the same time, renders it ineffectual as a 'public' organization traditionally charged with, among other things, instituting checks and balances to reign in market excesses. This simultaneous strengthening as well as weakening of the state where it emerges both as necessary and peripheral – essential and superfluous in relation to globalizing capital as it journeys to the last 'entrepreneurial frontier' – is central to BOP narratives on the state. While, traditionally, the state has been viewed as a 'coercion wielding organization' (Charles Tilly, quoted in Steinmetz, 1999: 8) under contemporary neoliberal-induced poverty regimes, the state continues to be coercive but in qualitatively different ways; that is, it acts more and more on behalf of markets, or more precisely, corporate capital (both domestic and foreign) helping to interpellate individuals and groups as consumers, entrepreneurs, and clients ensuring their rights to market participation. In this reading, management of the economic life of poorer communities by facilitating access to markets and credit and by making available infrastructures (social, economic, and political) attractive to private-sector investments emerges as the central task of governance. Indeed, the valorization of markets as sites of freedom, autonomy, and choice is the subtext that infuses BOP characterizations of the state.

The troubling ambiguity surrounding the state is also captured in the ways in which the BOP narratives historicize the state. That is to say, the BOP proposition presents a highly reductive history of the state, especially in the Global South, as part of its arguments for moving beyond the state as the main facilitator of poverty eradication efforts. Consider, for instance, the following excerpt where Prahalad (2006: 6–7) provides a historical framing of the state in India. He writes:

> The policies of the government for the first 45 years since independence from Great Britain in 1947 was based on a set of assumptions. Independent India started with a deep suspicion of the private sector. The country's interaction with East India Company and colonialism played a major role in creating this mindset. The experience with the indigenous private sector was not very positive either. The private sector was deemed exploitative of the poor. This suspicion was coupled with an enormous confidence in the government machinery to what is 'right and moral' … India's general suspicion of the private sector led to controls over its size and expansion … there were no credible voice in public policy for nurturing market-based ecosystems … [t]he focus of public policy was on distributive justice over wealth creation.

The above excerpt is problematic for two main reasons. First, it engages in simplification and dilution of histories of the state where a complex set of factors (economic, social, political, and ideological) behind India's post-independence turn towards a mixed economy is seen reductively as a historical reaction against the excesses of the East India Company. As per this view, the entire course of India's journey since independence turns on what might be called 'politics of suspicion' built around a deep mistrust of the private sector. Central to this politics of suspicion is the Indian state that has been unable to shake off what Prahalad calls 'the power of dominant logic' (that is, among other things, its reliance on distributive justice), rendering it archaic, intransient, and unproductive. Second, for Prahalad, the state remains an enunciative site of negative assumptions related to the private sector, in general, which has stifled the growth of market ecosystems in India. The state's emphasis on redistributive justice over wealth creation (the debates over public good versus private interests), according to Prahalad, has stalled robust private-sector development in India. In this reading, the state's focus on redistributive justice is misplaced as it failed to generate wealth (a nod to 'trickle-down' economics) necessary for addressing social challenges like poverty, unemployment, deprivation, and so forth. Such an anaemic and selective reading robs the state of its historical density obfuscating its embeddedness in larger regional and global contexts; not only that, it detracts attention away from the state's shifting alliances and coalitions across diverse and often contradictory sites under different historical conjunctures. Abstracted thus, the state is projected as a 'problem', a hindrance, requiring rehabilitation to accommodate the demands and dynamism of the private sector (domestic and foreign). Parenthetically, one may note that given the undermining of the state, terms like 'public', 'rights', and 'justice' are sparingly used in the BOP narratives. Stated differently, the enfeeblement of the state provides a convenient ideological cover for ignoring matters that have traditionally remained within the ambit of the state, that is, matters related to equality, social justice, human rights, or other public commitments that enhance collective well-being. Predictively, the space evacuated by the state is now occupied by markets that are offered as enabling sites of rights and freedoms where individuals and collectivities find meaning as sovereign-consumers, entrepreneurs, and clients. As mentioned earlier, time and again, within BOP narratives, dissimulation of the state goes hand in hand with reinforcement of markets where large multinational companies with their resources and capabilities are posited as an 'obvious' choice for finding 'commercial solution[s]' (Prahalad, 2006: 41) to most of the global challenges.

THE CORRUPT STATE

From its initial days, the BOP scholars have contended that corruption remains one of the most significant hurdles in creating market ecosystems at the bottom of the pyramid. Whenever the state is mentioned in the context of market-led poverty eradication strategies, issues of corruption immediately follow suit, making it appear as though corruption is synonymous with the state. For instance, consider this observation made in part to explain the difficulties associated with doing business at the bottom of the pyramid: 'Governments – especially local and provincial authorities – often do not function effectively or transparently. Corruption is widespread' (Hammond and Prahalad, 2004: 32). The notion of widespread corruption engulfing the states in the Global South is a recurrent theme in the BOP narratives. Even as Prahalad, in his best-seller (2006), condenses the histories of the state (that is, the Indian state) in one or two pages, a whole chapter is devoted to the need for reducing corruption and building 'transaction governance capacity' in the Global South. Notwithstanding variations in scale and scope, there is little doubt that corruption, in general, remains a challenge in all societies but to conflate 'the state', especially those in the Global South, with corrupt practices is to 'stereotypically and ritualistically' affirm its existence (Mateescu, 2001: 380), which results in the reification of the state as a monolithic and self-contained entity removed from the larger historical and socio-economic dynamics that provides the conditions of possibility for the political culture of corruption, in the first place. Moreover, the discourse of corruption also lends itself quite easily to Orientalism, where corruption is deemed endemic to certain societies systematically marked as immoral, irrational, and backward. On this reading, corruption becomes a 'particularly southern phenomenon' (Brown and Cloke, 2004: 280), a feature of societies lagging behind modern Western democracies with mature institutions capable of controlling corruption. The notion that corruption can be confined to the Global South is problematic as it flies in the face of the interconnections and interlinkages among different geographically located organizations, actors, and bodies wrought by contemporary globalization. At best, the intermeshing and criss-crossing of interests, alliances, and solidarities emanating from different sites, be it government, non-governmental agencies

(NGOs), multinational corporations, or supranational organizations, like the World Bank, makes any claims of corruption or malpractice as a geographically bounded phenomenon reductive and simplistic. At worse, it works as an ideological foil that mystifies the ways in which powerful Western entities and actors participate in corrupt practices beyond their own shores (explained as a necessary part of 'doing business' overseas) even as they denounce it, in theory. In their commentary on rising lawlessness and violence in postcolonial societies, anthropologists Jean and John Comaroff (2006: 134) contend that, in the African context, the prevalence of illicit activities along with the criminalization of the state must be viewed from the perspective of 'the change in the manner in which Africa is linked to the global order'; drawing in Mbembe, they claim, '[T]he continent ... has not so much been marginalized as entangled in a parallel pariah economy of international scale.' The authors highlight that, increasingly, multinational companies, especially in defence and construction, have been known to engage in graft and other illicit activities to secure contracts in African countries, which reinforces their point about the 'dangerous liaisons between the North and the South' (Comaroff and Comaroff, 2006: 139). Indeed, despite evidence that situates increasing criminality and coercion in African countries within the global scheme of things, international organizations like Transparency International mostly focus on bribe takers, invariably deflecting attention away from bribe givers.

What this means for the topic at hand is that the criminalization of the state, in general, cannot be viewed in isolation of the larger global shifts that unevenly and unequally connect different places and peoples in the scramble for investments and profits. To view the state in the Global South as endemically predisposed to bribery, malpractice, and nepotism is to engage not only in Orientalism but also in the politics of negation that refuses to acknowledge how global economic and political configurations rescale and recalibrate 'the state', in many cases collapsing the boundaries between the licit and illicit, legitimate and illegitimate. Writing on the neoliberal restructuring of the state through 'good governance' and 'transparency' in Turkey, Bedirhanoglu (2007: 1239) notes that the neoliberal conception of corruption is 'ahistoric, biased, contradictory, and politicized'. Corruption, according to the author, deserves 'critical attention since its specific neoliberal conception has fulfilled significant ideological and political functions within the post-Washington consensus, particularly at moment of financial crisis' (Berdirhanoglu, 2007: 1240). Berdirhanoglu (2007) makes two points that are relevant here: first, that discourses on corruption and measures for its containment in 'emerging markets' set-up agendas that are favourable to post-Washington consensus advancing neoliberal reforms (1240) and, second, that neoliberal conception of the state as a sum of profit-maximizing bureaucrats and politicians engaged in creating rents for their own private advantage promotes 'an individual universal conception of corruption' which refuses to see corruption as 'historically defined problem specific to modernity and capitalism' (1241). Coming from a Marxist perspective, Burawoy (2014: 973) ploughs a similar furrow when he writes that in studying corruption, one must pay attention to 'the thousand threads that connect the state to different fractions of capital', adding that 'corruption is inherent to capitalism, but it assumes different forms in different places and periods'. Drawing on his earlier ethnographic research on the copper industry in Zambia, Burawoy (2014: 974) notes:

> [T]he neoliberal attack on corruption 'hid' the effects of opening up of the economy to global economic forces, namely shifting the focus of corruption away from small-scale domestic capital to the benefit of international capital, benefits that hit their peak with 'Development Agreements' that governed the privatization of copper mines.

What comes into view here is that corruption, rather than being endemic to the states in the Global South (as the BOP authorizes), is intrinsically linked to the expanding circuits of neoliberal capitalism. In this reading, corruption appears to be a strategic response enabling adaptation and accommodation of neoliberal pressures and compulsions. As suggested by Burawoy (2014), the increase in corruption with the privatization of Zambian copper mining industries illuminates the collusion between state agencies and international capital seeking newer investments sites and markets. The point, here, is not to absolve the state of corruption in any society. Rather, it is to highlight that within neoliberal regimes of transformation, like the BOP domain, corruption functions as a prism through which states in the Global

South are refracted as the 'other' – opaque, murky, 'dirty', and irremediable. And, once positioned thus, the state has no other recourse except to take up the so-called market-like characteristics of *openness, accessibility, and transparency*. Viewed in this light, the vilification of the state and the emphasis on good governance and transparency becomes a Trojan horse through which neoliberal governmentalities are introduced and inaugurated in spaces hitherto resistant to market-based remedies.

What is noteworthy here is that within the BOP programmatic, the main issue with corruption is that it exacerbates the 'frictional losses of doing business at the BOP' (Prahalad, 2006: 77), increasing 'cost burden[s]' and business uncertainty. The focus on corruption as detrimental to business suggests that it is not as much an issue of morality as it is an economic issue – a constraint that hinders value creation through enterprise building. In this regard, early BOP advocates were emphatic that corruption impedes private-sector development because it undermines the 'capacity to facilitate commercial transaction through a system of laws fairly enforced' (Prahalad, 2006: 78). The remedy, as per the BOP proposition, lies in building 'appropriate institutional arrangements' that provide the infrastructural support for market creation. In this regard, the state becomes crucial for ensuring the 'rule of contract' (Prahalad, 2006: 79) facilitating conversion of assets into capital that could be, in Prahalad's words, 'sold, bought, mortgaged, or converted into other assets'. Here, BOP arguments about the need for regulatory framework protecting markets is seen to advocate what is known as 'economic constitutionalism' which 'treat[s] the market[s] as a constitutional order with its own rules, procedures, and institutions, operating to protect the market from political interference' (Jagsuriya, 2005: 8). Of particular relevance to us is that 'economic constitutionalism demands the construction of a specific kind of state organization and structure: a regulatory state, the purpose of which is to regulate and provide "economic order" within the global market' (Jagsuriya, 2005: 18). The emergence of the regulatory state instituting economic constitutionalism safeguarding markets from political pressures (legislative and executive) is central to the conception of the state within the BOP narratives. In this sense, within the BOP programme, the relationship between corporations and poor communities, to a large extent, is mediated by the state insofar as it provides the necessary conditions for enforcing contractual agreements and obligations. Indeed, this neoliberal disciplining of the state is crucial to the disciplining of the poor in market norms and rationalities underpinned by the 'rule of law' which frees up trapped assets, ensures access to credit, facilitates contractual relationships, and promotes transparency in transactions among different constituencies in a bid to create vibrant market ecosystems at the bottom of the pyramid.

At this point, it may be worthwhile to consider what has been the main response to the BOP formulations of the state. As an early critic of the BOP domain, Aneel Karnani (2006, 2007, 2009) has dealt with the issue of state in the BOP-led poverty alleviation agendas. In what follows, I turn to Karnani's[6] critique of the state within the BOP proposition to highlight how the response itself partakes in reconceptualizing the state in problematic ways.

READING THE CRITIQUE

Aneel Karnani's work (2006, 2007, 2009) highlights with particular clarity some of the popular objections to BOP formulations. Karnani's empirically driven re-examination of BOP claims and positions were important in opening a critical space for dialogue around the BOP proposition populated by scholars from diverse theoretical terrains and ethical standpoints. That said, Karnani's critique, by and large, operates within the larger neoliberal framework that informed the object of his critique, namely the BOP proposition. Given this, Karnani's criticisms of the BOP approach centres around contesting empirical fallacies and exposing untenable generalizations. While noteworthy, such a critique leaves undisturbed the theoretical and conceptual scaffolding of the BOP proposition and, in so doing, issues an endorsement of the premise upon which the BOP programme is based. Karnani's engagement with the state within the BOP domain exemplifies this. That is to say, even as Karnani criticizes the BOP proposition of undermining the state, he continues to valorize a reductive, neutral, and ahistorical understanding of the state, which paradoxically undercuts his own vision of the state vis-à-vis poverty alleviation.

Karnani (2007) has been unequivocal in his insistence that poverty alleviation cannot be solely entrusted to markets but needs the active support of governments engaged in creating and dispensing public provisions, especially to the poor. Lamenting about the tendency to downplay the importance of the state in poverty eradication efforts, Karnani (2007: 107) writes: '[A] by-product of the BOP proposition is its de-emphasis of the state in providing basic services and infrastructures.' The state, as per Karnani (2007: 106), must play a significant role in poverty eradication through the development of labour-intensive enterprises (small, medium, and large) by creating appropriate conditions through policies, infrastructures, and institutions. For Karnani, generating employment and employability is key to solving the problem of poverty. In other instances, Karnani (2006: 109) affirms the traditional functions of the government in the realms of safety, literacy, health, sanitation, and other public provisions as they have a 'direct and significant impact on productivity', which is an essential ingredient in combating global poverty. In a recent piece, Karnani (along with co-authors McKague and Wheeler, see McKague, Wheeler, and Karnani, 2015: 139) highlights what they call an integrated approach to poverty alleviation involving the private sector, governments, and civil society. This approach, as the authors put it, 'envisages a key role for government policy, institutions, and practices'. They claim that '[g]overnance institutions that are missing or weak should be strengthened rather than ignored' (McKague, Wheeler, and Karnani, 2015: 139) because government's role in 'four main areas of responsibility', that is, infrastructures, public services, job creation, and regulations, is held to be pivotal for the integrated approach to poverty alleviation.

What is instructive here is that while the state is deemed important, it essentially functions as a facilitator, an enabler of private-sector engagement in poverty eradication. So, for instance, the state is significant because of its role in infrastructural development easing private-sector participation in poverty remediation measures; enhancement of public services such as education and health (increasing employability), rendering commercially attractive an otherwise 'difficult' business environment; controlling costs of doing business leading to private-sector job growth; and instituting 'incentives, regulations, and standards' helpful in the creation of 'self-reinforcing cycles of productivity and employment growth for the poor' (McKague, Wheeler, and Karnani, 2015: 139–140). On this account, the state is instrumentalized as an apolitical vehicle for creating a board-based market economy without much analysis of the myriad processes, relations, and mechanisms that locates the state in differential power relations with respect to other institutions and entities in the society. Apart from ignoring the embeddedness of the state within the flows and ebbs of power and its constraints and enablements, the above formulations rehearse the ahistorical and depoliticized views of the state seen in the BOP narratives. Such a critical response, rather than moving away from BOP-led understandings of the state, reinforces from the backdoor the marginalization and peripheralization of the state. Where the BOP proposition, by and large, ignores or sidesteps the state (recall, that it is only part of the story) in a bid to foreground large private-sector involvement at the bottom of the pyramid; the response of the critics situates the state as a supplement to the market, a self-limiting entity cast, mostly, as a neutral dispenser of services and provisions beholden to national and international networks, links, and alliances that engender market-based solutions to intractable global challenges like poverty.

Towards the end of his recent book *Fighting Poverty Together*, Karnani (2011: 256) clearly states, 'To significantly reduce poverty requires resources. Only the business sector and the government can provide resources on the scale needed, it is impossible to eradicate poverty without the active involvement of both.' This excerpt is illustrative of how the government is invited back into the projects of poverty alleviation. It is hailed as a strategic partner to private enterprises in the fight against poverty. The issue, here, is that to draw an equivalence between governments and private-sector enterprise is to engage in wilful forgetting of the fraught relationship between the two and the collusions and complicities that mark their increasing interdependencies under neoliberal capitalism. The fiction of the 'ideal' state as representing the political will of the people steering social and welfare programmes and agendas to enhance social democratic traditions, a regulative body reining in excesses of the market through appropriate checks and balances is matched with its counterpart: that is, businesses as self-enlightened socially engaged and responsive entities ready to shoulder the burdens of public commitments like poverty alleviation. The positing of governments and businesses as occupying discrete domains of operations denies the blurred boundaries that exist between the two where powerful interests and stakes collide, collude, and coalesce to reinforce dominant economic and political ideologies. Under neoliberal conditions, public–private partnerships, even in extreme circumstances like disaster relief, have become increasingly steeped in market rationality 'more interested in profiteering than purely humanitarian motives' (Gunewardena, 2008: 4). Writing in the context of the aftermath of hurricane Katrina, Adams' (2012) work shows that, in a strange twist of neoliberal fate, public finances helped subsidize private enterprises leading to the deepening of crisis among the affected populations. The larger point here is: the question of state involvement in poverty eradication must recognize how neoliberal rationalities are wont to co-opt and instrumentalize the state for its own agendas and goals, which, among other things, renders poverty alleviation as yet another site of profit-making. If this be so, then can the state (now increasingly *neoliberalized*) be mobilized as an important player in global poverty management discourses? What comes to mind here are Audre Lorde's words (1984) from a different context: 'The master's tools will never dismantle the master's house' – meaning, the neoliberal state can hardly be entrusted to remedy or cure conditions that might, in fact, be a result of neoliberal social and economic policies and practices in the first place.

DWELLING ON THE QUESTION OF THE STATE: SOME CONCLUDING THOUGHTS

For the BOP paradigm, as well as its critics, there appears to be a degree of undecidability surrounding the state via-á-vis market-led poverty alleviation efforts. By and large, the state is depicted as inessential and inconsequential, relevant only to the extent that it serves as a strategic enabler of markets. Even when the state is considered central to the poverty alleviation efforts, it is positioned as a supplement to the resources and capacities of the private sector. Within the horizon of the BOP metanarrative insofar as the question of the state is concerned, the dominant imaginary conjures up a depoliticized, technocratic, and legalistic entity tasked with the work of supporting and maintaining robust self-sustaining markets. Clearly, such a state is accommodative of the newer social and economic regimes where, as Santos (2005: 26) put it, 'political therapy' entails a shift from 'the central state to devolution/decentralization; from political to the technical; from popular participation to the expert system; from the public to the private; and from the state to the market'. The BOP narratives on state vacillate between a bloated, wasteful, and intransient (fossilized) state hindering lean, flexible markets and a state that is a *natural ally* helping to enliven private-sector participation in poverty alleviation. Both of these accounts hide more than what it reveals about the fraught relationship between state and poverty. As suggested earlier, these scenarios obfuscate complex histories of the state, its omissions and commissions, silences and violations, and its deepening solidarities and alliances with the ever-expansive reach of global capitalism.

Perhaps an alternative way is to think about the state as a *pharmakon* – both remedy and poison mobilized and moderated under different historical periods by different groups to varying effects and outcomes. With Boaventura de Sousa Santos (2005: 26), we might return to the idea that 'state is a social relation and as such, it is contradictory and continues to be an important arena of struggle'. Such an orientation may encourage us not to relinquish the state to forces of globalizing capital in the context of poverty eradication but to take up moments of resistance and dissent as opportunities for aligning state's power for 'legal and juridical action' with counter-hegemonic causes (de Santos, 2005).

To recapitulate: the present chapter offered a close examination of the position of the state within the BOP metanarratives. As a neoliberal regime of power, the BOP proposition engages in systematically effacing the state only to rehabilitate it selectively as the promoter and facilitator of market economy. The dissimulation of the state in BOP discourses parallels the neoliberal restructuring of the state as subservient to the demands and desires of global capital. The ambiguities and uncertainties surrounding the state within the BOP narrative ontologize the state as ineffective, enfeebled, and apathetic. Enmeshed within the haze of incurable corruption, states in the Global South are rendered problematic in need of a healthy dose of neoliberal governance. As previously stated, the point is not to ignore state corruption but to problematize it in the context of the neoliberal dismantling of the welfare or interventionist state. On this reading, apart from evoking and invoking Orientalist themes, the notion of the state in the global South as wholly corrupt ensures its subordination and tutelage under Western neoliberal governance practices.

As mentioned earlier, on the question of the state, the critics of the BOP proposition, while raising important issues, fail to grasp how the reliance on neoliberal frameworks of thought undercuts their arguments about the centrality of the state in eradicating poverty. Under the present neoliberal conjuncture, the possibility that the state will be on equal footing with markets (domestic and international) is rather naive; it suggests a misreading of the ways in which unequal power relations shape, among other things, the relationship between state and globalizing capital. Indeed, the contention that state is intrinsic to capital accumulation, to escalating regimes of expropriation and violence, and to rising social brittleness and precarity warrants serious interrogation. In her critical analysis of the notion of social capital, sociologist Margret Somers (2005: 235) writes that under present historical conditions, there has been a reconfiguration of 'our knowledge and understanding of … what is the appropriate distribution of power among market, state, and civil society'. In the present context, the question of appropriate distribution of power among market, state, and civil society is seminal as it helps us to wrestle with the role of the state in relation to poverty eradication agendas. Also, we must remain wakeful to the neoliberal landscapes of power that have fundamentally altered the ways in which we comprehend notions of equality, rights, justice, emancipation, and so forth, and what might be its implications for state–poverty relations. In place of abstract, reified, and decontextualized formulations, what is called for is a deep knowledge of the materiality of the state; the different ways in which the state comes into being; and how state action (or inaction) infiltrates, shapes, and modifies lives of communities divided by caste, class, gender, sexuality, religion, and so forth.[7] Conceptually grounded, ethnographic research might help reveal tensions and fissures that need to be taken into account when rethinking the state in relation to poverty alleviation. To struggle against what Khare and Varman (2016) call the Kafkaesque state, its absurdities, and alienations, we must unpack the many *determinations* that constitute the conditions of existence of the state, be it historical, political, or ideological. Here, we are well-advised to heed Zizek's (2008: 6–8) plea that, instead of giving in to 'urgent injunctions' 'to act now', we need 'to withdraw' or 'take a step back' to 'engage in patient critical analysis' of issues – here, the relationship between democratic states and poverty alleviation. For the moment, then, let us pause over the notion of the state as pharmakon to see if we are able to reimagine the state – using James Tully's (2008) phrase from a different context – 'in a new key'. Analogous to jazz musicians playing classic compositions in a new key, improvising as they go along (see Tully 2008), rethinking the state in a new key allows for improvisations and dialogues with older, different understandings of the state in a bid to create possibilities for a transformative *state*. In closing, I return to the epigraph at the beginning of this chapter. In the direction suggested by philosopher Carlos Sini, the chapter hopes to dwell on the question of the state within neoliberal poverty regimes not to arrive at *answers* necessarily, but for the sake of initiating critical thinking about the state in relation to poverty under the present neoliberal times. The present chapter is a small step towards this end.

NOTES

1. While different theoretical traditions provide different definitions of the state, for our purposes, the state is defined as

   > the culmination of a process of concentration of different species of capital: capital of physical force or instruments of coercion (army, police), economic capital, cultural, or (better) informational capital, and symbolic capital ... this concentration as such constitutes the state as a holder of a sort of meta capital ... [enabling] the state to exercise power over different fields.... (Bourdieu, 1999: 57)

2. The question of the state vis-à-vis market-led poverty alleviation programme finds its clearest expression/treatment in the first-generation BOP study, and specifically in Prahalad's best-seller *Fortunes at the Bottom of the Pyramid* (2006). For this reason, the study draws extensively on Prahalad's culminating book.

3. Metanarratives can be thought of as 'big stories' that provide an interpretative umbrella under which smaller stories or narratives coalesce provisionally and contingently under certain historical moments. The BOP metanarrative gathers under its interpretative frame different narratives about the efficacy

of market-led poverty alleviation programmes, be it microenterprise, asset building, or social enterprise; see Chatterjee (2014).

4. Drawing on Foucault's posthumous work on neoliberalism, Lazzarato (2009) talks about 'enterprise society' where power exists through the creation of a new subject – an individual who is an entrepreneur competitive and self-managed taking on projects for continual self-improvement and well-being. The proliferation of possessive individualism, entrepreneurialism, and competitiveness in all walks of life is central to the making of enterprise society.

5. On this point, see Khare and Varman (2016).

6. My reason for focusing on Karnani is that he provides the most in-depth response to BOP's positioning of the state. In the spirit of academic dialogue, my engagement with Karnani's work should be viewed as signalling the importance of his critique to the burgeoning BOP scholarship.

7. Sharma and Gupta's (2009) work provides an entry into different ways of apprehending the state.

REFERENCES

Adams, V. (2012). The other road to serfdom: Recovery by the market and the affect economy in New Orleans. *Public Culture* 24(1[66]): 185–216.

Arora, S. and H. Romijn (2012). the empty rhetoric of poverty reduction at the base of the pyramid. *Organizations* 19(4): 481–505.

Bedirhanoglu, P. (2007). The neoliberal discourse on corruption as a means of consent building: Reflections from post-crisis Turkey. *Third World Quarterly* 28(7), 1239–1254.

Bradley, S. and M. Luxton (2010). Competing philosophies, neoliberalism and challenges of everyday life. In *Neoliberalism and Everyday Life*, ed. S. Bradley and M. Luxton. London: McGill University Press, 2–21.

Brenner, N., J. Peck, and N. Theodore (2010). Variegated neoliberalization: Geographies, modalities, pathways. *Global Networks* 10(2), 182–222.

Brown, E. and J. Cloke (2004). Neoliberal reform, governance, and corruption in the South: Assessing the international anti-corruption crusade. *Antipode* 36(2): 272–294.

Brown, W. (2009). *Edgework: Critical Essays on Knowledge and Politics*. Princeton University Press.

Bourdieu, P. and L. Wacquant (2001). Notes on the new planetary vulgate. *Radical Philosophy* 105(January): 2–5.

Burawoy, M. (2014). The color of class revisited: Four decades of postcolonialism in Zambia. *Journal of Southern African Studies* 40(5): 961–979.

Comaroff, J. and J. Comaroff (2007). Law and disorder in the postcolony. *Social Anthropology* 15(2): 133–152.

Conney, K. and T. Shanks (2010). New approaches to old problems: Market-based strategies for poverty alleviation. *Social Service Review* 84(1): 29–53.

Chatterjee, S. (2014). Engaging with an emergent meta-narrative: A critical exploration of the BOP proposition. *Organizations* 21(6): 888–906.

——— (2016). Articulating globalization: Exploring the bottom of the pyramid (BOP) terrain. *Organization Studies* 37(5): 635–653.

Davis, W. (2018). The neoliberal state: Power against 'politics'. In *The Sage Handbook of Neoliberalism*, ed. C. Danmien. Los Angeles: Sage, 385–398.

de Santos, B. (2005). Beyond neoliberal governance: The World Social Forum as subaltern cosmopolitan politics and legality. In *Law and Globalization from Below: Towards a Cosmopolitan Legality*, ed. B. de Santos and C. Rodríguez-Garavito. Cambridge: Cambridge University Press.

Dean, M. (2014). Rethinking neoliberalism. *Journal of Sociology* 50(2): 150–163.

Dolan, C. (2012). The new face of development: The 'bottom of the pyramid' entrepreneurs. *Anthropology Today* 28(4): 3–7.

Fernandes, L. (2018). Conceptualizing the post-liberalization state: Intervention, restructuring, and the nature of the state power. In *Feminist Rethink the Neoliberal State. Inequality, Exclusion, and Change*, ed. Leela Fernandes. New York: New York University Press, 1–31.

Gunewardena, N. (2008). Human security versus neoliberal approaches to disaster recovery. In *Capitalizing on Catastrophe: Neoliberal Strategies in Disaster Reconstruction*, ed. N. Gunewardena, and M. Schuller. New York: Rowman & Littlefield Publishers, INC, 3–16.

Hall, S. and D. Massey (2010). Interpreting the crisis. *Soundings* 44(44): 57–71.

Harvey, D. (2007). *A Brief History of Neoliberalism*. Oxford: Oxford University Press.

Hart, S. (2005). *Capitalism at the Crossroads: Next Generation Business Strategies for a Post-Crisis World.* New Jersey: Pearson Education.

Hammond, A. L. and C. K. Prahalad (2004). Selling to the poor. *Foreign Policy,* 1 May, 30–37.

Jayasuriya, K. (2005). Economic constitutionalism, liberalism and the new welfare governance. Working Paper No. 121, Asia Research Center, Murdoch University, National Library of Australia.

Jessop, B. (2012). Marxist approaches to power. In *The Wiley-Blackwell Companion to Political Sociology,* ed. E. Amenta, K. Nash, and A. Scott. Oxford: Blackwell Publishing Ltd, 3–14.

Karnani, A. (2006). Misfortune at the bottom of the pyramid. *Greener Management International* 51(September): 99–110.

——— (2007). The mirage at the bottom of the pyramid. *California Management Review* 49(4): 90–111.

——— (2009). Romanticizing the poor. *Stanford Social Innovation Review* 7(Winter): 38–43.

——— (2011). *Fighting Poverty Together: Rethinking Strategies for Business, Governments, and Civil Society to Reduce Poverty.* Athens: Ohio University Press.

Khare, A. and R. Varman (2016). Kafkaesque institutions at the base of the pyramid. *Journal of Marketing Management* 32(17–18): 1619–1646.

Lazzarato, M. (2009). Neoliberalism in action: Inequality, insecurity, and the reconstruction of the social. *Theory, Culture, and Society* 26(6): 109–133.

Lorde, A. (2003). The master's tools will never dismantle the master's house. *Feminist Postcolonial Theory: A Reader,* ed. Reina Lewis and Sara Mills. Edinburgh: Edinburgh University Press, 25–27.

Mateescu, O. (2001). 'Ours is a bandit state!' Power and corruption in postsocialist Romania. *Polish Sociological Review* 136(4): 379–395.

McKague, K., D. Wheeler, and A. Karnani (2015). An integrated approach to poverty alleviation: Roles of the private sector, government and civil society. In *The Business of Social and Environmental Innovation: New Frontiers in Africa,* ed. B. Verena, R. Hamann, M. Hall, and E. W. Griffin-EL. Switzerland: Springer, 129–145.

Mirowski, P. and D. Plehwe (2015). *The Road from Mont Pèlerin: The Making of the Neoliberal Thought Collective, with a New Preface.* Cambridge: Harvard University Press.

Omelsky, M. (2011). Chris Abani and the Politics of Ambivalence. *Research in African Literatures* 42(4): 84–96.

Ong, A. (2007). Neoliberalism as a Mobile Technology. *Transactions of the Institute of British Geographers* 32(1): 3–8.

Peck, J. (2010). Zombie Neoliberalism and the Ambidextrous State. *Theoretical Criminology* 14(1): 104–110.

Peck, J., N. Theodore, and N. Brenner (2009). Neoliberal urbanism: Models, moments, mutations. *SAIS Review of International Affairs* 29(1): 49–66.

Prahalad, C. K. (2006). *The Fortune at the Bottom of the Pyramid, Eradicating Poverty through Profits.* NJ: Wharton School Publishing.

Prahalad, C. K. and A. Hammond (2002). Serve the world's poor profitably. *Harvard Business Review*, September, 48–57.

Prahalad, C. K. and S. Hart (2002). The fortune at the bottom of the pyramid. *Strategy+Business* January, 1–14.

Roy, A. (2010). *Poverty Capital, Microfinance and the Making of Development.* New York, NY: Routledge.

Sassen, S. (2000). Spatialities and temporalities of the global: Elements for a theorization. *Public Culture* 12(1): 215–232.

Schwittay, A. (2011). The marketization of poverty. *Current Anthropology* 52(3), S71–S82.

Sharma, A. and A. Gupta (2009). *The Anthropology of the State: A Reader.* Malden, MA: John Wiley & Sons.

Sini, C. (2009). *Ethics of Writing.* Translated by Silvia Benso. Albany: Suny Press.

Smith, N. (2008). Neo-liberalism: Dominant but dead. *Focaal: European Journal of Anthropology* 51(1): 155–157.

Somers, M. (2005). Beware Trojan horse bearing social capital: How privatization turned solidarity into a bowling team. In *The Politics of Method in the Human Sciences: Positivism and Its Epistemological Others*, ed. G. Steinmetz. Durham: Duke University Press.

Steinmetz, G. (1999). Culture and the state. In *State/Culture: State-Formation after the Cultural Turn*, ed. Steinmetz. Cornell: Cornell University Press, 1–49.

Thorsen, D. (2010). The neoliberal challenge: What is neoliberalism. *Contemporary Readings in Law and Social Justice* 2(2): 188–224.

Tully, J. (2008). *Public Philosophy in a New Key: Democracy and Civic Freedom*, vol. 1. Cambridge: Cambridge University Press.

Wacquant, L. (2010). Crafting the neoliberal state: Workfare, prisonfare, and social insecurity. *Sociological Forum* 25(2): 197–220.

Žižek, S. (2008) *Violence: Six Sideways Reflections*. London: Profile Books.

10

A WOMEN-INCLUSIVE EMANCIPATORY ALTERNATIVE TO CORPORATE CAPITALISM?

THE CASE OF KERALA'S STATE-INSTITUTED KUDUMBASHREE PROGRAMME

GEORGE KANDATHIL
POORNIMA VARMA
RAMA MOHANA R. TURAGA

With the ongoing advancement of capitalism, corporate capitalism – a specific variety of capitalism that is grounded in neoliberal ideology (Harvey, 2007) – has been engulfing economic and social relations worldwide (Giridharadas, 2018). Simultaneously, the search for alternatives to corporate capitalism has been ascending in both academic (Bollier, 2014; Cruz et al., 2017; Kothari and Joy, 2017; Parker et al., 2014; Wright, 2010) and non-academic circles (Cumbers, 2017; A. Ferguson, 2009). A major focus of this search has been in 'developing' countries like India that face the onslaught of corporate capitalism (Kothari and Joy, 2017; Shrivastava and Kothari, 2012) while being ranked 103 out of 119 countries in the Global Hunger Index.[1] The neoliberal economic reforms introduced in India since the early 1990s have had a significant influence on developmental policies of even the states such as Kerala and West Bengal that have been governed by left-of-centre parties (for example, Communist Party of India–Marxist) (Das, 2019; Krishnamoorthy, 2010).

A central theme of inquiry on alternatives to corporate capitalism is of women-inclusive emancipation (Werlhof, 2007) and thereby the need to explore the emancipatory struggles of marginalized women who are involved in the creation of alternatives (A. Ferguson, 2009). In this chapter, we undertake such exploration through ethnographic field immersion in a programme called 'Kudumbashree' instituted by the Kerala state in 1998 with the objective of women empowerment and inclusion (NIPCCD, 2008).

The extant literature on Kudumbashree can be categorized into two broad streams. One stream evaluates the programme from the perspective of its ability to produce economic empowerment among women belonging to below poverty line (BPL) families, who are the primary targets for the Kudumbashree programme. This research uses traditional indicators of economic empowerment such as economic and financial asset accumulation and land productivity (for example, Agarwal, 2018; Chathukulam and Thottunkel, 2010) and finds that the Kudumbashree programme outperforms similar poverty eradication programmes elsewhere in terms of creating economic empowerment. The second stream of literature acknowledges the programme as being different from traditional anti-poverty programmes because of Kudumbashree's explicit focus on the participation of target groups in decisions that involve their livelihoods (for example, Williams et al., 2012). However, they show that even within the BPL groups, those who belong to the lower strata of the society in terms of both economic and social status are excluded (Devika and Thampi, 2007; Heeks and Arun, 2010; Williams et al., 2011). Even with an opportunity for self-employment, Kudumbashree failed to address the struggle for raising their voice within patriarchal relations (Aswathy and Kalpana, 2018). For example, this literature argues that as opposed to emancipation, Kudumbashree further reinforces the existing patriarchal relations within households (for example, Devika, 2016). Further, any openings for the emancipation of women within Kudumbashree are likely to be constrained by the neoliberal logic within which Kudumbashree is embedded (Devika, 2017).

This tension between considering women empowerment as an issue of access to resources versus transformation of disempowered societal structures and relations to release women's power is evident in the broader extant literature. The literature on women empowerment through access to resources ranges from diversity and inclusion in organization studies to resource-based inclusion in development economics, more so in the case of Kudumbashree (see Kalpana, 2017). In contrast, the feminist critiques have consistently shown how over-emphases on resources and economic welfare, and simultaneous discounting of structures of patriarchy, subordinate women (Acker, 1990; Cornwall, 2007). It leads to the reproduction of gendered social norms and structural exclusion of women (Derne, 2008; Srivastava, 2017).

For a deeper understanding of the issues of women (dis)empowerment, they point to the need to explore sociocultural dynamics that individuate women and create a subservient gender role for them (Cornwall, 2003; Fierlbeck, 1995), particularly in the case of Kudumbashree (Devika, 2016, 2017). As opposed to the neoliberal corporatist approach to women empowerment, the possibilities for an alternative approach stem from interrogating such notions and understanding the collective struggle of women for their rights and recognition (S. Ferguson, 2008). In this spirit, Kabeer (1999) notes that an instrumentalist approach to understanding gender inequality results in the loss of the political edge of feminism and undermines the potential to uncover possibilities of developing transformative alternatives (A. Ferguson, 2009; Ruether, 1995). Our study contributes by interrogating the notions of women empowerment and women emancipation in the context of possibilities of women-inclusive emancipatory alternative and identifying the conditions that may open up such possibilities. The specific research question we address is as follows: *How far does the empowerment envisaged in Kudumbashree initiatives lead to opening spaces for the emancipation of rural women, given these initiatives have been unfolding within potentially patriarchal relations and with the support of the state machinery that has increasingly come under the pressure of global corporate capitalism?*

Based on the analysis of our field explorations, we explore this question by examining the mobilization, collectivization, and collective actions of rural women through Kudumbashree initiatives. This structuring also helps to contribute to the extant Kudumbashree-related literature, which is largely silent on these processes within Kudumbashree programmes (Aswathy and Kalpana, 2018; Devika, 2017).

LOCATING KUDUMBASHREE HISTORICALLY

The Kudumbashree mission was launched by the Government of Kerala in 1998 with the stated primary aim of eradicating poverty by ensuring the transformation of women from being passive recipients of public assistance to being active leaders in development initiatives. Thus, the inclusion of rural women in the state's developmental project appears as the end for the mission.

The root of the Kudumbashree programme lies in the UNICEF-supported Community-Based Nutrition Programme (CBNP) that was implemented in 1991 by the self-claimed centrist government of Kerala to improve the nutritional status of poor women and children in the Alappuzha district. During the implementation of the programme, the idea of forming groups of local beneficiaries called neighbourhood groups (NHGs) came up (Kudumbashree, 2020; Raghavan, 2009). As the programme was assessed as successful, it was extended to another district in 1994 by the same government (Kudumbashree, 2020; Raghavan, 2009). However, as we explain next, Kudumbashree was created by the left government that came to power in 1996, partly as part of its strategy to mobilize the grassroots, its core electoral constituency.

Kerala has a long history of social actions taken by the members of the public along with state initiatives, and the well-acclaimed achievements on social indicators by the state (popularly called 'Kerala model of development') are attributed to this kind of public action (John, 2009). Direct state provisioning of public goods such as health and education, targeted at the poor and marginalized, has been at the centre of the Kerala model of development (Pillai, 2018). This is especially prominent during the regimes of left governments in Kerala since independence. This model thus was heavily reliant on public expenditures on direct provision while leading to middle classing of the society, which was amenable to the conditioning of neoliberal forces. The onset of neoliberal reforms undertaken by the Indian government in the early 1990s has significantly affected this model and the Kerala society in several ways (Mannathukkaren, 2010; Oommen, 2008; Williams et al., 2012).

First, the neoliberal regime gradually shifted the role of the state from an active welfare provider to a passive caretaker (Patnaik, 2014). At the same time, the centralization of resources in the hands of the federal government reduced allocation to states reducing the capacity of state government in Kerala to undertake public expenditures, particularly in education and health (Patnaik, 2018).

Second, the increasing participation of the private sector in sectors such as health and education made these services less accessible to the poor and marginalized (Educativa, 2014; Oommen, 2008) and relatively more concentrated in urban locations (Berer, 2011). Simultaneously, the creeping in of neoliberal policies led to agrarian distress, forcing farmers to leave agricultural occupation (Jeromi, 2007; Mannathukkaren, 2011). Third, market expansion and the rise of consumerists culture that came with the neoliberal reforms depoliticized the previously politically conscious society (Rammohan, 1998).

These, taken together, led to the alienation and demobilization of the grassroots – the core constituency of the left, making the left's grassroots mobilization strategies ineffective. Thus, the neoliberal reforms further aggravated the depoliticization process in Kerala that started as early as 1980 (Mannathukkaren, 2010; Williams et al., 2011). This forced the left parties to re-examine and re-establish their grassroots mobilization strategies. Therefore, the nature of democratic decentralization involving the many affiliates of the party – for example, the civil society organizations such as Kerala Shastra Sahithya Parishad (KSSP) or Peoples' Science Movement (Kannan, 2000) – built the foundation of Kudumbashree. When the left came to power in 1996, a facilitator for involving the public in state governance – the Panchayati Raj Institutions – had to be established by the state as per a constitutional amendment passed in 1992. The left used this opportunity to institute programmes that would help them mobilize grassroots, being informed by the success of the previous community-based initiatives. The strategic action resulted in the formation of Kudumbashree using the idea of NHGs as its grassroots building block while keeping its top-tier governance within the state machinery.

KUDUMBASHREE ACTIVITIES AND STRUCTURE

The major programmes executed through Kudumbashree are microfinance, microenterprises, health, education and child welfare, housing, and agriculture. The functioning of Kudumbashree is tied up to the development initiatives of the local government and follows a three-tier structure. Neighbourhood groups (NHGs) are formed at the village level with a minimum of 10 and a maximum of 20 members. The NHGs are federated at the level of a ward in the local government into Area Development Societies

(ADS) and further into a Community Development Society (CDS) at the level of the local government. The CDS members from each ward will select a woman chairperson for each *panchayat*. Even the three-tiered structure of Kudumbashree was directly adapted from the CBNP programme mentioned earlier.

METHODS

In alignment with our focus on exploring the Kudumbashree initiatives, we employed an exploratory multisite case study (Yin, 2011). Kudumbashree is a state-wide programme that has 2,77,175[2] NHGs. These NHGs, spread across 14 districts in Kerala, have heterogeneous effects with regard to women empowerment (Devika, 2016). Hence, students of Kudumbashree who explore women empowerment and collectivization suggest attending to the micro-dynamics of multiple specific sites within a specific geographical area that is not explored yet. Thus, we decided to focus on the Thrissur district, also called the cultural capital of Kerala,[3] which has not been explored in the extant literature on Kudumbashree. Within this area, for generating a more nuanced understanding, we applied three criteria for site selection: (*a*) both urban and rural sites, (*b*) sites that cover multiple activities of Kudumbashree, and (*c*) sites that are assessed as 'successful' and 'failure' by Kudumbashree officials in terms of the quantum of ongoing activities and participation of women. Consequently, we selected five sites in addition to the district office. The site access was often arranged by the Kudumbashree district officials.

All three authors (and a research assistant) together paid six site visits that spanned 12 days in May 2018. We spent approximately eight hours per day in the field, making direct observations and interviewing Kudumbashree members in groups and individually. The authors, together with the research assistant, created copious field notes that logged our observations and inference. We also created memos that contained our initial interpretations leading to a preliminary analysis. The preliminary analysis guided the subsequent round of interviews. We adopted a conversational style of interview (Turner III, 2010) that helped us frame questions not only around our broad focus on empowerment and alternatives but contextualize the questions depending on interviewees' response and their comfort level. This approach was particularly important since we wanted to include sensitive topics related to gender and patriarchy. The conversations were typically two hours long. While in the district office the conversations took place in the official's office rooms, we interacted with the NHGs at their workplace and home (when they invited us over).

The interviews were audio-recorded as the interviewees accorded permission after we built rapport with them through small talk. We transcribed the interviews and subjected them to thematic analysis (Van Maanen, 1998). We chose thematic analysis for the following reasons: the three authors conducted fieldwork together and analysed the data, although they come from different disciplinary backgrounds (organization studies, agricultural economics, and public policy) and methodological domains (econometrics and statistics, qualitative and interpretive methods). Pragmatically, this mix warranted a methodology that is relatively more flexible in choosing theoretical approaches and less procedurally fixated to leverage the advantage of multiple domain experience. In contrast to interpretive policy analysis (IPA) or grounded theory (and other methods like narrative, discourse, and so on), thematic analysis is not wedded to any pre-existing theoretical framework, giving it the flexibility to be employed within different theoretical frameworks (Braun and Clarke, 2006).

In the data that we analysed, although we identified a number of themes that went beyond the focus of this chapter indicating the relatively open nature of our conversations, for this chapter, we restrict ourselves to the following themes, which we consider as most relevant to the research questions of this chapter: mobilization, collectivization, collective action, alternatives, and empowerment. We chose latent thematic analysis, which allows a higher level of abstraction since our research questions focus on contested, complex, and abstract notions. Thus, the development of the themes involved interpretive work, and the analysis is already theorized, which indicates more of a constructionist than a realist or essentialist epistemology. We started jotting down ideas and potential coding schemes at the beginning of data collection and continued it right through the entire coding and analysis process. The analysis involved a constant back and forth movement between the entire data set, the coded extracts of data, and the analysis of the data. To identify patterns of meaning (or themes), we searched across a variety of data set, including group and individual interviews (primary), direct observations, and archival records.

Guided by our research question, we critically examine the claim of 'women empowerment', 'emancipation', and the potential for creating conditions for the alternatives to emerge. In the following, we present our examination as a thematically structured story that we created based on our field experience and reflective analysis.

MOBILIZING THE NEOLIBERAL GOVERNABLE SUBJECT

The aim of poverty reduction, thrift, and credit by each individual member of the group forms an integral part of Kudumbashree, making it the largest microfinance institution in Kerala (Kalyani and Seena, 2012). The members bring in small amounts and pool the money together for a corpus. This helps the members take loans from the corpus whenever they are in need, without relying on money lenders or other informal sources.

The procedural aspects of thrift contribution (such as the amount and time to collect) and income generation were decided jointly within NHGs. However, thrift as a central means for poverty eradication, and, in turn, 'economic empowerment of women' (Varghese, 2012), lies at the individual level for which each individual was made responsible through peer accountability. In other words, the NHGs emphasized 'self-help' for alleviating poverty by treating poverty as an individual issue (Kannan and Raveendran, 2017), depoliticizing it through an individualistic approach rather than adopting a politically sensitive redistributive approach.

In India and other developing countries, the individualistic approach to poverty alleviation through public action has emerged as a new form of developmentalism that is propagated and backed by global institutions such as the World Bank and International Monetary Fund (Brigg, 2006; Kannan and Raveendran, 2017). Interestingly, thrift, in terms of weekly cash savings (called *kudukka petty*) and informal chit funds (called *ari-chitti*), was a prevalent social practice in rural parts of Kerala, including our research sites (Job, 2003). The difference in the Kudumbashree approach is that while the cash savings were kept in women's or men's pockets, now it is deposited in a nationalized bank (as per the guideline provided by the state) in a joint account of Kudumbashree members, connecting the account holders to the vagaries of the market and linking the microprogramme to the world capital market in the globalized world. Of course, as Kudumbashree members repeatedly pointed out, now 'we (women) have money … and no need to beg (from husband)', which gave them some degree and feeling of economic independence, 'We tell our neighbours it is a great opportunity to earn some extra income without letting it affect their family responsibilities … and you then have your own savings in the bank.'

The discussions surrounding the new models of rural development and poverty eradication started in the early 1990s when the Indian government initiated a major process of neoliberal reforms. This provided ample time for a neoliberal imagination to take root in the minds of the people as Kudumbashree was instituted in 1998, a few years after Kerala had embraced the neoliberal policy regime. The desires and aspirations of the people were also shaped by the neoliberal notions of development (Gooptu, 2013). This social conditioning, in turn, legitimized the notions based on economically independent, self-reliant individuals and families that take care of themselves.

In addition to raising people's aspirations, the onset of reforms also led to a decline in job opportunities and an increase in the cost of living, prompting people to look for a viable economic alternative for supplemental income (Jeromi, 2005). As Kudumbashree members explained, the need for additional income was acute for several of them since they had negligible assets (including land) and low-paid jobs (husbands were mainly daily wagers, and women sometimes got paid work through MNREGS[4]).

> Rupees 270 we get [through MNREGS] is not sufficient … we are poor … others' status is better because their children grew up [to support the family]…. I used to do the job of culvert construction as part of MNREGS. At that time, my children were small. After some time, I felt the need for additional income [for which] I got into Kudumbashree.

The desirability of entrepreneurial, financially independent self or family was further reinforced in the training that the state provided to Kudumbashree

IMAGE 10.1   Snapshot of Kudumbashree website – stories of entrepreneurial successes

members, beyond 'technical skills' that included knowledge about operating within budget (partly provided by the state functionaries), as success stories of entrepreneurial Kudumbashree members were shared enthusiastically. The Kudumbashree website and training documents corroborate this experience sharing of Kudumbashree members (see Image 10.1).

We were also asked to meet such a 'heroine', who described to us in detail her transformation from a slum-dwelling housewife to an enterprising *dosa* maker (sort of rags to riches!) and a public functionary within the Kudumbashree set-up. Such personalities (including this heroine) were invited to share their experiences in various local forums and were looked up as benchmarks by other Kudumbashree members during our discussions.

On the one side, the Kudumbashree members were thus frequently invited to position themselves as self-capable autonomous individuals within the objectives that the 'empowerers' set for them, connecting them to 'to a subjection that is the more profound because it appears to emanate from our autonomous quest for ourselves, it appears as a matter of our freedom' (Rose, 1990: 256). As Williams et al. (2011) show, in the context of Kudumbashree, these techniques enable the state to free itself of social welfare obligations, creating a self-caring subject. More generally, they indicate mechanisms that create 'enterprising' 'responsibilized subjects' who are 'empowered' to self-discipline within a 'responsibilized quasi-autonomous' institution such as Kudumbashree that can be 'governed at a distance' (Barry et al., 1996; Miller and Rose, 1990; Rose, 1996). The technologies of budget and benchmark are vital for the conductance of the programmes of governing at a distance that characterized the Western-originated new public management under neoliberal rationality (Power 1995, 2000). These rationalities of government, in other words, governmentality, signify localized operations of a neoliberal project (Ferguson and Gupta, 2002). Thus, the creation of autonomy and empowerment in this context seems to indicate both 'export of technologies of subjectification' of neoliberal governmentality and enrolment of the 'developing world's' subject into the global neoliberal development project through such technologies (Brigg, 2006).

Through the continued participation in the Kudumbashree initiative, the income levels (saving and certain skills) of many Kudumbashree members have improved. Many participants felt that the increased income level gave them more 'voice' in the family decision-making:

Earlier, the male head used to make decisions in the family about expenses ... now women learned to work [means paid work] ... men have fewer jobs. There are many jobs in women's hands ... then, we have the freedom to spend (smiles). We can buy things we want. No need to ask anyone (look at others, and they nod their heads). They [husband/sons] know we have money with us now.

The 'male head' used to make family decisions since he had money power that accorded this right, which is now shared with females who should also be legitimate decision-makers by that logic. The primacy to capital (and not the stakeholder, for example, children or other family members) in such a thought process is striking. This reasoning and the related association of 'women empowerment' as 'economic empowerment' are central to neoliberal projects (Kabeer, 2005). Within such projects, this instance may be read as structural gain (financial independence) leading to women's 'empowerment' (Chavetz, 1990), as the predominant literature on Kudumbashree has argued

(Devika and Thampi, 2007; recent example, Banerjee et al., 2019). However, the Kudumbashree members in this process are legitimizing their voice in family decision-making based on the corporate market logic of 'higher income-higher value jobholder be accorded higher social status and thus more decision-making power' (George, 2015). This neoliberal programmatic logic was used to support the male domination and women's subordination in workplaces and labour markets (George, 2019), and thus the patriarchal relations in society (Eisenstein, 1979). The logic which was used to support patriarchal relations and the associated patterns of gendered practices is now seen as a currently accepted answer to the problem of legitimacy of patriarchy. The use of this 'hegemonic masculinity' (Connell, 1995) to apparently challenge the configuration of gendered practices (Connell and Messerschmidt, 2005) within the family ironically reinforces the legitimacy of the neoliberal programmatic logic.

An attendant creation (to independence and empowerment) is the discourse of 'flexibility'. Within Kudumbashree, the ongoing discourse framed and positioned the initiative as an opportunity for a 'housewife' to gain autonomy and flexibility in utilizing their labour time, while carrying out 'family responsibilities'. Many Kudumbashree members did not prefer a 'whole-day job' since it was difficult for them to 'discharge family responsibilities' with an eight-hour per day job. Their daily wager husband typically got 'works far from the house' which made the women do household work alone – this was the 'normal way of life, and therefore, fine'. Hence, 'work flexibility' and 'work site proximity to house' were crucial in deciding to take up a job, both of which 'Kudumbashree offered'. A participant shared:

> Men can leave for work even at 8 o'clock in the morning. We need to finish all the household chores before we leave. So, we start around 9.30–9.45 from home. We have also chosen work nearby home so that we can come back home by 4–4.30 [and sometimes in between]. We will have plenty of work even after coming back home.

Responsibilizing women for domestic labour thus forced them to look for 'flexible' jobs even if the jobs gave them less income (compared to men; particularly important for single mother or female sexed bodies) and bear low status and voice in the capitalist society (Rose, 1990). Then, on the one hand, probably, the responsibility for domestic work materially underpins the reproduction of women's inequality (Vogel, 2013) in this context. On the other hand, the state, through the quasi-autonomous Kudumbashree, seems to facilitate maintenance of the normalized gendered role of family caretaker, which leads to reproduction and reinforcement of the patriarchal relations (Radhakrishnan, 2015). If we consider women's domestic work as unpaid labour that procreates, feeds, and raises current and future generations of the workforce (Bakker and Gill, 2003), the role of the state and this ongoing gendering experience is in nexus with the capitalist forces. Another participant shared in a group discussion:

> Good that men can work longer. We should support [it] … our husbands nowadays do more skilled work [than ours]. So better payment and income. But even if they do the same work [as ours], it's better we stay back, and they go for full time [since they have better payment] … it's more income for the family.

This preference for male labour because of its higher market value has to be understood in a historical context of the state. There has been some pressure on the state (and other states) from big farmers (including industrialized farming) to mitigate the short supply of agricultural labour (mostly men) (George, 2015) that resulted in higher wages for agricultural, particularly skilled, labour (many Kudumbashree members' husbands, as mentioned previously, were skilled agricultural labourers). Then, it seems, in this context, in order for neoliberal capitalism to expand, women's domestic support that would release men's labour and, in turn, create a cheaper labour supply was a plausible condition (Vogel, 2013). Thus, beyond the issue of indirectly producing surplus value for the capital (and thus supporting the capital), reproducing gendered labour relations appears as a likely condition for the capital to retain its domination (Vogel, 2013).

The mobilization into already structured NHGs seems to have subsequently turned into a collective that created collective actions. As mentioned earlier, it is theoretically and practically important to explore the strategies and technologies of the 'women-empowering' 'women-inclusive' neoliberal project (and corporate capitalism) and the quest for alternatives within these processes, which the following section does.

ALTERNATIVE IMAGINATIONS MAROONED IN THE NEOLIBERAL COLLECTIVE

For many participants, once they became Kudumbashree members, beyond 'income-generation source, skill-training, and flexibility', Kudumbashree appeared as a space for sharing the experiences that they had in their families and larger society:

> There are discussions of savings, work schedules, and likes. But then, we also spent a lot of time sharing our personal and other experiences. More and more we feel that freedom to share because we can trust each other ... then many of us feel like that we are just one ... we have so much in common. We can, and we do, support each other and our families. That is Kudumbashree.

The overlapping experiences and a common feeling of social support – the 'shared space' (which is gendered) that helps them face their daily struggle for survival – functioned as a 'social glue' (Courville and Piper, 2004; Gelderloos, 2010), giving them an experience of a collective. This collectivization, therefore, was generated partly in the sharing of the gendering and gendered experiences as well as 'empowerment' in the labour relations both at home and outside. The experiences include both individual and collective emotions, decisions, and actions (NHG initiatives) that they recalled and enacted for our immersion which we explore next.

The Kudumbashree members' confidence – that their 'empowered state' through improved income and skill would be continued – was partly due to their shared trust in the collective called Kudumbashree.

> Participant 1: We never faced any issue of loan default as everybody is very cooperative. If somebody is in need of money for personal expenses such as marriage or kid's education, we take a loan in the group's name, and we are sure that there won't be any default.

Participant 2: In that (taking and distributing loans based on the bank saving), we look at the need. Not how much a person really deposited … I might have deposited more and the needy much less … doesn't matter … need is the point (gives examples of unexpected emergency needs of some Kudumbashree members in this NHG and the shared agreement to take a big loan to help members tide over such crises).

Participant 3: We do this in other NHGs also.… Then, see when making decisions, you have to give more weight to those who will bear the maximum effect of your decision. That is what we try in general.

The risk-taking based on the trust in the collective, the role of the 'principle of compassion', and the norm of keeping decision-making influence proportional to the consequence of the decision for one's lives are considered as aspects of operations of a participatory economic logic (Albert, 2003) – an alternative to the market-based logic of corporate capitalism (Wright, 2010). However, such snippets of alternative micro-imaginations and actions could wither away when they meet the operation of the neoliberal patriarchy within a family, as another NHG's experience shows. In this NHG, a new member who had rented a house in this locality joined. Her husband had got a job transfer (a member from an above-poverty-line family). Within a year, she took a loan for an emergency but then kept defaulting on the loan payment. In the name of peer accountability, some members raised concerns, but the defaulter convinced the majority that she would pay back the loan. One fine day, she and her husband vanished without any trace. The effect of this incident was not only members' gradual loss of interest in the NHG but in their words:

Participant 4: … then, we had no money with us … we are answerable to our husbands.…

Participant 5: Couldn't even look at the face of my husband and grown-up sons … now I have to ask them for money.

Participant 6: I don't make most family decisions … don't have a good job and for my daily expenses I depend on them (husband and son).

They say no more Kudumbashree, and I have to tell them lies for coming to meetings like this..

This case illustrates that not only do women not make decisions for the family but not even for themselves. The women do not have consent from the adult 'employed (paid)' males in the family for attending the 'women-empowering' Kudumbashree. Women legitimized and accepted the withdrawal of consent reproducing hegemonic masculinity as the legitimacy for their right to get 'empowered' and to assume the role of a family decision-maker itself rested on a neoliberal logic, as discussed earlier.

Conditions of possibilities for alternatives to emerge were marooned in the oceanic operations of the corporate neoliberal project in the context of another experience of collective action within the Kudumbashree: the Balasabha. With a care-taking intent, the social institutions such as schools and families often inculcate in children the dispositions and habits (thus forming a subjectivity) that would enable them to live best in the world they encounter. A consequence of such attempts is the reproduction of certain socially oppressive structures, including patriarchy (Kelly and Nihlen, 2017) and corporate capitalism (Apple, 2017; Bowles and Gintis, 1976). Pedagogically, unlike formal schools (which the children – mostly of Kudumbashree members – attend), the Balasabha operates informally using poetry (sometimes about working-class struggles), theatrics, and debates, mostly in the vernacular (Malayalam). The discussion involves issues of the importance of self-provisioning, organic farming, and corporate exploitation of workers and the environment that could create a subject who can question oppressive relations in society (Parker et al., 2014; Wright, 2010). However, the Balasabha activities also include banking, conflict resolution, mock run of the *panchayat*, running a children's council (in each Balasabha) that is organized hierarchically with positions such as mayor, deputy mayor, and so on, resembling the local state governance structure. In effect, as explained earlier, these activities produce a governable subject that would not discuss working-class control of the state or challenge the neoliberal patriarchal relations in families and schools. Dissent, if any, is contained within the 'democratic' processes (Mclaren, 1997) that Balasabha inculcates.

Such small ruptures in the totalitarian web of corporate capitalism, which can provide conditions of possibilities for the alternative to emerge, were more visible in other experiences of collective actions as well, for example, 'collective farming'. The notion of 'collective farming' originated outside the Kudumbashree programme and in the shared experiences of small landholders (less than 5 cents). As explained in the historical location of the Kudumbashree context, when food expenses went up, women started growing vegetable gardens around their houses independently to meet daily needs and to 'get our own produce'. As they faced difficulties with continuing independently, they started helping out each other in gardening and growing vegetables. They took this idea of 'growing together' to Kudumbashree meetings, and the state was willing to support the idea through Kudumbashree with subsidies and loan arrangements. As a participant shared:

> Before Kudumbashree [began], we did farming but individually in our small piece of land or labored in others' land. In Kudumbashree, we are together, and so we can take up bigger lands. More importantly, profit is our own now ... there is subsidies through Kudumbashree and loans from group [NHG]. If you are alone, you don't get these concessions.

While supporting such a bottom-up initiative, which seemed to mean not just cultivation but 'growing as a community' (yet it was vague), state mediation brought the initiative into a neoliberal project by connecting it to and making it dependent on banks loans and state subsidies. Although the larger mobilizing logic, the potential for increased income which motivated many to join Kudumbashree, was dominant among the members, there was also a feeling of sharing surplus value (profit) among themselves. In a group, one old ex-Kudumbashree member narrated the history (interspersed with the enactment and chipping in of other members):

> As the state leased bigger land, Kudumbashree women had to travel to these places far from their houses and use large farm implements. They were a bit scared to carry around the large implements [such as big pickaxe and wheelbarrow], least because of the physical weight but the symbolic weight of the dominating masculinity that was attached to

these artefacts within Kerala agricultural traditions. When the group walked away together carrying the artefacts, male relatives [including their spouses in some cases] and the public stared at the implements, saying 'Oh! Where are you guys [connotative meaning for males] going? No work at home?' Of course, they had made sure that they completed their 'due daily domestic responsibility' by 'waking up earlier' 'working faster'.

The women involved in the construction industry who worked as masons narrated a similar story. Gendering the labouring body and spatializing it (here, by normatively assigning female body to home space and kitchen garden) is a salient characteristic of capitalistic project (S. Ferguson, 2008) that accepts the 'scientific' assumption that male bodies are more efficient and intelligent (and thus more profitable) (Saini, 2017). To gain legitimacy for the body to labour (to do masculinized agriculture and construction work), it had to 'prove' its masculine 'efficiency to the society and the Kudumbashree or state authorities' and generate more income in both cases, collective farming and construction work. As some participants shared:

Participant 7: We drink tea and eat lunch while working as we need to finish our work at the earliest as the payment is based on a contract and not on a daily basis. So we don't waste time. See, we do our work and their [men's] work (pointing to another site). We did a better job often.

Participant 8: Now they had to accept that we also work. Yet it was tough for many to accept ... when we had repeated success, most of them accepted. [They] had no alternative!

The aggressive hard work, while 'not diluting household responsibilities', 'paid us off in fruits of the land, money, and acceptance' (by other females and males, including their spouses). The 'success', as defined within the masculine norms of the corporate capitalistic project, brought more Kudumbashree members into collective farming.

As collective farming became 'successful', Kudumbashree encouraged more women to come out and identify land for collective cultivation.[5]

Quite often, the cultivation took place in fallow land, which was supported by the state policy to encourage the use of fallow land to make it viable for cultivation, generating extra farm income (Harilal and Eswaran, 2018). This drive was important in the context of the shrinking size of cultivable land in Kerala. In towns, the land ownership mainly belonged to the rich (individuals or business houses), who were the new types of absentee landlords, which for some Kudumbashree members looked unjustifiable (from a group discussion):

> Participant 10: We don't have space for farming. Look, full of rubber trees [a few owned by members of the NHGs but mostly owned by outsiders]. We are forced to look for other places. All these (pointing to rubber plantations – a cash crop) and the government actions like demonetization hurt the poor, not the rich. They make us farmers suffer, yet we do farming.

> Participant 11: Yes, we don't have much land [empty cultivable land] here, but in towns, many lands lay unused. They buy land, and then they are all abroad. We go for those lands. Then we get only an 11-month [tenancy] contract. After that, they [the landowners] either increase the rent or do not rent. For submitting in Kudumbashree and for Krishibhavan subsidies, we need a tax receipt. This is a big challenge. We are not asking for big lands, but farmers must have land for farming. So that together we can farm. We can grow. We took this up with the Kudumbashree officials and the state. Nothing has happened so far.

> Participant 12: The 11-month contract demands a quick return. That is how the landowners and others [indicating state functionaries and other Kudumbashree members] see it: do the farming in such a way that you get a quick return. Quickly grow a crop, use chemical fertilizers, get the yield somehow. Never mind the harm – market and profit. For them, land is just that. A lifeless piece of [geographical] area to get profit.

In contrast with this corporate capitalist approach, these farmers explained their process in detail. First, prepare and nurture the land, like caring for a mother, through soil layering, de-layering, repeatedly moisturizing with the application of bio-fertilizers. Then wait for the land to become effective and cultivable (if it is a fallow land). Otherwise, they felt that they were harming the earth, which they did not want to, and could not, as they considered them as 'guardians with a responsibility to conserve the environment' (Escobar, 1996) and the earth.

Consequently, in order to see the fruits of their harvest, they needed a minimum of three years and hence the demand for a long-term contract and the government's intervention. Explicit in this latter approach is a shift from the logic of exploitation (of the lifeless) (Merchant, 1980) to the logic of nurture and caring, which other scholars found in alternative movements (Patel, 2013; Caggiano and De' Rosa, 2015). More important is the anti-patriarchal and more matriarchal underlining (Reuther, 1995). The earth, or specifically land, is considered a mother since, as a mother, the earth in its womb grows life. Within this reasoning, the use of chemicals, which could produce more profit, is considered as masculine violence (harm) against the mother and the life in her womb. Thus, we see, on the one hand, the reproduction of masculine hegemony and capitalistic patriarchal relations (for example, through a voluntary performance of 'domestic responsibilities' and the internalized masculine norm related to labour). On the other, in the experiences such as the ones described earlier, there emerges a resistance to capitalistic patriarchal relations between humans and the earth (Vaughan, 2006). The ruptures or inconsistency that this contradiction produces offers a condition for the possibility of alternatives to emerge (here in the form of reviving a matriarchal approach).

We now depend quite a bit on loans and subsidies. There have been so many government announcements about subsidies and loans to farmers. Their money goes into seminars, talks, classes by experts [a notion that some of them question – see later], and so on. Nothing reaches the farmers. Still, we do not and can't abandon farming because it is our livelihood. It is in our tradition, in our blood. Our past generations did it. We just cannot but do it when the rain comes. It's not just money. But we love it. Those who love farming will continue doing it even if you suffer losses, say, this year, with a hope that next year will be great. By the providence of the land. God's blessings!

In this spirit, 'friends of the earth' was a common imagination and feeling (although not largely shared) among Kudumbashree collective farmers in some rural NHGs, which glued them as a different collective. Thus, many Kudumbashree NHGs practiced organic farming and tried minimizing and recycling farm waste by making compost as fertilizer. They also tried to regenerate, use and preserve local seeds, plants, and practices sometimes in cooperation with a local research institute (for example, Mannoothy Agricultural University) – a connection that came through Kudumbashree – which made the local knowledge and source accessible to the public freely. Such imaginations and actions then seem to indicate remnant forms of commoning within the Kudumbashree initiatives. From a radical perspective, commons are considered as a place where the social (re)production of new (or old) practices of solidarity (re)emerge (Hardt and Negri, 2009). It, thus, is a space 'where there is a desire to constitute non-capitalist, collective forms of politics, identity, and citizenship'. They are created through a combination of resistance and creation and a questioning and challenging of dominant laws and social norms (Pickerill and Chatterton, 2006). From this perspective, farming on the unused lands that were kept for its real estate value (with big business houses or rich individuals) – an issue we discussed earlier – had both material and symbolic significance:

> We are not demanding the ownership [of this land]. But farmers should have a right to use it [the unused land]; otherwise, it is not even good for the environment, the earth and society. The state should take it or make them available to farmers for cultivation.

The ownership disclaimer is contextually salient since the Kudumbashree members informally came to know that (when they made such a proposal) the big businesses were concerned about a potential state takeover of their properties (as happened in Kerala during the land reforms period). In the participants' understanding, such concerns led 'big land owners' to deny joint liability groups (JLGs) renting the land for farming or discontinue the 11-month contract. Re-appropriation of unused lands through collective community ownership and bringing them under community land trust has been considered as an alternative to corporate capitalistic modes (Caggiano and De' Rosa, 2015). However, here the suggestion is not a concrete state takeover of the ownership but re-appropriation of the unused land. The issue of use is at its centre, which is argued to be defined not by an individual or a private business but by a community as per its need. The state is expected to act on behalf of the community fulfilling those needs. Connecting this point with the matriarchal socio-ecological approach to the land-farming relationship suggests a physical and cultural re-appropriation of spatial relationships (Escobar, 2008) linking symbolic, material and structural dimensions. In this imagination, there is also an attempt to reclaim the right to self-organize and facilitate communities' participation in the allocation and use of local resources (Wright, 2010). Yet this democratic impulse is largely circumscribed by the state democracy.

Further, the choice to practice collective farming combined the strong potential of agricultural activities to integrate 'problematic people' (Di Iacovo et al., 2006) with nature and community and thus appeared to promote community well-being and solidarity:

> This collective and the group activities connect us also to each other, not just JLG members or Kudumbashree but with the community. We come to know the issues in families, mental illness, deep debts, emergencies. We are not doctors, but from our experiences, we see that often mental problems here are coming from isolation. Many have their children migrated to the urban side or even to other states. No one to share, then. We invite them to get involved in farming and other such activities. Connect with nature and community is a solution. So we started using our activities to improve community awareness about environmental problems, sexual harassment, women's safety, and so on.

Within Kudumbashree's collective farming experience and beyond, a degree of women's solidarity (Banerjee et al., 2019), which seems to be rooted in a vague but feminist ecological ideology, is then producing a bottom-up communing-based socio-ecological relationship. This is similar to experiences within other alternative movements (Patel, 2013; Kothari and Joy, 2017). Such remnant interstices of commoning can be a favourable condition to open up possibilities for transformative politics (Bollier, 2014; Caggiano and De' Rosa, 2015). Yet, as seen earlier, these alternative imaginations and actions that are acclaimed to empower women exist within the ruptures of the ever-expanding relations of neoliberal capitalistic patriarchy.

DISCUSSION AND CONCLUSION

Our study presents Kudumbashree experiences as discrete moments within a corporate patriarchal capitalist totality which comprises 'a certain contradictory unity' (Bakker and Gill, 2003). Our exploration of the Kudumbashree experiences throws up this contradictory picture: on the one hand, there is the reproduction of a neoliberal self-caring autonomous (and thus 'empowered') subject who can be governed at a distance; a subject who is inscribed with a masculine hegemony that provides the ideological and material support for the reproduction of capitalistic patriarchal labour relations. On the other, there remains a struggling communitarian subject who positions herself inconsistently as anti-patriarchal within some experiences and capitalistic patriarchal yet empowered within some other experiences. This contradictory positioning and attendant imaginations indicate a rupture within the totalitarian web of capitalist patriarchal relations (Holloway, 2010; Parker et al., 2014; Wright, 2010). Within this rupture, we see micro emancipatory resistance, micro-challenges, and thus possibilities of alternative imaginations to the all-powerful capitalistic patriarchal relations among humans and between humans and the earth (Vaughan, 2006). The resistance and challenges can be in the form of anti-patriarchal questioning of land-labour relations and imaginations with matriarchal leanings that could create a bottom-up communing-based socio-ecological relationship. Such remnant interstices of anti-patriarchal communing, although they are sustained within the ever-expanding web of neoliberal capitalistic patriarchal relations, can offer favourable conditions for opening up possibilities for transformative politics (Werlhof, 2007; S. Ferguson, 2008). Yet these conditions that arise in the immediate and experiential are moments in a dynamic, historically changing set of corporate capitalist social relations.

These momentary conditions and the alternative imaginations that these conditions facilitate may lie beneath the more visible hegemonic domination of capitalism, which buries them down, as Gibson-Graham (2006) has argued. Yet the imaginations may keep themselves vibrant in the subterranean interstices, amidst all struggles, and become visible when we explore the unapparent ruptures within the totalitarian web of capitalist patriarchal relations. We identified and explored such interstices, which revealed the subterranean subversive imaginations that may facilitate experimentations in the politics of the possibility to organize social relations in a fundamentally different manner. These imaginations thus provide a way to perceive openings for a politics of possibility (Gibson-Graham et al., 2013). Hence, we agree with the argument (Scott-Cato and Hillier, 2010) that we need to look at the interstices within current institutions and ways of organizing to find transformational practices that could challenge and subvert the dominant status quo (Gibson-Graham, 2006; 2008). However, glorifying such emergence and romanticizing over the local communitarian imaginations unreflexively (see Böhm's, 2014, critique of Gibson-Graham et al., 2013), which appears as a rising trend (for example, Monbiot, 2017), may lead to discounting or ignoring the hegemonic domination and the attendant inequalities (DuPuis and Goodman, 2005; Harvey, 1996).

In this discussion, we might appear as seeking a middle ground between incremental micro-emancipatory politics and a fundamentally subversive antagonistic structural change, which is an ongoing tension within Critical Management Studies (CMS). The in-house critique of CMS for its near-exclusive focus on critiquing the hegemonic corporate capitalism without engaging with alternatives or not being performative (Spicer et al., 2016) has led to explorations and framing of alternatives to corporate capitalism (for example, Parker, 2017; Parker et al., 2014). The in-house critique, which suggested a pragmatic 'critical performative' engagement with management using notions of care and affirmation in lieu of the sustained antagonistic critiquing (Spicer et al., 2009, 2016), created a debate between 'negative' critique of capitalist management and the performative and 'progressive' engagement with the management. A related tension within this debate is between the dominant approach, particularly the post-modern or post-structural studies that advocated explorations of micro-emancipation-oriented incremental, cumulative changes to the dominant capitalistic organizing (Alvesson and Willmott 1992), and the search for more radical and structurally oriented subversive changes (Banerjee, 2008; Fleming and Banerjee, 2016). Pointing out the conceptual and pragmatic challenges to both these approaches, some scholars suggest a middle agonistic ground (for example, Parker and Parker 2017). We did not explicitly mobilize agonism as a normative framework for our exploration. However, as mentioned earlier, we do not see it pragmatic to reject or work outside the dominant capitalist system within which the alternative experiences are embedded (Mouffe, 2013), and our analysis indicates that within a neoliberal state-instituted 'alternative', possibilities for radical yet contingent alternatives could emerge in the struggles that attempt to expand possibilities for political engagement with the dominant hegemonic present by creating alternate imaginations and experiences. To this extent, our insights align with the agonistic approach (Mouffe, 2013; Parker and Parker 2017) that, for example, may consider interrelated clusters of worker-owned small-scale worker cooperatives as a potential alternative organizational form for its organizational and economic resilience (Kandathil, 2015), economic and workplace democracy (Kandathil and Varman, 2007), environmentally sustainable practices and continuous addressal of the workplace and larger inequalities (Parker, 2017).

Studies suggest that to resist dispossession, co-optation, and integration, alternative attempts like commoning needs an anarchist anti-statist approach (Escobar, 2008; A. Ferguson, 2009), such as organic social movements that should potentially lie outside the state (Holloway, 2002). However, consistent with other scholars on alternatives (Eid et al., 2001; Gutberiet, 2009; Harriss, 2019; Holloway, 2002; Wright, 2010), Kudumbashree experience indicates that there are conditions of possibilities for alternatives to emerge even within the sites of state–civil society relations to the extent that the interstices of alternative actions and imaginations are not sealed or swallowed up by ever-expanding capitalistic patriarchal forces. Along this line, as an alternative to corporate capitalism, among others, Wright (2010) suggests 'participatory socialism' wherein state and civil society jointly organize and control the production of goods and services. Within this alternative, similar to the Kudumbashree experience, the role of the state is to provide the template or parameters for organizing and controlling. However, Wright argues that further development and stabilization of such alternatives depend on two crucial conditions. The first is the presence of socially empowering institutional mechanisms with reasonable ideological coherence, which facilitate the exercise of social power to influence the state. However, if such mechanisms are instituted by the state (increasingly capitalist state), its social empowerment is a challenge. The second condition is that the civil society actors and the broader civil society should retain sufficient power (or influence) to function as a counter-check on the state power and economic power. Given the increasing neoliberal fabrication of the state, the civil society, and other societal institutions (including the media and family) (Derne, 2008; Ganguly-Scrase and Scrase, 2008), at least in the state of Kerala, this remains a serious challenge.

Within a women's inclusive emancipatory alternative, the roots of the alternative lie in questioning gender inequality and patriarchy. We agree with gender-focused feminist scholarship that despite structural gains and achievements in gender equality, patriarchal ideology may sustain even at the micro-level of patterned interactions between intimates (Hunnicut, 2009). However, what sustains patriarchy does not seem to be a gendering of work. Rather as ecofeminists argue and as Kudumbashree experience indicates, unpaid free modern domestic work (an invention of capitalism for Frank and Gills, 1996) appears to materially underpin the perpetuation of women's inequality in capitalist society (Vogel, 2013). Through historical analyses, more broadly, they have consistently argued that neoliberal capitalism is the finest expression of patriarchy (hence the term 'capitalist patriarchy') (Frank and Gills, 1996). The search for alternatives then should start with challenging patriarchal relations rather than class relations. Kudumbashree experience suggests that patriarchy, which is inscribed through domestic responsibilities, provides the ideological and material base for neoliberal capitalism.

Finally, while the scholarship on Kudumbashree either glorifies or vilifies Kudumbashree with respect to its potential to offer a women emancipatory alternative to corporate capitalism, our explorations show a more nuanced picture. We agree that set within the state institutional mechanism, Kudumbashree experiences can produce self-caring neoliberal subjects, devolving the state of its welfare obligations (Williams et al., 2011). Connecting this strategy to the global neoliberal project, we show how the production occurs through the export of subjectification technologies and its effect of producing not just a neoliberal project but one governable at a distance (Rose, 1990). Similarly, we also agree that in the name of women empowerment, the patriarchal relations are reproduced within the Kudumbashree experience despite structural gains (Devika, 2016). Our study indicates the crucial role of corporate, neoliberal project in the form of domestic responsibility that helps reinforce patriarchy. Yet, within the cracks of the totalitarian neoliberal project, our explorations show conditions for the possibilities of the emergence of alternatives. As one of our participants located her imaginations of alternatives in the providence of nature, we place our hope in the providence of the communities of activists, scholars, and provoked citizens at large.

ACKNOWLEDGEMENTS

The authors thank the members of the Kudumbashree programme, Thrissur District, Kerala, for generously sharing their experience with them and to the Research and Publication Unit, IIM Ahmedabad for funding the research project.

NOTES

1. See www.globalhungerindex.org/pdf/en/2018.pdf, accessed on 19 June 2019.
2. See www.kudumbashree.org/pages/171, accessed on 19 June 2019.
3. See www.thrissurdtpc.com/AboutUs, accessed on 19 June 2019.
4. MNREGS: Mahatma Gandhi National Rural Employment Guarantee Scheme instituted by the central government of India to provide 100 days per year of guaranteed employment to the rural poor.
5. The agrarian sector has been a relatively neglected area in Kerala's model of development, except for land reforms, which itself had a limited impact on agriculture (Harilal and Eswaran, 2018). This neglect led to underutilization of land as a means of production, and people retained land only as a relatively secure asset (Harilal and Eswaran, 2018). This resulted in people moving away from land, and consequently, large areas of cultivable land remained idle. On the other hand, thousands of poor families who are ready to

undertake agriculture as a livelihood option did not have enough land to venture into agriculture (Sajesh and Ramasundaram, 2013). In this context, Kudumbashree encouraged NHGs to undertake lease land farming as an income-generating activity.

REFERENCES

Acker, J. (1990). Hierarchies, jobs, bodies: A theory of gendered organizations. *Gender and Society* 4(2): 139–158.

Agarwal, B. (2018). Can group farms outperform individual family farms? Empirical insights from india. *World Development* 108: 57–73.

Albert, M. (2003). *Parecon: Life After Capitalism*. London: Verso.

Alvesson, M. and H. Willmott (1992). On the idea of emancipation in management and organization studies. *Academy of Management Review* 17(3): 432–464.

Apple, M. W. (2017). Reproduction and contradiction in education: An introduction. In *Cultural and Economic Reproduction in Education: Essays on Class, Ideology, and the State*, ed. Apple, M. W. London: Routledge, 1–31.

Aswathy, P. and K. Kalpana (2018). The 'stigma' of paid work: Capital, state, patriarchy and women fish workers in South India. *Journal of International Women's Studies* 19(5): 113–128.

Bakker, I. and S. Gill (2003). Global political economy and social reproduction. In *Power, Production and Social Reproduction*, ed. I. Bakker. and S. Gill. New York, NY: Palgrave, 3–16.

Banerjee, S. (2008). Necrocapitalism. *Organization Studies* 29(12): 1541–1563.

Banerjee, S., S. Carney, and L. Hulgard (2019). People-centered social innovation: An emerging paradigm with global potential. In *People-Centered Social Innovation: Global Perspectives on an Emerging Paradigm*, ed. S. Banerjee, S. Carney, and L. Hulgard. New York, NY: Routledge, ch. 1.

Barry, A., T. Osborne, and N. Rose (1996). Introduction. In *Foucault and Political Reason: Liberalism, Neoliberalism and Rationalities of Government*, ed. A. Barry, T. Osborne, and N. Rose. Chicago: University of Chicago Press, 1–18.

Berer, M. (2011). Privatisation in health systems in developing countries: What's in a name? *Reproductive Health Matters* 19(37): 4–9.

Böhm, S. (2014). Book review symposium: JK Gibson-Graham, Jenny Cameron and Stephen Healy, *Take Back the Economy: An Ethical Guide for Transforming Our Communities. Sociology* 48(5): 1055–1057.

Bollier, D. (2014). *Think Like a Commoner: A Short Introduction to the Life of the Commons.* Gabriola Islands, BC: New Society Publishers.

Bowles, S. and H. Gintis (1976). *Schooling in Capitalist America.* New York: Basic Books.

Braun, V. and V. Clarke (2006). Using thematic analysis in psychology. *Qualitative Research in Psychology* 3(2): 77–101.

Brigg, M. (2006). Disciplining the developmental subject: Neoliberal power and governance through microcredit. In *Microfinance: Perils and Prospects*, ed. J. L. Fernando. London: Routledge, 66–84.

Caggiano, M. and S. P. De Rosa (2015). Social economy as antidote to criminal economy: How social cooperation is reclaiming commons in the context of Campania's environmental conflicts. *Partecipazione e conflitto* 8(2): 530–554.

Chathukulam, J. and A. K. Thottunkel (2010). The Sen in the neo-liberal developmental programmes of Kerala. *International Journal of Rural Management* 6(2): 161–192.

Chavetz, J. S. (1990). *Gender Equity: An Integrated Theory of Stability and Change.* Newbury Park, CA: Sage.

Connell, R. W. (1995). *Masculinities.* Cambridge, UK: Polity Press.

Connell, R. W. and J. W. Messerschmidt (2005). Hegemonic masculinity: Rethinking the concept. *Gender and Society* 19(6): 829–859.

Cornwall, A. (2003). Whose voices? Whose choices? Reflections on gender and participatory development. *World Development* 31(8): 1325–1342.

——— (2007). Myths to live by? Female solidarity and female autonomy reconsidered. *Development and Change* 38(1): 149–168.

Courville, S. and N. Piper (2004). Harnessing hope through NGO activism. *Annals of the American Academy of Political and Social Science* 592(1): 39–61.

Cruz, L. B., M. A. Alves, and R. Delbridge (2017). Next steps in organising alternatives to capitalism: Toward a relational research agenda. *M@n@gement* 20(4): 322–335.

Cumbers, A. (2017). Creating the democratic economy. Accessed on 19 June 2019: https://neweconomics.opendemocracy.net/creating-democratic-economy/.

Das, R. (2019). Producing local neoliberalism in a Leftist regime: Neoliberal governmentality and populist transition in West Bengal, India. *Contemporary South Asia* 27(3): 373–391.

Derné, S. (2008). *Globalization on the Ground: New Media and the Transformation of Culture, Class, and Gender in India*. New Delhi: Sage Publications India Private Ltd.

Devika, J. (2016). The Kudumbashree woman and the Kerala Model woman: Women and politics in contemporary Kerala. *Indian Journal of Gender Studies* 23(3): 393–414.

——— (2017). Surviving in contemporary Kerala: Reflections from recent research in a fisher village. *Development and Change* 48(2): 364–386.

Devika, J. and B. V. Thampi (2007). Between 'empowerment' and 'liberation': The Kudumbashree initiative in Kerala. *Indian Journal of Gender Studies* 14(1): 33–60.

Di Iacovo F., Senni, S. and J. de Kneght (2006). Farming for health in Italy. In *Farming for Health: Green Care-farming across Europe and the United States of America*, ed. J. Hassink and M. van Dijk. Dordrecht, The Netherlands: Springer, 289–308.

Dupuis, E. M. and D. Goodman (2005). Should we go 'home' to eat? Toward a reflexive politics of localism. *Journal of Rural Studies* 21(3): 359–371.

Educativa, A. (2014). Privatization and its impact on the right to education of women and girls. CEDAW (United Nations Committee on the Elimination of Discrimination against Women), Written Submission. Accessed on 19 June 2019: www.campaignforeducation.org/docs/reports/GCE_Submission_Privatisation_CEDAW_2014.pdf.

Eid, F. and A. E. Bueno Pimentel (2001). Solidary economy: Challenges of cooperative agrarian reform in Brazil. *Journal of Rural Cooperation* 29(2): 141–152.

Eisenstein, Z. (1979). Some notes on the relations of capitalist patriarchy. In *Capitalist Patriarchy and the Case for Socialist Feminism*, ed. Z. Eisenstein. New York: Monthly Review Press, 41–55.

Escobar A. (2008). *Territories of Difference: Place, Movements, Life, Redes*. Durham/London: Duke University Press.

———— (1996). Constructing nature: Elements for a poststructural political ecology. In *Liberation Ecologies: Environment, Development and Social Movements*, ed. R. Peet and M. Watts. London: Routledge, 46–68.

Ferguson, A. (2009). Women, corporate globalization, and global justice. In *Feminist Ethics and Social and Political Philosophy: Theorizing the Non-Ideal*, ed. L. Tessman. Dordrecht: Springer, 271–285.

Ferguson, J. and A. Gupta (2002). Spatializing states: Toward an ethnography of neoliberal governmentality. *American Ethnologist* 29(4): 981–1002.

Ferguson, S. (2008). Canadian contributions to social reproduction feminism, race and embodied labor. *Race, Gender and Class* 15(1/2): 42–57.

Fierlbeck, K. (1995). Getting Representation right for women in development: accountability, consent, and the articulation of women's interests. *IDS Bulletin* 26(3): 23–30.

Fleming, P. and S. B. Banerjee (2016). When performativity fails: Implications for Critical Management Studies. *Human Relations* 69(2): 257–276.

Frank, A. G. and B. Gills (1996). The 5,000-year world system: An interdisciplinary introduction. In *The World System: Five Hundred Years or Five Thousand?* ed. A. G. Frank and B. Gills. London: Routledge, 3–57.

Frank, A. G., B. Gills, and B. K. Gills, eds. (1996). *The World System: Five Hundred Years or Five Thousand? Psychology Press*. New York: Routledge.

Ganguly-Scrase, R. and T. J. Scrase (2008). *Globalisation and the Middle Classes in India: The Social and Cultural Impact of Neoliberal Reforms*. London: Routledge.

Gelderloos, P. (2010). *Anarchy Works*. San Francisco, CA: Ardent Press.

George S. (2015). Gender and labour in Kerala. Unpublished thesis, ch. 5. Accessed on 19 June 2019: http://14.139.13.47:8080/jspui/bitstream/10603/166327/4/13_chapter5.pdf.

———— (2019). Globalization, workspace transformation and informal workers: A reversal of gender roles. In *Perspectives on Neoliberalism, Labour and Globalization in India*, ed. K. R. Shyam. Singapore: Palgrave Macmillan, 273–297.

Gibson-Graham, J. K. (2006). *The End of Capitalism (As We Knew It): A Feminist Critique of Political Economy*. Minneapolis, MN: University of Minnesota Press.

—— (2008). Diverse economies: Performative practices for other worlds. *Progress in Human Geography* 32(5): 613–632.

Gibson-Graham, J. K., J. Cameron, and S. Healy (2013). *Take Back the Economy: An Ethical Guide for Transforming Our Communities*. Minnesota, MN: University of Minnesota Press.

Giridharadas, A. (2018). *Winners Take All: The Elite Charade of Changing the World*. New York, NY: Alfred A Knopf.

Gooptu, N. (2013). Introduction. In *Enterprise Culture in Neoliberal India: Studies in Youth, Class, Work and Media*, ed. N. Gooptu. New York, NY: Routledge, 1–24.

Gutberlet, J. (2009). Solidarity economy and recycling co-ops in Sao Paulo: Micro-credit to alleviate poverty. *Development in Practice* 19(6): 737–751.

Hardt, M. and A. Negri (2009). *Commonwealth*. Cambridge, MA: The Belknap Press of Harvard University Press.

Harilal, K. N. and K. K. Eswaran (2018). The agrarian question and mechanisation of agriculture in Kerala. *Review of Agrarian Studies* 8(1): 2–27.

Harriss, J. (2019). The great transformation in our time and the possibilities for the renewal of social democracy. In *Perspectives on Neoliberalism, Labour and Globalization in India*, ed. K. R. Shyam Sundar. Singapore: Palgrave Macmillan, 123–143.

Harvey, D. (1996). *Justice, Nature and the Geography of Difference*. Oxford: Blackwell.

—— (2007). *A Brief History of Neoliberalism*. Oxford, UK: Oxford University Press.

Heeks, R. and S. Arun (2010). Social outsourcing as a development tool: The impact of outsourcing IT services to women's social enterprises in Kerala. *Journal of International Development: Journal of the Development Studies Association* 22(4): 441–454.

Holloway, J. (2002). Change the world without taking power. *New Politics* 9(1): 175–179.

—— (2010). *Crack Capitalism*. London, UK: Pluto Press.

Hunnicutt, G. (2009). Varieties of patriarchy and violence against women: Resurrecting 'patriarchy' as a theoretical tool. *Violence against Women* 15(5): 553–573.

Jeromi, P. D. (2005). Economic reforms in Kerala. *Economic and Political Weekly* 40(30): 3267–3277.

—— (2007). Farmers' indebtedness and suicides: Impact of agricultural trade liberalisation in kerala. *Economic and Political Weekly* 42(31): 3241–3247.

Job, S. (2003). A study of chit finance in Kerala with special emphasis on Kerala State Financial Enterprises Ltd. Unpublished thesis, Department of Applied Economics, Cochin University of Science and Technology, Cochin, Kerala.

John, J. (2009). *Kudumbashree Project: A Poverty Eradication Programme in Kerala.* New Delhi: Planning Commission of India, Government of India. Accessed on 19 June 2019: www.kudumbashree.org/storage/files/ort1w_kshree%20study%20report2.pdf.

Kabeer, N. (1999). Resources, agency, achievements: Reflections on the measurement of women's empowerment. *Development and Change* 30(3): 435–464.

—— (2005). Gender equality and women's empowerment: A critical analysis of the third Millennium Development Goal 1. *Gender and Development* 13(1): 13–24.

Kalpana. K. (2017). *Women, Microfinance and the State in Neo-liberal India.* London and New York, NY: Routledge.

Kalyani, K. and P. C. Seena (2012). Socio-economic changes of women through Kudumbasree: A study from Puthenvelikkara (GP) of Kerala state, India. *International Research Journal of Social Sciences* 1(2): 1–7.

Kandathil, G. M. (2015). *Contradictions of Employee Involvement in Organizational Change: The Transformation Efforts in NCJM, an Indian Industrial Cooperative.* Lanham, MD: Lexington Books.

Kandathil, G. M. and R. Varman (2007). Contradictions of employee involvement, information sharing and expectations: A case study of an Indian worker cooperative. *Economic and Industrial Democracy* 28(1): 140–174.

Kannan, K. P. (2000). People's planning, Kerala's dilemma. *Seminar.* https://india-seminar.com/semframe.html.

Kannan, K. P. and G. Raveendran (2017). *Poverty, Women and Capability: A Study of the Impact of Kerala's Kudumbashree System on Its Members and Their Families.* Thiruvananthapuram: Laurie Baker Centre for Habitat Studies.

Kelly, G. P. and A. S. Nihlen (2017). Schooling and the reproduction of patriarchy: Unequal workloads, unequal rewards. In *Cultural and Economic Reproduction in Education*, ed. M. W. Apple. London: Routledge, 162–180.

Kothari, A. and K. J. Joy (2017). Looking back into the future: India, South Asia, and the world in 2100. In *Alternative Futures: Unshackling India*, ed. A. Kothari and K. J. Joy. New Delhi: Authors Upfront, 627–645.

Krishnamoorthy, P. (2010). Development challenges of Kerala economy under globalization: A note. Accessed on 19 June 2019: https://ssrn.com/abstract=1722471.

Kudumbashree. (2020). History and evolution. Accessed on 19 June 2019: www.kudumbashree.org/pages/178.

Mannathukkaren, N. (2010). The 'poverty' of political society: Partha Chatterjee and the People's Plan Campaign in Kerala, India. *Third World Quarterly* 31(2): 295–314.

—— (2011). Redistribution and recognition: Land reforms in Kerala and the limits of culturalism. *Journal of Peasant Studies* 38(2): 379–411.

McLaren, P. (1997). *Revolutionary Multiculturalism: Pedagogies of Dissent for the New Millennium*. Boulder, CO: Westview.

Merchant, C. (1980). *The Death of Nature: Women, Ecology and the Scientific Revolution*. San Francisco: Harper & Row.

Miller, P. and N. Rose (1990). Governing economic life. *Economic Sociology* 19(1): 1–31.

Monbiot, G. (2017). *Out of the Wreckage: A New Politics for an Age of Crisis*. London: Verso

Mouffe, C. (2013). *Agonistics: Thinking the World Politically*. London: Verso.

NIPCCD. (2008). Gender framework analysis of empowerment of women: A case study of Kudumbashree programme. National Institute of Public Cooperation and Child Development. Accessed on 19 June 2019: http://nipccd.nic.in/reports/gender.pdf.

Oommen, M. A. (2008). Reforms and the Kerala Model. *Economic and Political Weekly* 43(2): 22–25.

Parker, M., G. Cheney, V. Fournier, and C. Land (2014). *The Routledge Companion to Alternative Organization*. London: Routledge.

Parker, S. and M. Parker (2017). Antagonism, accommodation and agonism in Critical Management Studies: Alternative organizations as allies. *Human Relations* 70(11): 1366–1387.

Parker, M. (2017). Alternative enterprises, local economies, and social justice: Why smaller is still more beautiful. *M@n@gement* 20(4): 418–434.

Patel, N. (2013). Islamic feminist reflection of pedagogy and gender praxis in South African Madaris. Master's thesis, University of Cape Town. Accessed on 19 June 2019: https://open.uct.ac.za/handle/11427/10649.

Patnaik, P. (2014). Neo-liberalism and democracy. *Economic and Political Weekly* 49(15): 39–44.

—— (2018). Trends of centre–state relations in India under the neo-liberal regime. *Studies in People's History* 5(1): 83–91.

Pickerill, J. and P. Chatterton (2006). Notes towards autonomous geographies: Creation, resistance and self-management as survival tactics. *Progress in Human Geography* 30(6): 730–746.

Pillai, N. (2018). Does quality qualify the Kerala model? Decentralised governance, human development and quality. Accessed on 19 June 2019: https://mpra. ub.uni-muenchen.de/id/eprint/85618.

Power M. (1995). *Audit and the Decline of Inspection*. London: CIPFA.

—— (2000). *The Audit Implosion: Regulating Risk from the Inside*. London: ICAEW.

Radhakrishnan, S. and C. Solari (2015). Empowered women, failed patriarchs: Neoliberalism and global gender anxieties. *Sociology Compass* 9(9): 784–802.

Raghavan, V. P. (2009). Micro-credit and empowerment: A study of Kudumbashree projects in Kerala. *Indian Journal of Rural Development* 28(4): 478–479.

Rammohan, K. T. (1998). Kerala CPI (M): All that is solid melts into air. *Economic and Political Weekly* 33(40): 2579–2582.

Rose, N. (1990). *Governing the Soul: The Shaping of the Private Self*. London: Routledge.

—— (1996). Governing 'advanced' liberal democracies. In *Foucault and Political Reason: Liberalism, Neoliberalism and Rationalities of Government*, ed. A. Barry, T. Osborne, and N. Rose. Chicago: University of Chicago Press, 37–64.

Ruether, R. (1995). Ecofeminism: Symbolic and social connections of the oppression of women and the domination of nature. *Feminist Theology* 3(9): 35–50.

Saini, A. (2017). *Inferior: How Science Got Women Wrong-and the New Research That's Rewriting the Story.* Boston: Beacon Press.

Sajesh, V. K. and P. Ramasundaram (2013). Effectiveness of collective farming under Kudumbasree programme of Kerala. *Journal of Community Mobilization and Sustainable Development* 8(2): 276–281.

Scott-Cato, M. and J. Hillier (2010). How could we study climate-related social innovation? Applying Deleuzean philosophy to transition towns. *Environmental Politics* 19(6): 869–887.

Shrivastava, A. and A. Kothari (2012). *Churning the Earth: The Making of Global India.* New Delhi: Penguin India.

Spicer, A., M. Alvesson and D. Kärreman (2009). Critical performativity: The unfinished business of Critical Management Studies. *Human Relations* 62(4): 537–560.

——— (2016). Extending critical performativity. *Human Relations* 69(2): 225–249.

Srivastava, A. (2017). Time use and household division of labor: Within-gender dynamics. Accessed on 19 June 2019: https://vc.bridgew.edu/may_celebrations/2017/session2/11/.

Turner III, D. W. (2010). Qualitative interview design: A practical guide for novice investigators. *The Qualitative Report* 15(3): 754–760.

Van Maanen, J. (1998). *Qualitative Studies of Organizations*, vol. 1. New Delhi: Sage Publications.

Varghese, M. (2012). Women empowerment through Kudumbashree: A study in Ernakulam District. Doctoral thesis submitted to Mahatma Gandhi University. Accessed on 19 June 2019: https://shodhganga.inflibnet.ac.in/bitstream/10603/25984/1/01_title.pdf.

Vaughan, G. (2006). *A Radically Different World View Is Possible: The Gift-Economy Inside and Outside Patriarchal Capitalism.* Toronto: Innana.

Vogel, L. (2013). *Marxism and the Oppression of Women: Toward a Unitary Theory.* Boston: Brill.

Werlhof C. V. (2007). No critique of capitalism without a critique of patriarchy! Why the left is no alternative. *Capitalism Nature Socialism* 18(1): 13–27.

Williams, D. G., B. V. Thampi, D. Narayana, S. Nandigama, and D. Bhattacharyya (2011). Performing participatory citizenship: Politics and power in Kerala's

Kudumbashree programme. *Journal of Development Studies* 47(8), 1261–1280.

———— (2012). The politics of defining and alleviating poverty: State strategies and their impacts in rural Kerala. *Geoforum*, 43(5): 991–1001.

Wright, E. O. (2010). *Envisioning Real Utopias*. London: Verso.

Yin, R. K. (2011). *Applications of Case Study Research*. New Delhi: Sage.

ABOUT THE CONTRIBUTORS

Suparna Chatterjee is an Associate Professor at the Sustainability and Global Cultures History and Williams College of Business, Xavier University. She examines the unequal geographies of globalization. Her work curates ideas from economics, history, business, and anthropology, to name a few, to study how ideas spread and impact the lives of people across the globe

Priyanshu Gupta is an Assistant Professor at the Indian Institute of Management Lucknow. He holds a PhD in public policy and management from the Indian Institute of Management Calcutta. He comes with around eight years of experience in areas spanning impact investing (Lok Capital), strategy consulting (A. T. Kearney), grassroots civil society engagement, and policy consulting. He has been associated with the Hasdeo Aranya region for the last six years. He holds a Post Graduate Diploma in Management (PGDM) from Indian Institute of Management Bangalore and a bachelor's degree in Electrical Engineering from Indian Institute of Technology (Banaras Hindu University), Varanasi. His research interests include property rights, forest governance, and environmental policies.

Maidul Islam is Assistant Professor of Political Science at the Centre for Studies in Social Sciences, Calcutta. Previously he has taught Political Science at Presidency University, Kolkata, and is the author of *Limits of Islamism* (2015) and

Indian Muslims after Liberalization (2019). He has a DPhil from the University of Oxford, UK.

Srinath Jagannathan is an Associate Professor at the Indian Institute of Management Indore. He completed his Fellow Program in Management from the Personnel and Industrial Relations Area of Indian Institute of Management, Ahmedabad. In his thesis, he focuses on insecurities experienced by workers in four different contexts – refugees, informal sector workers, contract workers, and workers with apparently stable employment contracts. His areas of interest include critical appraisals of Supreme Court jurisprudence on labour laws, workers' experiences of insecurity and injustice, resistance, critique of liberal practice such as discourses of access, and critique of the epistemological foundations of international business. His work, concerning the organizational apparatus that provides the infrastructure for police encounters in India, has been published in *Organization*.

George Kandathil is an Associate Professor of Organizational Behaviour at the Indian Institute of Management Ahmedabad. He obtained his PhD from Cornell University and MTech from the Indian Institute of Technology, Kanpur. He has worked in the spacecraft and automotive industries for a few years. His broad research interests lie at the interface of information systems implementation, organizational sociology, and critical management studies. Kandathil has published his research in some of the international management journals.

Apoorv Khare is an Assistant Professor at the Indian Institute of Management Tiruchirappalli. He obtained his PhD from the Indian Institute of Management Calcutta. He has worked in pharmaceutical and banking industries. His research interests are broadly in the fields of subaltern consumption, consumption behaviour in postcolonial societies, and consumer culture theory.

Ashish Kothari is an Indian environmentalist working on development, environment interface, biodiversity policy, and alternatives. He is one of the founders of Kalpavriksh, a non-profit organization in India which deals with environmental and development issues. He has been associated with peoples' movements like the Narmada Bachao Andolan and the Beej Bachao Andolan.

Kothari has also been a teacher of environment at the Indian Institute of Public Administration, New Delhi. He has also been a guest faculty at several universities and institutes and Mellon Fellow at Bowdoin College, USA. Kothari is currently coordinating the Vikalp Sangam (Alternatives Confluence) process, which provides a forum for organizations and individuals working on development alternatives across India to come together.

Prabhir Vishnu Poruthiyil is an Assistant Professor at the Center for Policy Studies, IIT Bombay. He teaches social policy usually through the lenses of inequality, sectarianism, and ageing in developing societies. His research has appeared in *Business and Society*, the *Journal of Social Quality*, *Critical Discourse Studies*, *Economic and Political Weekly*, and the *Journal of Business Ethics*.

Rajnish Rai teaches Business Policy and Strategy at the Indian Institute of Management Ahmedabad. His areas of expertise include value creation and appropriation in inter-firm alliances of simultaneous cooperation and competition, transaction cost economics in high-technology research-intensive industries, knowledge management in organizations, intellectual property rights, and the TRIPS Agreement and its impact on foreign direct investment. In his other life, Rajnish Rai is a member of the prestigious Indian Police Service (1992 batch). He earned his PhD (Fellow Program in Management) in the area of business policy from the Indian Institute of Management Ahmedabad and also holds a master's degree in patents law from the National Academy of Legal Studies and Research, Hyderabad, and another master's degree in public policy and management from the Indian Institute of Management Bangalore. He has published in leading journals such as the *Journal of Management, Organization, Economic and Industrial Democracy* and *Action Research Journal*.

Rama Mohana R. Turaga is an Associate Professor in the Public Systems Group at the Indian Institute of Management Ahmedabad (IIMA). Turaga holds a PhD in public policy from the Georgia Institute of Technology, Atlanta, and a master's degree in environmental engineering from the Indian Institute of Technology Kharagpur. Prior to joining IIMA, Turaga worked as a research associate at Dartmouth College, Hanover, USA, where he was a key researcher on the projects funded by the United States Environmental Protection Agency. Turaga's broad research interests lie in analysing the response of various societal stakeholders – governments, businesses, organized non-state actors, communities, and general public – to environmental issues associated with economic growth. His research has been published in reputed international journals such as the *Journal of Policy Analysis and Management, Ecological Economics, Journal of Industrial Ecology*, and the *Annals of the New York Academy of Sciences*.

Poornima Varma is an Assistant Professor at the Indian Institute of Management Ahmedabad. She has a PhD in economics (2010) from CESP, Jawaharlal Nehru University, New Delhi.

Rohit Varman is a Professor of Marketing and Consumption at the University of Birmingham. He holds a PhD from the University of Utah. His research interests are broadly in the fields of critical management studies and consumer culture. He uses interpretive methodologies, and his current interdisciplinary research focuses on violence, exploitation, and modern slavery.

Devi Vijay is an Associate Professor at the Indian Institute of Management Calcutta. Vijay's research spans questions of inequality, institutions, and collective action, with a specific focus on the healthcare sector. She completed her doctoral studies at the Indian Institute of Management Bangalore. She was a Fulbright–Nehru Postdoctoral Research Fellow (2016–2018) at the Mailman School of Public Health, Columbia University. She has co-edited *Alternative Organizations in India: Undoing Boundaries*, published by Cambridge University Press (2018).

Ram Manohar Vikas is an independent researcher. He earned his PhD and MBA from the Indian Institute of Technology Kanpur. He has worked in the construction and consultancy industries for several years. His research interests are broadly in the fields of consumer culture theory with emphasis on subaltern consumers. He has taught at the Institute of Rural Management Anand and the Indian Institute of Management Lucknow. Vikas has published his research in international management journals such as the *Journal of Consumer Research*, the *Journal of Macromarketing*, and *Consumption, Markets, and Culture*.

INDEX